Reclaiming William Morris
Englishness, Sublimity, and the Rhetoric of Dissent

Casting new light on the relations between nationalism, rhetoric, and revolution, Michelle Weinroth shows how the English legacy of William Morris was appropriated in the interests of political forces seeking hegemonic power. She argues that Conservative claimants readily disseminated Morris's aesthetic *oeuvre*, declaring it to be the embodiment of English sensibility. Communists, however, struggled to retain Morris's Englishness while promoting his political doctrine. Weinroth demonstrates that these peripheral ideologues were caught in a paradox: they could not grip the masses without the aesthetic appeal of Englishness, but Englishness was imbued with the very imperialism that they abhorred. Theirs was a propaganda strained by the conflict between political dissent and ruling-class cultural forms.

Moving through theoretical, historical, and exegetical analyses of propagandist texts, *Reclaiming William Morris* brings out the aesthetic underpinnings of nationalist ideology. Combining the philosophical substance of Karl Marx, Georg Lukács, Antonio Gramsci, and Ernst Bloch with Kantian aesthetics, Weinroth constructs a conceptual apparatus that explains the impassioned yet decidedly marginal rhetoric of early twentieth-century English communism.

MICHELLE WEINROTH is an independent scholar working in Ottawa.

Reclaiming William Morris

*Englishness, Sublimity, and
the Rhetoric of Dissent*

MICHELLE WEINROTH

McGill-Queen's University Press
Montreal & Kingston • London • Buffalo

© McGill-Queen's University Press 1996
ISBN 0-7735-1439-2

Legal deposit fourth quarter 1996

Bibliothèque nationale du Québec

Printed in the United States on acid-free paper

This book has been published with the help of a grant
from the Humanities and Social Sciences Federation of Canada,
using funds provided by the Social Sciences and Humanities
Research Council of Canada.

McGill-Queen's University Press is grateful to the Canada
Council for support of its publishing program.

Canadian Cataloguing in Publication Data

Weinroth, Michelle, 1959-
Reclaiming William Morris : Englishness,
sublimity, and the rhetoric of dissent
Includes bibliographical references and index.
ISBN 0-7735-1439-2
1. Morris, William, 1834–1896 – Political and social views.
2. Morris, William, 1834–1896 – Influence. 3. Communism –
England – History – 20th century.
I. Title.
PR5087.s6w45 1996 320.5'32'092 c96-900505-9

Typeset in Adobe Garamond 11/13
by Caractéra inc., Quebec City

*For my late father, Howard Weinroth, who combined
the rationalism and romanticism of the Communist intellectual.*

*For my son, Raphaël, whose innocent fantasies
have taught me the meaning of the imagined community.*

Contents

Preface and Acknowledgments

In this centenary year of his death (1996), when his name returns to prominence, William Morris remains a strangely elusive figure of English culture. Designer? Craftsman? Social reformer? Pre-Raphaelite? Morris cannot be defined readily. He has an omnipresence which is more felt than seen. Like a phantom, he lurks in Victorian furnishings, upholstered sofas, and floral wallpaper. Occasionally, he appears in the pages of the British daily press, hovering as an ideological muse for a socialist's lament on the fate of the working class. But his presence, which lies deeply embedded in British *popular memory*, has more significance than to astonish us with its endurance and varied appeal. Over the past hundred years, Morris's aesthetic and political *œuvre* has constituted a compelling symbol of English identity. In the 1930s, Conservatives, Social Democrats, and revolutionary Communists, *inter alia*, appropriated this national emblem to endorse and legitimize their own political agendas. But unlike mainstream ideologues, Communist propagandists faced perennial difficulties in their claim to Morris's nationalist legacy, a claim which they felt would facilitate their struggle to secure political dominance in Britain.

This book is about the fraught relationship between Englishness and the rhetoric of revolution, between the politically expedient power of nationalism and the propagandist endeavours of British Communists, notably those of the 1930s and 1950s. Conceived at Birmingham's Centre for Contemporary Cultural Studies, the study grew amidst discussions held by an academic collective (the "Popular Memory Group") whose aim was to analyse the purchase of conservative culture on British sensibility in the wake of the Falklands-Malvinas War (1983). The group's undertaking emerged as a response to the Left's disarray in the

1980s, its failure to wrest popular sentiment from the triumphalist euphoria which Thatcher had generated through her imperial exploits. Just as many thinkers on the Left were confounded by Labour's impotence in the face of Thatcher's political juggernaut, so the Popular Memory Group was baffled and sought to investigate "what went wrong" (Jeremy Seabrooke). In examining the cultural practices and customs of a British way of life, the Birmingham collective began an analysis of the disarming force of British conservative nationalism and its subtle penetration of private and public experience. But while the group's endeavour dwelled largely on the ideological process of Thatcherite hegemony, the question that held my own attention was why the Left – and specifically the Communists of the 1930s and 1950s – had laboured strenuously to secure hegemonic success yet could scarcely compete with their Conservative counterparts.

On 8 November 1989, the *Guardian* headlines announced the collapse of the Berlin Wall. The question which had launched my project on British Communists and their aborted efforts to achieve a political hegemony now seemed ever amplified, for it resonated with the rapid succession of crises in the Eastern Bloc countries. The events of that month in the former East Germany signalled the imminent demise of Communist Europe, and thereafter of the former Soviet Union. And while the fall of these regimes can hardly be conflated with the failure of British communism, for many, in Britain and elsewhere, the hopes for a redemptive socialist future were dashed.

Over the past six years, the Marxist doctrine and the political movements which it spawned have plummeted to oblivion. That Marxism constituted one of the major philosophical currents of the twentieth century did nothing to assure it a proper burial. Within political circles, there has been neither formal closure nor dénouement to this saga. The episode has been swept aside onto the rubbish heap of history. Such is the contempt which contemporary society has shown it.

Given this political climate, any serious invocation of communism could be deemed irrelevant. Yet while such a doctrine has now been shut out of contemporary ideological concerns, stamped as the cause of disastrous political regimes, the individual activists who devoted their lives to Communist social revolution remain, despite their orthodoxies and political miscalculations, undeniable heroes. They fought against fascism in Spain, resisted German nazism during the Second World War, struggled against the apartheid regime of South Africa. In their sustained commitment to world peace, they appealed strenuously for justice and ethical rectitude in the face of inhumanity. It would be both historically unfair and inaccurate to conflate these with politically corrupt leaders who ruled the reified State bureaucracies of Stalinism in the Soviet Union and the Eastern Bloc.

In this post-Communist period, ethnic cleansing has drenched Bosnia and Serbia in blood, neo-nazism has reared its face again in Germany and Austria, while fascism proliferates in France. As the Ku Klux Klan resurfaces more boldly in the United States, the Reform party of Canada schemes its own racist crusade in the spirit of Newt Gingrich. The reality of a viable system of democracy has been increasingly imperilled and a formidable question remains: Whither are we going? Eighty years ago, Rosa Luxemburg saw the fork in the road and predicted socialism or barbarism. But today it would be awkward to invoke the term "socialism" as an alternative to the *status quo*. The ideals of revolutionary Marxists would be simply mocked or heckled. Against a wave of popular cynicism, rugged individualism, and stubborn complacency, it is scarcely possible to restore belief in an equitable future commonweal short of being stamped quixotic or démodé.

Still, the vacuum left by the demise of socialist regimes has indeed, as Luxemburg predicted, become a sprawling, almost uncontrollable barbarism. Whatever one's political judgment of twentieth-century socialism, it is unlikely that society will recover from its present crises, short of revisiting the efforts and defeats of those who tried but failed to redeem the world of its ills during the earlier part of this century. In examining one specific contradiction which undermined British Communist propagandists – the conflict between revolutionary rhetoric and the discourse of Englishness – I have endeavoured in this book to contribute to that retrospective scrutiny and to rekindle debate on a subject that has been too swiftly cast aside. In the same breath, I hasten to emphasize that while this study is a critical analysis of Communist propagandist strategy, it was conceived with respect and admiration for the moral purpose and sustained political commitment of many revolutionary activists. On a personal level, I am indebted to those Communists who gave me their time and energy while I did my research in England. Ruth and Eddie Frow welcomed me frequently to their Working Class Library in Manchester, providing warm lodging, food, and friendship. I owe them enormous gratitude. I am also deeply grateful to Ann Schuman (the late Robin Page Arnot's secretary) for taping an interview with Arnot when he was alive in 1985, for inviting me to Forest Hill, London for further discussion and a viewing of a video of Robin Page Arnot, produced by Mary Ireland. Many thanks are due to John Kay, member of the William Morris Society, for valuable discussions and lending material. A.L. Morton, Andrew Rothstein, Ray Watkinson, Angela Tuckett-Gradwell, Alfred Jenkins, Christopher Hill, Eddie Hayes, George Matthews, George and Doreen Rudé, and Jack Lindsay were always prompt and informative in their correspondence with me, offering precious leads for my research inquiries. I thank them all for their conscientiousness.

Richard Johnson, my former doctoral tutor, ploughed through several drafts of this book. I am deeply indebted to him not only for his poignant criticisms but also for his encouragement and guiding spirit. In his loquacious manner, Bill Livant's imaginative mind always challenged and spurred me on to sharper and more penetrating theoretical analysis. Bill Schwarz generously procured material for me at the Colindale Newspaper Library, saving me a transatlantic journey to England while I was in Canada. The staff of the William Morris Gallery, the Marx Memorial Library, the Cambridge University Library, and the British Library proved most helpful and accommodating. Nola Brunelle of McLennan Library at McGill University and Cynthia Bullocks of the Industrial Relations Library at Michigan State University took out personal time to search historical references on my behalf. I thank them all warmly.

In the course of the first four years of my research, I received financial assistance from the Social Sciences and Humanities Research Council of Canada and Fonds pour l'aide et le soutien à la recherche. Both these institutions awarded me generous doctoral fellowships without which this project could not have been pursued. I am also grateful to the Aid to Scholarly Publications Programme which awarded me a grant for the publication of this book. Finally, I am indebted to all those at McGill-Queen's University Press – Philip Cercone, Peter Blaney, Joan McGilvray, Judy Williams, Roy Ward, and Susanne McAdam – who always gave me intelligent advice and encouragement.

My immediate and extended family endured the more difficult passages of this journey. My mother, Janet Weinroth, and stepfather, Jean Philippe Aubert, my sister Merav, and her daughters Anne and Beth all gave their support, particularly when the joys of motherhood drew my time away from writing. They greatly facilitated the task of bringing this study to fruition. My gratitude to Paul Browne is beyond measure. He nurtured my interests in German philosophy, offered judicious advice, read and reread the text with enormous precision, and gave unwavering emotional support. Most important, he believed not only that this project was possible, but that it mattered. I thank him profusely.

Reclaiming William Morris

Introduction

WHO are the english,
according to the definition of the ruling-class?
All you that went forth, lured by great-sounding names
which glittered like bubbles of crystal in your eyes
till they burst and you burst with them, shot to shreds
from one end of the shuddering earth to the other end,
shot that the merchant's pockets might clink and bulge,
shot that hoardings of imperial size
might fill each blank space of the motor-roads
with pink whore-faces beckoning the bankrupt to buy –
you are the english,
your ruling-class has said it,
you are the english,
keep then the recompense of a sounding name, for you have
nothing else.

...

Stand out one of the men who were not english,
come, William Morris,
you that preached armed revolt to the workers and said
of the men who died for us in the Commune of Paris:
We honour them as the foundation-stone
of the new world that is to be.
You that cried out after Bloody Sunday:
Not one, not one, nor thousands must they slay,
but one and all if they would dusk the day!

...

You were not english, we are not english either –
though we have loved these trees plumed upon the sunset
and turned back to the area-rails our prison-bars;
though we have followed the plough like a hungry rook,
with love for the brown soil slicing fatly away,
to haunt in the end the dingy rain of the street
where a prosperous spilth of warming music
trickled through drawn blinds on our beggar senses;

> though we have crept into the daisy-light of the dew
> to wake once more in the dripping tenements;
> though we have plucked hazelnuts of autumn,
> making faces at the squirrel, to kiss between laughters,
> that was not our land, we were trespassers,
> the field of toil was our allotted life,
> beyond it we might not stir though blossom-scents
> left tender trails leading to the heart of summer;
> though we have loved this earth where our sweat and our tears
> drained through the thankless centuries,
> … yet the bailiffs evicted us,
> it was all taken away, England was taken,
> what little of it was ours in desperate toil
> was taken …   (Lindsay 1936, 353–7)

IN AND AGAINST THE STATE

In an era of national chauvinism, they were internationalists. As strangers in their own land, British Communists of the 1930s were conspicuously distinct and socially forbidding. They embraced revolutionary ideas which challenged the quaint beauty of England's compact measure, shattering its blissful parochialism and summoning their fellow citizens to heed the evils of the day: the spectre of fascism and the belligerence of Western imperialism. Their "foreign" (Marxist) persuasion was deemed not merely formidable but perplexing, for it threatened to transform that "happy English isle" into a nation racked with rage and distemper. But however much they adhered to principles of dissent, promoting seismic social change, their propagandist efforts could neither escape nor eclipse a traditional Englishness, figuratively crystallized in the sensuality of the countryside where "the fields and hedges … are as it were one huge nosegay … redolent of bean-flowers and clover and sweet hay and elder blossom" (Morris 1889, 214). This fragrant bucolic place cradled the tender affections of their mainstream public and was thus a source of powerful rhetoric. But Communists themselves could never cherish this ruralist England naïvely. To them, the enchanting English bower was linked to a brutally iniquitous society.

Under capitalism, it would have been impossible for Communists to simply assert, as the Conservative statesman Stanley Baldwin did in 1924, that "England is the country and the country is England" (Baldwin 1924, 6). Such a pun on nationhood projected a societal oasis of perfect harmony in which the dissonance of class strife dissolved into a melodious chorus of patriots, pleasantly congregated under a company of oaks. To Communists, this conservative social imaginary was inadmissible. For it seized the very blitheness of the utopian countryside for an ideology that abetted the cause of an unjust liberal democracy. It was this "democracy" which Communists sought to challenge, and nationalism furnished the adversarial ground upon which they could stage their propagandist dissent.

The rhetoric of English Conservative nationalism, notably embodied in the speeches of Stanley Baldwin of the 1920s and 1930s, stood in stark contrast to Communist political interventions. It constituted a discourse of concealed self-empowerment and legitimation. Endowing its subscribers with a spirit of confidence and self-possession, it enabled them to peer vicariously through the window of an invented childhood, a prelapsarian social order that they had never experienced, but which they could fancifully herald as their legitimating source of authenticity. This *ersatz* childhood was an Arcadia detached from all concrete reality yet brimming with the aromas of private and communitarian experience. It was a prism of evanescent impressions forming the image of an exalted nation, a nation so enchanting that it devilishly precluded any veritable understanding of its jewelled form. Girded by a rhetoric which quashed quizzical thought and commanded a most consensual power, this Arcadia was swathed in panegyrical effusions, and in an all-encompassing idiom that simulated the concordant blend of elements intrinsic to a work of art. Disarming in its perfect totality, this national idyll elicited unequivocal unanimous applause and graced its citizens with a sense of utter plenitude that could only affirm their otherwise uncertain identity.

Wrought of the stuff of affect and imagination, and linked to moments of crisis and urgency, this nationalist discourse proved to be among the most compelling forms of political expression. Even in an age of cynical rationality and disenchantment,[1] the persuasive force of this rhetoric could be located in its manipulation of non-conceptual structures of thinking, aesthetic and dramatic elements that militated against cognitive inquiry while nonetheless addressing the rational sensibility of the modern individual – intellectual dignity and civic autonomy. These aesthetic features were capable of erasing the logic and objectivity of quotidian reality while engendering a momentary but consummate self-consciousness that compensated for the ethical and political mediocrity of routine life. In its simulation of the work of art, Baldwin's conservative nationalism satisfied its public's need for subjective enhancement, transporting it from the terrain of scepticism onto the dizzying plane of an imaginary stage – a place of powerful ideological persuasion.

But the insidiousness of this ideology was its tendency to masquerade as a universal doctrine delivered in the name of the "common people," while obscuring its own particular, indeed its privileged, class interests. Claiming to occupy a geographically bounded nation, Baldwin's conservative Englishness was rather a territory of the mind, a signifier open to much ideological contestation. For what it represented was less the citizen's self-identification and attachment to a homeland than the shoring in of these feelings of nationhood for the purposes of securing political consent.

In their efforts to build popular support, Communists could not, under the aegis of the "Third Period"[2] of the Comintern, entertain the use of such nationalist rhetoric for their own revolutionary ends. Indeed, the mystique and irrationalism which it promoted only strengthened the grip which capitalism had over popular consciousness. As heirs of Enlightenment thought, Communists sought to dispel what they saw as the obscurantism spawned by enticing aesthetic forms that betrayed an empty benevolence symptomatic of the "hollow equalities" of liberal democracy. In repudiating what was unethical, they opted for a rhetoric of agitation and unmitigated vehemence against the blandishments of the *status quo*. They forcefully exposed the clashing divisions of society, expunging all saccharine and irrationalist lyricism from their discourse, and with it any semblance of the enthralling sentimentalism so characteristic of conservative nationalism.

Yet they could hardly live by cognitive rationality alone. While their ethics and internationalist politics forbade them to adopt a mainstream nationalism as an instrument for securing popular consent, they yearned to be integrated within a national community. They hankered after approval from their fellow citizens but adamantly contested the political institutions that buttressed England's capitalist state. How could propagandists of the periphery become centrally positioned on the political stage while still adhering to their marginal beliefs? Conversely, how could they exploit a form of nationalism which perpetuated a social order that they vociferously deplored? How could they grip the masses when their propaganda consisted in dismantling the traditional ideals of Englishness, in advocating the virtues of an alien world ruptured from the bedrock of English ways of life? These are some of the conflicts between ethical rectitude and tactics which British Communist propagandists faced, most notably during the Third Period of the Comintern.[3]

Seeking control over public opinion, Communists were objectively caught between conscience and expediency, between their allegiance to the cold, austere laws of Communist morality and the tactics of winning warm approval from their audiences. Uneasy with the sentimental bonds of nationalism, they reproduced in their rhetoric the authoritative voice of a Communist superego. Yet, as Terry Eagleton has noted in his discussion of Burke's gendered notions of hegemony and aesthetics, "only love will truly win us to the law, but this love will erode the law to nothing. A law attractive enough to engage our intimate affections, and so hegemonically effective [such as the tenderness of nationalist lyricism], will tend to inspire in us a benign contempt. On the other hand, a power which rouses our filial fear, and hence our submissive obedience [like the Third Period Comintern], is likely to alienate our affections and so spur us to Oedipal resentment" (Eagleton 1990, 55). Burke's reconciling image for this paradox was the figure of the grandfather "whose male authority is enfeebled by age into a 'feminine partiality'" (Eagleton 1990, 55).

The Communists may not have *consciously* sought a solution to these contradictions in the identity of William Morris. But his legacy certainly proved to be a combination of the Burkean aesthetics of masculine austerity and female tenderness fused into the grandfatherly figure. Not that his posthumous image could be deemed in any way feminine. Yet the deep affection for the English countryside which he registered in both aesthetic and literary form rendered his legacy a repository of longings for the warmth associated with hearth and homeland. Simultaneously, Morris's self-proclaimed communism was marked by his masculinist posture, by his vigorous activism and commitment to a political cause. Together, his feelings for English ruralism and his political dissent *might* have enabled the radical propagandists of the 1930s to love a gentle Englishness and respect the formidable laws of revolution in one ideological thrust. But historical conditions and Morris's controversial legacy made this dialectical unity an almost impossible contingency.

THE BATTLE OVER NATIONALIST CULTURE

As a man of protean enterprises, William Morris was a poet, political reformer, designer, craftsman, Pre-Raphaelite artist of the nineteenth century, and more.[4] His rich and varied public life has been the object of biographical quests for his "essential" unity. Yet the search has exceeded the realm of pure scholarship. Numerous political institutions in distress, seeking to enhance their public image, have adopted Morris's legacy as their herald. In 1984, for example, London's Institute for Contemporary Art celebrated his 150th anniversary in an exhibition that edified Morris's art and socialist visions.[5] This provided a fortuitous yet expedient forum for redeeming the ideological identity of the Labour movement (cf. Jones 1984). It did so precisely by offering an aesthetic dimension to a political constituency that had been suffering from the pangs of electoral defeat (1983), as well as from the Conservatives' triumphalism over the Falklands-Malvinas War.

Fifty years earlier, the point at which the narrative of this book begins, another, even grander anniversary took place. In 1934, Morris's centenary was celebrated at the Victoria and Albert Museum. This setting of contemplative art lent itself to a panoply of centenary festivities which enabled the Conservative statesman Stanley Baldwin, as well as other publicly esteemed dignitaries, to vaunt the memory of Morris as a reincarnation of Victorian beauty and English character. Stressing the man's many facets and literary contributions to posterity, they paid homage to him in maudlin appreciations, worshipping him for his genius and aesthetic appeal. In an inaugural address that provided the overture to lavish praise, Stanley Baldwin spoke of Morris exclusively as a superior artist of eminent gentility and human warmth, dispensing with any reference to Morris's political role as founder of the British socialist movement. This omission represented the silent repudiation of another set of Morris admirers, the Communists who had revered and taken pride in the socialist struggles he pioneered in the 1880s–90s. To them, Baldwin's glaring lapse, his suave yet anecdotal discourse, constituted an infuriating myth that annulled the significance of Morris's political stature.

Nor was this partial Morrisania merely the work of Conservatives. Ethical socialists and Fabians who depicted Morris as a gentle Victorian, sentimentalizing him into a purely romantic and ineffectual dreamer, were wittingly or not being compromised to the Conservative appraisal of the man. Thus, as the centenary polished William Morris into a late

Romantic cameo of utopian sentimental idealism, it provoked the ideological fervour of Communists who regarded this one-sided portrayal as
a political offence to his memory as well as to his Communist disciples.
In *William Morris: A Vindication* (1934) – the central focus of this book
– a leading Communist party historian and journalist, Robin Page
Arnot, published a riposte that summoned back the trenchant edge of
the hero's lapsed politics.

Morris's legacy often acted as a source of conflict between those with
a Labour conception of socialism and those with a Communist one (cf.
MacIntyre 1975.) The battle was particularly vigorous with respect to
two streams of British radicalism: Labour socialists and Marxists. Morris's political thought came to represent their differing strategies for
social change, parliamentary reform versus radical revolution. This
divergence also expressed itself in the competing portrayals of Morris as
scientific communist and utopian socialist, posthumous identities
ascribed to him by vying admirers struggling to promote their respective
persuasions as overridingly superior.

Spawned by conditions of crisis, the furious appropriations of Morris's memory can hardly be seen as innocent redemptions of the hero's
cultural import, or as purely earnest efforts to save his life history from
oblivion. Clearly, various Morris institutions sought to "extort" a political, pragmatic value from his posthumous significance. In short, his
cultural worth lent itself to more than displays of memorabilia; it
fulfilled the needs of individuals and collectivities jockeying for political
power. In fact, close scrutiny of the propagandist claimants vindicating
the Morris heritage reveals that the essential object over which both
Conservative and Communist ideologues of the 1930s battled was a
nationalist dimension embodied in Morris's creative work. It became
the "catch-symbol" of their respective affirmations, rehabilitating or
endorsing the viability of their political programs. Morris's *œuvre* was
the symbolic treasure-house of Englishness, and the political expediency
of seizing his legacy came to define, on a more general level, the
necessary strategy for tapping a popular (read nationalist) sensibility
within the larger struggle to win or maintain hegemonic power.[6]

But for dissenting ideologues of the 1930s and even for those in the
1950s, the Communist Morris legacy betrayed an equivocal usefulness.
In theory, such a repository of culture and political history incorporated
both scientific-rationalist[7] and romantic-cum-utopian thought, and was
a worthwhile quarry of material from which to advance a Communist
philosophy. Yet in reality, Morris's memory was not easily deployed by

Communist ideologues; their relation to this national hero indexed a perennial dilemma of ethical idealism versus tactical pragmatism. Grounded in the idiom of a much-refined canon of bourgeois culture, Morris's aesthetic *œuvre* harbours a floridity which rankled with early Comintern propagandists. His romanticism is imbued with an English-ness which Conservative rhetoricians have stamped as decidedly ruling-class. Any marriage of this romantic identity with the praxis of revolu-tion could not sit comfortably in the minds of Communists, for such a blend seemed to compromise and dilute the vigorous essence of radical politics as well as to submit dissenting voices to the engulfing powers of the capitalist hegemony.

If Communist defences of Morris's legacy have been unwieldy, it is in part because his aesthetic proclivities conjured up for them the irrationalism of reactionary ideologies; but it is also due to a pre-existing Marxist critique of idealism which indirectly censored the aesthetic inclinations of Communist propagandists of the 1930s. The pre-eminent assault on idealism was that of Marx in respect to classical German philosophers (i.e. Hegel, Kant). These saw material reality as subordi-nated to the allegedly authentic identity of spirit and religion, a per-spective which according to Marx implied the demeaning of the most fundamental conditions of social being: material, social relations evinced in labour processes. The idealists failed to consider the contradictions between desire, freedom, and necessity in anything other than abstract terms, be it through objective idealism (Hegel) or through subjective idealism (Kant). As for the idealism of the Utopian Socialists in the nineteenth century, Engels launched his decisive and influential critique against their electicism and abstract concept of radical change in his *Socialism, Utopian and Scientific.* This tract bequeathed a whole ideology of scientific rationalism to succeeding Communist intellectuals of the twentieth century. As E.P. Thompson notes in the postscript to his major biography of Morris, the critique of utopian socialism in *The Communist Manifesto* and in Engels's celebrated treatise gave rise in the subsequent Marxist tradition "to a doctrinal antinomy: Science (good) Utopianism (bad). At any point after 1850, Scientific Socialism had no more need of Utopias (and doctrinal authority for suspecting them.) Speculation as to the society of the future was repressed, and displaced by attention to strategy. Beyond 'the Revolution' little more could be known than certain skeletal theoretical propositions" (Thompson 1976, 787–8).

With this antinomy, Morris's legacy (which incorporates a heritage of utopian romance literature compounded with his uninhibited advocacy of communism) provoked unending debate over the authenticity of his scientific Marxism. His both equivocal and elusive status compelled his Marxist advocates to vindicate his scientific Communist side, his revolutionary fervour and pragmatic effectiveness, in opposition to the highly apolitical, idealist versions heralded by Conservatives and Social Democrats.[8] Since Morris's legacy was an object of propagandist expression, any aesthetic signature that he lent Communist rhetoric could not, according to Comintern precepts, be conflated with the ideologies of political adversaries. Thus in an effort to protect the purity of Morris's scientific rationalism, Robin Page Arnot (Morris's prime vindicator) conceptualized and objectified the hero in terms that were distilled of all aesthetic niceties linked to utopian idealism and to a nationalism endorsing the *status quo*. The Communist portrait of Morris ultimately rendered the beauties of pastoral Englishness into the elemental forces of *Sturm und Drang*, the thunderclap of Romantic dissent. The hero's identity thus proved to be sublime and symbolic of the only possible aesthetic signature of Communist nationhood.

DREAMING OF UTOPIA

Revolution not only intervenes in the understanding, but equally in the fantasy, which has for so long been undernourished in socialism. It intervenes precisely in the fantasy of the understanding, in the extraordinary tension between processual reality and that which has not yet come into being within it – as our world.   (Bloch in Negt 1976, 69–70)

If the utopian facets of Morris's legacy presented ethical-tactical dilemmas for the Communist propagandists of the 1930s, this could in part be ascribed to the dissenters' conflation of the utopian aesthetic with purely fetishised, irrational thought. However, the presence of an "ideal" or utopian moment in both thought and activity does not necessarily amount to sheer idealist consciousness. Instead it signifies that non-rationality is rooted in both sensuous and epistemic moments of social being, in labour processes such as ideology itself. Rationalist philosophy cannot deny this without undesirable repercussions. Nor does such a claim privilege non-rationality over rational consciousness; it merely serves to underscore the point that the aesthetic ideal participates in an interactive relation with rational consciousness, and, in this interplay of forces, epitomizes the consummate dialectic of species-being. (Cf. chapter 5.)

Such an ontological consideration of aesthetics (cf. Lukács 1963) was not, however, a principal concern of the "scientific-Marxist" claimants of Morris's legacy – at least those of the 1930s. They displayed a certain "lack of moral self-consciousness or even a vocabulary of desire, [an] inability to project any images of the future" (Thompson 1976, 792). The censorship of traces of idealism, such as those expressed by utopianism, prevented Communist ideologues from overtly deploying aesthetic forms that would specifically delineate a community space beyond bourgeois society. Communist scientific utopia was literally "nowhere" to be "seen," only imagined through complex mediations of moral and hopeful attitudes of strength. Admittedly, if this repression of a sensuous aesthetic form occurred pervasively in Communist discourse, there were certainly significant exceptions.

In his treatise *Illusion and Reality*, a delineation of dreamwork and poetry, Christopher Caudwell wrote that dreams are not sites of serendipity where images associate "freely"; their imagistic restructuring of reality can be construed as a way of determining or propelling life in certain directions: "it … is possible to dream with accuracy of the future – in other words to predict scientifically" (Caudwell 1973, 298). From an orthodox Communist perspective, the idea that dream has the potential of predicting the future with "scientific accuracy" appears heretical. And yet, the dream factor to which Caudwell refers has (from its aesthetic vantage point) the capacity to rearrange memory images while being a reflective consciousness of the pattern and destiny of social reality. In the rearrangement of temporal poles, the moment of gratification or consummated desire is tentatively pitched in the immediate present, thereby prefiguring the future through aesthetic thought. Dream actively shapes and propels material practice, endowing social actors with a clairvoyance that enables them to navigate confidently through the myopia of the here and now.

Like Caudwell, Ernst Bloch sought to disentangle utopian*ism* as a static and idealist truth from the more general category of utopia; he regarded utopian projects as crucial for surviving conditions of duress and exploitation. In their anticipatory character, he claimed, dreams are emancipatory; they "manifest yearnings for transcendence and can function as symbols of human freedom and defiance regardless of social circumstances" (Kellner and O'Hara 1976, 25). Admittedly, Bloch did not advocate an indolent daydreaming or deluding fantasy. Strong desire incites action, yet it must be accompanied by a realism and a pragmatic perspicacity as to what and how desire can be realized. For as Blake had it, "he who desires but acts not, breeds pestilence" (Erdman 1965).

Concrete, grounded in history and committed to class struggle, Bloch's concept of utopia is distinguished from the idealism of the utopian socialists in that it does not imply epistemological leaps but rather the discovery of possibilities for change issuing from the interstices of the present; it is a coalescence of theory and practice which incorporates a rationalist scientific analysis of the present (the "cold current") and a non-rational, passionate component which appeals to the masses ("the warm current"). However, "the problem is that this warm current … has been suppressed by orthodox economistic or evolutionary Marxists who merely focus on the objective conditions for revolution and neglect the subjective factors" (Bloch in Kellner and O'Hara 1976, 30). What is required is some catalytic mediation between the cold current of rationality and the warm impulses of affectivity, those energizing forces which are indispensable for mass mobilization. Although demeaned or eschewed by rationalist ideologues, Bloch's principle of a warm current constitutes the utopian element which, Fredric Jameson has suggested, is intrinsic to "all class consciousness of whatever type … insofar as all … collectivities are themselves figures for the ultimate concrete collective life of an achieved Utopian or classless society" (Jameson 1981, 290).

If class consciousness is in its very nature utopian and if utopian impulses act as facilitating catalysts in social reproduction (cf. Caudwell and Bloch), then effective propagandists will reappropriate those forms of ideological consciousness and put them to use. For the utopian element is not only a guiding force of action but also a conceptualizing mechanism and a means of extricating the self from the tensions of immediate reality. In short, it feeds the passionate warm current that transports human subjectivity into an imagined realm of freedom. Admittedly, as an aesthetic structure which constitutes the vehicle of hope and driving force behind social activity, the utopian urge and the power of dream are necessary aspects of transformative praxis, but not sufficient in themselves. Still, they form the moment of elevation, clarity, and cohesion which every human endeavour requires for concretizing its ideals.

Like all human activity that is predicated on positing goals, propaganda foregrounds its ideal purpose (allegedly the achievement of the good) and illuminates it as a point of destination.[9] This illumination is performed by the utopian moment that proffers communities a pleasurable sense of future fulfilment, a prefigurative glimpse into the farther reaches of experience – a process crucial to enticing audiences and sustaining their belief in the legitimacy of a political discourse. For in their adherence to a particular message, audiences are engaged in an epistemic-imaginative journey; their compass is an aesthetic structure of consciousness which captures and maintains their interests throughout the numerous stations of an uncertain odyssey. Propaganda depends not merely on the logic of its discourse, but on its capacity to be affective, to endorse, dramatize, and enchant the experiences of a given social group – and this not merely in an abstract manner but in the very historical and cultural modes which constitute that public's disposition. Effective propaganda precludes the inscription of thought onto a *tabula rasa*; instead it requires as Jameson puts it "a complex strategy of persuasion in which substantial incentives are offered for ideological adherence" (Jameson 1981, 287). And if these incentives and utopian drives are to bear any effect, they must emerge from the texture and substance of immediate conditions, not *ex nihilo*. Any propagandist effort to deploy the utopian principle as a catalyst for mobilizing public opinion must also, then, be imbued with the kaleidoscopic workings of lived experience, an experience germane to the audience in question. Propagandist projects which are inherently bent on achieving hegemonic power are most successful when they reach out in all-embracing fashion, penetrating the depths of social consciousness, its tacit assumptions, its mores and customs, its unquestioned cultural forms. Harnessing these in aesthetic unities and fostering a conception of the world that is integrative, propaganda becomes most strategic when it produces a centripetal energy that gathers the public's self-consciousness into a whole *Weltanschauung*, a vision of shared history and determinate national destiny.

This is a Gramscian view of hegemony which avers that winning the consent and trust of a community can only occur if the concept of ideology is more than a doctrine of commonly held beliefs, orchestrated and imposed from above. Ideology is to be construed not only as an inverted consciousness which distorts popular perception of immediate reality, but also as an amalgam of mutually reinforcing customs and popular assumptions, practices, and experiences which reflect, confirm, and solidify the identities of social groups.[10] This affirmative impulse is linked to a social need for self-consciousness, a moment of self-perception where individual identity is cast as substantial, enduring, and free of constraints. It is a yearning for autonomy and self-validation which is satisfied aesthetically, thanks to the inversions that ideology exercises as it transposes objective contradiction into a harmony conforming to subjective desire. The ideological inversion can either be interpreted as a distorted consciousness of reality or as that imperative utopian factor from which human beings derive their confidence and enhanced self-image. The two perspectives on ideology are not mutually exclusive. On the contrary, they both often coexist, and the problem that ensues is that they can readily be conflated. What is but a blithe play of the mind, but an aesthetic liberty to pretend the impossible, may wax into an instrument of consensual persuasion. Under conditions of capitalist reification[11] in particular, the utopian factor (which is crucial for any consensus building) is wont to dissolve into an idealism that wreaks havoc. For in affirming subjective capability, the utopian ideal becomes a site of social control, notably in forums such as the pleasure industry (with all its materialistic enticements), Disneyland, hockey and other national sport tournaments, cultural anniversaries, commemorative occasions of heroism and national achievement, etc. While these fields of societal bonding and solidarity undoubtedly produce the comforting ambrosia of the political soul, enlivening the individual's identity, they are not merely community rituals which serve each and all in a disinterested and impartial fashion. The utopian aspirations which such collective experience enables, if only in aesthetic fantasy, are the source of political and commercial profit. Agents of power and social climbing derive consensus and material support for their individual interests precisely through their insidious clutch on the affective needs of public consciousness.

Dissenting propagandists of the 1930s recognized the pernicious duality of capitalist ideology, both its ability to affirm subjectivity and maintain a powerful hold over it.[12] Yet they could not enter the "sullied" terrain of rhetorical expediencies which their adversaries had monopolized, mastered, and deployed towards conservative ends. For the ethics of their dissenting doctrine would not readily sanction such a tactical manœuvre. Challenging the fundamental structures of bourgeois society, Communists were thus paralysed by a search for an authentic utopian moment that was pure of falsification. To adopt the existing forms of inspiration and solidarity that were acceptable because conventionally heralded in bourgeois ideology meant succumbing to the thrall of illusory blandishments. But to reject the only utopian factor available, namely, fetishized representations of collective and individual identity such as nationalism, romanticism, heroism, etc., was to jettison an indispensable component of political communication. Bloch put it bluntly: "the Nazis spoke deceptively, but to the people; the socialists spoke completely truthfully, but about situations; it is our task now to speak truthfully to the people about their situations" (Bloch in Negt 1976, 70). The antinomy registered here is crucial. On the one hand, conservative or fascist ideologues powerfully yet duplicitously tapped the visceral vulnerabilities of the people. On the other, Communist rhetoricians assumed an ethical integrity but failed to find the language of immediacy and direct access to win the full consent of their public.[13] They presupposed that mainstream society was steeped in the abstractions and idealisms of commodity fetishism, and that such reification could be dispelled through political enlightenment. But they failed to fully apply Marx's *Third Thesis on Feuerbach*, which refutes the premise that the transformation of human beings is an educative task where one section of society educates another. Society not only conditions humans but they too impinge on the environment. And since circumstances do not exist outside men, the transformation of an object by a subject must entail the transformation of the subject himself (Sanchez Vázquez 1977, 122).

In the role they espoused as tribunes of knowledge, the Communist ideologues dismissed the importance of securing a dialogical (Bakhtin) relationship with their audience, a relationship of mutual interaction. Instead they engaged in one-way communication, assuming a monological (Bakhtin) disposition that separated the "purity" of their scientific rationalism from the affective needs of their public.[14] Implicit in their proselytizing was the assumption that Communist ideology was a science, or at least could be presented in its pure logical form. Yet as I shall argue throughout this book, all ideology, though highly discursive in content, is profoundly aesthetic in structure and depends on certain pleasure principles of *immediate* gratification linked to aesthetic apprehension. (Cf. chapters 1, 2, 5 and 6.) However reluctant Communists were to appropriate the rhetorical devices of conservative discourse, however keen they were to preserve a rationalist rectitude, their rhetoric necessarily harboured its distinctive but nonetheless dramatic and aesthetic unities, as well as its tendency to reinvent nationalism in new apparel.

NATIONALISM, AESTHETICS, AND POLITICAL PROPAGANDA

Being the primary handmaiden and consummate catalyst of modern (particularly Western) propaganda, nationalism is not merely an aggregate of individuals circumscribed by a normative framework of institutions, economic activity, cultural experience, and identity; nor is it simply the abstract idea of nationhood marking the essential cohesion and driving force of a community in search of autonomy and legitimacy, be it self-determining or imperialistic. It is the particular coordination of these elements, integrated and brought to its final pitch through the dramatic and aesthetic structures of ideology itself.

There are many ways to skin a cat, and nationalism has proven to be not just any cat, but the one from Cheshire, omnipresent yet elusive, a source of mystery yet manifestly there before us. Despite the countless ways of addressing the phenomenon, sociologists and political theorists who have differed on the question of nationalism's either universal or specifically modern character generally agree that this creature of social reality is about political institutions and sovereignty. John Breuilly claims, "Nationalism is above and beyond all else, about politics and politics is about power. Power in the modern world is primarily about control of the state. The central question, therefore, should be to relate nationalism to the objective of obtaining state power" (Breuilly in Collins 1990, 106). In contrast with much sociological and political theory on nationalism (see, *inter alia*, Anderson 1983; Breuilly 1982; Gellner 1983; Greenfeld 1992; Kedourie 1966; Minogue 1987; Nairn 1981; Seton-Watson 1964, 1977; Smith 1983; Taylor 1991), my purpose here is not so much to describe how state power is obtained as to show that this "political" process is undergirded by aesthetic forms. The approach comes closer to literary and cultural examinations of nationalism (see, *inter alia*, Bhabha 1990; Eagleton 1990a; Jameson 1990; Said 1990; Wright 1985), and arises from the assumption that nationalism is pre-eminently *ideological* and therefore a *material force* inextricably, though not exclusively, linked to the workings of propaganda. Emphasis here is on the rhetorical moment of nationalism and the manner in which it manages the diverse facets of knowledge – science, ethics, and aesthetics; truth, integrity, and beauty – components essential to persuasive discourse, and thus, to achieving political power.

In contrasting Conservative and Communist rhetoric, I have sought to offset the quandary of dissenting British propagandists whose political discourse can be understood as an awkward unity of sublimated nationalist aesthetics and an ethical duty to scientific "truth." It is perhaps in the contradictory and aporetic nature of this rhetoric of dissent that the fundamental tensions of nationalism come to the fore. For only in an instance of imbalance and uncertainty can one begin to analyse the mechanisms of a discourse that is ever making claims to homogeneity and equanimity. The idealist veneer of nationalism is sustained by internal contrivances, aesthetic fictions that soothe the wounds of social distress and gratify the longing for a utopian redemption from crisis. Yet if nationalism can appease these desires, it must be subject to ethical judgment, for what it offers is always an illusion that deceives, not only within the bounds of fiction, but ultimately and most importantly within reality itself. The question is, then, how do we judge the aesthetic form ethically when it is ever sealing itself from political contingencies and ridding itself of all moral preoccupation? How do we reconcile ethics and aesthetics when truth is harsh and tragic? Kant's *Critique of Judgment* and preeminently his category of the sublime illuminate the query by beautifying sacrifice and agony and by embracing the aesthetic and ethical facets of judgment.[15]

But what of the relevance of Kant to the peculiarities of Communist Englishness? Apart from the useful systematicity with which it classifies aesthetic relationships, Kant's third *Critique* facilitates a typology of two forms of political propaganda, the one hegemonically centred (Conservative rhetoric), the other peripheral (Communist discourse). It serves as a useful repository of philosophical questions that now replay, now resolve the false polarities of utopia and scientific rationalism, as well as of class and nationhood which the Communists regularly confronted. But most important, in the Kantian category of the sublime reside the tensions between aesthetics and ethics which typify the dilemmas of Communist ideologues and thus exemplify in sensuous form the very essence of their predicament: how to *inspire* duty; how to give visible form to their abstract and often obscure doctrines of revolution; how to reconcile imaginative sensibility and moral rationality; how to retain ethical integrity in the face of the enthralling powers of an imperialist nationalism.

My use of Kant's third *Critique*[16] appears reminiscent of sections of Terry Eagleton's *Ideology of the Aesthetic* (Eagleton 1990, 196–233) which furnish a sensitive analysis of the sublime content of Marxist thought and praxis, as well as of the omnipresence of the beautiful in dominant bourgeois politics. However, in establishing that Conservative and Communist propaganda find their respective aesthetic correlates in the Kantian categories of beauty and the sublime, my emphasis has been less on the *ideology* of the aesthetic than on the *aesthetic* character of ideology, on its performative (rhetorical) dimension, which is capable of creating ideal constructs of reality and inducing an aesthetic apprehension of political thought. The homology which I posit between two forms of political rhetoric and Kant's aesthetic categories is preeminently an attempt to demystify the assumption that Marxist propaganda is purely rationalistic, cleansed of those slippery aesthetic flourishes associated with irrationalist conservatism; furthermore, whereas Communist propaganda has prided itself on its scientific rationalism, its monological tendency simulates inclusive societal dialogue, while only addressing its own converted community. Like its conservative counterpart, Communist propaganda does not persuade cognitively; it rather sways through tautology, for it is quintessentially a discourse of self-affirmation and inclusion, or conversely of moral repudiation and ideological exclusion. In such rhetorical communication, cognitive mediation is subordinated either to the pleasures of sharing in the warm embrace of community beliefs, or to the displeasures of adamant dissent where the marginality of difference is accompanied by the sublimated anguish of isolation.

HOW THIS BOOK IS STRUCTURED

To comprehend this book fully, the reader will need to follow the sequence of chapters chronologically, for each section is inextricably related to preceding and subsequent parts, and indeed to an overall pattern where aesthetic theory is closely woven with empirical history. Chapter 1 offers a theoretical framework of propaganda, including a detailed discussion of Kant's categories of beauty and sublimity. This introductory sequence should be construed less as a rehearsal of the traditional or pathbreaking debates on aesthetics than as a device for reevaluating conventional assumptions which relegate propaganda to a discourse of sheer deceit and instrumentality. My discussion of propaganda's ontic tendencies – those inexorable surges of self-affirmation – is intended to supplant pure moralizing on the duplicitous nature of instrumental and manipulative discourse. The analysis will concentrate on the discursive poetics of propaganda, those communicative devices that induce holistic, conceptless perceptions of reality. And I shall argue that these discursive elements, while replete with idealism and artifice, are nonetheless irreducible features of human epistemology, indeed the very irrational matrix from which political discourse gains its consensual power.

Chapter 2 launches the empirical narrative of William Morris's legacy, and paints a critical portrait of the centenary celebrations of 1934 and Baldwin's centenary speech. In this section, the category of beauty is posited as a correlative structure of common-sense Englishness (also indicative of capitalist consciousness) from which Stanley Baldwin draws his compelling rhetorical force and community consent.

Chapters 3, 4, and 5 concentrate on Robin Page Arnot's *William Morris: A Vindication, the* polemical reply to the 1934 centenary. These chapters trace the Communist reversal of the conservative appropriation of Morris's memory – a sentimental, mainstream portrait that Communists, notably Arnot, dismantled with particular adamancy yet also with an awkward vigour that disclosed the tension of their revolutionary principles and political practice. It is this tension which frames my analyis of Arnot's typically Communist rhetoric. Chapters 6 and 7 are devoted to the ensuing revolutionary discourse of the Popular Front[17] and of the Cold War. Chapter 6 consists in a detailed textual analysis of Jack Lindsay's poem "not english?" and chapter 7 discusses E.P. Thompson's lecture "William Morris and the Moral Issues of To-Day," a text delivered in 1951 as part of a conference on the American threat to British culture.

The treatment of the central text, *William Morris: A Vindication*, is a reconstruction of the character of Communist propaganda of the 1930s. Arnot's pamphlet can be understood metaphorically as a ruin endowed with traces of its formerly complete edifice. Its lost totality has been retraced and erected anew from an intensive analysis based on the paradigmatic import of one individual and his rhetorical relation to the pervasive currents of his Communist community: Arnot's Marxism-Leninism and its influence on his tract, and his cultural mentality (see the ascetic devotion to the cause of Communism which he adulates in Morris and which he no doubt applies in compliance with Party tenets, as well as his characteristic tensions as an intellectual proselytizing to the "masses"). Through these interweaving strands, Arnot's polemic ties together the fundamental political features of a Communist movement in the 1930s.

The propagandist lyric, "not english?," by the Communist writer Jack Lindsay (biographer of William Morris, among other things) was written in 1936 during the period of the Popular Front. It lends insight into the evolution of Comintern political invective. There the covert search for national identity is brought to its fullest expression in the utopian resolution of Lindsay's poem. Ideologically, "not english?" acts as a transitional piece, bridging Arnot's earlier pamphlet and the third text, E.P. Thompson's Cold-War Communist intervention ("William Morris and the Moral Issues of To-day"). Historically too, Lindsay's poem is significant in that its author was the editor of the *Left Review* and *Arena* journals and the very figure who inspired Thompson to write his speech on Morris for the *Arena* issue of 1951.

Lindsay's poem and Thompson's speech supplement Arnot's pamphlet in my analysis. Though they belong to the historical periods of the late 1930s, 1940s, and 1950s, they are not treated as autonomous entities, interesting in themselves, but as retrospective commentaries on the sectarian era of the Comintern. They provide evidence (1) that the suppression of nationalism or national self-identification could not be sustained beyond a certain point and that the floodgates of Englishness even for the erstwhile internationalists had eventually to burst open; (2) that under new conditions of political hegemony and sectarianism, namely those of the Cold War, nationalism once again could not be easily espoused by Communists; (3) that whereas in the 1930s, the colour and sensuality of the glories of Communist Englishness were reserved for a future point in history – some distant utopia – in the 1950s the sense of Englishness in all of its beauty and alleged authenticity was cast within the framework of a romanticized tradition of revolt. Even the poem "not english?" is compelled to articulate English communist identity in the form of a utopian projection – a space of negativity disjointed from the reality of everyday life. In each instance, a nationalist collective identity could never be registered with utter immediacy – it was always sublimated either by prospection or retrospection away from the profanity of the present, entrenched as each epoch (Class-Against-Class, Popular Front, and Cold War periods respectively) was in the ground of bourgeois society. These two supplementary texts must be seen, therefore, as the epiphanies of the sectarianism of the 1930s. What was not visible in the "obscurity of the lived moment" (Bloch 1977), i.e. in the Class-Against-Class period, can be witnessed with hindsight in the later moments of the Popular Front and the Cold War.

But in addition, these two discourses function as extensions of the argument developed in chapters 2 to 5 in which the aesthetic of the sublime (with its intrinsically ascetic and internationalist ethos) is traced beyond the parameters of the sectarian period of the Comintern. Representing two further examples of the ongoing dynamic of sublimity, these texts reflect the vicissitudes and reversals of an earlier (1930s) revolutionary propaganda. The movement from Arnot's sublime rhetoric through Lindsay's poetic discourse to that of Thompson constitutes an expansive development replicated by the aesthetic category which shifts from its character of pure dissent and polemical protest to one of aristocratic aloofness and chauvinist self-affirmation reminiscent of bourgeois nationalism itself. The crucial function of the last chapter on Thompson's rhetoric is to explore the ambiguous character of the sublime within the boundaries of Communist discursive practice and thereby identify the dynamics which forestalled any veritable consummation of revolutionary ideals.

It is of course perilous to overstate the case of three ideologues whom I have categorized as ideal types. They do not in themselves carry the weight of all the Communists of their respective epochs. And indeed, there is the danger that the reader will interpret the notion of typicality in a sociological sense. However, it must be underscored that the methodology and interpretive analysis which have been deployed here entail an analytical approach stemming more from the humanities than from the social sciences. Within this disciplinary context, the term typology does not refer to the conclusions drawn from an investigative process akin to sociological surveys in which a large sample from a given study is scrutinized in terms of a scale of predetermined criteria. Indeed, my approach has been one of intensive rather than extensive analysis. In this respect, I have had to restrict myself to a small number of (model/ ideal) propagandist discourses. Clearly, in the fields of sociology or history, such a small selection of empirical examples would seem too scant to be considered worthy of scientific validation. But since I have not undertaken a sociological experiment, additional empirical examples of Communist propaganda/ists would not be integral to my method. Nor is my purpose here to engage in pure textual exegesis or meticulous empirical biographies of rhetoricians as a means of delineating Communist propaganda. Instead, I propose a strategy of validation that emerges out of a non-Foucauldian literary archaeology. Chapter 3 is a case in point. The treatment of Arnot's political tract is first and foremost a reconstruction of a dissenting discursive practice. It is an analysis which draws out the depth and three-dimensionality of the polemical text, amplifying its intertextual resonances and revealing its multifarious (political, aesthetic, psychological, and philosophical) layers. In a polyphony (Bakhtin) of mutually echoing references, Arnot's tract can be construed as more than a single/singular voice. For while his discourse appears to be but one among many propagandist pieces, it is in fact a typical[18] instance of Communist rhetoric – neither the sum nor the average of a whole ensemble of texts, but a concrete universal (Hegel) that harnesses the most essential features of its political community.

If I have focused upon the 1930s, it is not with the intention of mapping a local history of propaganda; my hope has been to yield new ideas on the ramifications of sectarian dissenting rhetoric. Arnot's text is a discursive aperture through which a whole ideological mentality may be perceived. And the category of the sublime, which endows Arnot's tract with typicality, extends the *Vindication*'s relevance beyond the specific era of Comintern sectarianism, revealing a continuity in the disposition of Communist ideologues throughout various historical epochs.

In an interdisciplinary way, I have attempted to show the links between aesthetics and politics, non-rational and rational thought, and more specifically between German aesthetics and British Comintern and Cold War rhetoric. It must be said, however, that these relationships lend themselves to a discussion of a wide variety of subjects to which I have not accorded the same degree of attention. This is not a cultural-cum-historical monograph on either William Morris or his claimants. Nor is there any pretence of an orthodox treatment of Kantian philosophy. It is rather an attempt to engage with English political culture through philosophical categories that highlight the epistemological and ontological underpinnings of a proto-revolutionary discourse.

Nor do I claim to resolve or supersede the conflicts and paralysing dichotomies which the subject matter raises. Yet, perhaps the dynamic of an alternative, dialectical method that this book seeks to adopt may contribute in some minor fashion to weakening society's "mind-forg'd manacles," to liberating contemporary thought from what is now a sclerotic scientistic idealism, theoretical and aloof from praxis, now an eclectic and fissiparous empiricism, saturated with the fetishisms of the *status quo*.

CHAPTER ONE

Philosophical Reflections:
Towards a Theory of Propaganda

PROPAGANDA AND BOURGEOIS IDEALISM

Propaganda is often considered a politically motivated enterprise in which attempts to transmit ideological values are realized by affecting people's thinking; it has come to represent a method of persuasion involving psychological manipulation, deception, and political coercion. Familiarly used pejorative terms such as these have tended to lodge the discussion of propaganda almost exclusively within a genre of human wilfulness, thus thwarting a more "objective" account of what propaganda represents beyond its seemingly unmitigated maliciousness. Yet while it would be naïve to suppose that propaganda does not (either consciously or unconsciously) distort the object of its statement, it is worthwhile recalling that even the most rationalist of discourses is implicated in the use of aesthetic niceties and potential fictions. Public discourse cannot readily be split into truthful versus deceptive persuasion. Indeed, to trace the border between manipulative and merely convincing information seems beside the point. For that suggests a division of discourse in which the chastity of absolute truth would stand pitted against the evils of falsity: a Manichean battle between the knights of honesty and the dragons of deception. Of course, avoiding categorical antinomies does not mean that we should jettison all ethical perspectives in favour of sheer relativism. Still, it is important to underscore the fact that no one vantage point can be wholly rationalist or utterly objective. "Every determination is a negation," as Spinoza has it; every self-vindication is forged at the expense of something or someone else. Propaganda takes this maxim to its ultimate pitch, for in its desire to promote a given advocacy it is never casual or conversational. Its determinations are far from neutral. On the contrary, propagandist discourse often waxes destructive of otherness while aggrandizing and idealizing its own perspective. This inflated self-importance constitutes a seminal moment in a rhetorical self-empowerment that dramatizes the virtues of the propagandist ego and shunts aside the value of the other. It is this epistemological narcissism which is at the heart of what we conventionally perceive as distortion. It is this epistemological imbalance which would also suggest that distortion cannot be purely ascribed to ideological conspiracies or to indulgent aestheticism. Indeed, if we treat the Manichean idealism of propaganda in terms of its origins rather than exclusively in relation to its nefarious effects, we may be able to liberate the concept of political discourse from the cage of its demeaned status as a purely slanderous and dubious process; we may shed light on the ontological character of propaganda as an activity of self-vindication.

Like Hannah Arendt's notion of politics, propaganda can be construed as a form of collective disclosure, "a realm of appearances in which human agents, acting together, disclose who they are and what they wish the world to look like" (Beiner 1983, 12). The preeminent issue here is that propaganda represents that social process in which political actors construct a public stage, delimiting a sphere open to view, yet controlled by those very ideologues[1] whose intent is to dramatize their collective identity in the most ideal apparel. Propaganda provides the forum in which a given community identity may be projected boldly as autonomous, free from perturbing constraints and elevated to incomparable superiority. Clearly, such a phenomenon is not only discursive but fundamentally ritualistic and theatrical. As a transmission of knowledge, propaganda is both a performative deed and a verbal dis-play; its narration is condensed into quasi-palpable unities of idealism, glorified cameos of its authors' desires and self-perception. It is a public stage where actions and speeches are aesthetically gathered into a patterned whole, carved out, smoothed over and polished to a lustre that reflects the glamourizing projections of a self-affirming community. Nor is this phenomenon incidental. For in the midst of pervasive conflict, loss, human ephemerality, and societal dislocation, the natural human inclination is to fabricate aesthetically pleasing artefacts, celebrative events, symbols of solidarity that conjure up a place of desired social harmony. Through multiple artifices of heightened expression, aesthetic culture endows human communities with dignity and value, with the stability of tradition and with a defined sense of belonging. Similarly, as an artifice of politics, propaganda acts as an enhancing mechanism for parties and social groups in distress. It is an aesthetic process which fabricates meaning where there is often merely contradiction; it idealizes its own subjects' prowess and moral capability when they are deeply flawed and deficient; it creates a mock world[2] in which its truth becomes impervious to the alternate claims of the other, and in so doing, draws an imaginary line between its own laws of justice and those of the outer world. In this regard propaganda harbours something of the essence of a work of art.

But if this aesthetic process which propaganda shares with works of art is understood as a *sine qua non* of social being (not some frivolous act of self-adornment), then it is also a phenomenon linked to the human yearning to eclipse mortality. It is a condition that crystallizes humanity's self-assertion in the face of loss and strengthens its moral determination to override the disruptive breaks posed by dissolution. Similarly, political discourse finds itself frequently caught within the vital struggle of life versus death, particularly in the context of international rivalries. Yet even when this ontic battle is not overtly at issue, a residual urgency may be detected in propagandist communication. The imperative dynamic of such discourse predicates that it must be wholly approved, existentially felt, highly charged, and intolerant of the elasticity of casual conversational exchange. Endowed with the ambition to disseminate a given advocacy as effectively and as widely as possible, propaganda assumes an incontrovertible importance that engulfs its audience in the intensity of its statement.

But the successful outcome of propaganda cannot derive exclusively from a subjective willing of desire, from an insistent discourse that imposes its vantage point as an all-consuming voice of truth. However finely wrought in content and in form, the performative quality of this communicative process equally depends on the evaluative judgments implicitly and explicitly proffered by a given audience. The latter furnishes the delimiting markers of a propagandist performance, since it is the value system by which a community accepts or rejects a rhetorical intervention that determines the guiding principles of the ideologue's discursive mode. The propagandist's expression and an audience's reception are in fact interrelated, depending for their convergence and harmony on the degree to which speaker and audience share a common value system. Thus the epistemic and the performative facets of propaganda coalesce to form an interactive set of operations.

Political discourse must create that exquisite balance between an expression of subjectivity (aesthetically wrought and framed within a dramatic performance) and the reflection of community values and long-held assumptions. The interpenetration of these two poles is dialectical, for the historical, existential moment of the performative act is aesthetic, forged out of a subjective will, while the aesthetic reception of the communicative event is socio-historical and predicated on the specific and local value judgments of the given epoch. It is this intermingling of the politico-historical and the aesthetic which marks the quintessential character of propaganda, most specifically as a discourse of modernity. Indeed, while propaganda appears as a transhistorical phenomenon, its specific dialectic of authorial individualism versus common-sense values joins it to that duality of subjective freedom and civic-ethical obligation to the collective will of the state, as embodied in the bourgeois citizen. Such is the modern blend of autonomy and bondage that typifies the nature of propaganda.

Standing upon the fulcrum of two historical periods, propaganda reveals its modernity through a bifurcated self-consciousness. Its conjunctural position splits its *Weltanschauung* in twain. Chronologically, it is born with the emergence of the modern state (the late eighteenth century). Epistemologically, it harbours a nostalgic yearning for its ancestral roots, classical Greek rhetoric. In its retrospective longing for an epoch when political education was merely a rhetorical reinforcement of the existing societal conditions, when oratory was largely a reenactment of the dominant ideology, propaganda is both regressive in its desire for simplicity and innocence, and progressive in its historical kinship with pathbreaking movements such as the French Revolution.

The conjunctural character of propaganda, namely its coalescence of old and new politico-philosophical perspectives, is analogous to the nostalgic propensities of German philosophical idealists such as Hegel and Schiller. These treated the period of ancient Greece as the summit of exemplary *Sittlichkheit*, the beautiful, good, ethical life, which they contrasted with the "soulless mechanism of the modern state" (Gadamer 1986, 14). This aesthetico-ethical value of Beauty, ascribed by the eighteenth-century philosophers to the Greek political system, intended to represent how people from former eras found their ethical ideals concretized in their everyday lives. The virtues of the political state were said to coincide with the particular existence of each citizen, allowing these members to recognize themselves both individually and through society as a whole.

Whether such a coincidence of state ideals and real society was historically true seems less important than the fact that eighteenth-century philosophers deployed a concept of societal harmony as an exemplary model against which their modern state could be pitted. A putative societal unity which linked the general social outlook of the people with their actual life experiences was conceived by those in the modern period as commenting upon the divisive character of their own political orders. The fissiparous nature of modernity was marked by the split between civil society and the state, a split which incurred the loss of the naïve *Sittlichkheit* which had harmonized the constituent parts of premodern society into a form of alleged beauty. As Z.A. Pelczynski has pointed out, the emergence of civil society in Western Europe towards 1789 formed a sphere of the nation-state in which a complex of social and political practices and institutional relations served to promote the rights of the individual. Indeed, "[civil society] was bound up with the conception of an abstract, atomistic individual, pursuing his selfish interests through work, production, contract and exchange and enjoying morally and legally guaranteed rights to free activity in the economic, social and cultural sphere" (Pelczynski 1984, 263).

But while it enabled the individual to fulfil himself privately, civil society was inadequate for his complete self-realization, since it dismissed his capacity for public action, his ability to act on behalf of shared interests and ideals. The rupture evinced here between private and public interests, between civil society and the state, characterizes a crucial aspect of capitalist alienated social relations, relations which thwart any veritable convergence between ethical ideals and real labour processes (Pelczynski 1984). A harmonious relation, such as Hegel might have visualized it through his invocation of the Greek polis, could be recon-stituted as a modern *Sittlichkeit*, yet only through the idealism of nationalist consciousness, which beckons individuals to the public, polit-ical arena and seemingly restores the lost "unity" of ancient democracy.

The above contrast between ancient and modern forms of political organization lends us an analogy upon which propaganda and classical rhetoric may be theorized. Ancient political rhetoric can be understood in terms of the shared values and interlocking relation of society's public and private interests. From this it may be presumed that such political discourse carried a reiterative function, that is, one in which rhetoric aimed merely to inflect the ideological presuppositions generally held by society at large. Here a substantial common sense linked the speaker to his audience. Propaganda, by contrast, breaks forth with the capitalist epoch, with the advent of nationalism and romantic individualism. As the illegitimate child of ancient rhetoric, propaganda comes into existence through the schisms of societal re-formations, through revolutionary sunderings of old feudal structures and through the reversal of whole *Weltanschauungen*. It finds itself caught in the cleavage which Hegel announced as the separation of civil society and the state, and as such, it replicates the alienated features of bourgeois individualism, of private and common interests severed into incommunicable polarities.[3] Here then, modern rhetoric (or propaganda) stands devoid of an *inherent* common sense which would otherwise bond the propagandist to his audience.

In its modernity and anchorage to a fragmented, class-riven society, propaganda betrays the political desire to recuperate some semblance of community consensus, some coincidence between state ideals and actual societal relations. This does not imply that all propaganda expresses its nostalgia for a "pre-lapsarian" epoch in overt uniformity. Depending upon the nature of the ideologue, propagandist forms differ according to whether they are of ruling-class origins or of anti-institutional dissent. Still, the common element in differing types of discourse is that, as with philosophy, they are really forms of homesickness marked by an "urge to be at home everywhere" (Lukács 1978, 29). In other words, propaganda ideally manifests itself as a political struggle by rhetoricians to harmonize their ethical ideals and the real lived experiences of the social majority. Being at home constitutes being at one in all capacities of life, epistemological, social, as well as political. And the expression of this desired oneness is embodied in the self-enclosed perfection and self-sufficient totality of aesthetic forms – forms such as the Hegelian concept of Beauty and its ascription to the ideal Greek political state. Seen in the context of the ancient Athenian democracy, the aesthetic structure of Beauty represents an innocent or naïve form of absolute harmony. Yet within the setting of modernity, the aesthetic structure of Beauty is sentimental, for it consists in merely the appearance of total perfection.[4] In truth, it represents a desire for a unity between ethical ideals and political reality in an age when such a consonance is no longer possible.

In the interpenetration of propagandist polarities (epistemology and political practice), the aesthetic structure of Beauty acts as a catalyst to represent the form of a given society, yet never the form which corresponds to what is but rather that which corresponds to what ought to be. The aesthetic component is expedient for visualizing and delivering aspirations towards new social orders. Such aspirations are, however, not realist depictions but rather portraits of the contradictory world of modernity, elevated to the stature of ideal, harmonious conditions. Propaganda creates this idealism in its deployment of aesthetic structures which mask the tensions present in the forced (and thus incompatible) coalescence of outmoded, unitary world-outlooks and political states of the modern era. Consequently, in mediating between political theory and praxis, propaganda reveals itself as a form of self-enhancement that eclipses material discrepancies and appropriates those aesthetic structures most suitable for idealizing its form and content. The aesthetic structure which facilitates propagandist communication is a type of judgment, a category of endorsement. Such a catalyst is indispensable to modern political discourse, bereft as the latter is of tacit approval, and fated with a continual search for consensual recognition from its community. Propaganda is ever pursuing an ideological home, a concord between the unsubstantiated claims of the bourgeois individual (the ideologue) and the evaluative judgments harnessed in common sense (the audience). Part of this search for consensus entails the construction of an illusion that the propagandist odyssey has already been completed and a unity between the authorial subject and his audience soundly secured. Indeed, the cunning technique of the propagandist is to offer the impression that his discursive statement is not tendentious but universally accepted, and that the gulf which separates the ideologue from his community has been superseded even before the rhetorical enterprise has begun. The sleight of hand occurs as the propagandist assumes the voice of dogmatic truth rather than that of dithering relativity. To comprehend the details of this feat, which dispels the ideologue's subjective stance and transforms it into a widely accepted standpoint, we must probe the judgment of taste, specifically the aesthetic of the beautiful which Kant delineates in his third *Critique*. For it is this aesthetic category which will illuminate the propagandist manœuvre of winning consent through tautology rather than through meticulous rational persuasion.

PROPAGANDA AND AESTHETIC JUDGMENTS

As a discourse germane to the modern state, propaganda reproduces the schisms and alienations of contemporary society, a society bereft of that much-sought *Sittlichkeit* uniting citizen and community. Liberal democracy pretends to cherish the virtues of a harmonious union between individual and collectivity; with the niceties of political rhetoric, it legitimates itself through a recuperation of the alleged congruence of premodern social orders, apparently superseding the hiatus of modern society – that chasm between ethical ideals and fragmentary social relations. In this ideological vindication of the capitalist state, hegemonic propaganda pursues a course of elaborate and often subtle persuasion in which three fundamental principles stand out:

(1) the production of idealist visions of society. These are substantiated through an iconography and discursive imagery that is culturally and historically determined by the predisposition of its audience;
(2) the invocation of subjective, sensuous perceptions, experiences of reality that serve to infuse the idealist projections of the propagandist message with an accessible, plausible realism;
(3) the application of evaluative forms and commonsensical topoi, structures that endow propagandist claims with a seeming ground of objectivity and legitimacy.

These three strategies in no way exhaust the corpus of propagandist operations, yet they form a skeleton upon which other unspecified elements may be fleshed out. The encounter between (2) (individual assertions expressed as subjective experience) and (3) (the structures or standards for validating such assertions) forms a relationship between quality and quantity respectively. It is on this interactive couplet that factor (1) (the idealist vision of society) is produced. In other words, the degree of endorsement received for a propagandist message will depend upon the natural convergence felt between the quality of experience expressed (the subjectivity of the discourse) and the objective structures of validity that are deployed in its defence. For, ultimately, it is not sufficient that the content of a propagandist message project an idealist image which embodies the worth of society; it is also imperative that the rhetorical form appear as well integrated and harmoniously wrought as possible. It is the interpenetration of the components of quality (subjective expression) and quantity (objective validation) that determines the fluency and internal consistency of this element of form and, by extension, the degree of wholesale approval awarded to the propagandist intervention.

If we turn to the aesthetic categories of beauty and the sublime which Kant classifies more generally under the rubric of judgments of taste, a similar relation between *subjective perception* and *objective validation* may be discerned. The aesthetic judgment is divided, as in the above model of rhetoric, according to the relations of quantity and quality.[5] In the division of quality, Kant presents the branch of the aesthetic judgment which pertains to individual, subjective perception. In the division of quantity, he articulates the element of universal communicability, an imperative factor for consummating the judgment, rendering it spontaneously pleasurable and universally valid. The two facets of the judgment constitute the poles of particularity and universality, and their special convergence comes to define the specific nature of the aesthetic judgment itself.

A judgment, according to Kant, is "the union of representations in one consciousness"; it is the faculty of subsuming the particular under the universal (the faculty in which particular cases are grouped under a general structure). But this definition of how the universal and the particular coalesce through a process of subsumption applies specifically to the concept formation of logical judgments.[6] The latter are formed through a causal superordination and subordination of elements, through "the exposition of an unbroken coherence of conditions, which can be conceived as the analogue of a connection between premises and conclusions" (Cassirer 1981, 309). Aesthetic judgments, or judgments of taste, are not, however, judgments of *concrete* cognition; in this respect they issue out of a representation of a given object whose empirical, objective properties are denied, or held at bay. The aesthetic judgment does not concern itself with the ground or consequences of its objects, but compels a contemplative attitude which instantly unites the manifold character of its object through intuition. Seizing a purely timeless meaning, it eclipses the causal relations of temporality that are normally registered in a cognitive judgment (Cassirer 1981, 310). Still, such a judgment can claim *objective* legitimacy even while it disregards the material qualities of its considered object, for it replaces a logical structure of validity with a structure of affective satisfaction. Satisfaction is the experience which accompanies the representation of an object, and, as such, becomes the determining measure for validating the aesthetic judgment. In brief, that which is judged is neither the object *per se* nor the subject contemplating the object but the *subjective relation* of the subject to its object.

Unlike experiences of satisfaction which are either sensually "pleasant" or morally "good," the aesthetic judgment of beauty is indifferent as regards its object of contemplation. The former two are bound by some interest or purpose. The "good" refers to a concept of a specific object. For "in order to find anything good, I must always know what sort of a thing the object ought to be, i.e. I must have a concept of it" (Kant 1951, 41). Similarly, that which is deemed "pleasant" rests on material sensation (e.g. I must smell a flower to know its fragrance). But paradoxically, the judgment of the beautiful (as a judgment of taste) succeeds in achieving universal assent for its subjective claims – indeed, succeeds in granting its judgment an air of objectivity – even while it has refused to say anything particular about its object *per se*. In its indifference to its object, the judgment of taste is disinterested;[7] it overrides private interests in favour of a general satisfaction that appears aesthetically valid for everyone. And based on what can be presupposed in every other person, and contingent on the belief that there is cause for attributing a uniform satisfaction to everyone, the judgment of taste will speak of the "beautiful" as if beauty were characteristic of the object and as if the judgment were logical. An aesthetic judgment thus assumes the appearance of a logical judgment because it has appropriated that characteristic feature of universality, namely the presupposition of its validity for all men/women.

In succeeding to claim validity for its subjective satisfaction without in any way grounding the universality of its judgment in objects, it acquires the status of *subjective universality*.[8] For even as it does not furnish a grounded, objective validity for its claims, its impartial and disinterested character gains universal approval. This affords it a universality of commonly held subjective attitudes which stand in for an actual, objective truth.

The universal acceptability of the judgment of taste is contingent on its capacity to proffer total satisfaction universally and with impartiality at that. This satisfaction is not a pleasure based on the plenitude of material sensation, or on that of moral contentment, but on a satisfaction contingent on the universal consensus and communicability of a judgment. Such communicability derives from the more quintessential or ontological pleasure linked to social inclusion within a given community.[9] Access to and identity with the *sensus communis* is not merely a linguistic or cultural immersion in the ideology of a social group, but a quasi-filial membership in the warmth of a community. As Kant points out, "the power of communicating one's state of mind, even though only in respect of the cognitive faculties, carries a pleasure with it, ... we can easily show [this] from the natural propension of man toward sociability (empirical and psychological)" (Kant 1951, 53).

The qualitative aspect of satisfaction in communicating a judgment intersects with and depends on its quantitative character, that is, with the manner in which a subjective attitude is deemed universally communicable and acceptable to all. Indeed, "[i]f the determining ground of our judgment as to this universal communicability of the representation is to be merely subjective, i.e. is conceived independently of any concept of the object, it can be nothing else than *the state of mind* [added emphasis], which is to be met with in the relation of our representative powers to each other, so far as they refer a given representation to *cognition in general*" (Kant 1951, 52). But the judgment of taste seems to enjoy the benefits of both concept-determined and non-conceptual judgments. It preserves the autonomy of an Olympian disinterestedness, unsullied by the resistances of the empirical world, yet in spite of its non-cognitive status, it retains a share in the harvest won from structures of universal validity. The judgment of taste consequently dons the robes of "cognition in general" and secures a communicability that rescues it from the questionable worth of pure subjectivity. This *cognition in general* is recuperated through the harmonious interaction of the imagination (the coalescence of various intuitions) with the understanding (the conceptual moment which unites representations according to the imperatives of Kantian reason; cf. below). It is the harmony of the cognitive faculties which engenders a purposiveness[10] or adequate logic that guarantees the validity of the aesthetic judgment. The judgment consequently makes sense in general without being riveted to any material object or condition of interest.[11]

AN AESTHETIC TYPOLOGY OF PROPAGANDA

To claim as Eagleton does that "the aesthetic judgment is ... a kind of pleasurable free-wheeling of our faculties, a kind of parody of conceptual understanding, a non-referential pseudo-cognition which does not nail down the object to an identifiable thing, and so is agreeably free of a certain material constraint" (Eagleton 1990, 85–6) is to suggest that it is a traitor to logical judgments. Indeed, it is true that the aesthetic judgment does not subsume its particular subjective experience under the universal in a cognitive (deductive) fashion and that its disinterested posture forbids it to engage with its object directly. It is equally true that the aesthetic judgment asserts its universal validity by lending its claims an air of probability and internal consistency. Short of veritable proof, it violates the scientific nature of logical judgments while borrowing their general principle of cognition as a guise of validity. However, this violation in no way casts a shadow on the ethical character of the aesthetic judgment, since the latter never pretends to be anything other than aesthetic, and can thus exonerate itself of an otherwise condemnable artifice.

Throughout, the judgment of taste evades material confrontation with objective discrepancies. If the judgment is able to voice its claims universally on behalf of everyone, it does so not by postulating "the agreement of everyone (for that can only be done by a logically universal judgment because it can adduce reasons)"; instead it "*imputes* this agreement to everyone, as a case of the rule in respect of which it expects, not confirmation by concepts, but assent from others" (Kant 1951, 50–1). Here the judgment, which refuses to enter into cognitive inquiry, does not expect or intend from others a confirmation of its concepts, but rather requires assent. The universal voice, therefore, hovers above material interests and as such it cannot be interrogated or called to justify the grounds upon which it rests its case.

Were we to transpose the structure of the aesthetic judgment to the relation that a propagandist holds in respect to society, we would find the individual propagandist and his community analogous to the singular judgment of the beautiful with its subjective universality. (The analogy is of course contingent on the potential that this propagandist has for winning universal consent.) In seeking to marry his own subjective stance with the validating norms of a given audience, he must in effect violate rational proof in the same way as the subject of an aesthetic judgment does. In so far as he has no full mandate from the people to apply as law, his method is not a deductive one. Unable to demonstrate his logic to his audience from a solipsistic, or idiosyncratic, stance (one must always mediate with one's audience), his method is an aesthetic mode where universal objectivity appears to have been subsumed under a particular claim, and through a particular object. But in fact, only the appearance of objectivity has been engendered. Thus, a propagandist who in a modern era seeks to win if not preserve hegemonic power must assert his singular appeals as if they were authoritatively and objectively true. His discourse must achieve an immanent quality akin to an aesthetic judgment if only by his very appropriation of rhetorical forms which *demand assent*, expect *universal endorsement*, and thus, exempt him from the cognitive processes of deductive or inductive proof. The propagandist has neither the time nor the space to engage in actual logical demonstrations; he has only condensed moments in which to foster an air of rational and objective truth. This, indeed, is his performative feat.

The assertiveness and seductively coercive character of the aesthetic judgment (specifically the beautiful) which does not hope for accord but rather gracefully secures it by dint of pleasurable enticements can be relocated in the confident spirit which fuels a propagandist discourse. Here the self-affirming rhetorical voice is such that the discursive message is delivered as if it were already generally valid and widely upheld. The propagandist form avoids tentative, hypothetical gestures, hesitancies and internal rifts in logic. Unlike scholarly treatises that are constrained by the barriers of stylistic courtesy, propaganda betrays a robust, illocutionary character, achieving its effect with self-possession and untrammelled self-evidence.

As an aesthetic judgment, the category of the beautiful is particularly suited to demagogues who are endowed with a hegemonic power that enables them to voice their persuasion as if it were the confirming echo of the popular will. In this, they replicate the very tautological structures of the beautiful, which elicits mere contemplation, a free mental play that rehearses the said virtues of the state and refrains from tortuous analyses of society's flaws and deficiencies. And even when there may be divergences between ideological representations of political affairs (as delivered by august statesmen) and real, popular experiences, the beautiful enters in as a matrix of legitimizing common sense, frequently embodied in the abstract concept of "the people," that imagined community of hegemonically incorporated citizens that is invoked as a sign of prevailing consensus.

But not all demagogues possess the privilege of wielding such rhetorical forms as the judgment of the beautiful, a judgment which constitutes the correlative structure of ruling-class nationalist discourse. For those representatives of the national community who differ with the ruling-class hegemony, the aesthetic of the beautiful and its political equivalent (nationalism) cannot and will not be unequivocally espoused (Rosa Luxemburg, for instance). These propagandists are not in a position to assert national consensus when they stand against the *status quo*. Ethically, they cannot presume to appropriate rhetorical forms that are produced through some sleight of hand, through the pseudo-objectivity of prejudice and custom that affirms what is "right" by way of moral law and not by scientifically generated claims. Nor can they accept the artifices endemic to this aesthetic judgment which is but a mock version of some authentic perfection. It must be recalled that the category of the beautiful does not correspond to the naïve beauty reminiscent of Greek antiquity. In reality it is a sentimental aesthetic whose hankering after an innocent unity between ideal human values and lived experience involves an artificial façade of natural harmony. Such an aesthetic category betrays its own anachronism and discomfort with the fissiparous character of the modern state. Against the ascendancy of capitalism, the mentality intrinsic to the judgment of the beautiful clings to the naïve epistemologies of past eras; and in carrying over antiquated forms of consciousness into modernity, such a judgment engenders the illusion that the past societal relations can coincide unequivocally with those of a new epoch.[12]

As the crystallization of a conservative mentality, the judgment of the beautiful stands as the object of Kant's inadvertent disapproval. (Cf. Beiner 1983, 61–2.) In other words, while Kant would not readily admit to impugning the value of the judgment, it becomes evident that he is doing so unwittingly, since the judgment of the beautiful bears a structural resemblance to the object of his overt critique, namely to the assumptions of pre-Enlightenment metaphysicians (Leibniz, Plotinus, Plato, etc.). As an Enlightenment thinker of the French Revolution, Kant criticizes premodern metaphysicians for their dogmatic obscurantism, for their unscientific search for objective knowledge, and for their resignation before the alleged givenness of cognition. Rather than take knowledge for granted, Kant's "Copernican revolution" entails a conscious investigation into how the structures of the mind operate. Similarly, the judgment of the sublime (the second of the two aesthetic judgments in Kant's *Critique of Judgment*) dismantles the unquestioned presuppositions of the judgment of the beautiful. The self-enclosed unity of the latter never seeks to prove its own claims through material objectivity, just as the dogmatism of pre-Enlightenment metaphysics asserts scientific knowledge even while only a speculative form of reason. We may thus conclude that Kant condemns the dogmatic metaphysicians in the same fashion as the judgment of the sublime unearths the unprobed depths of the judgment of the beautiful.

In discarding the philosophies of premodern metaphysicians, Kant offers (albeit within the parameters of his epistemology, which refuses to engage with contradiction) a meticulously honest and systematic statement on the limits of human cognition. Uncompromising in his effort to be accurate about the possibility of knowing reality, he avers that even the complete knowledge of the phenomenal world would amount to no more than a grasp of appearances, for reality in itself cannot be known (Kant 1986).

The judgment of the beautiful epitomizes Kant's disillusionment with the possibility of knowing reality; for him all that is knowable is the appearance of things, precisely that which characterizes the beautiful.

The latter proffers us merely the *form* of objectivity, the *appearance* of totality, while never confronting the material essence of the "thing in itself." This judgment is but a subjective ideal, and insufficient for an absolute apprehension of reality. In its partiality, but particularly in its artificial objectivity (its subjective universality), the judgment of the beautiful may be regarded as the aesthetic structure which captures the complacent and fetishistic essence of bourgeois consciousness. For ultimately, a judgment that presents itself as universally valid in default of rational proof can only resort to large measures of non-rationality in order to assert its claims.

Seen as the aesthetic form which marks the incipient religiosity of social consciousness within a secular capitalist order, the judgment of beauty is a crucial component of a bourgeois ideology: it offers an antidote to the individualism of civil society, contrasting with callous market relations which eclipse the affective bonds of human solidarity; it furnishes that compensatory ideal of a *Sittlichkeit* which raises the bourgeois individual from his mean posture as *homo oeconomicus* to a member of society endowed with a spirit of fraternity and civic duty. But where the aesthetic of the beautiful provides a humanitarian flourish, an appearance of intersubjective harmony and collective good will, where it seems to comment critically on the private interests of the market and its normative laws of exchange, it is also strangely complicit, through its internal workings, with the very economic determinant of capitalist society: the commodity form. Paradoxically, this aesthetic category is ambiguously both distinct from, and convergent with, the sphere of the market. A close scrutiny of the aesthetic judgment and the commodity form reveals that they share a strikingly common structure.

The judgment of beauty appears to reflect a qualitative condition of pleasure; in reality it mediates a qualitative/quantitative relation and subordinates the former to the latter. It appears to concern itself with subjectivity, translating the particularity of sensuous experience into a universal form. Like the commodity, the aesthetic category lets private experience fall prey to the consuming power of a social value; the materiality of the particular is thus distilled into the abstraction of the universal. Just as in the commodity, where exchange-value dominates use-value, so in the judgment of the beautiful, a quantitative representation of pleasure prevails over a qualitative experience which is renounced or left phantom-like, hovering as a lingering memory.

In essence the judgment of the beautiful compromises its link with sensuous immediacy in shifting from its material origins to an ideal, hollow shell of subjectivity. Yet this transmutation is utterly occluded. Like the commodity, which is seemingly a simple thing, a finished product with an exchange-value that obliterates real labour and itself with false immediacy, the judgment of the beautiful appears as a unitary object, a compelling but inexplicable value of seeming spontaneous generation. In fact, it is the product of a series of social, economic, and political conditions which have generated certain predispositions and cultural tastes. Yet its superficial allure is that of an impenetrable structure of gratification that fosters the sentiment of absolute pleasure – absolute because all-consuming and universally felt. Such a perfection is secured in appearance only, courtesy of the judgment's purposeless purposiveness,[13] a totality and state of completedness which is utterly abstract, above material discrepancy and partisanship.

The success of the aesthetic judgment as it achieves absolute fulfilment in the contemplative subject is contingent on its capacity to produce a seamless coincidence between subjectivity and objectivity, between the feelings of a receiving subject and an aesthetic object. In fostering this identical subject-object, the judgment creates a miraculous unity of differences, indeed a perfect fit of form and content. But in so doing, it proffers merely a formal equality of relations, never a material one. The purposiveness of the beautiful is purposeless, because abstract and detached from purpose, that is, from the substance of life. Similarly, the equation which exchange-value establishes between two commodities constitutes a standardized measurement which irons out differences into a subsuming unity – a rational unity of workers' labour time. But here, as with the beautiful, reference to material activity is jettisoned. Instead, a numerical form is ascribed to labour power, distilling the content of work into the pure form of abstract labour. Thus a seemingly disinterested mathematics is created out of material effort, exploitation, and social inequality. The latter contingencies amount to a "contaminating" content which "interferes" with the perfection of form, indeed with that *form*-ula of exchange. Reference to the particularity of labour is subordinated to some higher force while the labourer becomes invisible within the purely quantitative and formal terms of exchange.

The judgment of the beautiful is equally predicated on a formal totality. For the experience of beauty only emerges as an immediate and intuitive surrender to a consensus of commonly held tastes, a consensus which acts as an *ersatz* of real sensuous and subjective experience of fulfilment. Just as exchange-value is a social relation in which a standard measurement has been established between two objects of commerce, so the aesthetic judgment is a social relation where agreement has been cemented into a socially held form of beauty; but just as exchange-value makes no reference to its material sources, so the aesthetic judgment remains taciturn as to particular experience, conveying a universalizing structure of common pleasure that is alienated from personal subjectivity.

In their formal perfection, both the category of beauty and the commodity form offer the illusion of a social accord as if it were a preestablished harmony with no apparent origins. In both instances the autonomy of such accords or ratios of exchange assumes a force to which human subjects readily and blindly surrender. Social and historical geneses of value, whether pecuniary or aesthetic, become naturalized into fetishes, destinies, and laws that inhibitingly govern public consciousness. Such collective thought genuflects before appearances and limits its own expansive capacity to explore knowledge. Little wonder then that Kant, who may have had no articulate sense of commodity fetishism, was cognisant that the judgment of the beautiful belongs to the realm of sheer appearance. As an uncompromising rationalist, he would sooner have admitted with honesty to the impossibility of knowing or judging reality wholly than delude himself with a mirage of aesthetic (subjective) idealism. While his critique does not refer to market forces and the fetishism therein, he nonetheless defends a righteous morality that implicitly repudiates the judgment of the beautiful, leading it off-stage, and inviting in its stead the category of the sublime: the judgment of the supersensible which comments silently on the cognitive inferiority of the sensible world.

With the sublime, Kant presumes that real truth may be sought, and that the veritable questions of total knowledge may be addressed. Whether the grasp of such objective knowledge is ever realized remains to be seen. What, however, persistently begs interest is that the sublime judgment becomes the uninhibited critique of a judgment of appearances (i.e. the judgment of the beautiful); for with the sublime, it is not consonance but dissonance which is at work in a set of contradictions which are thrown into relief. These index the impossibility of making "real" sense of appearances short of a total succumbing to faith.

For comparable reasons, Kant and the dissenting propagandists may be seen to deploy the judgment of the sublime as an ethical aesthetic, symbolizing the desire for unadulterated truth. If the judgment of the beautiful suggests a spurious quality that characterizes the propagandist's operations in the bourgeois state, then it becomes incumbent upon the social critic to apply the aesthetic of the sublime as an indictment of contemporary society and as a gesture towards some alternative ideology.

Although derivative of the judgment of the beautiful, the judgment of the sublime blatantly exposes the contradictions of capitalist society; it foregrounds the discrepancy between the societal harmony represented by the judgment of the beautiful (analogously by nationalist rhetoric) and the veritable character of bourgeois society as an aggregate of atomized individuals, dislocated and individualistic in mentality. The characteristic feature of the sublime judgment is that, in its ethical critique of bourgeois consciousness, it is unable to express itself meaningfully and directly through conventional language. In Kantian terms, the sublime cannot formalize its judgment by referring to the visible structures and objects of the natural and social setting, but only by reaching out towards a space devoid of recognizable objects, a sphere beyond common sense. It is a judgment that represents itself through formless entities with the aim of negating the aesthetic of the beautiful and disrupting the parochial enclosures of a world of charm and appearance. In its repudiation of society's conventions, it provides a medium in which to comprehend the actions of dissenting propagandists whose rhetoric rejects mainstream sensibility and imagistic forms associated with the *status quo*. Bereft of a legitimate language by which to represent their alternative ideological views, these innovating rhetoricians are compelled to subvert conventional structures of consciousness through an ironic vision and multiple inversions of dominant thought. Such negativity arises out of their ideological marginality as well as out of their specific antagonism towards the ruling class. Lamenting their peripheral status, they exhibit their claims as unsung, *universal*, and *authentic* truths. Unlike conservative rhetoricians, who merely reinforce or echo preestablished social and political ideals, these dissenting figures must project a viewpoint that is credible, appealing, and endowed with apparent objectivity, and all this in default of the immediate recognition that a community would otherwise unthinkingly proffer the tribunes of common sense.

Dissenting propaganda is thus undermined in a twofold fashion: first in its failure to accede fluently and readily to the pregiven attitudes of its following; and secondly, in its paucity of sensuous expression. Indeed, sensuousness is crucial for political persuasion, not only in contributing to the vivid evocation of an ideal vision but also in its aesthetic capacity to foster that desired contemplative unity between ideologue and public where "perceiving and representing powers [are brought] into direct resonance" (Cassirer 1981, 316). But in dissenting propaganda, such enhancing and enabling sensuous material is often absent or overshadowed by a resolutely moral rather than expressive rhetoric, by a discourse that ruptures with commonplace consciousness and imposes an opaque if not unthinkable utopian space (e.g. Communist society) on its audience.

The sublime aesthetic, like the rhetoric of a revolutionary ideologue, expresses an ethically compelling message, but in so doing, it projects ideals that are wanting in consensual support and so unique that they exceed the limits of everyday consciousness. The sublime is therefore most suitable for dissenting propaganda, since it emblematically mirrors the efforts of an oppositional ideologue who must confer truth upon an *unrecognized* and often incomprehensible persuasion; conversely, the judgment replicates the audience's endeavour to grapple with far-reaching mental constructs delivered by the innovating rhetorician. More will be said about this below and in chapter 6. For the present, we must consider the distinctive features of the sublime itself.

Unlike the beautiful, which aims to demarcate a boundary around the movement of the imagination so as to engender aesthetic form, the sublime fails to trace a *visible* contour around the imagination, since it knows no object that will represent its intended meaning, a meaning which is boundless and beyond the immediacy of sheer appearances. The contrast between the sublime and the beautiful resides in their different conformity to the structures of the imagination: "Natural beauty (which is independent) brings with it a purposiveness in its form by which the object seems to be, as it were, preadapted to our judgment, and thus constitutes in itself an object of satisfaction" (Kant 1951, 83). The sublime, on the other hand, appears "as regards its form, to violate purpose in respect of the judgment, to be unsuited to our presentative faculty, and as it were to do violence to the imagination" (Kant 1951, 83).

In claiming that natural beauty is preadapted to our judgment (it brings with it an object whose form is adequate and harmonious), Kant presents the imagination as a faculty of cognition whose criteria for defining purposiveness are determined by *existing* social values and presuppositions. In order for the imagination to accept a given object as beautiful and thus totally purposive, the object must conform to those preestablished values. The sublime also seeks a consonance between the imagination and its object. Yet it must do so in default of social conventions; here lies its quandary. For when it intends to express its judgment in totalizing form, the sublime is thwarted. At its disposal are merely forms of representation emanating from the sensible world – forms unsuitable to its intractable object. Yet some form of totality or legitimacy, some recognizable medium of representation is indispensable.[14]

Having failed to realize its goal through the preconceived structures of consciousness belonging to the realm of appearances, the sublime is compelled to relinquish its search for measures of legitimacy in the sensible world and pursue its quest in the sphere of the supersensible. For if the sublime cannot locate its purpose, or consummate its judgment within the material world in the manner of the beautiful – a judgment whose totality issues out of a ground external to the subject – then it must search for form in an attitude of thought, within subjective consciousness (Kant 1951, 84). This transfer from the sensible world to the supersensible arises also in response to the displeasure experienced when the mind is confronted with discordance incurred through an explosive conflict between the imagination and the concept of a boundless object. A feeling of pain emerges, accompanying the imagination's perceptual confusion. But after strenuous efforts to attain an idea, it capitulates and a sentiment of respect ensues (Kant 1951, 84). Respect arises out of the imagination's inability to adequately grasp its object. Exhibiting an almost despairing sense of helplessness and paralysis in comprehension, the imagination surrenders to Kantian reason. The latter enters at this juncture to impose a law which imperiously demands that the imaginative faculty comprehend its object in one thrust of intuition. Coerced by this virtual categorical imperative, the imagination is urged to reach a magnitude more extensive and thus more *authentic* than any possible within the sensible world. Through the intervention of reason, its perceptual discomfiture is suddenly transmuted into a paradoxical pleasure which arouses respect and awe for an internalized external force, Kant's law of reason. This superego predicates that all meaning must ultimately be grasped through an absolute totality.[15] It is a categorical fiat that compels the imagination to accept its own self-abnegation so as to resolve the mind's conflictual predicament. But such a surrender to the laws of reason does not occur until the imagination has displayed a voluntarist energy in seeking to overcome its cognitive impasse, indeed its tussle with its counter-faculty, the understanding.

The understanding is a form of cognition that entails logical comprehension. It proceeds to grasp reality in *syntagmatic* fashion (*Auffassung*). When it is confronted with problems of the supersensible realm, it is satisfied to analyse these merely by enumerating and thus mathematically describing the endlessness of an incommensurable infinity. But the imagination fails to operate thus. Indeed its cognitive character is *paradigmatic* (*Zusammenfassung*) and demands a certain synthesis of perceptions in order to seize the logic of unfolding infinity. Yet the understanding does not afford the imagination any such correlative unity within its mathematical representation of boundlessness (Weiskel 1976, 39). A conflict emerges here between the imagination and understanding. Dissatisfied with the syntagmatic character of understanding, the imagination requires that the manifold (and in the case of the sublime, the countless) perceptions of its object be gathered in one thrust of intuition. The understanding, by contrast, is content to apprehend the infinite without this paradigmatic unity. Given this impasse in mental processes, reason enters the scene to arbitrate the cognitive faculties: it imposes a law of unity on the imagination and understanding and, like a gallant knight, seems to rescue the mind from total cognitive failure. But this salvational act, in which reason swiftly dictates the imperative of a totalizing boundary, involves a moral law that is both destructive yet edifying for the imagination. Indeed, the imagination's resurrection from the ashes of cognitive defeat occurs courtesy of reason, but with the proviso that the imagination annul its sensible perceptions. Empirical scepticism must be renounced if the boundlessness of infinity is to be imaginatively grasped. In this self-denial, the imagination must in fact forfeit its own capacity to perceive its object so as not to contradict the ultimate law – the law of the higher and larger ethical community embodied in reason's dictates – that there should be total unity in the representation of the infinite. Such a ritual self-sacrifice, which extracts a portion of "flesh" (subjective perception) for a more sustaining moral and ideological identity, marks the quintessence of the sublime – a judgment based on a type of ritual sacrifice, an aesthetically painful moment that is articulated overtly in the name of a higher truth (the commonweal), and covertly or unwittingly in honour of reason's priesthood. Enduring its own self-abnegation before reason, the imagination's Oedipal self-blinding is not merely a humble bow of ignorance but a submission to a religious belief. For now bereft of its vision, it acquires an ever more acute insight, yet with it has come a giant leap of faith and a capitulation to the authority and prestige of reason itself.[16]

The imagination's surrender to reason is to be registered on the one hand as a moment in which the imagination is receptive and submissive. On the other hand, it is a moment in which the law of reason forces the imagination to act, and thus perform its own resolution of cognitive contradictions. This performance is related to the dynamic sublime, to that affective and practical moment in which some external, natural object is said to inspire a sense of danger in the mind of the subject (Kant 1951, 99–100). Here, in the definition of the dynamic sublime, Kant elucidates the moral elevation which a subject experiences in overcoming its own helplessness before the magnitude of nature.[17] Through a process of sublimation, the formidable quality of nature becomes the semiotic expression of the affective duress which the imagination experiences in relation to its cognitive inadequacy. Allegorically the outer setting represents an invisible process of reversal in which the feelings of fear, inadequacy, and defeat are transformed into moral exaltation. Analogously, on the cognitive level, the loss of control and identity inflicted on the imagination when it is denied its perceptual strength – sensible vision – results in a moral vindication. Such an enhancement of the imagination is admittedly an illusory power, yet it enables it to supersede its vulnerability before the terror and awesomeness of the natural world. (Cf. Beiner 1983, 59–60.)

Let us now turn to the scenario of a propagandist event and the attempt by an audience to seize the meaning of a political message that disrupts commonsensical notions of social well-being. In what way is the cognitive conflict of the sublime judgment pertinent to an audience rallying before a dissenting propagandist? Imagine a scenario in which an audience seeks to comprehend an unfathomable problem, an abstruse political discourse; then consider the propagandist as an enlightening figure seeking to steer his audience through a cognitive labyrinth. In this relationship the audience's struggle with a dense conundrum corresponds to the mathematical sublime, while the rhetorician's role as salvational figure, resolving the audience's cognitive quandary, refers to the dynamic sublime. In other words, the relationship between audience and propagandist is equivalent to the efforts of the imagination and the law of reason respectively. On one level, and on one level only, the analogy shows that there is an inner dialogue that unfolds within the mind of the audience. Like the imagination, the public responds to the presuppositions and the ethics of a given community; these ethics are trumpeted by priestly figures such as the rhetorician and reason itself. Incarnating the moral law of the community, both ideologue and reason are types of superegos that act upon the subjective cognitive efforts of their audiences. They represent the voice of a socially upheld ethos, an ethos that provides the articulacy and guiding structures through which an audience can grasp the meaning of its own identity and surmount its socio-political impasse.[18] It is the aim of the rhetorician to help break this immobile state of affairs by delivering his audience from their affective unease and despair and by raising them to a sense of defiance and political empowerment.

Related to the catalytic role of the rhetorician is the authoritative position which he holds *vis-à-vis* his audience. Like the patriarchal posture of reason, which elicits reverence from the submissive imagination, the dissenting rhetorician not only draws respect from his audience, but also a necessary trust. For in encountering cognitive difficulty, such an audience comes to believe (through a series of rhetorical interactions) in the propagandist promise that trust in the victories of dissenting struggles guarantees a utopian resolution for the future. Awe and respect result from the audience's ignorance, and mark its quasi-religious belief in the final statements of the rhetorician. For in his persuasive endeavour, a dissenting rhetorician must infuse his audience's imagination with hope and optimism, even while he rails at common sense and calls for a wholly new political outlook. He must inspire and energize their beliefs in a higher cause of revolutionary activity as well as in their own moral identity. Just as reason orders the imagination to forfeit its perceptual pleasures for moral grandeur, so the rhetorician must encourage his public to sacrifice itself in the name of ethical rectitude and emancipatory autonomy.

To complete this analogy between the sublime and dissenting rhetoric, we must turn now to the function of Kant's reason within the final stage of the sublime judgment. Strangely, at the apex of its odyssey, the sublime rises to a supersensible height, distancing itself from the charms and appearances of the beautiful, only to plummet into the depths of irrationality, the site which seemed originally to circumscribe beauty alone.

In its imposition of assent upon its audience, the judgment of the beautiful civilly and gracefully insists upon a surrender of scepticism and a withdrawal of distinctive opinion; indeed, it nudges its audience through the pressures of consensus and the pleasures of community inclusion to comply with the majority voice (recall that the judgment of taste expects universal agreement as to its subjective claim to beauty). This unspoken but profoundly felt demand reproduces itself in the sublime through a sterner and starker decree issued by reason. Imposing a law of moral agreement upon an otherwise confused and conflicted mind that struggles to fathom the infinite, Kantian reason resembles the uniting force of the judgment of beauty, a category of taste that disdainfully excludes, if it does not approvingly include its disciples. Indeed, the supersensible judgment of sublimity is aloof to the world of the sensible, just as the disinterested aesthetic judgment is *detached* in its own empirical sphere from the clash of material interests. In both these positions of superiority and detachedness, judgment is formed out of an intuitive impulse. Indeed, the moral dimension of the sublime proves to be but a sophisticated irrationality before which concrete cognitive judgment is relinquished through awe and respect for fundamental human values: justice, fellow feeling, and duty to an ethical common-weal. Consequently, we may say that the aesthetic judgment, be it sublime or beautiful, always carries with it a component of faith, often manifesting itself in the artifices of aesthetic beauty, or simply in a genuflexion before a law of stern morality (sublime).

In the movement from the judgment of the beautiful to the judgment of the sublime, the suspended disbelief intrinsic to the beautiful is echoed by a subscription to faith within the moral sphere of the sublime. The similitude between the apparently divergent judgments consists in their dismissal of concrete objective proof, and in their capacity to secure validity through a powerful consensus or community law that seemingly *authenticates* subjective claims. The sublime's invisible and ineffable truth is given meaning and substance because reason has endowed it with an ethics of dignity and virtue, and has compelled the imagination to dutifully subscribe to a law of high morality. This *conformity* to some abstruse but profoundly categorical law entails an enormous faith, a belief that the cognitive sacrifice is ultimately in the interests of a general good, the betterment of human subjectivity at large, embodied in the figure of reason and the community spirit. Similarly, the judgment of beauty expects that a given object will be readily accepted as beautiful without specification or concrete empirical proof; intrinsically, it depends on an unspoken set of unquestioned but authoritative assumptions as to an ideal totality. Such a matrix of irrational legitimacy enables the judgment of the beautiful to rest its case confidently. Thus with the laws of custom and revered tradition, the judgment induces society's members to pledge their allegiance and withhold their scepticism and cognitive inquiries. For what overrides here is the universal sense of plenitude and togetherness engendered in the very contemplation of beauty, as they drink at the fount of its abstract pleasure.

Fostering a complacency in social consciousness when it pretends to assert a universal truth on the basis of sheer appearances, the judgment of beauty masks its internal discrepancies and thereby undermines its audience's critical spirit; in short, it constitutes the aesthetic index of an epistemological condition of bourgeois society in which individuals are deprived of the possibility of understanding reality in its overall complexity. They are able to accede merely to a partial aspect of their own social relation to others and to the mediations that constitute capitalist societal organization. It is this partial vision that ideologues perpetuate by parading selected representations of reality under the apparel of objective truth. And in promoting a spurious sense of comprehensive knowledge, they gratify and appease their public, but constrain the expansive potential of social consciousness.

Yet it is against such complacency and self-deluding thought that Kant's epistemology responds. Claiming that total knowledge would be impossible were it sought, he resorts to an open admission of religious faith. Giving prior and exalted worth to a world of objectivity that society cannot gauge from immediate sense perceptions, he dispels all questions of pretence. The ethical rectitude which the judgment of the sublime seeks to enforce (with the spirit of Kant's refusal to claim knowledge of an elusive objectivity) becomes an implicit indictment of the spuriousness of bourgeois consciousness, a critique of the arrogance of modern subjectivity whose self-liberating energy makes ambitious claims to conquer new worlds of knowledge. To Kant, this ostentation of human capability needs to be humbled by a more ethical and self-critical awareness of human limitations. As a compensation for the recognition of these inhibiting structures of consciousness, Kant finds solace in the redemption of religion as the moral enhancement of human righteousness.

In essence, one might say that the judgment of the sublime encapsulates Kant's rational indictment of bourgeois consciousness. But by extension, it also embodies Kant's ambiguous relation to knowledge: on the one hand, a scepticism before sensible appearances and their falsity; on the other, a surrender to the irrationality of a religious idealism. What cannot be known in any concrete fashion is relegated to the thing-in-itself, to a sphere of unknowability which only some higher omniscient force can master and comprehend. Strangely then, Kant's rationalism moves from a critique of one irrationality located in the sensible world to an endorsement of another irrationality situated in the supersensible realm of the sublime.

Now what of the analogy drawn thus far between the sublime judgment and dissenting revolutionary rhetoric? If it holds true, then we are left with a compelling consideration. For it can be argued that just as the category of the sublime follows a movement from rational criticism to religious self-exaltation, so the scientific rationalism which is inherent in the philosophy of revolutionary praxis must at some point surrender (within the parameters of its own dissenting discourse) to an irrationalism or a religious idealism. That this dialectical reversal and reversion to idealism is a feature of counter-hegemonic rhetoric can only be conjectured formally from the correlation posed between the sublime aesthetic and dissenting ideology. As yet, it is but a hollow hypothesis, an abstract prognosis. But it is the task of the ensuing chapters to determine in more pointed and detailed fashion whether this projection is valid. For it is the vissicitudes of the aesthetic of the sublime, as it weaves its way through the poetics of revolutionary discourse, which will disclose the limits and contradictions, the ironic reversals, the weaknesses and strengths of a stringent propaganda caught between the tensions of ethics and praxis. Such an epiphany can only unfold through an inquiry into the empirical object of this study – William Morris's legacy and its cultural appeal for rivalling factions of British society during the 1930s and 1950s. It is to this political saga that we now turn.

CHAPTER TWO

Conservative Propaganda and the Legacy of William Morris

They parted warmly and affectionately at Paddington, and the last vision of him in his recollection was, as Morris was waiting for a slow train that went to Oxford, seeing his back bent over Smith's bookstall. Those were early, happy, and sacred recollections.   (*The Times*, 1934)

IDEALISM AND THE MORRIS CENTENARY

On 9 February 1934, the day Stanley Baldwin gave his inaugural address at the Victoria and Albert Museum in honour of Morris's centenary celebrations, *The Times'* art critic commented on Morris's art at the anniversary exhibition. It "brings home," he claimed, "the enormous range, versatility, and fertility of Morris as designer and craftsman, and it 'places' him firmly in relation to the British school as a whole. Different as they are in subject matter, nobody can pass from the Exhibition of British Art at the Royal Academy to this one and fail to recognize that he is in the same artistic atmosphere" (*The Times* 1934a).

Although the centenary exhibition was by no means the exclusive commemorative event of Morris's anniversary, it was indicative of the overwhelmingly aesthetic (i.e. arts and crafts) penchant of the tributes honouring the cultural hero. Nor was the description by *The Times'* art critic unrepresentative in its reinforcement of the exhibit's English character. Yet in leaving the preview at that, the public was given to believe that Morris's whole legacy consisted only of aesthetic creativity. The impression was widely reinforced by similar partisan attitudes towards Morris's art and design work.[1]

Stanley Baldwin was the most notable contributor to this pervasive view of Morris's identity. He acclaimed Morris for being the "greatest craftsman of all times." His words were recorded in *The Times*, and, together with the art critic's commentary, the opening of the centenary exhibition stood flanked by two feature items from the national press. The legacy of William Morris received its almost indelible seal as a repository of artistic genius and English character. Nationalism and beauty were coalesced in one cultural profile.

The Victoria and Albert Exhibition put forward Morris's legacy in its artistic versatility, but, in so doing, it singled out his aesthetic preoccupations as preeminent. In this, it reinforced the partial character of the centenary overall, offering an incomplete rendition of Morris's *œuvre*. Few of the exhibits gave any exposure to Morris's social and political radicalism.[2] Few sought to engage with the history of the man who became "increasingly depressed by his dependence on the patronage of the 'idle privileged classes.'" In fact, it was "the conviction that he might be producing 'nothing but dull adjuncts to meaningless pomp, or ingenious toys for a few idle rich men' that drove him to political commitment" (Naylor 1981, 58).

It is true that a series of tributes to Morris's legacy (compiled by G.E. Roebuck in a book of appreciations commemorating Morris's birth) faintly gestured to his politics. Yet his socialist struggles were alluded to in such abstract and idealist fashion that the substance of his political doctrine could scarcely be felt.

The contributors to this compilation were a set of eminent men and women, designers, literati, art connoisseurs, architects, scholars from Oxbridge with well established reputations – in short, the cultivated members of upper-class English society. Their tributes largely concerned Morris's art and poetry. If reference was made to Morris's politics, it was soon distilled into an idealized discussion of the hero's utopianism. Nor were the means of acceding to Morris's projected commonweal ever articulated. For these were anathema to the ideological sensibilities of the commemorators, who were all averse to concepts as "violent" and un-English as revolution, indeed, averse to Morris's views on how to realize his aspirations.[3] The concept of class struggle never once entered into these tributes. Instead, the commemorators preferred to hush that aspect of Morris's thought which prescribed a program for the social transition from capitalism to communism.

Clearly, Morris's political persuasion caused his conservative admirers discomfort. But they sequestered perturbing considerations (such as revolution) in a suspicious silence, creating a gulf between the unsavoury character of their actual world of strife and strain and the glories of Morris's utopian ideals. In one respect this resulted in a hero-worship that thrust him high above his eulogizers. He stood ahead of them because of his lucid insights – insights which made him the "implacable enemy" of "the ugliness, waste, and vital impoverishment that underlay ... the pomp and commercial prosperity of Victorian civilization" (Shaw in Roebuck 1934, 35). But in another respect Morris was still held to be a part of the society on whose behalf he struggled. He constituted a "typical"[4] figure, a synthetic unity of universality and particularity; through his *œuvre*, he gathered together a conservative community of admirers and joined them to his own extraordinary individuality. Standing at the periphery of mediocre society, he was distinctively himself, yet he was also deemed a member of that social group which edified him. He embodied their projected aspirations and incarnated their self-consciousness in inverted form, endowing them with a utopian élan. But he was also the fruit of grief, for the adulation of his memory was born out of a rueful recognition of the distressing realities of the 1930s.

In a plaintive tenor, the commemorators poured scorn on a decade marred by economic and class strife, declining imperial Englishness and attendant waning cultural values. Yet this did nothing to induce the worshippers to question the nature of their capitalist world. That would have been inconsistent with the genre of their celebrative texts as well as anathema to the idealism which the centenary occasioned. The latent dissatisfaction with modern society (a discontent which commemorators expressed in their adulation of Morris's alternative visions) emerged almost exclusively in a regret that eschewed the disruptive questions of political struggle and surrounded Morris's legacy with resonant hymns of maudlin worship.

In a quasi-religious ambience of civil and self-subordinating acts of duty, the celebrators deplored their "real" political life as a world of sin and dissolution, while endowing their hero with the virtues so wanting on their own "mortal" turf. By aspiring towards the ideals which they imputed to their idol, they sought an ennobling experience that might elevate them to a higher though ultimately only imaginary community.

The worship of Morris throughout the centenary celebrations was thus a religion of a secular kind, the sigh of the "oppressed creature, the heart of a heartless world and the soul of soulless conditions" (Marx 1843–4, 244). It produced a legacy that was redemptive in aim and inverted in consciousness, disclosing that community's ideological disorientation. Conversely, the edification of Morris's legacy stood as that social group's "general theory," "its encyclopedic compendium, its logic in popular form, its spiritual *point d'honneur*, its enthusiasm, its moral sanction, its solemn complement and its universal basis of consolation and justification" (Marx 1843–4, 244).

Yet if Morris's legacy was the universal ground for truth of conservative commemorators, it could only be a spurious universality. It was made to assume an air of objectivity even though it was only subjectively determined. His commemorators put forth a subjective universality whose seeming validity issued out of tacit assumptions of ideal beauty, ethical rectitude, the good life, etc. But their claims could only be "groundless," since the constitutive material of their judgment, namely, the real social relations and historical substance of Morris's identity, were eclipsed. Only the popular *form* of beauty – commonsense and abstract renderings of Morris as Victorian luminary and utopian visionary – was retained. Like the aesthetic judgment, which is in no way dependent on the material conditions of its object, the centenary celebrations avoided confronting the political struggles of Morris's utopian aspirations, and dwelt instead on the beauties of a future England wrought out of their subjective fantasies.

The cultural legacy of the conservative Morrisania appeared to carry the value of utopian beauty quite independently of its commemorators' ideological predispositions. A definite relation between men assumed the fantastic form of a relation between things, "where the productions of the human brain appear as independent beings endowed with life" (Marx and Engels 1978, 31) – a case of fetishism not unlike religion. Under such conditions, it was also easy to pretend that, in lyrically articulating the virtues of the man and his work, the commemorators could transport themselves into the farther reaches of his utopian visions by way of some fanciful will. Here the mediations between the "is" of the present and the "ought" of some future world would transpire for them through suspensions of disbelief, as if the incantations of Morris's poetic spirit and enthralling art could magically wish away the present and unfold the future upon a distraught and conservative socio-political order.

The idealism of the celebrative appraisals and the general ambience of the centenary lent itself to an exploitative political intervention – the inaugural address delivered by Stanley Baldwin. Chosen as the main speaker, Baldwin no doubt drew more than innocent pleasure from the anointing festivities. The centenary enabled the statesman to exalt himself politically yet unobtrusively within the halls of the Victoria and Albert Museum. The stage was set for him to intervene and promote his version of Morris in a context where minds had already been prepared to accept Morris's legacy in purely aesthetic terms. Here was a setting which served as a theatrical forum for suspending disbelief, for entering an imaginary place of desire extracted from the disturbances of social reality, an enclave where audiences could feel enhanced by pleasurable fantasies in a mythologized world of Merrie Englishness.

Without this matrix of predispositions, Baldwin's rhetorical intervention and his title as statesman might not have been regarded with much sympathy or respect. For his inducement to address the opening ceremonies was his close affiliation with the Morris circle, his filial link with Edward Burne-Jones, the artist friend of William Morris. But in his typical style, Baldwin exploited his intimate connection with the hero to secure credibility, even while his discourse was highly personal and wanting in biographical accuracy. Proliferating anecdotal fictions and contributing to that long-standing myth that Morris was but an eminent Victorian of gentle civility, Baldwin nonetheless delighted his audience and won popular respect. How did he succeed? The question demands a close appraisal of Baldwin's rhetoric, his style and approach to propaganda, his philosophy and political ethos, as well as his status as Conservative ideologue.

THE ANTI-PROPAGANDIST STATESMAN

Among his rhetorical assets, Baldwin had a crucial advantage, his aide Tom Jones, a Welsh-speaking former professor of economics whom Lloyd George had brought into his new Cabinet secretariat in 1916 (Mackintosh 1977). Baldwin regarded him as an expedient devil's advocate who proffered valuable insight into both the Welsh mind and the mentality of Labour. He also respected Jones for his able services in writing speeches. As a man with a talent for rhetoric, Jones helped compose those disarming turns of phrase for which Baldwin was so celebrated (Mackintosh 1977, 204). Besides investing his energies in crafting such political discourses, Baldwin also stressed his public image through radio, which "was especially suited to his supposedly non-political low key chats" (Schwarz 1984, 9). In an era when the radio newsreel gradually came to usurp the mass meetings as the medium through which politics was disseminated, Baldwin's participation in the BBC could only have accentuated his possibilities of greater electoral popularity. In his studied public relations, Baldwin felt he had superseded oratory, a forum which he deemed outmoded and which he condemned furiously:

The rhetoric of to-day, the rhetoric we have to consider, is the rhetoric of "Bulging corn bins." I suppose that this gift has been responsible for more bloodshed on this earth than all the guns and explosives that have ever been invented. If we look back only over the last century, was there anything more responsible for the French Revolution than the literary rhetoric of Rousseau, fanned by the verbal rhetoric of Robespierre and others, just as the Russian Revolution was due to the rhetoric of Kerensky – flatulent rhetoric which filled the bellies of his people with the east wind? ... It is because such forces can be set in motion by rhetoric that I have no regard for it, but a positive horror. (Baldwin 1924a, 95–6)

His antipathy towards political oratory can be traced to his anti-militant posture. He preferred to cradle the *status quo* with a subduing rhetoric which he deemed non-propagandist. Thus he avoided alarmist language and managed his crises by infusing a paternalist tone into his discourses, a tone that served to alleviate the tensions of disparate class elements in British society (Schwarz 1984, 7). Baldwin's rhetoric was linked to his conciliatory leadership and to his capacity to build consensus by arresting political conflict, exuding a relaxed disposition, and finally, displaying trust in his ministers. In conceding to the autonomous responsibility of others, he was greatly favoured. "Birkenhead was able to write to Baldwin without exaggeration, 'Your own personality has converted a Cabinet, which assembled upon the crater of some bitter and recent memories, into a band of brothers'" (Mackintosh 1977, 202). In his low-key manner, Baldwin managed to achieve a charismatic presence that altered the state of Conservative politics in the twentieth century (Schwarz 1984). But if he repudiated political oratory, he indulged in another form of public speech which he deemed immune to the rabble-rousing propensities of "subversive" (i.e. Bolshevik) elements. Although highly personal in his speeches, Baldwin sought to give the impression that his convictions were value-free yet all the more valuable for their alleged disinterestedness.

It is hardly surprising then that Baldwin's hostility towards the hustings address should compel him to gear his rhetoric to "non-political" forums such as the aesthetic celebrations of the centenary. But for the same reason, one is led to ask: did his inaugural speech at the centenary offer him a covert opportunity to engage in political rhetoric so imperceptibly as to make his contribution seem purely aesthetic? Was there a hidden political agenda – intentional or not – which emerged from an apparently blithe set of reminiscences on William Morris?

A RHETORIC OF PLEASURE AND IRRATIONALITY

Here *in extenso* are the two articles which reported on Baldwin's speech, a speech which was never published or kept in full in Baldwin's memoirs.

Genius of William Morris: Mr. Baldwin's Vivid Tribute –
"Greatest of the Craftsmen" – Recollections of Forty Years Ago

Mr. Baldwin delighted an audience with recollections of his friendship with William Morris – "the greatest craftsman of all time" – when he opened an exhibition in celebration of Morris's Centenary at the Victoria and Albert Museum yesterday.

Incidentally Mr. Baldwin spoke of himself as "chief of the common people." Among those on the platform was Miss May Morris, younger daughter of the artist.

Mr. J.W. Mackail, who presided, mentioned that Mr. Baldwin was a nephew of Burne Jones, and grew up in the intimacy of the circle in which Burne Jones and Morris were the central figures.

Mr. Baldwin said that he was all in favour of centenaries. In the first place, he thought it was good for them to praise famous men and to call a halt for one second from the eternal crabbing that was so characterisitic of much work that was done at the present day.

He was quite unconscious of having an uncle in Burne Jones who was anything essentially different from other people's uncles and thought it was an avuncular function to paint.

"In the same way Morris to me in those days was a perfectly natural phenomenon and exactly what you would expect your uncle's friends to be" he said. "There seemed to me nothing odd or unusual about him. I do not remember the time when I did not know him and of him, because he was a friend of my mother's.

The Child in the Studio

"My Mother was an exceedingly pretty and precocious child and when she was about nine or ten she was a great pet of Morris, Burne-Jones, and Rossetti. Extraordinary as it seems, they used to allow this child to sit in their studio with them and talk to her, and what is still odder allow her to talk to them.

"I have one or two delightful tributes of those doings, one a drawing given to her on her eleventh birthday, 'With the affectionate regard of Rossetti' written in the corner; and another a most beautiful bit of of illuminated manuscript worked on vellum, which I always understood was Morris's first attempt – and infinitely better than most men's last – given to her as long ago as 1857 during which year she had her 12th birthday.

"Nothing seemed more natural than that a friend of mother's should write volumes of poetry by the time he was thirty, nothing seemed odd that the same man should make wallpaper, that he should do illuminated manuscripts, and that he should begin where other people left off.

"All these things seemed perfectly natural, just as it was natural for my mother to ask him when he paid his first visit to Iceland to bring me back an Icelandic pony which he tried to find me but came to the conclusion that it would cost so much to ship that I must be content with a Welsh one.

"In those years, a mighty long time ago, it was, he seemed part of that life in London which I saw when I came up from the country. I lived in the country and came to London but little, and from those years of early boyhood I saw nothing of him. I went to work, and then when I was 27 or 28 I saw him once again. As it turned out it was near the end."

Mr. Baldwin then spoke of the last time he parted from Morris in 1896, and added, "those were early, happy and sacred recollections."

Hater of Cant

Mr. Baldwin spoke of the variety and volume of Morris's work – a storyteller from boyhood, a story writer and poet from the dawn of manhood, painting, drawing, modelling, designing, illuminating, decorating and making furniture and stained glass and tapestry, rugs, carpet and wallpaper.

"And all these things he was doing in full blast by the time he was thirty years of age. When you study his work, I think that first and foremost the conclusion you come to is that he was essentially not only a great craftsman, but from the variety of his work, and from the skill of it, probably the greatest craftsman of all time.

"What strikes me as so extraordinary is that he did not go to technical schools, or put through examinations boys or men whom he chose to work with him. He just went out into the highways and ditches, seized some lad by the seat of his breeches, dumped him down in front of a loom, and the man became an artist. Contact with genius did that.

"What struck one too, was the supreme absence of any form of self-consciousness, pose or humbug in a man who was a very great artist and a profound hater of every form of cant and humbug and what to-day would be called a snobbish form of highbrowism.

"And he was capable of dealing with windbags and humbugs, and all those people who are not here, but always with us (laughter). I often wish that with a few of his trenchant sentences he could visit us again if only for a short time.

Chief of the Common People

"One saying of Morris – it is equally true in every walk of his life – was: 'If a man is not thinking about himself he is himself.' It takes a minute to let that sink in, but it is quite true."

Morris had that essential quality of genius, fertility – the creative power that never stopped.

"What I liked about him so much," said Mr. Baldwin, "was that he never used jargon of art. He used English and English that could be understanded [sic] of the common people of whom I am chief. And another phrase of his of which I am very fond was 'One's head is rather like an everlasting onion. You peel off the idea you see and there is another underneath it, and so on.'

"That exactly describes the process, and it is eternal until you get down to that little white essence of the onion.

"He took great joy in the common things of life, beer, tobacco; he thanked God for having made anything as strong as an onion. He liked just the ordinary simple fun of life. I can hear his laughter now in those far off days, fond of practical jokes, of horseplay, and all mixed up with his work – a great, glorious, jolly, human being.

"If we ask ourselves what may be seen in this world of ours as the result of his life, we may fairly say that there are many more today than there were sixty or seventy years ago who seek and desire what is beautiful and what is clean; that there are many people, too, who feel discontent with what is mean and what is ugly and vulgar, and insofar as that leaven works it will hasten the day when the beautiful will thrive.

"That widely diffuse feeling, due to many causes, has yet been due largely through the inspiration of his life and his work, a life lived for beautiful, clean honest work in which there was nothing mean in any sense of the word."

Miss May Morris proposed a vote of thanks to Mr. Baldwin.

(*Morning Post* 1934)

William Morris
The Legacy of Beauty
Mr. Baldwin's Tribute at Exhibition

Mr. Baldwin yesterday opened in the north court of the Victoria and Albert Museum, South Kensington, the exhibition which is being held in celebration of the Centenary of William Morris. A description of the exhibition was given in the Times yesterday. Mr. J.W. Mackail presided, and was supported by Mr. Ormsby-Gore, First Commissioner of Works, Mr. H. Ramsbotham, Parliamentary Secretary, Board of Education, Mrs. Baldwin, Miss May Morris, younger daughter of William Morris, and Sir Eric Maclagan, Director of the Museum.

The Chairman said that one inducement for Mr. Baldwin to open the exhibition was the fact that he was a nephew of Burne-Jones, and that he grew up in the intimacy of the circle in which Burne-Jones and Morris were central figures, and that his mother was, from her early girlhood, one of Morris's closest and most attached friends.

Mr. Baldwin said that he was all in favour of centenaries. It was good for them to praise famous men and to call a halt for one second from the eternal crabbing that was so characteristic of much work that was done at the present day.

The eyes of childhood were very different from those of maturity. He was quite unconscious of having an uncle in Burne-Jones who was anything essentially different from other people's uncles. He knew that he painted and that he enjoyed it. In the same way, Morris to him, in those years, was a perfectly natural phenomenon, and exactly what they would expect their uncle's friend to be. He did not remember the time when he did not know him and of him, because he was the friend of his mother. She was an exceedingly pretty and precocious child, and when she was nine or ten she was a great pet of Morris, Burne-Jones, and Rossetti, and, extraordinary as it seemed, they used to allow this child to sit in their studio, talked to her, and what was still odder, allowed her to talk to them. He had one or two delightful tributes to those days. It seemed perfectly natural that his mother should ask Morris, when he paid his first visit to Iceland, that he should bring back an Icelandic pony. He tried to find it, but came to the conclusion that it would cost so much to ship that he must be content with a Welsh one. (Laughter.)

Mr. Baldwin referred to Morris's life in London, and said when he (Mr. Baldwin) was about 27 or 28 he had the great pleasure of seeing him again. He said "pleasure," but that was only half that one felt, because, as it turned out, it was near the end. It must have been in the spring or summer – he kept no diary – of 1896, when he was at Rottingdean, and Morris came to spend a night or two with his aunt. Even under his unskilled eye he could see that he was ill. That well-known blue reefer jacket was hanging loosely on a shrunken frame, and he was obviously very, very tired. But he (Mr. Baldwin) had a vivid recollection of the happiest, most affectionate, and the gentlest talk throughout the afternoon and evening, and the next day they travelled together as far as Paddington. No one could have been more delightful to the raw young man than he was on that occasion. He seemed to take him, after a lapse of years, as the child of the child he had loved so many years before. They parted warmly and affectionately at Paddington, and the last vision of him in his recollection was, as Morris was waiting for a slow train that went to Oxford, seeing his back bent over Smith's bookstall. Those were early, happy, and sacred recollections.

Variety of Work

The first point he would concentrate on was the volume and the variety of Morris's work. He was a story teller from boyhood, a story writer and a poet from the dawn of manhood, and yet, while poetry poured from him, he did not think he really regarded the making of poems as work, but thought it was not worth doing unless doing something else at the same time. He was painting, drawing, modelling, designing, illuminating, and decorating, making furniture and stained glass, tapestry, rugs, carpets, and wall paper. All those things he was doing in full blast by the time he was 30 years of age. When they studied his work the first and foremost conclusion they came to was that he was essentially not only a great craftsman but, from the variety of his work and the very skill of it, probably the greatest craftsman of all time. He loved craftsmanship because he could not keep his fingers still. He loved it for the joy of it.

What struck him if he tried to project an elder mind into what one unconsciously saw as a child was the supreme absence of any form of self conscious pose or humbug in a man who was a very great artist, and a profound hatred of every form of cant and humbug of what to-day would be called a snobbish form of high-browism. He was a man who went through life on a perfectly even keel, swayed not to the right nor to the left, but just living for his work and for every kind of work. There was one saying of his of which he was very fond. He used it probably in connexion with artists, but it was equally true in every walk of life. "If a man is not thinking about himself he is himself." It took a minute to let that sink in, but it was quite true.

"Jolly Human Being"

Having described Morris as a "great, glorious, jolly human being" Mr. Baldwin said that he passionately desired beauty to be within the reach of all people, and that they should have, as he had, a discontent in the presence of everything that was either ugly or vulgar, or as they so often were, both together. Perhaps if they asked themselves, not so much what his legacy was in work, as what might be seen in this world as a result of his life, he thought they might fairly say that there were many more to-day than there were 60 or 70 years ago who sought and desired what was beautiful and clean – that there were many too who felt discontent with what was mean, ugly, and vulgar. In so far as the leaven worked it would hasten the day when the beautiful would thrive. (*The Times* 1934)

Peaceable in mood, Baldwin's speech is saturated with personal reminiscences that lyrically draw the image of Morris into focus, generating an aesthetic ambience and luring the audience into a world of wistful memories. His intimate contact with Morris – a privilege Baldwin had enjoyed as a youth – lends him an expedient rhetorical hook. Courtesy of this personal contact, his autobiographical speech assumes an innocence akin to that of a child whose eyes are open wide in amazement before the world, yet who paradoxically also accepts extraordinary events as wholly natural. Such a frame of mind, in which sophistication is shed and a childlike acquiescence before wonderland is deemed both necessary and natural, encourages Baldwin's audience to withhold cynicism and critical doubt, to receive the statesman's speech as a cinematic blend of part-adult, part-childlike nostalgia. For here various reminiscences and temporal registers converge indiscriminately, leaving little possibility for construing Baldwin's discourse as a rationalist biography of Morris's persona. Indeed, his anecdotal tribute to Morris is a rhetorical fantasia, rhythmically punctuated by the ebb and flow of memories and juvenile perceptions. Baldwin "was quite unconscious of having an uncle in Burne-Jones who was anything essentially different from other people's uncles. He knew that he painted and that he enjoyed it. In the same way, Morris to him, in those years, was a perfectly natural phenomenon, and exactly what they would expect their uncle's friend to be" (*The Times* 1934).

The spontaneity and nonchalance with which Baldwin accepted these family mementoes reinforced his assumption that "(n)othing seemed more natural than that a friend of mother's should write volumes of poetry by the time he was thirty" (*Morning Post* 1934). In pronouncing these words, Baldwin betrays a conceit in enjoying the close contact with the Morris circle. But while he feels the thrill of association with the great master, he understates the privilege so as to naturalize his hero's genius. He replays not only the memory of what transpired in his past but also the youthful perception of a child innocently delighting in the marvels of the world, yet never probing beneath the mystery of their outward form, lest critical knowledge dull their scintillating appearance. In this childlike frame of mind, where Baldwin implicitly offers the parameters and guidelines for interpreting his centenary tribute, the most unlikely portrait of Morris can be irrefutably presented. For it is composed out of the idiosyncratic laws of cohesion inherent in the playful "surrealism" of personal recollections and altered perceptions of reality that characterize the work of art.

This aesthetic (non-rational) apprehension of Morris which Baldwin induces (and its attendant pleasure) exempts him from the ethical responsibility of probing further into Morris's personal history, his Renaissance versatility and its import to culture and politics. The more this "aesthetic" sensibility is reinforced in Baldwin's speech, the more his audience is dissuaded from considering the thornier issues of Morris's political profile. Indeed the sheer casualness of Baldwin's rhetorical form encourages his audience to accept his claims as unquestionable. Implicit in his discourse is the notion that truth need not justify itself but may simply declare itself and dispense with scientific proof. His discussion of the role of the university as a school of character makes this assumption explicit:

The ideal character is a harmony of many virtues, and it is a tradition amongst us to give truthfulness the position of the cardinal virtue. Hence, for example, the curious power of Lord Althorp, who was known to have said to the House of Commons, "I know this to be right. I cannot remember why – but you may take it that it is so." And they believed him. And if the noblest exercise of freedom is the pursuit of truth, the best equipment for the search is to be truthful. The inculcation of the practice of truthfulness no less than the acquisition of knowledge is the motive force of an educational system. The student is here to learn the habits of accuracy in measurement, precision in statement, honesty in handling evidence, fairness in presenting a cause – in a word, to be true in word and deed.   (Baldwin 1925, 77–8)

In his centenary speech, Baldwin conveys the idea that he knows Morris viscerally and that the alleged honesty with which he describes the hero is intrinsically self-justifying. He draws assent by presenting his version of Morris as a declaration of absolute truth and the very self-evidence by which he proclaims his opinion becomes synonymous with authority and rectitude.

Coupled with this tautological, yet demonstrative, expression, Baldwin intensifies the irrationalism of his discourse with the melancholic strains of pathos and nostalgia.

It must have been in the spring or summer – he kept no diary – of 1896, when he was at Rottingdean, and Morris came to spend a night or two with his aunt. Even under his unskilled eye he could see that he was ill. That well-known blue reefer jacket was hanging loosely on a shrunken frame, and he was obviously very, very tired. But he (Mr. Baldwin) had a vivid recollection of the happiest, most affectionate, and the gentlest talk throughout the afternoon and evening, and the next day they travelled together as far as Paddington. No one could have been more delightful to the raw young man than he was on that occasion. He seemed to take him, after a lapse of years, as the child of the child he had loved so many years before. They parted warmly and affectionately at Paddington, and the last vision of him in his recollection was, as Morris was waiting for a slow train that went to Oxford, seeing his back bent over Smith's bookstall. Those were early, happy, and sacred recollections.   (*The Times* 1934)

Morris's affection for Baldwin's mother is a crucial aspect of the centenary speech. The affective component allows the statesman to present himself – even by proxy – as a recipient of Morris's tenderness. Son of the "little pet child" (i.e. Baldwin's mother), Baldwin ensures that his affiliation to the genius, Morris, is unequivocally clear. Simultaneously, he evokes the relation between Morris and himself with a muted false modesty, recollecting encounters with the great artist as soberly pleasant. In this understated but nostalgic portrayal of the intimacy felt between the two men, Baldwin also underscores the affection which Morris displayed. Thus while the specialness of feeling is crystallized in a phrase such as "happy, and sacred recollections," Baldwin tends to dissolve any marvelling experience into everyday life as if to claim that the "extraordinary" for him was the norm, and that he (Baldwin) belonged to the upper echelon of English society. In naturalizing and celebrating his hero, Baldwin incurs respect for Morris's talents, but also blocks all threatening cognitive inquiry into the hero's qualities.

It sufficed merely to remark upon and admire the hero's gifts and never to probe too deeply into the "perilous" depths of reason. Thus Baldwin declared: "What strikes me as so extraordinary is that he [Morris] did not go to technical schools ... He just went out into the highways and ditches, seized some lad by the seat of his breeches, dumped him down in front of a loom, and the man became an artist. Contact with genius did that" (*Morning Post* 1934).

Averse to intellectualism but enamoured of pragmatism and notions of spontaneous genius, Baldwin revered Morris's uncomplicated philosophy of aesthetic practice, not least because it coincided with a populist and "unadulterated" type of English culture: "'What I liked about him so much,' said Mr. Baldwin, 'was that he never used jargon of art. He used English and English that could be understanded [sic] of the common people of whom I am chief'" (*Morning Post* 1934). This implicit glorification of the common people contrasts radically with Baldwin's hostility to the "non-ordinary," dissenting citizen. Similarly, his depiction of Morris is made to conform to a popular (conservative) English sensibility. For ultimately Baldwin's intent here is to market a public symbol for national acceptability. In this, he must define his hero as a genius yet not emphasize his distinctive marginality. He must portray Morris as anti-intellectual and pragmatic, moderate and sober, profoundly English in his empiricism, and removed from the "sullied" demagogy of politics.

Reinforcing these values, Baldwin produces an "innocent" mode of rhetoric which paints a benign image of Morris, a representation which coincides with the naïveté that Baldwin seeks to engender in his nonrationalist discourse. The more he justifies turning a blind eye to life's contradictions, the more he legitimates a mindless apprehension of reality, a complacent and limited world-outlook. And when proffering political commentary on the advent of a new social order, his discourse waxes conveniently vague and ambiguous, specifically in respect to the concept of the beautiful: "there are many people, too, who feel discontent with what is mean and what is ugly and vulgar, and insofar as that leaven works it will hasten the day when the beautiful will thrive" (*Morning Post* 1934).

Since Baldwin's strategy entails conciliation, his concept of the beautiful is rendered opaque enough to be elusive, yet precise enough to connote some form of moral virtue. (Thanks to the disarming tenderness with which he delivers his recollections of Morris and his own childhood naïveté, his abstract claims stand untrammelled.) But this notion of the beautiful is not truly an emblem of universality; it is only deceptively consonant with that of Morris. In the latter's eyes, "the beautiful" constitutes a symbol of societal commonweal in which social iniquities would be erased. For Baldwin, however, "the beautiful" implies that disparate social groups conform to the *status quo*. Such a vision entails a hierarchically rigid class system where worker uprisings are contained and all social groups are kept intact, "happily" working in their respective spheres and submitting to an external law of harmony. Hence, Baldwin's prototypical worthy citizen is one who does not meddle in politics and remains tolerant of difficulties by maintaining a stiff upper lip. In his lectures, this cross-section of British national character is made clear.

> As a nation, we grumble, we never worry, and, the more difficult times are, the more cheerful we become ... We are always serene in times of difficulty. We are not a military nation, but we are great fighters. We have staying power, we are not rattled ... the Englishman has a profound respect for law and order – that is part of his tradition of self-government. Ordered liberty – not disordered liberty, nor what invariably follows, tyranny; but ordered liberty, at present one of the rare things of this topsy turvy world.   (Baldwin 1933, 12–14)

As a representative of the ruling class, as a Conservative with political clout, Baldwin blends a desire for quelling unrest with his portrait of Morris as a "moderate" fellow whose exemplary status is intended to didactically convince others of the value of an individualistic philosophy and of the need to preserve existing societal relations: "He was a man who went through life on a perfectly even keel, swayed not to the right nor to the left, but just living for his work and for every kind of work" (*The Times* 1934). In reality, Morris was hardly a man of even temper, though he displayed admirable fidelity to his underlying philosophies of life.

But Baldwin's portrayal of Morris does not aim to deliver the hero's veritable identity, but rather a conservative ethos clothed in human garb. Indeed, Morris's imputed moderation coincides with Baldwin's conciliatory politics and rhetorical mode, genteel, calm, and reassuringly confident. As a representative of the ruling class, Baldwin is graced with the privilege of deploying aesthetically pleasing rhetoric that sustains an air of harmony and balanced certainty and figuratively replicates Baldwin's political hope: to maintain the equilibrium of the *status quo*. For the latter is mimetically conveyed by a tranquil and seemingly "disinterested" discourse. Gentle in form, it nonetheless belies an underlying coercion that is constitutive of Baldwin's concept of beauty in which any ethos resistant to conservatism is deemed contemptible and ugly. Through an affective principle, Baldwin marks a dividing line between those conforming and dissenting members of his public. Creating a family ambience out of the nation-state, he invites his followers into a territory of consensus and putative fellowship, dismissing all rebellious forces who openly grieve their economic plight. Thus what struck Baldwin was Morris's profound hatred of "every form of cant and humbug" and his alleged ability to deal "with windbags and humbugs

and all those people who are not here, but always with us (laughter)"
(*Morning Post* 1934).

Nor is the quashing of dissent by rhetorically exiling "crabbing"
protesters Baldwin's unique mode of preserving the symmetry of the
status quo. If the enemy within must be silenced for his antagonistic
relation to the family nation, so must the enemy without, who allegedly
threatens the beauty of the British country landscape. Thus in striving
to be reelected in 1935, Baldwin sought a mandate from the electorate
to spend more money on armaments. On 1 October 1935, he delivered
a speech (ironically) to the Peace Society. With masterful eloquence, he
declaimed: "We live under the shadow of the last war and its memories
still sicken us ... That swathe of death cut through the loveliest and
best of our contemporaries; public life has suffered because those who
would have been ready to take over from our tired and disillusioned
generation are not there." In evoking that "dear, dear land of ours,"
Baldwin intensified the anguish of loss by depicting "the level evening
sun over an English meadow, with the rooks tumbling noisily home
into the elms." Finally, in his decisive coda, he warned: "Make no
mistake; every great piece of all that life that we have and hold and
cherish is in jeopardy in this great issue" (Young 1976, 115). With
commingling tones of pathos, serenity, and imminent loss, Baldwin
succeeded in securing his mandate for rearmament.

Thus the revered English way of life which Baldwin cherished and
vaunted through his manicured depictions of the countryside was
scarcely innocent. Domestically, English civilization was preserved
through the containment of discontented social elements. Internation-
ally, the "eternal essence" of English rural peace was guaranteed through
an increase in military defence and potential warfare with other nations.
And if such violence underlay the politics of Baldwin's speeches, his
discourse was carefully crafted with cameos of ruralism to dissimulate
the harshness of its bellicose intent.

But the rhetorical device can be seen as more than a veiling process.
It consists in a somewhat more complex set of dynamics, readily graspable through Kant's category of beauty. Take Baldwin's depiction of the
level evening sun over an English meadow with its peace and equanimity. The representation is couched in the first person plural, indicating
that such a "good life" is consensually endorsed: "every piece of all the
life that *we* [added emphasis] have and hold and cherish." By referring
to this imaginary "we" as well as by expressing some general but sensuously evocative image of "that cherished life," Baldwin produces an

idealist portrait of some would-be English nation, a portrait whose vacuous character is not felt, since he has gilded it with the stereotypical features of a much-mythologized English countryside, suggested briefly here through the image of the "rooks tumbling noisily home into the elms." But paradoxically, like Kant's category of beauty, Baldwin's references to a state of harmony entail an aesthetic pleasure that is divorced from the material pleasantness of sensation. The rhetorician induces a non-empirical subjectivity which stands as a universalized form symbolizing the fulfilment of pleasure in each individual.

Yet a universalized form is never the actually lived experience of pleasure; it is rather a hypostatizing symbol that is all things to all people. Consequently, the pleasure of an aesthetic attitude (in Kant's judgment of the beautiful, as in Baldwin's lyrical reflections on the countryside) does not consist in a pleasantness of feeling, but in a detached image of *plenitude*. Baldwin deploys a rhetoric of pleasure which is free of the existence of real history and which represents an abstract relation to the beautiful. For by erasing temporal causalities and social distinctions within the community, by bringing the empirical world to a standstill as is the case in all aesthetic attitudes which dispel unwanted movement from their idealist sphere, he offers not what is subjectively pleasant to each individual, but rather an unspoken agreement as to what is universally desirable.

Just as the category of the beautiful in Kant's *Critique of Judgment* is based on the disinterestedness of a contemplative attitude that is free of the discrepancies of the object to which it refers, so Baldwin deploys a rhetoric that conjures up images of social accord and national superiority (cultural instances of "beauty") while eluding the intricate complexities of reality. In his pleasing and emollient speech forms, he is responsible for engaging his audience so totally that his discourse must rid itself of justification, of references to determinate concepts. As with the category of beauty which precludes cognitive inquiry, Baldwin's rhetoric forbids investigation. To probe into the mystique of the beautiful is to destroy the aura of plenitude surrounding an object and thus to diminish its satisfying appeal. Similarly, Baldwin creates immediate delight in recollecting Morris's extraordinary attributes, and avoids any analysis that might tarnish the joy of sheer contemplation.

The statesman's rhetoric is consequently wrought out of enticing pleasure on the one hand, and irrationalist qualities on the other. These two facets are intertwined. Suffice it to note how Baldwin's philosophy echoes the mysticism of nineteenth-century German vitalism where "experiencing the world is the ultimate basis of knowledge... [where life itself] behind which [one] cannot penetrate, contains structural connections from which all experience and thinking is explained" (Dilthey in Lukács 1980, 418). Comparably, rhetoric was sufficient and at its most effective for Baldwin when it simply showed the truth without analytic explanation: "Truth, we have always been told, is naked. She requires very little clothing" (Baldwin 1937, 94).

It was the irrationalist philosophy to which Baldwin (wittingly or not) subscribed that allowed him to remain sufficiently detached from his subject of discourse, thus eluding the inadequate empirical evidence which he deployed as instant proof for his rhetorical claims. The putatively value-free politics under which he masqueraded enabled him to cast his statements as blithe, aristocratic truths, impervious to contestation.

BEAUTY AND POLITICAL HEGEMONY

Baldwin's rhetorical method was not foreign to his status as a Conservative bourgeois ideologue with hegemonic power. His popularity and entrenched position within the establishment were factors that granted him the licence to pursue a rhetoric of irrationalism with impunity. But it was the specifically bourgeois character of his public role as ideologue defending the *status quo* that enabled him to cast history aside and to pontificate with mellifluous ease while expecting immediate approval for his claims. This type of rhetorician secured the possibility of delivering a beguiling discourse with utter legitimacy precisely because of the disjuncture intrinsic to his Conservative posture. This disjuncture is evidenced in the tension between his defence of the pecuniary interests of the market and his ideological status as statesman claiming disinterested concern for the commonweal of the nation. As Barthes has it, the bourgeois ideologue names himself without difficulty, openly declaring his capitalistic affiliation; ideologically, however, his status dissolves into a nebulous anonymity (Barthes in Sontag, 1982). Moving from reality to representation, the ideologue expels all concrete meaning from his position in order to assume the "classless" character of a nationalist identity. Thanks to the veil of abstraction lent by nationalist rhetoric, he is able to suppress the particularity of his economic ethos and appear as an equal, fraternal member of the state, promoting interests that are allegedly common to all his fellow citizens. (Cf. Newbold 1923, 109–14.)

To conceal his selfish motives with an air of magnanimity, he must adhere to the following modes of persuasion:

(1) the separation of his ideological status from real ideological contingencies;
(2) the preservation of a disinterested air secured in the promotion of universal rights and equal civic relations in a discourse that gratifies its public with a clear vision of communitarian experience and fulfilment;
(3) finally, this projected vision of the good life must be offered in terms and imagery that are couched in a legitimate and appealing vocabulary, one that is endorsed by tradition and current consensus.

In toto, these three modes of argumentation preclude all effort to persuade strenuously and intellectually. For in the abstract projections of bourgeois rhetoric, the ruling-class ideologue shunts aside discrepancies and material weaknesses, while focusing his message on superlative attributes. The gulf between the ideal and the real facets of the bourgeoisie is tactically preserved in order to sustain the superiority of the dominant class over threatening opposition. This crucial buffer zone keeps at bay any challenge to the ideologue's claims, thus enabling him to avoid confrontation with dissent.

Such an irrationalist form of persuasion allows him to present assumptions in a confident tenor and with tautological assertiveness. Added to this, his discourse of national harmony serves to ply a public with promises and pleasures of communion otherwise absent in the conflictual realm of everyday life in the market and civil society. Finally, the Conservative appropriation of conventional common-sense idioms, of long-held assumptions and traditional values, provides the ideologue with a reflexive endorsement of his advocacies, a reflexiveness that arises from the pregiven legitimacy associated with the veneration of time, seniority, and permanence. Through these modes of argumentation, Conservative rhetoric succeeds in promoting an immediate reception among its following, broadcasting its claims from an Olympian pedestal and securing a chasm between the material interests of private man and the "glorious" disinterestedness of public citizen. For economic and universal man constitute the polarities of a bourgeois antinomy whose hiatus between the real and the ideal conceals an interaction that, if disclosed, would shatter the whole edifice of bourgeois ideology. Such a hiatus preserves the aura of the state from the mediocrity of the market and replicates the gulf between exchange-value and use-value, a dark hole that lets duplicity slither in, *incognito*, to keep the poles of ideal societal harmony well at bay from the venal interests of the market sphere.

The dissimulations with which the ideological moment is activated as it occludes the material underworld of economic reality are ultimately constituted out of a flourish of abstractions, a tapestry of formal totality and perfection reminiscent of aesthetic processes. It is not therefore incidental that ruling-class ideology adopts as its expedient handmaidens aesthetic categories with which to enchant its audience and advance its persuasion through discursive seduction. In bourgeois society, the aesthetic form has always appeared removed from labour, prised out of the realm of material interests, and as such treated as a clear antidote to the pecuniary character of commodity relations. What a seemingly innocuous device with which to ensure the validity of an ideology whose main purpose is to sequester its exploitative and economic philosophy behind walls of rationalization! But curiously, if aesthetic categories (such as the judgment of the beautiful) appear as expedient mechanisms of conservative ideology, they do not serve only to camouflage the relations of use-value to exchange-value, or merely to rescue something of the sensuousness of use-value from the formal laws of commerce. If it is to act in accord with the interests of bourgeois ideology, the aesthetic structure must suspend reference to class discrepancy and political injustice while replicating and reinforcing the fetishism and deceptive blitheness of exchange-value.

The category of beauty, which constitutes a subjective universality, seems to slip gracefully into the workings of bourgeois rhetoric. Because of its abstractness – its purposeless purposiveness – this aesthetic judgment of pleasure and universality contains all the mechanisms by which the Conservative rhetorician can defend the established order imperceptibly, appearing in fact as if he were merely celebrating and inflecting a familiar song of widely held renown and popularity. As a structure of consensus, the beautiful is eminently useful for a persuasive act that seeks to appear laden with pregiven legitimacy. Its implications in the realm of concrete social practices are most markedly felt in the discourse of nationalism, a discourse that represents the non-rational yet most powerful validation of a given political community.

Manipulating the reflexive reception of his middle-class audience, Baldwin's perorations on the English countryside are a case in point. Summoning forth a well-canonized image of England of yore, and

appropriating rhetorical tropes from a well-rehearsed repertoire of ruralist discourse, his conservative ethos is apt to be smoothly admitted with
but a nod of the head or an inner pulse of recognition.

The Englishman is made for a time of crisis, and for a time of emergency. He
is serene in difficulties, but may seem to be indifferent when times are easy.
He may not look ahead, he may not heed warnings, he may not prepare, but
when he once starts he is persistent to the death, and he is ruthless in action.
It is these gifts that have made the Englishman what he is, and that have enabled
the Englishman to make England and the Empire what it is …

To me, England is the country, and the country is England. And when I
ask myself what I mean by England, when I think of England when I am
abroad, England comes to me through my various senses – through the ear,
through the eye, and through certain imperishable scents. I will tell you what
they are, and there may be those among you who feel as I do.

The sounds of England, the tinkle of the hammer on the anvil in the country
smithy, the corncrake on a dewy morning, the sound of the scythe against the
whetstone, and the sight of a plough team coming over the brow of a hill, the
sight that has been seen in England since England was a land, and may be seen
in England long after the Empire has perished and every works in England has
ceased to function, for centuries the one eternal sight of England. The wild
anemones in the woods in April, the last load at night of hay being drawn
down a lane as the twilight comes on, when you can scarcely distinguish the
figures of the horses as they take it home to the farm, and above all, most
subtle, most penetrating and most moving, the smell of wood smoke coming
up in an autumn evening, or the smell of the scutch fires: that wood smoke
that our ancestors, tens of thousands of years ago, must have caught on the air
when they were coming home with the result of the day's forage, when they
were still nomads, and when they were still roaming the forests and the plains
of the continent of Europe. These things strike down into the very depths of
our nature, and touch chords that go back to the beginning of time and the
human race, but they are chords that with every year of our life sound a deeper
note in our innermost being.

These are the things that make England, and I grieve for it that they are
not the childish inheritance of the majority of the people of to-day in our
country. (Baldwin 1924, 3–7)

This most celebrated of Baldwin's addresses, entitled "On England," was
presented to the Royal Society of St George[5] in May 1924, several
months after Baldwin's resignation from office (22 January 1924), but

several months prior to his reelection (4 November 1924). The timing of this speech suggests that it was geared towards enhancing and legitimizing his electoral campaign and ambitions to become prime minister.

As a lyrical adulation of "authentic" Englishness, the speech mawkishly plucks the heart-strings of its patriotic and conservative audience. In an effort to ensure a faithful following, Baldwin waxes effusive over England's rustic quaintness, aiming to reaffirm and reshape the values of a much-threatened and weakened British conservatism (cf. Langan and Schwarz 1985, 33–61). His strategy is wholly anti-intellectual, but viscerally powerful in its consensual process. Instead of protracting abstruse political arguments, it validates identity and personal subjectivity, creating an emotive affinity with the audience – a ground of common sense which is intended to suture the objective gap that separates the ideologue from his addressees. As a point of encounter, an aesthetic universe of harmony and societal well-being, this discursive sphere of social contentment is meant to induce a consummate pleasure, leaving the public vulnerable to the attractions and wiles of the ideologue's political statement, and thereby provoking a quasi-unquestioning acceptance of his claims.

Nevertheless, such a receptive response cannot be guaranteed in the mere invocation of a utopian sphere. Baldwin's ideal England is a representation of plenitude, but it is scarcely a whimsical symbol of subjective delight. It is rather a specific totality whose imaginative free rein must adhere to aesthetic laws which can be located once more in Kant's judgment of beauty. Indeed, the innocent air of the imagined nation and its inexplicable emergence are the result of a complex of (at least) two intersecting forms of perception that are correlative with the Kantian beautiful: the one qualitative, the other quantitative. As we saw in chapter 1, (at least) two essential criteria predicate the consummation of Kant's category. The first is an immediate, non-conceptual and disinterested apprehension of an object, a perception that may be imaginatively inspired and shaped by the evocative impact of an object's sensuous properties, but which is in no way materially affected by these contingencies. The judgment of beauty depends in this respect on a disinterested, contemplative appreciation of an object. Its other criterion is universal communicability. More pointedly, the particular character of a subjective perception of an object must be transcended and transformed into a universally communicable symbol of pleasure – in short, into a *sensus communis*.[6] The judgment of beauty is, therefore, predicated on an alchemical process which distils a qualitative experience of personal gratification into a quantitative measure – a commonly shared experience where personal gratification and total communicability converge in a stroke of utter harmony and collective satisfaction. Thus the effortless delight[7] of instantly grasping an object's meaning or sensuous impact is compounded with the feeling of inclusion in a social group's warm embrace, an embrace contingent on sharing in the community's prevailing common sense.

The qualitative and quantitative aspects of the judgment of beauty can also be construed as two levels of reception: the one subjective, the other objective. Both forms of reception constitute examples of immediate apprehension. Both embody direct structures of understanding that are vital to Baldwin's rhetorical project, a project which celebrates the public's ego by eliminating cognitive labour and by performing a ludic rehearsal of its familiar customs and commonly held social values. It is the intersection of these qualitative and quantitative modes of reception that forms a beautiful totality of non-conceptual apprehension – i.e. Englishness in her seductive grace – which an ideologue such as Baldwin must adopt if his nationalist address is to sway and capture his public's visceral sensibility.

A closer look at that rhetorical process shows that Baldwin's imagined nation ("England is the country") bifurcates into two entities: (1) an object of sensuous beauty with empirical properties that are perceived by the senses ("England through her sights and sounds"); (2) a concept of dramatic space where an audience can recognize itself as an accepted member of the community. Thus in reference to his public, deemed an emotively bonded clan of Englishmen, Baldwin declares: "there may be those among you who feel as I do." Together the objective/sensuous reception of the nation and the subjective/commonsensical understanding of the portrait of Englishness are moments of recognition and thus of instant comprehension, of cognition rehearsed rather than strenuously laboured. Objectively, the audience grasps the meaning of the nation as an "other," recognizing it within its own familiar experiences from a childhood past. Subjectively, this same audience is viewed, interpellated, and incorporated by that other (the ideologue and his discourse) into the nation itself. Consequently, the ideologue and the audience perceive each other and their respective selves in a mutual process of self-contemplation. The sensuous and the commonsensical apprehensions of the nation seem to interpenetrate in a harmonious unity.

This intersecting of perspectives is reinforced by Baldwin's construction of the nation as a *childish inheritance*,[8] a coinage pregnant with ambiguity. On the one hand, the idea of inheritance as property suggests that the meaning of the nation is an object to be owned, seized, and appended to one as a medal of excellence and self-identification. On the other hand, *childish* (read more accurately as childlike) inheritance resonates with the idea of organic, filial, or natural membership within a given community. Together these two facets of *childish inheritance* define Baldwin's personal concept of *belonging*, a concept which encapsulates the convergence of the two levels of immediate reception as incorporated in the judgment of beauty: apprehension and commonsensical comprehension. For the mental grasp of a concept finds its equivalent in the seizure (appropriation) of a piece of property – the nation as an inheritance – while commonsensical comprehension represents the immediate inclusion or comprehension of the individual within a social group.

Dancing on its own grammatical dualism, the term *belonging* refers both to the idea of *being part* of (cf. the gerund of the verb *to belong to*) a community and to the idea of a possession, as in the noun *belonging*. The nominal form of *belonging* (an object to be owned) is the product of a transformation of the verbal form (i.e. the act of participating in a social ensemble). Here the processual character of social participation is congealed into an objective entity, into a property endowed with a value that serves the purpose of social affirmation. Thus, Baldwin's notion of *childish inheritance* can be seen as a phenomenological convergence of the subjective and objective receptions which correspond to the qualitative and quantitative facets of the judgment of beauty. When these two receptions interact in a mirroring relation, they form an idyllic encounter, a perfect *Sittlichkeit* of particular and universal that marks the consummate moment of an ideal community, an imagined nation, a symbol of beauty crystallized as an inheritance or cherished property. As such, this national entity is appropriated by each individual as his/her own. And it is just such a jewel of ownership that the ideologue must craft if he is to endow his audience with a revitalized identity, with an exaltation capable of mollifying that public's potentially obdurate scepticism.

Thus far we have witnessed an integrative discourse that reflects the inclusive quality of Baldwin's speech: its invitation to the audience to recognize itself within a given ideological territory, an imaginary space which affords the public its sense of legitimacy. But such a spatial structure of inclusion and validation is contingent on its coherence and perfect coincidence with the sensibilities of its subjects. The imaginary community in which the public is placed must conform to their tastes and must harmonize with their predispositions so as to ensure that approval is unequivocal and unchallenged by the slightest dissent. In essence, the dramatic space through which the public is included and affirmed is not an objective but a subjective universal matrix, not a real, concrete place or community but a subjective mental landscape *invented* and *constructed* by the ideologue on the basis of certain cultural dispositions shared with his audience. And to ensure that this imagined space function as the absolute affirmation of the public's sense of identity, the ideologue's rhetoric must centralize its own predilections and moral values and weed out the gnarled contradictions that might hamper the purposiveness of this imagined community. Like the beautiful, the Arcadia of nationalist discourse is not a veritable union of self and otherness, but an identity of self and *imagined* otherness. Here the audience is brought back to an invented or *ersatz* childhood in which harmonious relations are contrived, not resurrected. Validity emerges through a subjective universality, through an endorsement that has been guaranteed because the subject (Baldwin and his public) has created its own community in its own image to suit its subjective will. Like the beautiful, Baldwin's nationalist rhetoric constructs its own measure of universality through a process of self-centralization that necessarily excludes unwanted debris – elements that do not fit within the parameters of its normative judgment. Such a persuasive feat hinges on three factors: (1) a suspension of disbelief; (2) an exclusion of contradictions; and (3) a centralization of its own claims.

Preeminently, the ideologue draws his audience into a world which is intensive and set apart from mundane distractions that might challenge his discourse. Like the category of beauty, which is disinterested and above the sphere of contradictory everyday life, Baldwin's portrait of the nation remains unquestionable and naturalized because it belongs to a world of the imagination, predicated on its non-empirical laws of coherence, and on an unmitigated contemplative pleasure. As with the judgment of beauty, the transformation of subjective claims into apparently incontrovertible (because widely accepted) fact depends on creating an aesthetic universe of cohesion and unadulterated pleasure. This effect is achieved through formulations and syntactical structures that dispel doubt and cognitive inquiry. By silencing oppositional judgment, such linguistic constructions elicit immediate understanding. Baldwin's sensuous depiction of the nation and his reinforcing claim that England is to be seized through the senses – the generic form *par excellence* of immediate reception – compel a mode of comprehension which yields to the authority of unquestioned yet preestablished assumptions. Here is an irrationalist rhetoric which vindicates the ludic delights of sheer recognition, a mimetic act that is in perfect consonance with the seemingly effortless character of the judgment of beauty itself. Significantly then, Baldwin regulates his audience's reception by stressing simplicity and sense perception as the guiding hermeneutics of his statement. If his discursive world order is to be received with beneficial results, his public must adhere to these simple but imperative caveats. Thus, by addressing the idea of England through the senses, Baldwin adopts a style and tone of childlike innocence, a tranquillity that defines the appropriate pace and form of reception that can secure immediate consent. His smooth, untrammelled rhetoric replicates the peace and seemingly unsullied beauty of a "pure nature," cleansed of dissenting thought. In his nostalgic and mellifluous language, he shifts the register of audience reception and expectation from rational, quotidian consciousness to aesthetic apprehension.

Baldwin's authority is also secured rhetorically in his use of dramatic centrality. Raising his discourse with ostentation to the status of pomp and ceremony, he prefaces his statement on the beauty of the nation with the declamatory pronouncement: "The sounds of England." His subjective reminiscences are suddenly granted central status. The "sights and sounds" of Englishness are Baldwin's specific examples of the national identity, but they have been exalted by dint of their syntactic and aesthetic complexion into cameos of ruralism, evocative of an implicit English community and readily acceptable as universal emblems of quaint English country life. To oppose this consensus is to suffer the sense of exclusion from the seductive bower which Baldwin invokes; it is also to fall victim to the pangs of solitude which come from being exiled into the camp of otherness, a camp linked with the discomfiture of decentred subjectivity. The magnetic power of inclusion which Baldwin's nationalist rhetoric is able to produce discursively coerces, if not nudges, his public into a reflexive acceptance of his message. For it is the strong reluctance felt towards being excluded from the national utopia that elicits unthinking abidance by its laws and acceptance of its sanctity. Conversely, it is the pleasure of inclusion which seductively entrances an audience to abide like dutiful citizens by the laws of the discourse.

Yet to heighten the public's sense of belonging to the circle of Englishmen, the ideologue must centralize their participation within the ideal community of the nationalist discourse and endow them with another audience that will act as a mirror of recognition. Such another audience can only be an imaginary public evoked initially as the central protagonist, a conservative Englishman with whom the real audience may identify. With this identificational link, the real audience comes to inhabit the epic role of the stereotypical hero and assumes its presence on the imaginary stage.

Consequently, by duplicating his audience, Baldwin renders his following both actors in and witnesses to the same drama – actors by proxy and identification, and self-admirers who draw approval from an imagined community derived from the ideologue's interpellating artifices. The imagined community which provides this desired approval is, of course, no more than the projection of the public's yearnings. It is a community predetermined and extended outwardly from the very ego of the real audience. Being an extension of that public's fantasies, it can readily guarantee spontaneous applause. Thus the possibility of a perfect reciprocity of recognition produces a validation of subjectivities that is so complete that fictional protagonists and audience are indiscernible; they are an identical subject-object. This *identity* manufactured between the public, the ideal nation, and the ideologue himself forms a *homogeneous medium* (Lukács 1981) of social relations encapsulated by the purposiveness of the category of beauty. So total is this medium that it leaves no discursive space for inquiry. It is predicated on a wholesale trust and on a sphere of utter plenitude that empties the public mind of sceptical thoughts and caresses it with affirmations of its rational autonomy. The public's desire for rational self-sufficiency is thus paradoxically ensured through a *simulacrum* of logic which only the imaginary sphere of the beautiful can engender; for the latter's logic is so self-enclosed and autonomous that it dispenses with discursive explanation. Still, it grants the appearance of coherence and rationality.

Like nationalist discourse, the beautiful engages in a tautological process of celebrating the socially determined presuppositions of identity and subjectivity. Supplanting doubt and criticism with the pleasurable experience of self re-cognition, it seemingly reconciles identity and difference. But the harmonious totality both of the aesthetic judgment and of nationalist rhetoric remains a counterfeit reconciliation of opposites. For just as the beautiful is a *sentimental* reconstruction of the *naïve* symmetries and consonance of some prelapsarian totality (cf. Lukács 1968, 101–20), so nationalist discourse is only a false mimesis of a naturally integrated childhood, a copy produced out of subjective contrivance, tragically unable to shrug off the artifices which betray its continual hankering for an authentic home.

SENTIMENTAL NATIONALISM

Baldwin's discourse on childish inheritance and experience of English ruralism lets the floodgates of sentimentalism burst forth. Comparably, his centenary speech on Morris swells with nostalgic yearning for the golden epoch of childhood days, those "sacred, happy" times. The plangency that runs through his recollections of Morris harmonizes with the tone of eulogies and obituaries written in Morris's honour around the time of his death in 1896. These forged the first strains of a conservative Morrisania, a common sense upon which Baldwin could rest his own disquisition.

Whether of conservative or socialist penchant, the obituaries dwelled largely on Morris's worth as a humanitarian figure; they paid little heed to his alleged artistic deficiencies (cf. controversy as discussed in Litzenberg 1936). Instead, these tributes elevated Morris's qualities onto an idealist plane, glorifying him in unashamed terms. But, principally concerned with a moralizing purpose, they depicted Morris with maudlin detail only to subordinate his persona to that of the English nation.

The most ostensible nationalist appropriation of Morris's public stature occurred in *The Times*, it being the central voice of the hegemonic press.[9] The portrait of Morris's physiognomy as an emblem of prototypical Englishness was equally pivotal to the obituaries. His eccentricity, fiery countenance, and distracted air were ascribed to his artistic mentality, a feature anchoring him to English "genius."

As I write I seem to see Morris in the study of his house at Hammersmith ... several pages of manuscript on the blue foolscap paper before him. With a quick upward glance he would drop his pen, and begin to talk. His eyes were blue-grey in tint, and in repose they might be described as meditative, not, however, even then without a something in their glance that betokened the boundless energy of the man. But when his face was absolutely still one noticed rather the lofty uprightness of the brow than the eyes. The change which came over his features on commencing to speak reminded me of a similar change which my uncle (who, as a law-apprentice, had seen Sir Walter Scott while still a Clerk of Session) told me came over Sir Walter's features in animation – a change that transformed, as it were, the whole man.

When Morris spoke, especially when the theme was anything in which he had real interest, his eyes gleamed, and he became engrossed with that one theme, and generally that one theme was exhausted before another was introduced. (Bell 1896, 693–702)

The portrait of Morris's artistic stature was not, however, restricted to mental distraction, nor merely to association with other cultural figures from the English stockhouse of writers. His general disposition was also made to blend with the setting in which he dwelt. The descriptions both of Morris's study, endowed with the English classics, and of the London setting which the library overlooks recall the union of man and country, of artist with English place.

Sometimes in the midst of his flow of brilliant conversation, and without ceasing to speak, he would rise and, passing his fingers over his beard or through his hair, rough and curly, would pace swiftly across the floor of his uncarpeted study, and look for a few minutes at some volume taken from a long antique book-case – a book-case containing many precious tomes, some in black letter, as well as rare editions of the English classic poets. His study windows commanded a picturesque view over the Thames, which, at this place, and conspicuously its opposite, is not without some touches of beauty. (Bell 1896, 697)

Morris's social philosophy was also specifically intertwined with an English ruralism. Descriptions of his physique and personality were mingled with the attributes of his domestic surroundings and with his own lyrical visions of utopian settlement. A celebration of man and nation transmuted the otherwise affectively charged discourses on Morris's demise into grief for the loss of a national epoch.

Kelmscott, the riverside village on the Upper Thames, just below Lechlade, where the poet and craftsman is to be buried, had been his country home for twenty-five years, and he was greatly attached to it. The old manor – an ideal "haunt of ancient peace" – is rich with associations of Rossetti and others of his circle ... In the poet's Utopia – *News from Nowhere* – he drew a picture of it, very little idealised; and in a recent contribution to one of the magazines he gave a detailed description of the house and grounds, and his love for them – "a reasonable love, I think for though my words may give you no idea of any special charm about it, yet I assure you that the charm is there; so much has the old house grown up out of the soil and the lives of those that lived on it

– needing no grand office-architect, with no great longing for anything else than correctness, and to be like Julius Caesar; but some thin thread of tradition, a half-anxious sense of the delight of meadow and acre and wood and river; a certain amount (not too much, let us hope) of common sense, … and perhaps at bottom some little grain of sentiment." (*This Morning's News* 1896)

The funereal descriptions of Morris's death reproduced the atmosphere of requiem solemnity and religious reverence through a glorified tapestry of autumnal beauty. With the use of pathetic fallacy, death was glamourized in the imagistic innuendoes of dying foliage.

The train arrived at Lechlade soon after eleven, and in the midst of a driving rainstorm. The body was transferred, characteristically, to an open farmer's wain decorated with branches of willow and alder, with an open canopy of vine leaves. For three miles or more, the road lay through the country he had loved so well and described so often, between hedges glorious with the berries and russet leaves of the guelder rose, hips and haws and dark elder berries, broken by the dying silver leaves of the maples and the stone hedges made of upright slabs, which are as characteristic of the district as the weathered stone roofs. At last, within a few yards of the house where he was happiest, he was borne to the porch of the little church of St. George, and laid for the last time among the friends who loved him.   (Obituary 1896)

Out of the burial description, the hard reality of interment was aestheticized into a vision of Morris at peace and at one in his English earth. Kelmscott "commiserated." The vegetation invoked highlighted Morris's passing in the "dying silver leaves of the maples," and in the deathlike imperviousness of the stone hedges that stood opposite the living glory of the "russet leaves of the guelder rose," of "hips and haws and dark elder berries."

Seemingly passive background to the report on the burial event, the obituary is in fact imbued with a nostalgia that recalls Morris's predilections, and his intimacy with friends and English landscape. As the man and his environment are made to merge, the affective touches and those mentions of his happiest times at the porch of the little church of St George bring the pathos of his passing into an appealing admixture of bittersweetness and tragic beauty, one that inspires a sense of enduring Englishness. What is lost in the man's death becomes reincarnated in more magnified form through his posthumous resurgence as a cultural object endowed with ideological resonance.

As Morris was deified, he became an embodiment of English value and thus profitable material for Baldwin's Conservative political rhetoric in 1934. Indeed, if the statesman's centenary speech was inherently a eulogizing form, it could only have benefited from the elegiac lyricism of obituaries and commemorative tributes. As with his speech "On England," Baldwin's address on Morris is imbued with a damp romanticism. Recollections of the hero at Rottingdean are marked by the imminence of his passing. In this context of approaching death, Baldwin frames his "happy" and "sacred" recollections. Yet his feelings of grave regret are only partially directed at the loss of Morris, whose death is but the occasion to lament the disappearance of those olden days of Merrie Englishness. So too in "On England," Baldwin grieves that certain bucolic niceties are no longer the childish inheritance of all, but merely those of a waning Anglo-Saxon elite. England has become "adulterated" by the infiltration of foreign elements that cannot appreciate her "essential" beauty. In this imperial doctrine of nationalism, Baldwin's self-privileging discourse selects only that audience which has "authentically" lived alongside and within English nature in all of her sensuality. Only such an audience can claim the right to remember Baldwin's real (read Conservative) England. So too, in the statesman's centenary speech, only the children related to the Morris circle, such as Baldwin and his mother, can gain special access to that world of excellence and unselfconscious genius. For Baldwin, nothing other than that sensuous contact will allow for a "veritable" comprehension or legitimate claim to Morris, and by extension to Englishness at large. That such a sensuous contact is filiative and incommunicable to foreigners renders it all the more irrational, exclusive, and hermetically sealed in its prism of narcissism.

This aristocratic self-depiction deploys a mildly pathetic voice, drawing out its own rarity and threatened state. On the grounds of some putative loss, Baldwin's discourses "On England" and his opening address at Morris's centenary hanker after an earlier, "pure" community, a mythical entity typical of ideal constructs of nationhood. With a saccharine lyricism, his speeches urge the public to resurrect old conservative values. Through a romanticized portrait of the past, he generates the public's aesthetic delight in dwelling on the niceties of a glorified era, a period of bounty and peace that inspires desires for psychic fulfilment. Of course, the return to a mythical past remains caught in an empty idealism, a purely contemplative pleasure. Nonetheless, the very lyrical pathos intrinsic to Baldwin's rhetoric also infuses his preferred conservatism with an endangered and thus elect quality. For pathos tentatively suspends an audience's rational scepticism and tenderizes their feelings, warming them towards the subject of loss (Morris/conservatism.) Pathos also compels the public to identify with the rhetorician and vicariously feel his sense of bereavement. It may even induce them to offer consolation as an act of moral approval or sym-pathy. Seen in less emotive terms, the act of sympathizing is none other than a non-rational agreement expressed towards the afflicted. Thus Baldwin's use of lamenting flourishes serves to gain immediate, unthinking endorsement for an otherwise wholly subjective experience, ascribable purely to himself and to those whom he embraces under the canopy of true Englishness. While lyricism is the subjective note expressed by the bereaved, it is also the sentiment that endows Baldwin's rhetoric with a certain legitimacy, for the sympathy which it wins gives objective form (social character) to a biased admiration of conservative Englishness.

CONCLUDING REMARKS

I have sought in the above to foreground a sample of Conservative propaganda through Baldwin's ruling-class rhetoric. A significant feature of this discourse was its self-reflexive rhetorical expression. Stylistically and formalistically, it replicated the ideals of Baldwin's hegemonic ruling class. When unity and harmony were advocated as the utopian essence intrinsic to an Englishness of Conservative hue, the category of beauty was summoned in order to convey the political creed of national cooperation and economic prosperity. Yet while this aesthetic category had a political dimension in so far as it provided the enhancing images of societal reward (retributive utopia), it was also a symbol which was deemed disinterested and thus conducive to a ruling class seeking to appear unimplicated in party or class strife.

The category of the beautiful which mediates the aesthetic forms of Conservative rhetoric not only suggests fellowship, national belonging, tranquillity, and plenitude, but most significantly tacit consensus, the institutionalized legitimacy of a ruling class. For even while its economic philosophy does not correspond to the needs of society at large, the aesthetic judgment affords Conservative propaganda the device through which to secure consensual validation for its claims. The deployment of Morris's legacy as an emblem of totality becomes an expedient not only to conjure up utopian peace and commonweal, but to engender a non-rational, symbolic standard by which a social group consolidates its system of beliefs. Simultaneously, the aesthetic category must be seen in terms of its denial of contradictions. Witness the centenary, where a conservative vision of beauty quashed the Marxist Morris. In 1934, the conservative legacy produced a mausoleum of cultural power erected on the very ground of an ideological battle. Yet, silently excluding the Communist Morris heritage, the celebrations hushed all sign of actual hegemonic warfare, and this because the aesthetic mode of Baldwin's ruling-class legitimacy entailed a denial of class conflict.

If the statesman quelled disturbances, such a manoeuvre was possible thanks to certain structural conditions. Baldwin's rhetoric could not credibly silence contentious matters linked to Morris's legacy simply through an appeasing style of address. To be able to digress on personal reminiscences was in itself a privileged discourse not readily available to all public speakers. It remains that Baldwin was blessed with several advantages: first, political legitimacy freed him from justifying his overly subjective perorations. He represented a Conservative institution with preestablished hegemonic dominance. He was lord president of the national government when MacDonald was prime minister. Yet the latter often depended on Baldwin's advice and expedient interventions (Young 1976, 100). Secondly, Baldwin's appraisal of Morris was endorsed by a well-entrenched conservative Morrisania, incipient during the emergence of the obituaries. Thirdly, he treated his audience as a family of mutual trust and won consensus most effectively through his use of a lyrical nationalism. In brief, Baldwin exploited the predisposing forms of consciousness forged by tradition and custom, as well as by the disarming poetic flourishes of ruralist Englishness. In tapping the irrational sensibilities of his audience, he elicited approval for a revered English culture so intertwined with the precepts and shibboleths of his own politics that endorsement for the latter could only ensue.

His desire to propound truth rather than vigorously argue for it can be grasped in terms of the conceptless nature of the aesthetic of beauty, a category that symbolizes the idealized conservative nation and reveals the privilege of its subscribers, who assert their own political visions as universally beautiful. In this vein, the domination of the William Morris centenary by Baldwin and company represented the extent to which tradition and legitimacy prevailed in the court of the ruling class. There a social elite could pontificate upon a well-canonized appraisal of Morris without any recourse to reasoned thought or substantial historical evidence. For theirs was a propaganda of pacification, irrationalist persuasion, and disarming seduction.

CHAPTER THREE

Propaganda of the Third International and the Emerging Marxist Morris

Bourgeois critics have condemned art which reflects the dialectic contradictions with society as "propaganda." They raise the reactionary slogans: "Art for art's sake" and "Art above politics." They forget that bourgeois art itself, under the conditions of its first vigorous development, was "propaganda," the expression of a class striving for its revolutionary liberation from the restrictive property relations imposed by feudalism upon the further development of the productive forces of society. That modern bourgeois critics should attempt to deny the value of art as a revolutionary weapon, as a weapon of social transformation, merely betrays their lack of consciousness of the objective fact that the historical movement of contradictory class forces which emptied the content of feudal culture, now empties the content of their own culture.
(Davis and Kemp 1934, 77)

HISTORICAL TANGENTS OF COMINTERN RHETORIC

If Baldwin's propaganda aimed to dissimulate its political motivations, Communist rhetoric of the 1930s in no way intended to obscure its ideological purpose. On the contrary, it sought to expose its philosophical tenets and revolutionary goals as lucidly and vigorously as possible. Thus when Robin Page Arnot undertook to respond to the Morris Centenary, he composed a pamphlet entitled *William Morris: A Vindication* (1934). The text aimed to enlighten the public. In its uninhibitedly forceful tone, it debunked the Conservative and reformist versions of Morris's memory and showed them to be distortions of history. Simultaneously, it attempted to reclaim Morris as a revolutionary socialist and, in so doing, disarticulate his legacy from its mainstream canonization. But the process was fraught with the politico-aesthetic tensions of Marxist propaganda of the Class-Against-Class period (1928–35). Considered closely, Arnot's text can be seen as a microcosm of the dilemmas that Communists faced in their desire to exploit an appealing form of nationalist culture (e.g. the Morris legacy) yet one which was not fully compatible with their stringent adherence to revolutionary internationalism and their decidedly anti-Social-Democratic stance. Entrenched in an Englishness that Communists repudiated as bourgeois, Morris's cultural import was nonetheless a most seductive and pragmatically useful icon for promoting the revolutionary cause; however, it had to be selectively used for winning Communist consent, particularly a sectarian Communism of the Class-Against-Class period. But whence this sectarianism and how did it impinge on Marxist discourse?

As the year 1934 reached the brink of world conflagration, it inevitably rekindled the scenario of 1914, evoking for Communists such as Arnot the ideological collapse of the Second International and Lenin's critiques thereof. Nor were Lenin's preachings against social-opportunists and reformists merely a matter of theoretical interest. Arnot applied these commentaries concretely by adamantly opposing conscription during the First World War. Incarcerated twice, once in 1916 and again in 1919, he became sensitized to the principles of war resistance, which in turn fuelled his activist journalism[1] in the 1930s (Winter 1974, 124–5). At this time he insisted that the historical watershed of the Great War need not recur, for the fateful memory of the Second International should dispel working-class gullibility before imperialism (Arnot 1934, 488).[2] Nor was his attitude singular. In fact, the invocation of the Second International and its encapsulation of the Social Democrats' capitulation to bourgeois imperialism was part of a shared Communist consciousness, a hallmark of Marxist-Leninist education. (Attfield and Williams 1984, 103)

The sectarian stage of the Third International, otherwise known as the Third Period or Class-Against-Class era, ran from 1928 to 1935. In identifying fascism as the "right wing" of finance capital, and social democracy – or "social fascism" – as the latter's "left wing," it directed Communists to dissociate from all Labour alliances and engage in continual propagandist attacks on Social Democrats. Such an ideological context rendered the political scenario of the First World War propitious for Arnot's journalism. The political climate offered the possibility of paralleling 1914 and 1934 and rehearsing an indictment of Social Democracy. Thus when Arnot wrote in 1934 on the secrecy of diplomatic and military preparations for war which British Liberal statesmen concealed in their utterances, he recalled the events of twenty years before: "The masses in Britain were bulldozed into accepting British imperialism as a protagonist of peace at the very moment that the finishing touches were

being made for the outbreak of war ... The precise duty of the proletariat
was confused with bourgeois pacifism and the working class came more
and more under the influence of the bourgeois pacifists. And there were
no greater adepts at the game of 'pacifism' than Mr. Lloyd George and
his tail of Nonconformist Ministers" (Arnot 1934, 491–3).

Arnot's denunciation of "pernicious" pacifist phrase-mongering was
marked. Rhetorically he asked whether the situation in 1934 would entail
a repetition of the vague verbiage of pacifism only to be "swept up and
consumed like stubble in the fires of war" (Arnot 1934, 496). Being
aware of the residues of "classless" reformism, he urged unequivocal
clarity as the decisive mode by which the working class could oppose
the coming war, and demanded that the nebulousness spawned by
bourgeois pacifism be extirpated from the anti-war camp.

Arguing that reformist tactics only helped to secure fascist victory,
Arnot derided with impassioned tones the untrammelled calm of moderate reformism and parliamentary negotiation that underlay the codes
of "honourable" British diplomacy. Others too, such as Arnot's prominent comrade Rajani Palme Dutt, a member of the Communist party's
executive committee, claimed that the looming shadow of a fascist wave
could only be forestalled through concerted campaigns against reformism. Liberal reasoning was regarded as futile if not strategically fatal in
resisting fascism. At best it was "a measure of the complacent humbug
that can still be indulged in by high priests of parliamentary deception"
(Dutt 1934, 584).

Dutt sustained his propagandist zeal by alerting public consciousness
to the imminent dangers of barbarism. In his preface to *Fascism and
Social Revolution*, he declared: "Present society is ripe, is rotten ripe for
the social revolution. Delay does not mean pacific waiting on the issue.
The dialectic of reality knows no standing still. Delay means ever-
extending destruction, decay, barbarism. The words of Lenin on the eve
of October apply with gathering force to the present world situation:
'Delay means death'" (Dutt 1935, 17).

Compounded with their call to action, Communist propagandists
sought to expose the reformist liberal conscience that reviled the barbaric
extremism of Hitlerian fascism but simultaneously cowered beneath it
with irrational terror. Dutt claimed that this liberal ideology saw fascism
"not as the logical working out of the class-struggle, of the methods of
capitalist dictatorship, at one extreme stage, but as a sudden irruption
of an alien force from nowhere breaking in upon the imagined 'rule of
reason'" (Dutt 1934, 587).

To Communists, a cure for this "malady" of irrationalism meant radical social change, feasible only through energetic praxis, agitation, and a compelling propaganda that would combine both poignant analyses and vigorous critiques of the capitalist world. Such proselytizing persisted beyond the Class-Against-Class period into the late 1930s. Here are Arnot's remarks just prior to the Second World War.

The alarming feature of the present situation in summer 1938 is that the workers and the people of Britain are not fully awakened to the nature of the dangers before them ... It is as though there were two years 1938, in one of which the five years growth of fascism has reached a point when its furious offensive threatens to drive the workers and all mankind into the slaughterhouse, and another year 1938, seven years removed from the second Labour Government, and twice seven years from the first Labour Government, and presumably on this reckoning, nearing a third Labour Government; in which old policies are as valid as ever; in which all are living in an island, sundered from the war-torn world ... Now, of course, there is no such imaginary island of time or geography. The whole world is threatened this year by fascism and war and we are part of that threatened world. Not only so, but in world politics, Britain so far from being on the fringe, is actually the centre of gravity.   (Arnot 1938, 483)

Arnot's rhetorical tone is not remote from the urgency expressed in 1932 by Dutt, writing with polemical flair in the editorial pages of the *Labour Monthly*.

What then is the lesson for the working class in relation to the present particular crisis in whose midst we find ourselves? Not to waste time to listen to the bourgeois left reformist (ILP) speculations as to whether or not this is the "final collapse of capitalism." Still less to listen to the bourgeois and reformist pratings of a hundred capitalist solutions (cancellation of debts and reparations, currency and credit reform, planned economy, etc.) and supposed harmonious reconciliation of capitalist contradictions. But to *utilise the present intense and still increasing particular crisis for the maximum revolutionary purpose*, to press forward the active struggle, to build the workers' fighting front, to awaken the workers to the meaning of the crisis and the issues before us.   (Dutt 1932a, 14–15)

In 1933, the Communist poet John Cornford reflected on the divide between reformism and decisive revolutionary action, most particularly in respect to literary culture. Just as Arnot and Dutt sought to dispel the public's political inertia through galvanizing language, so Cornford

condemned the artist's "impartiality." In his efforts to expose the specious neutrality of culture, he declared: "As the crisis deepens, the
situation more and more urgently demands a choice between revolution
and reaction. The collapse into subjectivity of Eliot, Joyce or Pound
shows more and more clearly the fate of those who admit the necessity
of choice. The traditional artist's 'impartiality' is unmasked as a denial
of class struggle – as a powerful instrument in the hands of the possessing class who would prefer to keep in their hands the means of production without a struggle" (Cornford 1933–4, 25).

Cornford's critical assessment came in tandem with his departure
from Stowe public school and coincided with his rapid immersion in
London's Communist community. In 1934 he joined the Communist
Party and became editor of *Student Vanguard*. His thoughts were voiced
at a peak of radical ebullience when Marxist theory was diffused through
the then dynamic *Daily Worker* and satellite forums: the Worker Theatre
Movement, the Academy Cinema with its Soviet classics, political car-
toons, and literature for children, not to mention the Marxist theoretical
output of *Labour Monthly*'s Leninist readings, as well as plentiful con-
ferences and socialist summer schools. A mushrooming culture of Communist activism organized formally and informally in the artisan areas
of Soho and Holborn secured a dynamic public interest in world politics
as well as a beavering animation of Marxist ideology (Howkins 1980,
248–50). This effervescent Communist world contrasted radically with
the tranquil quarters of the Victoria and Albert Museum where the
centenary of William Morris dissolved into a distant Merrie England,
into an imaginary island all too reminiscent of that insular British
enclave to which Arnot referred in *Labour Monthly*, four years later.

From a Communist perspective, the centenary was surely a symptom
of that British quiescence before, and detachment from, political
involvement. For the event lent a sanctuary to conservative and liberal
idealists – an ensemble of contemplative artists – who eschewed all active
responsibility for the fight against fascism. As a site of retreat, the
centenary was also an occasion for reformist and conservative rhetoricians to reinforce quietist attitudes and render the Morris anniversary a
consolatory escape from the adversities of 1934.

Such cultural distraction could be secured imperceptibly in Baldwin's
poignant but subtle claim that it is good for centenaries "to praise
famous men and to call a halt for one second from the crabbing that
was so characteristic of work that was done at the present day" (*The
Times* 1934). The remark only reaffirms Cornford's lucid point that the

possessing class would prefer to keep in their hands the means of production "without a struggle." By evading controversy, the Morris centenary confidently unfolded its celebrations with an air of political neutrality intrinsic to a self-preserving ivory tower of literati and dignitaries. And yet, as a cultural event, it helped to cement public ideas and social values already prevalent and touted by the major institutions of British society. It fostered an appearance of independence from the corporate class that controlled the celebrations, thus succeeding in creating a false divide between culture and the economy. In actuality, the business and politics of the centenary could not be disentangled from its cultural *façade*. Nonetheless, in an ideological way they were. For the organizers fostered a myth which elevated culture and wrested it from the politics and cash nexus of that ruling-class hegemony.

With its contrived "disinterestedness" and feigned innocent omission of Morris's Marxist legacy, the anniversary depoliticized its own celebrations in keeping with its conciliatory politics. And at a time of crisis, such depoliticization was deplorable to Communists who advocated public enlightenment; the centenary, in the eyes of Arnot and like-minded Communists, was but a plethora of biographical memorabilia that obscured the essential questions of Morris's legacy.

But triumphant as Social Democrats and Conservatives may have been in their monopoly of the centenary stage, they were unable to silence Marxist voices altogether. On the contrary, they provoked a riposte which Arnot initiated in his pamphlet, *William Morris: A Vindication*. In it, he sought to conquer the establishment Morris legacy and pronounce a Communist version as preeminent.

The tract was no casual retort. With stridency it scorned the biographical memorabilia, the "prattle" of discourses, speeches, and newspaper comments that depicted Morris as "a great poet, a great craftsman, a great influence, a great what not" (Arnot 1934a, 4) and that gave short shrift to Morris's politics. In an oral interview, Arnot indicated that his *Vindication* was not only a response to the official celebrations of the Centenary but a reaction to "all the talk which went on for the greater part of a month and which celebrated William Morris as any other big figure from the past" (Arnot 1985).

Laconically, the *Vindication* reveals (as many of Lenin's polemical tracts express more elaborately) a disturbance with the narrow-mindedness and limited news of bourgeois journalists and political demagogues – and their urge to replace discussion of urgent political issues with tittle-tattle about politics and a specific category of personality (Baluyev 1983, 29).

Responding to the dilution of a legacy which he regarded as significant for Communist ends (namely the political crusade that the hero William Morris led in the name of socialism), Arnot denounced the peripheral comments on Morris's persona, not merely as trivial biographical details, but as the veneer of reformist, Menshevik obfuscation. His pamphlet functioned as a propagandist skirmish, aiming to puncture the inflated centenary speeches and to hack at their mystificatory trappings.

In keeping with its ideological principles, the *Vindication* proved to be a highly charged settling of accounts in which Arnot sought to dismantle the Conservative and "Menshevik" – i.e. Social-Democratic – Morrisanias. He rebuked the centenary for its cultural debauchery, for its "orgy of canonisation" in which "the hash of 'Appreciations' written for the Walthamstow Centenary Celebrations in several cases [carried] the myth into wildest travesty" (Arnot 1934a, 5). And in declaring that Morris was being hoisted up to his niche as a "harmless saint," as "a great Victorian," Arnot parenthetically exposed the irony in these bouquets. Amidst the endless tributes to Morris, he wondered whether the eulogizers and worshippers of Victorian values ever read what Morris wrote of Queen Victoria herself (Arnot 1934a, 5).

Bristling with anger and invective, the *Vindication* calls attention to its subjective mood. In the tonal qualities of his polemic lies the key to understanding why Arnot was so irked by the conservative centenary. For as Bakhtin has it, intonation "is always at the boundary between the verbal and the non-verbal, the said and the unsaid. [It] is the most supple and most sensitive conduit of social relations that exists between interlocutors and a given situation" (Bakhtin in Todorov 1984, 46). The now plaintive, now trenchant tones of Arnot's text resonate beyond the surface of his polemic; they point to a larger political context which we must now consider.

THE MARXIST RESPONSE TO THE MORRIS CENTENARY

Robin Page Arnot – whom I hadn't yet met in 1934 – would often say with some energy that when he wrote the *Vindication* he was very much vexed at the treatment of Morris to "de-politicise" him by overstressing the pre-Raphaelite connections and laying bare all their weight on "art" of various skills etc. – (Indeed it's pretty apparent as a tendency if you go today to Kelmscott Manor; it would be hard strolling through it to find any indication that he was a red-hot socialist activist.)   (Tuckett-Gradwell 1985)

If Arnot's outrage before the centenary was palpable to Angela Tuckett-Gradwell years after the publication of the *Vindication*, one can confidently imagine its powerful intensity in 1934 when he first deplored the commemorations for having obliterated the Marxist William Morris, and for polishing the legacy of the hero into a cameo of idealism that shamelessly denied his public engagement in political strife. Significantly, Arnot's response was provoked by more than an aesthetic or academic disfiguring of the Morris legacy. His anger focused on the politics of the centenary, which appeared as a form of cultural barbarism where, as Walter Benjamin had it, "Whoever has emerged victorious participates to this day in the triumphal procession in which the present rulers step over those who are lying prostrate" (Benjamin 1969, 256).

From the early statements on the conservative canonization of Morris, Arnot's authorial voice identifies with the victims of cultural misrepresentation. The pamphlet resonates with the pathos of an elegy for revolutionaries misappropriated by posterity. It opens with a quotation from Lenin's tract, *State and Revolution*, that bemoans the bourgeois abuse of the legacy of revolutionaries: "During the lifetime of great revolutionaries the oppressing classes have invariably meted out to them relentless persecution and received their teaching with the most savage hostility, most furious hatred and a ruthless campaign of slanders" (Arnot 1934a, 4).

It is of interest to note in this overture that the subject of oppression is neither William Morris nor revolutionaries *per se*, but rather their legacy, their "teaching," which is received with the "most savage hostility, most furious hatred," etc. And after their death, because "attempts are usually made to turn [revolutionaries] into harmless saints," the "real essence" of the heros' revolutionary theories is emasculated and vulgarized, its sharp edge blunted.

For Arnot, the centenary's real "crime" was less the exclusion of Morris's Marxist followers or the occlusion of Morris's political character than the throttling of the Marxist heritage as a whole. The *Vindication* appears to be a biographical account of the revolutionary Morris. Yet in identifying with the victims of cultural hegemony, with those exiled Marxist Morrisites, it stands preeminently as a lament for a demeaned Marxist doctrine. Admittedly, Morris remains an important catalyst. Indeed, he is not wholly superseded; for any unmediated defence of Marxism would feature as the transparent sentimental voice of a self-pitying political community. Through the Morris vignette, this maudlin note is quashed; distance and mediation enable Arnot to imbue his text with a certain emotive quality while not lapsing into self-indulgent pathos. In short, Arnot's rhetoric issues overtly from his anger over the marred Morris legacy. But more crucially and obliquely, it is the Communist cause that captures Arnot's expression, fuelling his intense authorial involvement as well as the aggrieved tone of his polemic.

In being relegated to a periphery of silence, Arnot compensates for his affrontedness through the vigorous language of his pamphlet. The *Vindication* breathes the anxiety of the Communist party, strained by the strictures of an ultra-left line: the Class-Against-Class stance. The latter entailed the disaffiliation of the Communist party from all Labour forces, trade unions, and broad left alliances. Prior to 1928, much of Communist support emanated from its interaction with the rank and file of the Labour movement and non-sectarian Party-dominated organizations. But as Alun Howkins demonstrates, the new line of Communist independence "alienated a whole area of 'left' support" (Howkins 1980, 242). In short, with the change in line, "the Communist Party was forced to isolate itself from the rest of the Labour movement. The 'non-sectarian' contacts of the past came to an end, the social and especially cultural movements which the party had supported, but which were largely social democratic, now became the enemy, and areas of support which the party had come to rely on, the Left of the trade unions, sections of the Labour press and so on were now denied to it" (Howkins 1980, 245). Given these conditions, the task of winning consent waxed all the more challenging.

Marxists were also faced with the awkward enterprise of adjusting their theory to an empiricist English culture. In this, they were often at pains to capture consensus. Ever torn between national and international tempers, they avoided a nationalist profile, but sought an identity that would fuse Marxism with British sentiment. Indeed, as they recognized themselves, the "alien" political doctrine needed to be implanted in British soil if revolutionary propaganda was to succeed. As Jack Cohen wrote in 1932, "It remains a truism that England, the country where Marx and Engels lived and died, and where all their important works were written, is the country where Marxism is least rooted among the masses. The vigorous propaganda of the principles of scientific socialism, of Marxism-Leninism, amongst the workers, is one of our most important tasks – a task which we must admit, to our shame, that we have tremendously neglected" (Cohen 1932, 295–6).

Concurrently, Ralph Fox advocated "translating Bolshevism into English" (Fox 1932, 204–5).

> We are inclined to simply laugh when charlatans like Middleton Murry and Ethel Mannin appear in the *New Leader* as saviours of the British workers. But it is not the persons who matter, only what they represent. And their aim is obvious, to put up again the old story that Bolshevism is wonderful for Russia, only for Britain it is not necessary ... The appearance of Mannin and Murry, though it is a sign of the ideological bankruptcy of the ILP is no excuse for failing to destroy the illusions they attempt to perpetrate in the minds of the workers.
>
> How can that exposure be accomplished? ... in showing that Bolshevism is not a purely Russian phenomenon not only by our works but by our deeds. That is to say we must learn to translate Bolshevik experience into terms of British reality, overcoming the ... mechanical application of *general* directives without making them concrete for the given country and the given incident of class struggle.   (Fox 1932, 204–5)

This meant heralding a tradition of indigenous revolutionaries that would offer the British Communist recruit a familiar model with whom to identify. History was encapsulated in the legendary feats of proletarian resistance. Thus Fox underlined that "the best traditions of the revolutionary proletariat, including the British proletariat with its great memories of Chartism, are expressed to-day in the Communist International, the undisputed leader of which is the Party of Lenin, the Bolshevik Communist Party of the Soviet Union" (Fox 1932, 205).

Like the memory of the Chartists, the legacy of Morris as a British revolutionary acted as an important strategy of political persuasion. More than a dissenting figure, he was a man of versatile accomplishments, endowed with cultural legitimacy and thus useful for capturing mainstream sensibilities. Both through his artistic reputation and his Englishness, he had been widely accepted, and could potentially serve as the seductive embodiment of Marxist theory. Consequently, any potential capitulation of the Morris legacy to Conservatives and Social Democrats would be deemed a pragmatic loss for Communist cultural politics. Not surprisingly, Arnot's tract exudes a sense of urgency in its desperate effort to retain the Morris symbol and to guard it against the hegemonic interests of Conservative and reformist claimants. For ultimately, "the fight over the body of Morris was a fight against the influence of Marx inside the Labour movement" (Arnot 1934a, 6).

Yet if the *Vindication* sought to retrieve Morris, to win him back (Arnot 1934a, 31) from the clutches of a ruling-class foe, it could not realize this objective unproblematically. For one, it could not retain the Morris icon as it had been canonized at the centenary. To reproduce the portrait of the English artist would potentially result in the conflation of the revolutionary socialist with the Victorian, sentimentalist Morris which Conservatives and Social Democrats had constructed. As a result, Arnot's polemical intervention could only be unwieldy. In its awkwardness, the *Vindication* indexed the propagandist predicament of the Communist party during the Class-Against-Class period, its self-exile, as well as its anger at and distrust of the collusive forces of reformism.

In Morris's alleged misnomers, Arnot is continually reminded that Social Democrats were promoting their political cause in order to destroy the revolutionary Communist movement. Bruce Glasier's suggestion that Morris was a utopian socialist whose convictions were steeped in a literary ethical socialism, consonant with that of Ramsay MacDonald, rankled with Arnot's Marxist sensibilities (Arnot 1934a). In retaliation, Arnot denounced Morris's "traducers" and defined the hero as a distinguished prototype of revolutionary socialism. "Morris did not become a literary Socialist or an artistic Socialist, or any kind of middle-class parody of a Socialist ... When in 1883, he declared himself to be a Socialist, or, as he once said, 'become one of the Communist folk,' it was precisely in the meaning of the last words of the *Communist Manifesto*, written by Marx and Engels thirty-five years before" (Arnot 1934a, 15). Thus against the opportunism of the British bourgeois "Philistine" Hyndman, and against the ethical religiosity of the Glasiers and MacDonalds, Arnot casts a shadow of disapproval so as to illuminate the "authentic" Morris. In this, his polemical demonology of the leaders of Social Chauvinism recalls Lenin's multiple revisitations of "class betrayal" and the Second International, a subject that is integral to the politico-aesthetic underpinnings of the *Vindication* in its war on bourgeois propaganda.

THE BAN ON SENTIMENTALISM:
RESISTANCE TO REFORMIST PROPAGANDA

The exasperation which the *Vindication* expresses towards the centenary obliquely reveals the centrality of its author. The subtext discloses passionate undertones, signs of an intense authorial subjectivity. What appeared to be solely a vindication of Morris is equally and perhaps preeminently a covert self-defence of the author as Communist ideologue. As to its more objective concerns, the pamphlet betrays an acrimonious note that is symptomatic of the marginality of the Communist party and its pressured condition under the shadow of fascism; the tone of the polemic is, consequently, as much a refraction of the author's subjectivity *vis-à-vis* the Party's dilemmas and instabilities as it is a mirror of his own activist relation to the Communist movement. The tract absorbs Party policy as its nourishing ethos and is thus acutely averse to the ideological programs of social democracy, whose capitulations to and compromises with capitalism are said to block the Communist project of wholesale revolution.

In its retaliation against reformism, Arnot's critique of the centenary is levelled at the bourgeois press, in particular at those chatty columns which Communists regarded as digressions from the science of high politics. As an active journalist, covering issues in various pamphlets and contributing regularly to the *Labour Monthly*, Arnot sought with persistent energy to expose the mendacious character of the media and to provide incisive analyses of the *status quo*, in an effort to lay bare the workings of bourgeois institutions.[3] It is here that his critical attitude as a journalist brings him close to Lenin.

Leninism marks a theoretical tradition among British Communist intellectuals, whether formally or informally trained in the teachings of Marxism. The theory of the *Communist Review* and the *Labour Monthly* is imbued with excerpts from Lenin and articles written in the latter's ideological spirit. In short, one might say that the popular memory and political *Weltanschauung* of Communists of the 1920s and 1930s are deeply entrenched in Leninist analysis. To recall this heritage is to contextualize the *Vindication*, but also to introduce a hermeneutical tool for probing the polemic, otherwise quite cryptic in its textual brevity. The pamphlet can only be grasped in its full extent by being magnified through the lens of other contemporary or homologous texts. Indeed, in order to decipher Arnot's more obscure allusions, it is necessary to juxtapose the *Vindication* with an equivalent polemic, Lenin's eulogy to Tolstoy in which Lenin responds to the writer's posthumous subjection to the capitalist press. Just as Morris's conservative claimants hushed his sharp critique of capitalism, so Tolstoy's liberal Narodnik publicists and eulogisers eschewed the writer's condemnation of Russian liberalism.

Look at the estimate of Tolstoy in the government newspapers. They shed crocodile tears, professing their respect for "the great writer" and at the same time defending the "Holy" Synod. As for the holy fathers, they have just perpetrated a particularly vile iniquity; they sent priests to the dying man in order to hoodwink the people and say that Tolstoy has "repented." The Holy Synod excommunicated Tolstoy. So much the better. It will be reminded of this exploit when the hour comes for the people to settle accounts with the officials in cassocks, the gendarmes in Christ, the sinister inquisitors who supported anti-Jewish pogroms and other exploits of the Black-Hundred Tsarist gang.   (Lenin 1910, 326)

In the hypocritical eulogies of Tolstoy published in the government newspapers, Lenin locates the dissimulations of the press, the recreation of a writer's cultural identity in conformity with the politics of the ruling class. Most prominent here is Lenin's assault on the duplicit piety of the religious orders that blessed Tolstoy as a repenting soul and exculpated him for his subversive conscience. Not only does Lenin's invective show that this holy anointment was but an institutional sign of quashing the writer's political dissent and symbolic menace to capitalist rule; the virulent article also demystifies the saccharine sentimentalism of crocodile tears evidenced in these spurious panegyrics of the bourgeois press.

Look at the estimate of Tolstoy in the liberal newspapers. They confine themselves to those hollow, official-liberal, hackneyed professorial phrases about the "voice of civilised mankind," "the unanimous response of the world," the "ideas of truth, good," etc., for which Tolstoy so castigated – and justly castigated – bourgeois science. They *cannot* voice plainly and clearly their opinion of Tolstoy's views on the state, the church, private property in land, capitalism – not because they are prevented by the censorship; on the contrary, the censorship is helping them out of an embarrassing position! – but because each proposition in Tolstoy's criticism is a slap in the face of bourgeois liberalism; because the very way in which Tolstoy fearlessly, frankly and ruthlessly *poses* the sorest and most vexatious problems of our day is a *rebuff* to the commonplace phrases, trite quirks and evasive, "civilised" falsehoods of our liberal (and liberal-Narodnik) publicists.   (Lenin 1910, 326)

By extricating Tolstoy from the morass of liberal praise which served to contrive a benign public profile, Lenin depicts the writer as an anti-hero, excommunicated from the Synod. In this respect, he is able to redress the ill-conceived appraisals of the writer – appraisals which drowned Tolstoy's recalcitrance in grandiloquent praise and disguised the liberals' embarrassment over a thinker who challenged the integrity of their political institutions. In identifying with Tolstoy, Lenin rescues the misrepresented writer from a deluge of "trite quirks" and "civilised" falsehoods. Simultaneously, his vituperative indictment of the Narodnik publicists serves to jolt his readership into political alertness.

With similar intentions, Arnot defends the Communist Morris, elliptically revealing his hatred for the hypocrisies of the Conservative and Social-Democratic commemorations: "The centenary of his birth was turned into an orgy of 'canonisation'; books poured forth 'in his honour'; newspaper articles were written in dozens; and this 'great Victorian' (did they ever read what Morris wrote of Queen Victoria?) was hoisted up to his niche as a 'harmless saint'" (Arnot 1934a, 4).

The grammatical relief of quotation marks conveys Arnot's profound cynicism towards the centenary discourses. But by presenting an alternative portrait of Morris – the epitome of rebelliousness – Arnot pierces the deceptive blitheness of the centenary canonization and stresses, as Lenin does with Tolstoy, the bristling contrariness which Morris displayed towards the dominant bourgeois institution.

When modern "Socialists" hasten to defend the British monarchy and are found dancing attendance on pregnant princesses; when so many, too, of Morris's old associates have taken knighthoods from "the Fountain of Honour," it is refreshing to quote Morris's own attitude on the monarch of the day, who was not to be given the gratification of snubbing her Liberal ministers for nominating Morris Poet Laureate.

"What a nuisance," he says "the monarchy and court can be as a centre of hypocrisy and corruption, and the densest form of stupidity."

The Jubilee of Queen Victoria is for Morris "hideous, revolting and vulgar Tomfoolery." "One's indignation," he says, "swells pretty much to the bursting point."

"The Great Queen," Victoria, for him was a representative of capitalism; and her life was that of "a respectable officer who has always been careful to give the minimum of work for the maximum of pay."   (Arnot 1934a, 24–5)

References to Morris's disgust with the "loathsome subject of the Jubilee" express Arnot's parallel revulsion before the orgy of the centenary and its status as "vamped-up excitement" linked to the distractions of Armistice Day (Arnot 1934a, 25). But simultaneously, such pointed allusions to Morris's intolerance of the state of Victorian capitalism flesh out the hero as a persistent rebel, as a figure whose dissent crystallizes through agitational, anti-sentimental language, reminiscent of Lenin's polemical depiction of Tolstoy's frank but defiant subversion of the bourgeois political system.

Communist portraits of revolutionary heroes are consciously opposed to the hypocrisy of liberal sentimentalism; in their representations of cultural heroes, the Marxist-Leninist ideologues prefer to deploy the disturbing revolutionary impulse, to explode the deceptively harmonious world views of bourgeois society, and provide an aperture into the class antagonisms and dialectical forces of the nation-state as it really exists beneath its abstract models. The Communist Morris is thus an anti-hero, revered for his barbed anti-Victorianism, for his outspokenness and "revolutionary edge." Any alleged saintliness imputed to him by Conservative and Menshevik claimants is as brusquely spurned by Arnot's rationalist refutations as by his subjectively charged discourse.

ASSAULTS ON THE GENTLE SOCIALIST

The *Vindication* delivers the identity of Morris with a robust style even while it harbours an elegiac tone. Its underlying plaintive substance is transmuted into wrath and protest. In one respect, the pamphlet is a political eulogy, a cousin of those lyrical discourses which heaped praise and glory on the Morris hero in 1896 and shortly thereafter. But the decidedly anti-sentimental character of the tract prohibits maudlin romantic language. This censorship is more than superficially stylistic. It is fundamentally cultural and political. And it finds its preliminary purging task in the eradication of the "gentle socialist" image of William Morris. The latter is specifically the product of the Menshevik appraisals, versions that were consonant with what Ramsay MacDonald said of ILP socialism: "that it was based not upon economics, but [on an] historical, ethical and 'literary basis'" (Arnot 1934a, 5). In a caustic pastiche, Arnot rebuts this position:

The usual explanation is to treat Morris's "excursion into Socialism" as some sort of aberration of the poet, one of these things which show what fantastic fellows artists are. When this usual explanation is furbished forth in its Labour Party variety it is the revolutionary character of his Socialism which is regarded as the aberration. This essentially Philistine view of the development of every great artist or fighter is buttressed up by sentimental reflections on struggles that Morris had to carry through inside the Socialist body to which he belonged – all written in the kindly offensive manner of a doctor descanting on an imbecile patient – and on the other hand by sham versions of the history of the 'eighties and the three preceding decades.   (Arnot 1934a, 8)

What are the elements in this Menshevik myth that offend Arnot's sensibility? Consider, for a start, the "gentle Morris," the aesthetic embodiment of ethical socialism. Here in this cast, the hero is revealed as an intensive ideological summary of his makers, namely ILPers, whom Arnot regards as traducers. Among them, Ramsay MacDonald and Bruce Glasier "constructed a Morris that never existed, a sickly dilettante Socialist" (Arnot 1934a, 5–6). Arnot believed that Morris's imputed attributes were merely the projections of his claimants' self-fancying ideals. Utopian and ethical socialists were abhorrent to Arnot, since they were caught deep in "the swamp of religiosity" (Arnot 1934a, 5–6). Bruce Glasier, in particular, "had the effrontery to suggest that the treatise *Socialism, Its Growth and Outcome*, by Belfort Bax and William Morris represented the views of Bax but not those of Morris, who 'belonged to the old Utopian school and not to the modern Scientific-Socialist school of thought'" (Arnot 1934a, 7).

Arnot's disgust with the "gentle" Morris icon is clearly a function of his repudiation of the enemy, symbolically encoded in the hero's Labourist cast. Such a reaction compares readily with Lenin's polemical fireworks: i.e. attacks on Ramsay MacDonald and related cronies. The "gentle" Morris symbolizes a pseudo-pacificism. Recall how Lenin vents his spleen in respect to those who distorted the essentially proletarian sympathies of Tolstoy. Such a polemical anger is also evident in Lenin's critique of Ramsay MacDonald's political writing, in which MacDonald betrays "that smooth, melodious, banal, and Socialist-seeming phraseology which serves in all developed capitalist countries to camouflage the policy of the bourgeoisie inside the Labour Movement" (Lenin 1924, 142). The image of the "gentle socialist" conjures up such a conciliatory discourse and can be seen as a symbol of labourite collusions with imperialism.

Historically, Lenin's outrage before MacDonaldism resides, as Arnot's does more mutedly, in the action of "Social Chauvinists."

Those Socialists who, during the war of 1914–18, did not understand that this war was criminal and reactionary, that it was a war of rapine, in which both sides pursued imperialist aims, are social patriots, i.e., they are Socialists as far as words are concerned, but patriots in deed; they are friends of the working

class only in words, in reality they are lackeys of their "own" national bourgeoisie, assisting the latter to deceive the people by depicting as a "national
war," "a war of liberation," "a war of defence," "a just war," etc., the war
between the two groups of English and German imperialist bandits, both
equally foul, equally mercenary, equally bloodthirsty, criminal, and
reactionary.   (Lenin 1924, 145)

Portraying these socialists as underhanded imperialists, "ignoramuses or
hypocrites" who deceive the workers by repeating commonplaces on
capitalism, Lenin identifies in particular the disciples of the Berne
International – "yellow," "perfidious" conceders to the bourgeoisie –
among whom Ramsay MacDonald stands out prominently. Prototypical
of "that nursery and pattern of opportunism," MacDonald is said to
deliver his political message with the "entertaining naïveté of a parlour
socialist" (Lenin 1924, 145) pretending to disregard the compelling
nature of his oratorical effect.

It is not incidental that the resonances of MacDonaldism buzz around
the title "gentle Morris," suggesting a sham pacific rhetoric, indeed a
discourse that disguises its bellicose intentions and surrenders to imperialism by engaging in a conciliatory verbal waltz. Such language is
entrenched in all the propriety and protocol of "those countries of
longstanding democratic parliamentary culture [where] the bourgeoisie
has acquired the fine art of acting not only by violence but also by means
of deceit and bribery and flattery" (Lenin 1924, 147).

If the "gentle socialist" evokes memories of "genteel" classes, of
excessive pomp and vacuous ceremony, then Arnot's disgust may be
attributed to the submergence of the Morris legacy in this bourgeois
world where injustice masquerades under the seemingly innocent smiles
and handshakes of international diplomacy. And so long as the memory
of the First World War is rife with the history of class betrayal, Morris's
"gentle" aspect can only conjure up a spurious gentility, a charge inexorably linked to the political acts of his "peace-loving" admirers. To
Communists, the "gentle socialist" is thus an emblem of duplicit pacifism, a product of emollient language whose tender style conceals an
underlying aggression that is directed as much at dissenting social forces
as at countries beleaguered by imperialism.

In the vague generalities of chauvinist discourse, the civil strife
between socialists and capitalists is dissolved under the pressure of
national harmony. Such dissimulation occurs in the workings of "social
opportunism" through a confusion engendered and preserved in the

opposition between war and peace. It is an opposition which contains two possible tensions: a struggle for socialism within the national setting under times of peace; and the struggle between nations – a state of war which inhibits the fight for socialism. Lenin shows that the root of this confusion resides in the very concept of class struggle and its relation to the nation-state, a confusion which Marx and Engels identified as a discrepancy within the representation of the class struggle – between its apparent form and its actual content (Pêcheux 1975).

But the confusions incurred are not innocent consequences of political discourse. They are the product of an evasive and imprecise language that tends to dodge the thornier aspects of the political economy and the machinations of heads of state at whose mercy the uninformed public is caught. Consider Arnot's comments on the slippery character of Labour party campaigning which dilutes its own socialist commitment.

How unimpeachable the election programme is, how free from any reproach of setting class against class, is very noticeable in another respect. That is the extraordinary vagueness of its phrasing. Instead of presenting in crisp unmistakable words exactly what Labour stands for and what it stands against, it gives, in spite of its apparent detail, the impression of a rigmarole of meaningless generalities, such as any tired speaker utters when informed that there are persistent and awkward hecklers in the audience.

Now this is not unintentional. The drafters of the Labour Party programme are perfectly well aware of the value of words, vague words as well as precise words: and vague words have been chosen in this case just because it *is* an audience that is being thought of, an audience that might be alienated by a crisp statement of working-class policy. Here we have the clue to the tone of the election programme. It is tuned to reach the ear of the middle-class voter.   (Arnot 1922a, 335)

Not only is the "gentle socialist" Morris a reminder of those foggy forms of rhetoric with their propensity for deception, he also recalls the labourite electoral strategy of winning votes by softening the tones of an otherwise militant propaganda. In short, the "gentle socialist" is used by a Labour program to gesture towards a middle-class audience, to treat it tenderly so as to avoid ruffling its sensibilities with the robustness of revolutionary speech.

The rhetorical effect of vague generalities used to deliver a conveniently non-committal set of political ethics lends itself to negotiating a cooperative and unifying relation with the electorate at large. By consciously blurring distinctions among class factions, the rhetoric of Labourism trumpets a propaganda of social harmony, just as "from the end of 1917 onwards ... Labour was made to stand for all sections of the nation and not only for the labouring masses" (Arnot 1922a, 337). To Arnot, as to his Marxist triadic ancestry (Marx, Engels, Lenin – as well as contemporaries such as Caudwell), this potpourri of Labourite programs represented a travesty of Marxist perceptions of society: it signalled a homogenization of those class structures which Marxist philosophy deemed incompatible and irreconcilable. The phenomenon of confluences in Labourite ideology recalls the philosophies of early utopian socialists, which Engels regarded "as a kind of eclectic, average Socialism ... a mish-mash allowing of the most manifold shades of opinion; a mish-mash of such critical statements, economic theories, pictures of future society by the founders of different sects, as excite a minimum of opposition; a mish-mash which is the more easily brewed the more the definite sharp edges of the individual constituents are rubbed down in the stream of debate, like rounded pebbles in a brook" (Engels 1880, 61–2).[4]

As Engels repudiates the erosion of difference into homogeneity (consider the imagery: "individual constituents" *rubbed down* in the stream of debate"), so Lenin speaks in *State and Revolution* of "the real essence of revolutionary theories" being *blunted* (Lenin 1932, 7). Both Marxist thinkers take issue with the bourgeois eradication of revolutionary contradictions. They take offence at the erasure of dialectics and its replacement by eclecticism, since the latter fosters a naïve and thus restrictive view of social reality. In their contrasting but essentially equivalent metaphors, both Lenin and Engels express a refusal of apparent, "phenomenal" continuity. Eclecticism, one may say, becomes that devilish twin of dialectics, falsely similar yet fundamentally distinct. In its apparent congruity with dialectics it actually masks those crucial divergences which Marxist science wishes to highlight. And if Lenin and Engels note this conflation of epistemological perspectives, it is not to engage in metaphysical quibbles, but rather to show that when

dialectics are replaced by eclecticism, – as when Engels's notion of violent revolution is misconstrued – it typifies the most widespread practice of "present day Social-Democratic literature in relation to Marxism ... In falsifying Marxism in opportunistic fashion, the substitution of eclecticism for dialectics is the easiest way of deceiving the people. It gives an illusory satisfaction; it seems to take into account all sides of the process ... whereas in reality it provides no integral and revolutionary conception of the process of social development at all." (Lenin 1963, 400)

The "gentle socialist" is distasteful to Arnot as much for the multiple resonances which mingle in that phrase – soft, pliable discourse, agile but dubious diplomatic negotiations and nebulous epistemology – as for the effects that this title bears on a Marxist perception of the socialist agent. The "gentle socialist" is the product of a savaged revolutionary, a symbol of an emasculated activist, whose adamancy and political astuteness have been compromised. This "gentle socialist" is also incapable of delivering an unequivocal project of cataclysmic social change, for he bends and concedes too readily to the bourgeois system and is left impotent in the face of Marxist imperatives. In the vein of Fabianism, as A.J. Morris describes it, he would sooner hymn "the virtues of the inevitability of gradualness, a lyric sweetly tuned to the English genius for moderation in all things especially change" (A.J. Morris 1974, 1) than trumpet the sounds of revolutionary fury.[5]

THE WORKINGS OF SENTIMENTALISM

The debunking of the "gentle socialist" Morris amounts to a rejection of sentimentalism and to the birth of an anti-sentimentalist aesthetic, a prime impulse of the *Vindication*. But the resonances of the title "gentle socialist" suggest that the anti-sentimentalism of the political tract is not an idiosyncratic feature either of Arnot's character or of his Leninist ancestors, but a culturally determined aesthetic preference. Nor is this predilection primarily addressed towards aesthetic forms in themselves, but rather towards the far-reaching implications that these forms harness semiotically. Consequently, sentimentalism stands in for a range of epistemological, propagandist, and hegemonic concerns: genteel discourse, electoral sycophancy, supine reformism, social chauvinism, irrationalist eclecticism – elements wholly incompatible with a Marxist political philosophy.

In its attempt to conquer the illusory, peace-loving aspects of the "gentle socialist" icon, the pamphlet also marks an attempt to puncture the silence so characteristic of bourgeois propaganda which elides "unsavoury" discussions of the political economy through sentimentalist obfuscation. The *Vindication* proposes to drive a wedge into the illusory screens of such propaganda, introducing a demystificatory breach. In so doing, it throws into relief the class struggle that would otherwise stand unnoticed beneath the benign apparel of bourgeois discourse. The text's destabilizing rhetoric is a direct reaction to the contrived continuity of sentimentalism, to a sensibility so irksome to Arnot in that it borders on irrationalism. Although no overt analysis of this saccharine mentality is given, the *Vindication* suggests that sentimentalism is the handmaiden of a political rhetoric which compels an audience to assume a vulnerable and regressive posture before its enrapturing discursive qualities. Intoxicating forms of address foster pleasure but also expel all critical consciousness, reducing the public to utter submissiveness. Thus when Labour party Morrisites spout "sentimental reflections on struggles that Morris had to carry through inside the Socialist body to which he belonged," they deliver these thoughts in an "offensive kindly manner of a doctor descanting on an imbecile patient" (Arnot 1934a, 8); in other words, in the manner of a patronizing ideology addressing a gullible audience.

With respect to the "Menshevik" Morris myths, Arnot argues indirectly that much of this sentimentalism is also lodged in the commonplace worship of Morris's utopian literature, a genre which he claims has been classically misapprehended. In the case of *News from Nowhere: Or an Epoch of Rest, being some chapters from a Utopian Romance*, "the poison ivy of the myth has completely hidden the oak. Almost everyone appears to have read *News from Nowhere* under the domination either of the bourgeois, Labour Party or ILP myth, and have, consequently, read not what was in the book but what they expected to find" (Arnot 1934a, 25).

Presupposing that within Morris's utopian romance lies an inner, authentic truth, Arnot removes the "poisonous" layer of pleasure of *News from Nowhere* and focuses on the sequences which depict class struggle. By seeking to disclose the vital "essence" of Morris's work and salvage it from the onslaught of mythmongers, he repeats Lenin's redemptive gesture towards Marxism: "Thirty years later it took all the force of Lenin's genius and profound knowledge of Marxism to restore in a revolutionary epoch, the actual teachings of Marx and Engels. So much the easier was it for the mythmongers to smother up the teachings of Marx forty-five years ago" (Arnot 1934a, 25).

The reference is to Lenin's *State and Revolution* and to his demystificatory task therein; but the allusion is equally an assertion of Arnot's comparable duty to resurrect the Marxist Morris who had been "smothered" by the stifling weight of the Menshevik Morrisania. Nor is the imagery gratuitous. The smothering of the "real" Morris coincides with

Arnot's figurative descriptions of poison ivy which allegedly strangled Morris's Marxist legacy. Thus he castigates Labourite rehearsals of Morris's imputed utopian socialism, rehearsals which he claims misconstrued Morris's utopian romances (specifically *News from Nowhere*) with their overemphasis on the idyllic serenity which "so overpoweringly assails the senses already drugged by the Labour Party–ILP myth that, seemingly, many who may wander there hear the *News from Nowhere* but do not hearken to it; remember the fragrance of the garden, but nothing of the men who dwell therein. It was as though the readers of the Dialogues of Plato were to remember only their setting – the shady plane tree beyond the banks of the Cephisos and Socrates paddling his feet in the burn – but forget what the Dialogue was about" (Arnot 1934a, 28). Here is an example of the type of utopian sensuality to which Arnot was referring.

We were soon under way and going at a fair pace through the beautiful reaches of the river, between Bensington and Dorchester. It was now about the middle of the afternoon, warm rather than hot, and quite windless; the clouds high up and light, pearly white, and gleaming, softened the sun's burning, but did not hide the pale blue in most places, though they seemed to give it height and consistency; the sky in short, looked really like a vault, as poets have sometimes called it and not like mere limitless air, but a vault so vast and full of light that it did not in any way oppress the spirits. It was the sort of afternoon that Tennyson must have been thinking about, when he said of the Lotus-Eaters' land that it was a land where it was always afternoon.   (Morris 1890, 157–8)

Although aware of the hermeneutical pitfalls of the genre of utopia, Arnot's concern is with the impact which the lulling and chimeric qualities of *News from Nowhere* may have had on Morris's mythmongers. As he saw it, the descriptive texture of this bucolic utopia engendered an enthralling beauty, exploited ideologically by ethical socialists and their kind to dull society's critical senses and sanctify aesthetic niceties to the detriment of political analysis. In this, Arnot's association of romanticism with bourgeois literary subjectivism, apolitical fantasy, and cloistered individualism forecloses any possibility of integrating Morris's romantic facets with his revolutionary identity. The *Vindication* subordinates Morris's flights of aesthetic delight in sensuous pleasure to Arnot's prior considerations, to his political objectives which, in 1934, are directed more towards a prospect of revolution than to literary

romance and its social value. Thus, in selecting the political graphics of
Morris's legacy, Arnot chooses to highlight a "realist" (cf. Lukács 1963)
portrait of Morris's identity, rather than the naturalistic details of some
individualist biography. For such features are deemed superficial trappings to be jettisoned in favour of a more "substantive" analysis.

SENTIMENTALISM AND IRRATIONALISM IN THE FASCIST CONTEXT

We, who can look back over the developing years since Morris wrote, we can
see with what insight he beheld the class struggle in Europe. Had he lived
another ten years he would have seen many features of his chapter on "How
the Change Came" enacted in the year 1905 in Russia, from the massacre of
Bloody Sunday through the mutinies of the armed forces and the General Strike
to the creation of Soviets (Workers' Committees, Morris called them), the
formation of the Black Hundred (the Friends of Order, Morris called them)
and finally the armed rising.

Again, in 1934 in Britain, the growth of Fascism (both Governmental and
Blackshirt) pays tribute to the insight of Morris.   (Arnot 1934a, 28–9)

As the various factions ventured into the William Morris battlefield,
Arnot's intervention came as a skirmish, which for all its marginality
and relative impact on middle-class society (Morton 1985) aimed to
enlighten popular consciousness as to the cultural reach, not only of
reformism and conservatism, but of a fascist trend insidiously unfolding
during the 1930s. Indeed, in his commitment to the anti-fascist campaign, Arnot contributed numerous articles to the Communist journal,
the *Labour Monthly*. Here he reminded the public that the year 1934
stood like a precipice before a wave of totalitarianism. Although primarily a rebuke to the Morris centenary, the *Vindication* is written in this
political climate. As such, the polemic reveals Arnot's sensitivity not
only to the fascism of his day but also to its manifestation in previous
periods of history. In his commentary on Morris's utopian romance,
News from Nowhere, Arnot links Morris's insights on "Bloody Sunday"
with British fascism of the 1930s. (Cf. Morris in Arnot, 1934a.) However,
while this pervasive anti-fascist consciousness underpins the *Vindication*,
it is not against totalitarian ideology *per se* that the pamphlet stages its
arguments. Rather, the polemic is an indirect castigation of a "dying
culture" open to cooptation by fascist ideologues (Caudwell 1938).

Repeatedly Arnot displays his eagerness to show that Britain is not immune from the influences and even the infiltration of what was commonly assumed to be an exclusively foreign totalitarianism (Arnot 1938). A decrepit capitalist condition is traced back to the Victorian epoch. The continuous impact which capitalism had on society's welfare (from the nineteenth century onwards) enables Arnot to use Morris's disgruntled attitude towards the degeneracy of the Victorian period as an intertextual voice from which to pour scorn upon the political realities of the 1930s. It is through Morris's reflections on the state of the arts, a condition which indexed some deeper socio-economic malaise, that he establishes the links between the Morris centenary and a society susceptible to irrationalism and ethical decrepitude.

The centenary, in Arnot's view, is a locus of cultural decay, and it is to this malaise that he turns with a "breath of discontent" (Caudwell 1949) to expose the seeds of British social vulnerability before the ideological powers of fascism. Indeed, a principal concern of his Communist rhetoric is that Conservatism and Social Democracy are the political tempers which may bring British society to the threshold of an irrationalism that would glorify and indeed sanction genocide in the name of religious rites (Rickword 1934; Stead 1935). According to Communist ideologues, the material horror of such a pending reality is prefigured in the contamination and vitiation of the human mind. In the *Vindication* Arnot warns against the deceptively moderate character of British sensibility. In the texture of non-"extremist" rhetoric, he locates the blitheness and seemingly non-political propaganda of bourgeois ideologues, implicitly responsible for a moral vapidity such as that occasioned by the centenary. He sees this society as quasi-inebriated with the cloying sentimentalism of a ceremony that acts as the compensatory boost or "vamped-up excitement" (Arnot 1934a, 24) for an alienated bourgeois world. Such sentimentalism in collective celebrations also functions as a cosmetic disguise of the underlying adversities of the state, its imperialist imbroglios and its tyrannical rule abroad.

In its dissimulation of the imperialist and exploitative character of capitalism, the sentimentalism of the centenary's celebration of British culture becomes a religious distortion of social consciousness forbidding society to penetrate the "spiritual aroma" (Marx 1843–4, 244) and secular halo with which it has swathed itself. Arnot's pamphlet represents an endeavour to grapple with this religion where society conceals its own malaise with a sentimental aura, offering itself consolatory and thus "imaginary flowers" (Marx 1843–4, 244). His diatribe serves to dismantle this illusory veil of cultural pleasures and rhetorical niceties that Conservative ideologues and Social Democrats have spun around their own political condoning of the capitalist state.

In this light it can be argued that Marx's notion of the imaginary flowers (by which a society's disorientation is temporarily assuaged) constitutes a metaphoric correlative of sentimentalism where the putative unity of some former Elysian world is imperceptibly appropriated and becomes the condition through which harmonious societal relations crystallize. This epistemological attitude assumes prominence in the political visions of bourgeois ideologues, and particularly of aesthetes and literati of the 1920s and 1930s, whose retrospective itineraries were pursued as crusades for a primal unity – a unity of blood and instinct and finally of racial pedigree (cf. D.H. Lawrence and T.S. Eliot). These searchings were the products of a will to salvage the "dignity of man" amid the shattered ethical values of the twentieth century during an epoch riven by war and societal disarray (Gloversmith 1980). But as such, these philosophical and ideological pursuits of coherent value and transcendence were also aimless ambles through the realms of mysticism, revelation, and individualist escape. Sentimentalism constituted the foreshadowing of these more overtly irrationalist symptoms, a poultice that granted temporary relief from the drudgery of the postwar world, yet a balm that also desensitized and inhibited the moral health of humanity.

As the precursor of irrationalism, sentimentalism can be seen as the product of modern alienated society. Here the subjective consciousness of individuals is increasingly estranged from both their social and natural environments; it is "the sigh of the oppressed," yearning for a unity which is markedly absent in an era of societal fragmentation. In short, it is the attribute of the judgment of the beautiful which provides the appearance of totality and creates the "feeling of perfect accord between the self and the world, a feeling of vibrant stillness and animated rest" (Kurrik 1974, 48); but it is an experience which is in fact no more than an artificially induced state of naïve pleasure and absolute harmony.

Desirable as such a state of serenity and oneness may be (even to the sensibilities of a rationalist individual), this condition of the "beautiful" (a judgment that is conceptless) is all too problematic. As a state of consciousness, sentimentalism favours a retrieval of a childlike past; it hankers for a non-rational immediacy and simplicity of mind which is static and contemplative. Epistemologically, such a stance is duplicit, since it replaces veritable cognition with but the appearance of true rational thought. Like religion, sentimentalism produces a distorted knowledge of reality, a consciousness that denies material causalities and legitimates an idealism where the apprehension of objectivity is ultimately violated and skewed.

As a contemporary of Arnot, Christopher Caudwell sheds light on the ramifications of false innocence and spiritual simplicity in his remarks on the problem of contemplation as the primary canker in a dying bourgeois culture: "It is a human weakness to believe that by retiring into his imagination man can elicit categories or magical spells which will enable him to subjugate reality contemplatively. It is the error of the 'theoretical' man, of the prophet, of the mystic, of the metaphysician, in its pathological form the error of the neurotic. It is the trace of the primitive believer in magic that remains in us all" (Caudwell 1938, 2).

Repeatedly Caudwell expresses disgust with the irrational, "infantile regression" of his society in crisis. The recourse taken to mythology, racialism, hero-worship, nationalism, and mysticism offends him profoundly. He sees these tendencies as a return to the womb of primal nature in wholesale abandonment of intellectualism. Thus sentimentalism with its pseudo-innocence is similarly the unhealthy or degenerate attempt by an advanced culture to revert to the naïve in search of an unmediated totality; it is but the fabrication of the "old bourgeois pastoral heaven of the 'natural man' born everywhere in chains, [yet a 'natural man' who] does not exist" (Caudwell 1938, 70).

Like Caudwell, and other committed Communists of the 1930s, Edgell Rickword expresses a concern for the "moral" but also humanitarian destiny of society enraptured by the emotionalism of fascist fantasies and adolescent devotion to leaders. Rickword sees the charismatic power of figures such as Hitler, Moseley, and Mussolini as corrupting the public consciousness with a mystical aura of patriotism that weakens intellectual opposition to war: "Minds are being prepared not merely to think that war is not so bad but even to applaud when it is being as blatantly glorified as it ever was by a Prussian philosopher like Treitschke, who was so soundly abused in 1914" (Rickword 1934, 44).

Clearly, Communist rejection of this irrationalism and its link with fascist and fascist-tending ideologies was more than academic. It was determined by an underlying resistance to imperialist aggression. "National or Coalition Governments are bound to make war in the end, and in a state of war what little liberty the intellectual has now will inevitably be taken from him. There must not be any hesitation in resisting these two things, not only in their most obvious physical manifestations, but in the subtler emotional forms they take in literature, philosophy and art" (Rickword 1934, 45).

That Communists sounded the knell to warn against fascism was no doubt an act based on material political realities: the advent of world war. But the fields of protest were not strictly political and economic. In the "superstructural" sphere of humanist culture, Communists were keen to extract all signs of ideological submission to fascist thought. *Ipso facto*, they placed a high premium on their scientific rationalist ethos, regarding such a philosophy not only as ethically superior but as a crucial defence against the enslavement of popular minds to the force of totalitarian regimes. Thus they sought the subtler and seemingly non-political (aesthetic and literary) snares of irrationalism that would capture the sensibilities of lost "souls" wandering through the pewter bleakness of world war, depression and socio-economic upheaval.

THE AESTHETICS OF AGITATION

The aesthetic and rhetorical qualities of Arnot's *Vindication* acquire their legitimacy and constitutive logic in the light of these historical conditions. The pamphlet is virulent and confrontational for pragmatic reasons: it mimetically reproduces a mood of urgency in order to sensitize its audience to political crisis, countering the soporific side effects of sentimentalism with the dynamic impulse of agitational rhetoric. What is possibly an implicit, or unconscious, propagandist approach in 1934 later develops into an explicit method. For in 1938, Arnot openly refers to the need to awaken public consciousness and to instil a sense of the onrush of fascism as well as a more acute perception of contemporary events (Arnot 1938).

Admittedly, the relation between the centenary and proto-fascist culture is not a dominant object of Arnot's pamphlet. Nonetheless it can be regarded as a determining political setting. The more immediately striking concern is Arnot's critique of capitalist culture and the deceptively superficial appearances engendered by the commodity form germane to that system. Yet if the Communist is preoccupied with this epistemological reawakening of public awareness, his agitational strategy does not collapse into the apparently radical ruptures into which the artistic avant-garde stepped during the 1920s and 1930s. The *Vindication* does not approach any threshold of surrealism, for instance. The latter's "convulsive effort to split open the commodity forms of the objective universe by striking them against each other with immense force"

(Jameson 1971, 96) is aesthetically anathema to the discursive style of the *Vindication* even while it may conceivably resonate with the principle of shock and conflict that characterizes the pamphlet. Nor can one claim that the agitprop theories of the Workers Theatre Movement are directly applicable to the tract. Yet, there too, one locates an aesthetic philosophy whose anti-sentimentalism (cf. Samuel et al. 1985) it is tempting to equate with the self-conscious virility of the pamphlet.

Despite its convergence with modernist aesthetic theories of the 1920s and 1930s which ostensibly accord with Arnot's rejection of bourgeois institutions, the *Vindication* is unable to absorb these vanguardist trends unproblematically. For while Arnot advocates an unequivocal break with bourgeois culture, his political tactics must be distinguished from his aesthetic principles, which remain anchored in traditional forms of literary expression. He does not engage in surrealist subversion of linguistic or narrational syntax. He only challenges a particular form of historical reportage – a historiography which he deems unscientific. While one may argue that the agitational tones of his text are strongly affected by the contemporary aesthetic tendencies of revolutionary art, the *Vindication* ostensibly falls into the category of Brechtian didactic estrangement (*Verfremdung*),[6] since it seeks to enlighten with crisp clarity rather than entertain with levity. It aims to reveal the apparatus of social-democratic institutions rather than conceal it. The avant-gardist aesthetics which it integrates are not immediately those associated with agitprop theatre, German expressionism, surrealism, or Soviet constructivism – indeed that host of revolutionary forms which display their resistance to the dominant cultural institutions. One might rather situate the pamphlet in the tradition of polemical tracts of dissent, seasoned with the philosophies of Marxist-Leninism. But finally, as a genre, the *Vindication* is caught between the narrative structures of the bourgeois novel and the intensity of the plaintive lyric. It possesses a socialist-realist[7] force and pivots on a heroic principle that underlies the aesthetic trends of Marxist-Leninist art and literature.

Still, Arnot's immediate recalcitrance remains apparently comparable to those rebellious forms of art which typify the avant-garde. His anti-institutional position is an upheaval of social protocol, an irreverence before British quietude. His rhetorical discordance is agitational, highlighting a disconcertingly new and unfathomable perception of reality, an epistemological *Verfremdung* that strikes a note of foreign exuberance and a revolutionary temper which British common sense has tended to stamp out of its ruling-class canon.

DIALECTICS AND NARRATIVE STRUCTURE

If the *Vindication*'s stylistics remain distinct from their contemporane-
ous modernism, they are not bereft of the confrontational character of
anti-traditionalist art. The pamphlet repeatedly highlights Marxist battles against reformism. It inscribes these ideological wrangles as the key
codes of a dialectical narrative, as the class antagonisms of a Leninist
vision of society.

First, we have Arnot's warfare with the MacDonalds and the Glasiers,
a classic opposition between the Marxist crusader and his ethical-socialist
adversaries. Then, in a second section, Arnot sweepingly revisits Morris's
conversion to socialism, pivoting this narrative sequence on the decisive
theme of class struggle, the motif which lends itself to a logical dénouement, in short, to a revolutionary messianic promise of imminent
commonweal. In a third section, Arnot focuses on a specific moment
of Morris's political history, namely, the breach with Hyndman and the
Social-Democratic Federation. This marks a sequence which mirrors
Arnot's resistance to his contemporaries, to his ethical-socialist opponents. Once more, the division between Marxist and reformist persuasions is advanced. Finally, Arnot considers Morris's legacy in a
comparable opposition of ideological forces. Here, a statement on the
posthumous battles over Morris's memory, the polarized predilections
for his aesthetic or political writings, returns to echo the conflicting
relation between Communist and reformist ideologies.

Just as shock and dialectical movement in Eisenstein's montage[8] are
evidenced in the warring collision of disparate images, in the kinetic
impulse of dialectical art, so a similar juxtaposition occurs in Arnot's
narrative sequences: the dramatic conflicts recounted between Communists and Labourites, ILPers and Social Opportunists provide the pattern
of dualities through which Arnot designs his layout of class alliances.
This narrative pattern serves as an aesthetic determinant of his style,
since it provides the structural foundation for his ensuing aggressive
dialogue with contemporary bourgeois adversaries. His idiom is closely
linked to that *zerbrechend* (demolishing) impulse which typifies Leninist
discourse both in form and in content: e.g. Lenin's belief that the masses
need to be imbued with a sense of violent revolution is a notion self-
reflexively reproduced in the formalism of his violent linguistic devices,
in rhetorical tropes that contrast with the saccharine and tenderizing
language of social-democratic propaganda. Similarly, Arnot pits his
idiom of sharpness against sentimentalism; he brandishes a rationalist

appraisal of Morris by denouncing the emasculated Labourite renditions and by foregrounding the "vital essence" of Morris's political prophecies. Implicitly, he warns against the ancillary niceties of Morris's utopian romances in which the perilous ambiguities of literary style block the clear reception of a political message.

The discursive vigour of the pamphlet is most immediately felt in the clipped and often blunt character of Arnot's phraseology. The *Vindication* adopts a disruptive grammar-school diction which violates the genteel forms of "civil" language. This is executed in the intertextual chorus[9] of voices which Arnot creates by citing the expletives, tempestuous and scathing asides, and informal speech patterns of a host of characters: Lenin, Morris, Engels, as well as a motor mechanic denouncing the oppression of factory labour. These voices mingle with Arnot's sporadic aspersions, expressed in contemptuous remarks rather than in the high-flown flourishes of upper-class language. Note his pejorative diction in castigating the mythmongers.

The main burden of this myth ... is that Morris was "not a Marxist," and if there is now some assimilation of Morris and Marx in their *scribblings*, [added emphasis] it is only because they have at length created a mythical Marx to fit in with their mythical Morris. (Arnot 1934a, 5)

there is a manuscript in the handwriting of Morris, being a short precis of one of the "economic portions" of *Capital* which, for those so *blind* that they cannot see the results of a study of Marx in *John Ball*, should be an incontestable proof enough that Morris *swotted* [added emphasis] at Marx. (Arnot 1934a, 7)

Here too in the preface to William Ferrie's depiction of factory oppression, Arnot injects a derogatory turn of phrase:

To this *twaddle* [added emphasis] there was given a terrible answer from William Ferrie, a motor mechanic, whose statement, – duly banned by the British Broadcasting Corporation – might well be an additional footnote to Part IV of *Capital*. (Arnot 1934a, 10)

Arnot seems also to privilege Morris's critiques of the middle- and upper-class sectors of British society.

The upper and middle classes as a body will by the very nature of their existence resist the abolition of classes ... I have never underrated the power of the middle classes, whom, in spite of their individual good nature and banality, I look upon as a most terrible and implacable force.   (Morris in Arnot 1934a, 18)

In his less polemical moments, Arnot's style harbours a somewhat self-conscious plainness, an understylized idiom that precludes, indeed censures, baroque ornament. "Morris, with his grasp of the results of the application of machinery by the capitalist method of production, concentrated his attention on the products and especially on the consumption of goods produced by capitalism in the mid-nineteenth century. He looked and saw that it was ugly: and he pierced through to the root cause in the division of labour and the toilsome life of the exploited worker" (Arnot 1934a, 11).

Aesthetic flourishes are mostly derisive images or textual borrowings that are markedly fierce in character. Arnot appears to relish rehearsing the lines of revolutionary apostles. Quoting from the *Communist Manifesto*, he deploys the formidable eloquence of Marx and Engels to his own rhetorical ends: "Let the ruling class tremble at the prospect of a Communist revolution" (Arnot 1934a, 15). Similarly, Morris's writings serve Arnot's agitational role as they evoke the orator rabble-rousing to incite political action: "[to] further the spread of international feeling between the workers by all means possible; to point out to our own workmen that foreign competition and rivalry, or commercial war, culminating at last in open war, are necessities of the plundering classes; and that the race and commercial quarrels of these classes only concern us so far as we can use them as opportunities for fostering discontent and revolution" (Morris in Arnot 1934a, 23). Here the shock effect of Arnot's idiom rests more on horrifying bourgeois sensibility, on puncturing the propriety and hypocrisies of civil etiquette, than on disturbing a conventional set of cognitive references.

At face value, the aesthetics of agitation constitute the phenomenal features of political indignation. Substantively, however, they betray an anxiety and a quality of loss hidden under the veneer of wrath. In this respect, the *Vindication* arises out of the tensions of a dialectic between grievous sentiment and defiant self-assertion. In content, the *Vindication* presents a plea for the consensual approval of a Communist ideology, a plea which solicits the recognition of a political movement strenuously preserving its identity under the pressures of its counter-hegemonic isolation from the broad left alliances. In form, however, the pamphlet refrains from adopting a language which might otherwise secure wider endorsement for Communist politics. Such a language would belong to a traditional Englishness, often sentimental and defined by ruralist aesthetics which mark the iconography of early British Socialism. The latter deployed the imagery of bucolic peasants and artisans as the emblem of a Golden Age, a solidarity of labour and brotherhood of man. Socialism, the term epitomizing a cult of beauty, was exemplified in the flowing robes and goddesses of Walter Crane's engravings (Samuel et al. 1985). But such versions of beauty, redolent with the aroma of English Romanticism, were totally anathema to the aesthetic precepts of the Comintern of 1928–34. Bucolic niceties were too reminiscent of a conservative and ethical-socialist sensibility which Communists were denouncing in their campaign against Social Democrats and reformists. Here one observes a correlation between the visual beauty evoked in the floral motifs of Walter Crane's art, often illustrating Morris's poetry, and the rhetoric of a Baldwinian demagogue. Suffice it to recall that in his sentimentalist rhetoric, Baldwin used a nostalgic idiom which evoked images of national harmony in English country landscapes with cameos of rural labourers. The resemblance between Baldwin's political speeches and the ideologically distinct but pictorially similar Crane iconography with its pastoral women, floral garlands, and peasant labourers reveals a common ground of propagandist discourse, deceptively harmonious yet ideologically disparate. Both, however, induce a lulling sentimentalism which Communists regard as the treacherous moment of irrationalism.

But by breaking away from Labourist alliances, Communist propaganda dismissed the cultural storehouse of aesthetic motifs from which British socialism took place. Communist discourse repudiated the conventional forms of beauty that formed the Romantic and ruralist fabric of British culture, replacing these with a set of sublime aesthetics whose moral overtones spurned the alluring poetics of ideological seduction. Arnot's Communist defence of Morris is consequently a problematic affirmation of national culture. For in seeking to win consent, the pamphlet's doctrinal content and vituperative mode remain intrinsically alienating and disruptive of English sensibility. Like the Proletcult art of its epoch, and like its political philosophy, Arnot's text is marked by its Leninist qualities – agitational language which can be seen as the glimmering of a sublime aesthetic style. Such a dissenting discourse refuses the integrating flourishes of a Baldwinian speech, since bucolic beauty is not only deemed sentimental but also effeminate and ineffectual, indeed wholly anathema to a Marxist-Leninist disposition.

Divorced from the political networks of Social Democracy, Arnot's polemic remains pure of ideological compromise, yet drastically hampered by a limited iconographic and rhetorical common sense through which to be socially endorsed. In aiming to dispel all sentimentalism from its rhetoric, a Communist tract such as the *Vindication* displays its removal from the national cult of rural romanticism and harmonious community integration. The political dynamic of the pamphlet is intransigent in asserting its revolutionary creed, relentless in its deconstructive style, and defiant in its conquest of sentimental style. But these signs of a Communist sublimity with its moral repudiation of the aesthetic of beauty also foreshadow the obstacles which thwart the project of winning political power. Fervently anti-nationalist in its precepts, the Communist rhetorical form (exemplified thus far as an ardent and recalcitrant attitude) forfeits the very ground upon which public persuasion and hegemonic consent can be realized.

THE OPTIMISM OF MARXIST RHETORIC

The aesthetics of resistance and agitation come to define the formalistic identity of the *Vindication*. Yet as previously noted, this polemical style does not collapse into an unmitigated modernist dispersal where an aesthetic shattering of bourgeois culture myopically becomes an end in itself.[10] Such a phenomenon is incompatible with the Marxist praxis which Arnot advocates. Nor will the nineteenth-century subject-matter – William Morris – suffer any modernist rendition short of engendering a risible and self-defeating pamphlet. The positive and earnest tenor of Communist rhetoric prohibits aesthetic playfulness. So, too, the divisive effect of a polemic that intends to smash, indeed disintegrate, the continuities of sentimentalist Morrisania must finally surrender to a reintegrating, unifying principle. The *Vindication*, in short, cannot remain a purely destructive and deconstructive tract. Instead, it is compelled, for its own political dignity, to rebuild its ideological edifice upon the ruins of its adversaries.

To the utterances of doom of the capitalists, … we do not look for our perspective. What these utterances reveal is the consciousness of the capitalist class, the consciousness of their approaching end, the guilty consciousness of a damned and doomed system, a dying class. So much the more do these utterances of despair of the capitalists only give to the proletariat the great confidence and determination. The facts of breakdown which bring despair to the capitalists bring hope to the proletariat. "That which hath made them blanch, hath made me strong; What hath quenched them, hath given me fire." (Dutt 1932a, 8)

Just as the submergence of sentimentalism is a function of subordinating the individual subjectivity to the collective structures of Communist organization, so the constraint placed on individualist anger is equally a measure of an overriding party ethos. The pamphlet reflects the movement of some self-lamenting "I" to a collective "we" that gives shape to formless agitation. For just as soulful subjectivism is anathema to the polemic, so the Marxist pamphlet cannot dissolve into the chaos of subjectivist nihilism. The *Vindication* is fuelled by its intersubjective philosophy and its transformative principles, which are wholly incompatible with the isolated and quiescent character of narcissistic grief – "the torment of a creature condemned to solitude and devoured by a longing for community" (Lukács 1978, 45).

In contrast, the pamphlet conquers its isolated subjectivity by blending it into the politics of the Communist party. The latter lends cohesion and unity to a tract which would otherwise lapse into a purely disruptive moment of protest, anger, or individualist acrimony. Governed by an optimistic impulse and by a belief in freedom through political praxis, the pamphlet remains defiant in the face of alienated society. Its confrontational jousts are spurred on by a hopeful and ceaseless resistance to world holocaust, social reification, and moral decay.

With dynamic energy, the *Vindication* forecloses both the melancholy of a sullen lament as well as the relentless negations which it might inflict upon its enemy out of vindictiveness. The text is neither a tragic lyric nor a vendetta; it is a self-assertion, a vindication whose success depends on sublating its inner disquiet into the promise of some retributive justice. Such a promise provides the psychic integration necessary for gathering the centrifugal energy of revolutionary activism into a moment's stability. However, a promise of some future Communist commonwealth, imagined as a bucolic English setting, remains beyond the immediate bleakness of 1934 and scarcely credible to a Communist anti-utopian sensibility.[11] Yet a surrogate resolution is introduced via the potent and unifying force of the human agent – the Communist activist. It is he who brings the elements of class struggle into positive form, coalescing the dialectics of society and individual into a meaningful and inspiring unity while the English utopia is postponed to some post-crisis moment. A hero such as Morris acts as a prefigurative reminder of that much-sought place of Communist desire. Through his Englishness, he suggests a national setting in which these political aspirations may be charted, while in his praxis he retains the revolutionary resistance to conservative nationalism and stasis. In the guise of William Morris, the Communist hero holds both the settled space of Englishness and the continual flux of history in the prism of an activist stature.

CHAPTER FOUR

Martyrdom and
the Communist Intellectual

Not one, not one, nor thousands must they slay,
But one and all if they would dusk the day
From "A Death Song"
(William Morris, written for the funeral of Alfred Linnell, 1887,
in Arnot 1934a, 32)

THE COMMUNIST INTELLECTUAL:
CONSCIENCE, DESIRE, AND DUTY

In his polemical anger, Arnot indirectly registers the plight of his party. Yet, however much his actions are intertwined with the larger political Communist movement, his grievances also reflect his personal challenge to single-handedly deliver an unprecedented political statement. In 1934 no other member of the Party contributed to the debate on the reformist-conservative "mythology" of Morris (Morton 1985). Arnot's fury can thus be seen as a compensation for an unsupported and unwieldy endeavour: to counter a massive backlog of preconceptions which coloured the Morris hero with strains of conservative sentimentalism and covert anti-Marxism. Voiced in shrill and solitary cries, Arnot's message reverberated in subsequent defences of Morris, particularly those of A.L. Morton, Andrew Rothstein, George Thomson, and E.P. Thompson, to mention but a few.

Compounding his unique position in 1934, Arnot was confronted with the resistance of his Communist audiences, who, in such a period of radical militancy, could not be wholly disposed to the Morris symbol. For while Morris was recognizably a figure of esteem and popularity among the senior Communists of the 1930s, and while his poetry often served as the coda to many an oration at political rallies (Arnot 1985), his aesthetic temper conflicted with the cultural ethos of revolutionary heroism, fervently forged as the iconographic idiom of propagandist inspiration of the Class-Against-Class period. Represented in his Pre-Raphaelite designs of floral and lyrical voluptuousness, Morris's Bohemian Victoriana was anathema to the masculinist rigour of, for instance, the Workers' Theatre Movement and its aesthetic criteria for proletarian art (Morton 1985). The Class-Against-Class period proved to be a moment in which any propagandist style which imbued itself with traces of middle-class leisure and contemplative serenity was regarded as betraying agitprop vanguardism, the Soviet exemplar of legitimate aesthetics. These aesthetics unequivocally delivered the proletarian virtues of scientific rationalism. Morris's cultural import could not, therefore, be hailed easily without being accommodated to the aesthetic sensibility of that sectarian Comintern phase.

With such constraining conditions, Arnot's efforts to project the image of William Morris appeared manifestly frustrating; these strictures were in part a source of tonal intensity which the *Vindication* exuded as the sigh of an affronted Communist advocating his political convictions with fidelity to the Party's honour. In part too, these historical conditions were the weights which inhibited Arnot from being able to trumpet Morris's Englishness in the aesthetic forms which typified the hero's national belonging. In a sense, the *Vindication* was both an overt eulogy of Morris's Communist identity and a defence of Marxism-Leninism, whose philosophy of active revolution was endorsed with images of heroic dissent. Through diatribe and passionate appeal, the pamphlet objectified Arnot's political convictions while also providing a forum in which his subjectivities of suppressed Englishness and disdained irrationalism could be channelled and aesthetically condensed.

As we probe the *Vindication* more deeply, increasingly from Arnot's personal perspective as a Communist intellectual, his grievances (which upon a first hearing resemble the inflammatory notes of sensationalist journalism) assume a more complex and penetrating character. Meanwhile, the subject of his polemic – the defence of William Morris as Marxist – undergoes a reversal, only to be subordinated to Arnot's master plan, to his definition of an optimum Communist praxis and its attendant practitioners. Now, Arnot emerges as the principal hero grappling with his identity as a Communist intellectual, as a committed rhetorician serving the cause of the Party and the larger vision of an alternative society.[1] Yet while devotion to that cause produces a *raison d'être* and governing principle for the activist, what this devotion entails remains an often intractable problem. For the nature of this intellectual is that of a social hybrid, a locus of tensions between a bourgeois middle-classness and a desired working-class identity.

In his aspirations to fulfil the demands of Party doctrine, the Communist intellectual is confronted with an internal rift in conscience: he is required to retain his intellectual acumen while discarding his middle-class refinement; he must incarnate the mental leadership of the Party yet avoid dissolving into an intellectual aristocrat.[2] In a series of precepts and critical comments on Communist intellectuals, published in the *Communist Review*, Palme Dutt spelled out the covenant of Marxist-Leninist activism.

Adherence to the Communist Party is an expression of intellectual conviction of the correctness of Communism and of the determination to fight for it. But much more is needed to make the Communist, to make the fully effective Party member. Particularly in the case of these comrades, there are often many misconceptions and old associations to be cleared away; and tendencies can appear, which, if uncorrected, can become dangerous. Many of these comrades have come to Communism by a process of reasoning and argument on general conceptions, from an interest in philosophical questions, etc., but have not yet had any experience of or contact with the working class movement … The majority take part with painstaking good-will in the so-called "local work"; but this often in practice only amounts to the performance of a few mechanical tasks of selling the paper, attending a local group, etc., without any real closeness to the workers and the workers' struggle; this inevitably cannot draw out and occupy their active thought and interest.   (Dutt 1932b, 423)

Judging Communist intellectuals for perfunctory performance in Party activity, Dutt identifies their contradictory social place. As nomadic converts from Oxbridge academes, moving to the arena of activist struggle, these Communists to whom Dutt preached were in some measure the disillusioned individuals of the 1920s, bourgeois literati whom T.S. Eliot had inspired in his irrationalist despair over man "isolated in the wasteland of a mechanical civilization" (Wood 1959, 101). Towards the 1930s, they turned their backs on self-indulgent solipsism and chose the road to social responsibility and active protest against capitalism. Yet as recent converts to the Communist movement, such intellectuals were deprived of political experience in mediating revolutionary theories with practice. Still, they displayed enormous zeal and commitment, relinquishing the contemplative existence of closed university circles, and discovering in Communism a ready-made instrument of action to be wielded in the denunciation of bourgeois values.

But suffice it to say that in their transition from the realms of esoteric thought to radical activism, these proto-Communists were compelled to comply with new ideological principles that were often difficult to absorb in practical terms. When they joined the Party, they faced the task of divesting themselves of bourgeois consciousness and of adopting a proletarian spirit, radically detached from their previous life-style and world-outlook. They were obliged, according to Duttian prescription, to "break their chains, to break their isolation and separate their character as 'intellectuals,' as a few have already done, and enter fully into the life and fight of the Party in the same way as every Party member" (Dutt 1932b, 424).

Dutt was a severe critic of intellectual isolationism. He berated intellectuals for their inability to adapt to the new Party setting which in reality was an island of ethical rectitude in the midst of an alienating capitalist environment. He regarded the segregation of the intellectuals from wide-ranging political involvement with the rank and file as a pernicious atomization which merely reinstated the esoteric coteries of the élite intelligentsia. It also weakened the Communist intellectual's understanding of the fight for a Marxist revolutionary doctrine "against opportunism, against imperialism, against bourgeois influence in the working class, against religion, against all those manifestations of idealism in every sphere of thinking, politics and activity" (Dutt 1932b, 427).

Dutt's warnings against professional segregation were underpinned by the crucial issue of class distinctions, distinctions which appeared to divide the Party. In urging more vigilance in the case of intellectuals where he saw "a real danger of a class factor ... [rendering] ... any sign of segregation or differentiation far more serious" (Dutt 1932b, 427), Dutt imposed the weightiest challenge on the intellectual. This protagonist had to fully grasp the principles of Communism and subsequently repudiate any traces of self-interest, demonstrating objective self-criticism.[3] Yet with all of these principles and directives, Dutt failed to address the needs of the new recruit, an individual still caught within the mesh of bourgeois common sense.

His method of indoctrination and conversion, one could argue, entailed a martyristic self-suppression, a radical and thus undialectical rupture from bourgeois consciousness. In his promotion of a dire break between bourgeois idealism (or common sense) and a Marxist philosophy of praxis, he edified the latter and refused all contact with the former, neglecting to see the value of common sense as an object of criticism which could nonetheless be deployed as a catalyst of change. As Gramsci had it: "A philosophy of praxis ... must first of all be a criticism of 'common sense,' *basing itself initially, however, on common sense* [added emphasis] in order to demonstrate that 'everyone' is a philosopher and that it is not a question of introducing from scratch a scientific form of thought into everyone's individual life, but of renovating and making 'critical' an already existing activity" (Gramsci 1971, 330–1).

But Dutt's insistence on avoiding ritual execution of Party tasks implied that those members who were intellectually equipped with knowledge should apply their political articulacy to propaganda in order to strengthen the revolutionary process. They should never, however, supplant their revolutionary activity with intellectual expertise. Embedded in these expectations was an imperious judgment which hauntingly berated the intellectual for the slightest self-absorption in philosophical speculation. Unlike Gramsci, who counsels that criticism of such class consciousness should depart from and base itself upon the human needs of individuals locked in bourgeois common sense, Dutt's transformative politics involved an extirpation of bourgeois residues from Communist activism, a priest-like imposition of dogma from a lofty moral altar. But such dogma remained insensitive to the interests and mentality of aspiring Communist intellectuals.

Communist self-realization was rigorous and morally challenging. It set a perfect political-cum-ethical balance in activism that was difficult to achieve save through aesthetic projections. Arnot's portrait of William Morris as a revolutionary fighter of middle-class origins is one such aesthetic prism of ideal political praxis. It is the expression of a Communist's fervent commitment to the rank and file, compounded with a versatile yet discrete deployment of specialized knowledge. With Morris as a guiding impulse, Arnot defines his own Communist posture, and thereby formulates the basic tenets of his political doctrine within the framework of Marxist activism.

His defence of Morris cannot be dissociated from Dutt's precepts pronounced in 1932. Indeed, a close textual reading of the pamphlet releases echoes of Dutt's Communist counsel to intellectuals. Here is the opening paragraph of the *Vindication*:

The revolutionary Socialist fighter, William Morris, artist, craftsman and poet; born in London on 24th March, 1834, of a well-to-do bourgeois family; went through the routine of his class at public school and Oxford University. He wrote poems, became a master craftsman in one kind after another, from furniture to designing to printing; became a manufacturer; took up the secretaryship of an anti-war association in the 'seventies; in 1883 joined a Socialist organization, agitated and organised; edited the *Commonweal*, to which Frederick Engels and Eleanor Marx contributed; and, worn out by a life of intense and ceaseless activity over many fields, died at the age of sixty-two, having remained to the end a revolutionary Socialist.   (Arnot 1934a, 3)

Tireless as an activist, all-rounded as a man of diverse vocations, and faithful as a Socialist to his ideals, Morris scarcely falls short of those Communist virtues vaunted by propagandists such as Dutt and his followers. In fact, Morris is portrayed as the optimum type that qualifies for the heroic role, "fighting for the overthrow of capitalism and for the victory of the working class" (Arnot 1934a, 5). The role is *ipso facto* cast as a dynamic one; for as Dutt's predilections and formulations indicate, the ideal Communist intellectual is an individual bent on revolutionary praxis, averse to bourgeois idealism, armchair radicalism, and contemplative modes of thinking.[4]

The depiction of the activist is not, however, restricted to an enumeration of the hero's activities and Communist accolades. The pamphlet's style is intense and exudes the vicarious ardour of the historian portraying the hero as a socialist fighter. The rhythm of the prose is clipped and mimetically replicates the unceasing pace of Morris's life.[5] The fast tempo effect is created in the seemingly endless spill of Morris's prodigious endeavours as a man engaged in multiple public activities. Despite his bourgeois origins, he breaks from the drawing room of leisure and lunges forth into a world of rugged strife. Despite statements to the contrary, he remains unstintingly faithful to his revolutionary ideals.

The importance of this opening paragraph is its stress, both in stylistic form and in content, on the hero's activist profile. Nor is it an incidental emphasis. The cutting edge of the *Vindication* lies in its trenchant contestation of the conservative image of Morris: the genteel, contemplative artist of utopian zeal and English humanity. In lieu of this ruling-class version, Arnot foregrounds a nineteenth-century shadow of a would-be twentieth-century Communist intellectual who adheres faithfully to the theoretical precepts of the Party. Thus Morris becomes Arnot's rudder, governing a practical application of class consciousness and facilitating a unity of theory and practice. Whether in fact Arnot concretized such theoretical dogma within everyday life cannot be fully determined; what is certain, however, is that Arnot was able to apply an aesthetic version of Duttian prescriptions through the evocation of Morris's activist stature. By deriding the contemplative version of Morris, Arnot implicitly asserted his predilections for a practical politics and for a rejection of over-professionalism within the intellectual sphere of the Communist community. In the light of Communist orthodoxies, it may now be grasped why the bourgeois idealism so prevalent in the conservative Morris legacies jarred with any revolutionary appropriation of the hero.

As an aesthetic exemplar of the Communist intelligentsia, Morris can only be cast as a praxis-oriented figure; he cannot be partisan to a leisurely engagement with bourgeois idealism, nor can he for that matter be a working-class character, devoid of the intellectual's dilemmas. His value to Communist propagandists must correspond to an aesthetic solution for these self-critical intellectuals, on the one hand shackled to a bourgeois class consciousness, on the other aspiring to achieve a proletarian epistemology that was emancipatory and inspirational. But since the political-cum-ethical project of Communist ideals remained non-viable short of favourable societal conditions, the hero is necessarily an aesthetic representation of a utopia. His aesthetically embodied scientific rationalism is brought to an idealist pitch removed from the reality of everyday social practices. In this respect, Morris's identity ultimately flips from its association with materialist activism into an idealist martyrdom, a reversal that marks the first signs of bourgeois idealism peering through an ardent but nevertheless sectarian Communist practice.

REVOLUTIONARY PRAXIS: ACTIVISM OR IDEALISM?

At a *prima facie* level, the traits with which Arnot endows his hero are diverse. But in reality, they are held together by a dialectical interaction of Morris's moral and physical facets. In short, Arnot's depiction of the hero's political involvement is pinned to a vision of continuity and to a unity of manifold activities. Any alternative impression of disjointedness or dilettantism is dispelled by the sustained rhythm of the opening text. Note how continuity is palpably expressed in the extended last line of the paragraph, where Arnot brings the pulsating effects of his hero's life to its culminating breath: "and, worn out by a life of intense and ceaseless activity over many fields, died at the age of sixty-two, having remained to the end a revolutionary Socialist" (Arnot 1934a, 3).

The concept of physical stamina is highlighted here in the rhythm and the tempo of the text, as in the sheer description of physical exertion. "Ceaseless activity" is transformed into a moral, ethical, and ideological stamina, eclectic public activity into unified versatility. Morris's tireless-ness is literal, but its final impact bears significantly on his fidelity to a cause and to its implicit philosophy of revolutionary socialism.

The fundamental ambiguity in the hero's physical and moral facets is crucial to the alternating material and idealist imagery with which Arnot characterizes the dualism of contemplative and praxis-oriented epistemologies. Such an opposition is implicit in Arnot's continual repudiation of bourgeois idealism and conversely in his consistent adu-lation of revolutionary militancy. The narrative of Morris's life-history is expressed in the pamphlet precisely as a battle of the individual against the corrupt politics that underlie the bourgeois individualism of the Victorian era. With a crescendo of sublime imagery, Arnot dramatizes Morris's scornful sentiments towards the nineteenth-century capitalist world. An accruing passion marks the incipient transformation in the hero's persona as he subsequently enters the political terrain of revolu-tionary activity.

Under these circumstances it is not surprising that a gifted young artist, with powers yet unexplored, should from the very beginning show a fierce hatred of capitalism. At first the expression of this attitude takes various forms: it takes the form of delight in other periods of history. It is shown in his attempt to change completely the whole expression of capitalist civilisation in its arts, in his hatred of conventions of bourgeois society, its customs, its costumes, its furniture, its decorations and patterns, its cant and hypocrisy. Not until twenty years have passed does this hatred of capitalism begin to take on a political form. But this hatred endures all the time, increases, deepens and grows to be a fiery inextinguishable fury against capitalism, an unquenchable hatred, "a lightning flame, a shearing sword, a storm to overthrow." (Arnot 1934a, 9)

The final lines of this passage bring the descriptive details of Morris's self-consciousness to an effusive pitch; they serve to intensify the emo-tion which Arnot invests in his prose, a fury towards the iniquities of the 1930s which parallels Morris's hatred of Victorian capitalism. In his discursive flights and flourishes, Arnot draws upon Morris's own idiom in order to indict both nineteenth- and twentieth-century stages of capitalism; his identification with Morris is profoundly linked to the discontent which he shares with Morris not only towards the political system but also towards its degenerative impact on humanity. Yet in condemning capitalism and its attendant idealism, Arnot carefully selects a robust, masculinist imagery that is consonant with the aesthetic precepts of the Class-Against-Class period. His stylistic enhancements are necessarily those of volatile storm and of a virility that is aggressive and elemental in mood. The severe discursive forms are used to conquer any semblance of supine gentility conventionally lingering in the plea-surable floridity of British maudlin literature, so deeply engrained in aspects of Morris's writings. Consequently, while literary ornament is not utterly discarded, the stylistic material of the *Vindication* is replete with an anti-sentimentalist passion, but one that remains strenuous and aesthetically consonant with the practical vigour of the activist hero.

The portrayal of Morris's epic mission to redeem his age from moral disorder ultimately converges with Arnot's heroic duties as a Communist intellectual. Thus Arnot's attempt to quash the resurging aesthetic and contemplative propensities within himself may be witnessed obliquely through his projection of an inner conflict present in Morris's torn relation to artistic pursuits and ethical goals: "the gifted artist, poet and craftsman, hater of capitalism, casts by his hesitation and sets out himself to slay the ravening monsters, leaving behind him forever 'the idle singer of an empty day'" (Arnot 1934a, 13).

Hatred for the cultural decadence of Victoriana, which Morris hith-erto spluttered forth in renowned tempestuous fits,[6] is finally channelled into defiant bellicosity. Morris's slaying of ravening monsters (a phrase deriving from his *Earthly Paradise*) symbolizes the ideological battle which his activism enables him to consummate; for while his attack on the monster of capitalism constitutes the assault on the external social environment, Morris's mission is equally one of destroying that part of himself which was embroiled in the external malaise. Being part of his capitalist society, any transformation of its condition necessarily incurs a conversion within himself, an evolution from his status as idle singer to the fiery posture of a revolutionary socialist fighter.

Through material interaction with society, Morris acquires a higher consciousness which had previously been frustrated by his social detach-ment as a cloistered poet-artist. His "ascent into politics" (Arnot 1934a, 13) – a phrase which significantly reveals the propagandist's preference for politics over aesthetics – occurs through a crucial phase of transition which biographers have repeatedly located in the poet's Icelandic voy-ages and in his subsequent involvement in the *Eastern Question*. In the stark, barren landscape of Iceland, Morris sought inspiration and hope for nerving himself "for the epic struggle of the classes in Britain" (Arnot 1934a, 14) – a far cry from Baldwin's Icelandic pony! There he identified with the harsh qualities of the Icelandic setting and discovered a cathartic relief in the simplicity and strains of a courage germane to the Spartan milieu. His absorption with this world of rude but metallic strength served as a tonic for his distress and discontent with the overwhelming ambience of social ills in Victorian Britain, ills that manifested themselves most prominently in the "anaemic" art of a bourgeois middle class and which symbolized the epitome of frivolous waste and moral vacuousness. In his fascination with, and pursuit of, this Nordic space (with communities still unaffected by class strife yet caught in a perennial battle with the austerities of nature) Morris began translating the *Volsung Saga*, "the epic story that was to the other sagas what Homer had been to the classic literature of Greece" (Arnot 1934a, 14). Emphasizing Morris's enthralment with the epic mode, Arnot writes: "The towering courage and spirit of the epic is unmistakable, and tells something of what its writer was becoming" (Arnot 1934a, 14). Morris's greatest epic poems, *Sigurd the Volsung* and *The Fall of the Niblungs*, reveal a sense of renewed and immense energy, a strength yielding the possibility of action and political salvation. The epic attraction of Nordic sagas galvanizes Morris to come like Agamemnon's son "to assert the transcendence of a moral vigour and rescue the age from moral collapse" (Dale 1977, 35). Thus, in his return to Britain, Morris involves himself in the *Eastern Question*, where his participation in the anti-war association and "Anti-Scrape" (Morris's term for the Society for the Preservation of Ancient Buildings) constituted his first forays into political activism. His shift from expressing dark poetic moods in *The Earthly Paradise* to his anti-war manifesto addressed to the working men of England, urging them to fight British imperialism in the Middle East, a shift from aesthetic lyricism to vigorous invective, demonstrates how his early recalcitrance was transformed into activist protest. (Cf. appendix.) Here, according to Arnot, Morris's bourgeois idealism begins to shed its skin. The process was already initiated by his journeys to Iceland, where spatial qualities presented the inspiring motifs through which Morris's self-contemplation and accruing politicization transpired. Iceland metaphorically represented the ideological sacrifice of bourgeois individualism, a sacrifice over which Dutt's precepts for Communist intellectuals hover with ghostly authority. Perhaps Arnot's own dilemmas and self-conscious efforts to espouse his Communist persuasion with utmost rectitude[7] filter through his depictions of Morris's Icelandic experience.

For the notion that the bourgeois individual must relinquish all activity contaminated by the corrupting conditions of capitalist society is a belief that permeates Morris's critique of Victorian aesthetic taste with its denunciation of the socio-political iniquities of capitalist profit. "All that art had meant in the life of mankind had become narrowed down to fine arts for fine ladies and gentlemen. Morris detested the flat ugliness of the ordinary consumption of products of capitalism. So he reached the two-fold conclusion: first that art must perish unless it be a people's art; secondly that the worker must be an artist and the artist must be a worker" (Arnot 1934a, 11). "Shoddy art" was the consequence of the exploitation of workers under capitalist economic conditions. These determined the chaotic and moribund state of aesthetic activity, an art that was destined to perish if it was not radically transformed.

Morris saw his excursions to Iceland as essential for comprehending the links between art and the state of the economy. Images of ascetic rigour and moral strength were embedded in the northern landscapes and they often evoked the vision of a sparse sensuality that he could pit against the excesses of Victorian society. Nor was the opposition between the Nordic culture and Morris's contemporary England an incidental contrast: the stark physical environment of the north became the aesthetic correlative of a process of purging Victorian capitalism of its depravities. Morris suggested that there be a wholesale eradication of bourgeois individualism based on the efflorescence of a new art germane to a revitalized classless society. Such societal sacrifice and regeneration became Morris's projection of cataclysmic revolution. On a personal scale this assumed the form of renunciation of self-interest and class privilege.

Morris's militant address to the working men of England and his final channelling of discontent into public action grants Arnot's self-defining activism an exemplary direction. Not only can he identify with Morris's propagandist enterprise as an agitator of the masses, he can also emulate his hero, the middle-class figure who continually sought to divest himself of bourgeois tendencies and veered from his Liberal penchant to revolutionary socialism. In this transition, Morris revolutionized himself and challenged the status of the middle class. In a letter to his friend C.E. Maurice (1 July 1883), who believed that "change depended on individuals of good will belonging to all classes" (Arnot 1934a, 18), Morris flatly averred: "The upper and middle classes as a body will by the very nature of their existence resist the abolition of classes ... I have never underrated the power of the middle classes, whom, in spite of their individual good

nature and banality, I look upon as a most terrible and implacable force"
(Arnot 1934a, 18).

Clearly Morris's words reveal his discontent with his own class, but
implicitly also his adamant will to reinforce the antagonism of classes
as a necessary means of destroying the very system which engendered
societal iniquities (cf. Arnot 1934a, 18).

In so far as he is torn between his bourgeois past and his devotion
to a future Communist cause, the tension and self-denial that the
activist must endure precipitates an "ideological martyrdom." Admittedly, such a martyrdom does not entail physical persecution or death
at the altar of an enemy class. Still, the activist suffers from a perturbed
conscience, and his compulsion to drive his energies ever forward to a
given cause is undeniably an act of selflessness. But while the activist's
submission subordinates his particularity to a larger universal structure
(a political movement or doctrine), his self-abnegation is scarcely a
unilateral act. For such withholding of immediate interests is contingent
on an ulterior return. Even here, altruism pivots on a reciprocal
exchange in which the ascetic figure is blessed with moral grace for his
magnanimity of spirit. Thus at his most self-sacrificing, the Communist
intellectual recuperates his reward, namely a gratification in the glory
that "justifies" his total submission to the Party. In Arnot's case, a
desired activist role is aesthetically seized through his projected image
of Morris. His vindication of Morris's virtues enables him to present
an icon that others will emulate and which is no doubt Arnot's self-
portrait in the making. Thus, in a tradition of hero-worship, he extols
Morris as Ralph Fox hails Henri Barbusse and other admirers wax lyrical
over Lenin's memory (cf. Fox 1935, 3–6; "Editorial Review," *Communist
Review* 1926, 343–418). The prevailing element in each of these dual sets
is the relationship between the propagandist-activist and his heuristic
model. The latter is undoubtedly the object of discussion and the focus
of rhetorical attention; but the former, the eulogizing agent, is the
subject fantasizing over his own desires to embody the very hero of his
panegyric.

Increasingly the materialist activist becomes a martyr shot through
with idealism. Implicitly as well, his morality is given primacy over his
sensuous needs. Indeed, the extent to which Morris is conceived as an
ideological devotee to the cause is an index of the moral superiority
which Arnot ascribes to the role of activism. Relentless practical engage-
ments are not construed as mindless but as self-conscious submissions
to higher values which grace the activist-martyr with an ennobling depth

of spirit. An idealist morality is intrinsic to this justification of human suffering and endurance, not only for the Communist propagandist himself (e.g. Arnot) but also for the Communist recruit before whom the activist hero is exhibited.

In so far as Morris acts as a guiding principle for Arnot's own Communist identity, he also lends an instrument which facilitates Arnot's propagandist role. It is therefore hardly incidental that the rhetorical value of historic martyrs and heroes (such as Morris) plays a significant part in Communist propaganda of the Third Period of the Comintern: "Notions of 'revolutionary genius,' personified first by Lenin and Trotsky, were common currency in the early days of the Third International. The succession of heroes and martyrs thrown up by the first decade of its existence; then the rise of the Chinese Red Army, with its galaxy of 'proletarian commanders' and 'proletarian statesmen'; and finally the magnificent figure of Dimitrov all served to renew notions of heroic leadership" (Samuel 1986a, 107).

As an ideological and moral educator, the Communist Arnot cultivates both the political acumen of his following and their ethical standards of conduct. In this respect, the rhetorical image of revolutionary heroism becomes his major heuristic device. For while Morris's profile holds up a mirror to Arnot's own sense of identity, it is also a reflection that has acquired a rhetorical instrumentality. Initially, Morris's heroic stature had use-value, enabling Arnot to objectify himself through emulation. Now Morris acquires the status of a rhetorical object of exchange between Arnot and his audience. Morris (the man) is eclipsed from discussion while his posthumous social value as an ideological martyr surfaces for the purposes of propagandist intervention.

THE MARTYR HERO TRANSFORMED:
FROM EMPIRICAL FACT TO JUDGMENT

Presented as a legacy that has been marred and savaged by mythmongers, Morris's posthumous identity is not that of a real man, but of a rivalry over his symbolic value. Implicit in Arnot's strokes of invective is the exposition of an ideological lesson, a fable encapsulating Lenin's words of wisdom on revolutionaries and their social fate. Thus, in tandem with his own aesthetic reconciling of Communist intellectual dilemmas, Arnot produces the rhetorical material with which to enhance his hero, less as a person than as a value judgment. Morris becomes the incarnation of disinterestedness, firstly in so far as he is treated as a legacy, and thus as a coalescence of social relationships, and secondly, in so far as the activist posture which he assumes entails the subordination of all his private enterprises to a single end, beyond his own personal needs. Both types of disinterestedness frame him as a paradigm of totality, moral virtue, and societal purposiveness.

Although disinterestedness is already present in Morris's selfless activist years, such a trait is further accentuated after his demise. Here he is transformed into a legend. And by becoming an object of ideological interest, he is dehumanized, now into an object of political controversy, now into one of consensus. He is no longer treated *in himself,* rather the living content of his personal history becomes the servant of some ulterior will, of societal powers seeking to deploy him as an aid to facilitate the swaying of public opinion.

The rhetorical crystallization of Morris's identity has a specific social purpose, namely to assemble the details of his endeavours, including his personal vagaries and strengths, into a structure of validity that signals neither physical nor sensuous beauty but rather moral perfection. Whereas Baldwin elevated his hero to the sphere of a judgment of the beautiful, to a category of disinterestedness predicated on a visible and pleasurable commonsense beauty, Arnot produces a sublime judgment out of his protagonist, one where the social concept of universal validity is rendered in moral rather than sensible terms. Just as Baldwin deployed Morris's legacy for the enhancement of a conservative ideology, and in so doing derived immediate, non-rational acceptance for his claims, so Arnot eagerly strives for immediate recognition for his political appeals to Marxism by enriching the concept of activism with Morris's various humanist gestures to the cause.

The multiple features of the martyr-hero provide the adequate structure of purposiveness to legitimize Arnot's pronouncements. But this adequate structure, this emblem of goodness and societal totality, is culturally determined and historically specific. If the martyr-hero is to conform to such an ideal, his characteristic features will only do so if he complies with a cultural concept of social harmony and ethical integrity. As an idealist structure of goodness, the exemplary portrait of Morris must fulfil several criteria. Firstly, it must display his constancy to a political cause; secondly, it must be in social harmony with the community; thirdly, it must become the symbolic incarnation of the community's optimum ethical values; fourthly, it must demonstrate a dialectical epistemology which is wrought out of a totalizing vision, sustainable even beyond the abyss of death.

In the Communist tradition of the later 1920s, affiliation to the Party's goals entailed nothing less than absolute persistence. It was claimed that

Those who join to-day join in full consciousness of the necessity of unflinching struggle against Labour's enemies.

A Bolshevik is not one who joins the Party when the revolutionary wave is at its height. A Bolshevik is he who takes part in the work of building a C.P. in the course of years, and if need be of decades, in years of slow development of revolution. ("Osip" 1926, 190)

In order to mark Morris's unflinching activist spirit, Arnot declares, in the vein of the inherited orthodoxies of Bolshevism, that Morris "died at sixty-two having remained to the end a revolutionary Socialist" (Arnot 1934a, 3). This constancy of revolutionary activism assumes the rhetorical function of ensuring a movement's viability and of validating its ideological presuppositions. Fidelity becomes the ethical incarnation of a driving impulse which motivates and sustains the political struggle. So, in his quasi-religious commitments, Morris reveals an endurance whose intensity constitutes the necessary individual power required to overthrow the capitalist state. Not that this one hero will suffice; rather the effort which he displays is the symbolic quota of energy that every other activist will need to expend in order to consummate a potential revolution.

The Communist prototype marshals a devotion to the cause such that all of his acts and his every facet are permeated with his political mission. In applying Agnes Heller's remarks on the bourgeois citizen to the revolutionary, one might say that the latter constitutes the "whole housekeeping of feeling [in which every] feeling receives light from the Cause, every emotion refers to the Cause" (Heller 1979, 221). Comparably, Morris is said to have "swotted at Marx" and eventually his reading of *Capital* began to "shine through [his] writings, letters and speeches" (Arnot 1934a, 18). In physical and moral stamina Morris displayed a commitment to a sole purpose, and the ailments which he suffered are deemed the testimonies of his relentless political efforts: "At the age of fifty-seven [he] set himself to build a new Socialist organisation ... but he was rapidly becoming an old man ... Hardly had the new society begun when he was prostrated by his worst attack of gout, with disabling kidney disease added thereto. He continued to speak and give lectures, but his most active period was over" (Arnot 1934a, 21).

Concentrated energy and commitment to the cause are also part of the sheer process of achieving the aims of the struggle and of overcoming the necessities of rigorous circumstance. The latter foster an ethos of mental strength and unswerving fortitude. The imperative to create a strong party affects the moral sensibilities of the activist who assimilates this concept of endurance into his very ascetic mentality. His fervour is an intensive emotion which musters all secondary feelings towards the final objective. Any feeling that detracts from the enthusiasm of the activist is regarded as a sign of weakness. Once again Agnes Heller's concept of the bourgeois citizen analogously expresses the point: "All feelings belong to the Cause, there is no 'waste' involved ... all wavering of feeling is particularist which stems from 'private' roots" (Heller 1979, 221).[8] Such an all-consuming subservience to the revolutionary will may be witnessed here in Morris's political literature, an area of aesthetic creativity which is legitimated by its conscious subordination to the proletarian movement.

In all Morris's writing during his great revolutionary period of the 'eighties, the poet has become the revolutionary artist, whose special skill, energies and insight are devoted to the class struggle. *The Dream of John Ball* is revolutionary. *A King's Lesson* – that marvellous picture of the life of the lord and the serf – is a revolutionary lesson. The poems he wrote were short revolutionary chants for Socialists, or, as in his larger, unfinished poem, *The Pilgrims of Hope*, devoted to the life of a proletarian and the struggles of the workers, culminating in the Paris Commune. His poetry, his whole high power of expression in prose and verse, had been turned by Morris into a revolutionary weapon.   (Arnot 1934a, 30)

Unwavering and undaunted resolution is displayed in the disinterestedness of this faithful hero. These traits of continuity form the willpower that coincides with the overall set of dynamics operating in accord with the direction of the political movement. As he struggles and dies for the community, the virtue of the martyr is largely due to his purposive action. His efforts are aligned with the will of others and harmonize with their desires for political and social liberty. His goodness is judged conditionally upon the self-fulfilment which he enables others to experience. For as he devotes all of his energies to a universal ideal, he denies his private interests in the name of their absolute commonweal and postures as a symbol of hope for a feasible revolutionary outcome. His unremitting toil turns into Arnot's rhetorical device for promoting an optimism of spirit; his enterprises represent the precedents of human possibility by which Arnot can galvanize others to act in similar cooperative fashion. Indeed, Morris's life-history and its revolutionary pulse become the repository from which Arnot's source of rhetorical truth is wrought. It is also the point from which followers resume their struggles with refuelled strength as they pursue their own contributions towards that revolutionary end. Such a hero's exemplary status is the oasis of rest and regeneration for the contemplative admirers of his activism; and as the source of replenishment, he disseminates his identity like holy bread or a sacrificial lamb who bequeaths life to others as Lenin bequeathed his memory to the Russian people. "Through his coolness, the unstudied carriage, the pleasant voice which went on, reasoning, convincing, was shining an intense fire and implacable will. And it was not the fire, the will of an individual; it seemed as though the aspirations and determination of a class were in Lenin. It was as though he had been made the vehicle for the driving will of the awakened workers. Through him spoke the Revolution" ("Editorial Review," *Communist Review* 1926, 395).

Like Lenin, the Morris figure embodies the mass man through whom the collective desires of a community can be both perceived and conceived. By displaying the staying power of his revolutionary will, the activist hero provides not only inspiration but an extended vision which draws parameters far beyond the immediate flux and nebulousness of everyday life. The benefits reaped from his unflinching belief in a future commonweal are those elements of cognitive possibility lent towards a community's sense of optimistic redressal. The clarity and coherence which his faith proffers are the necessary components for enabling social movements to rationalize the farther reaches of future history. For intrinsic to his martyr role is both the embrace of the processes of life struggle and the overcoming of long-term historical adversity.

In his tribute to Rosa Luxemburg (the Polish Communist martyr who suffered an abysmal fate amid "Social Opportunists" of the Second International), Georg Lukács elaborated on the nature of Communist epistemology, its clairvoyance and historical breadth.

It is this clear-sighted certitude that guides Rosa Luxemburg in the campaign she waged for the emancipation of the proletariat ... Her death at the hands of her bitterest enemies, Noske and Scheidemann, is logically the crowning pinnacle of her thought and life. Theoretically she had predicted the defeat of the January rising years before it took place; tactically she foresaw it at the moment of action. Yet she remained consistently on the side of the masses and shared their fate. That is to say, the unity of theory and practice was preserved in her actions with exactly the same consistency and with exactly the same logic as that which earned her the enmity of her murderers: the opportunists of Social Democracy.   (Lukács 1971, 44)

In this panegyric to the martyr, death surfaces with vestigial romanticism as the quintessential criterion for unifying a revolutionary theory and praxis. And in punctuating the end of a human life in absolute, irrevocable terms, the fatal blow crowns Luxemburg with honour for the genuine constancy of her devotion. Death and only death can determine the ultimate measure of fidelity to the cause.

Such unshakeable faith is seen by the Communist as an ideological stamina that subsists on a totalizing vision which remains undaunted by episodic crises. In this respect, Lukács's assessment of Luxemburg stresses the close affinity between an uncompromising commitment to a political goal and the dialectical continuity of a proletarian epistemology. Raphael Samuel has pointed out that Communists, as they saw it, "were the only people with a 'strategy.' They brought, in Lenin's terms, 'sober calculation' to their tasks, combining 'tremendous passion' with 'great coolness.' They linked economic issues to political questions, they elevated the struggle for immediate demands into stepping stones on the road to power. Above all Communists had a sense of 'perspective' – an ability to take the long-term view" (Samuel 1986a, 105).

Being a function of the rational lucidity of model Communists, this long-term view is aesthetically evoked in the martyr's silhouette. For even in the face of death or precarious fate, the sacrifices which he suffers are construed as minor wounds endured for the more far-reaching end of the political cause. Even when suffering suggests failure and separation, the heroic scope of martyrdom projects meaning and coherence onto the disturbances of episodic defeats.[9]

With the aura which the martyr acquires for his acceptance of the role of collective spokesperson, the material sacrifices of his revolutionary deeds are materially annulled; yet they are distilled into a moral and privileged stature of an exclusive and superior hero. The incomparability of this figure induces an engaging mimetic process. With his mystique and romantic posture, his exemplary form is enhanced, seemingly as a gratuitous ornament, yet, in truth, as a useful enthralment. For precisely in that extra-human halo reside the impulses and incentives for emulation. Muted envy impels his worshippers, admirers, or awe-inspired onlookers to apply the formula of heated activism and self-sacrifice and to struggle ardently for individual and collective glory. For it cannot be denied that the mobilization of social forces at large is contingent on the sensitive stimulation of human subjectivities. In this respect, the hero is wielded as a psychological instrument that taps the moral prestige, the civil honour, and the desire for social approval present in each individual. He guarantees not only the possibility of realizing the cause but also the individual gratification – however imaginary – of personal celebrity fantasized by others. (Cf. the commemoration of the martyred Communards and their exemplary stature in Sara 1926; Luxemburg 1915, 17; and Marx and Engels 1958, 536.)

In this sense, he grants a promise and injects a sense of viability into the social movements beset by despair and political defeat. In the words of the Bulgarian martyr Dimitrov: "It was necessary to offer the example of a living man standing up to fascism. It was necessary to restore courage to the people, to help to reassemble the forces of the proletariat in the midst of the struggle, and to instil ferments of hesitation and bewilderment among the mass of National-Socialists" (Dimitrov 1935, 343).

The shift that Morris's cultural profile entails, from its innocent status as object of cognition to its role as rhetorical trope, represents a movement from empirical fact to value. This metamorphosis suggests that the simple identity of the hero (in its various appropriations) eventually assumes an exchange-value. Whether he is portrayed as a Victorian artist-poet or as an ideological martyr, Morris's multiple attributes yield the more significant structure of endorsement – the aesthetic judgment – indeed the very device which both Baldwin and Arnot deployed in their production of consent. While in the Conservative discourse it was an aesthetic judgment of beauty that ensured consensual approval, in the Communist polemic it was the sublime that predicated a painful sequence of mediated apprehensions. But as such the sublime aesthetic, with all of its attendant discomforts, proffered returns. As the signature of an oppositional political mentality, it symbolized the long-term vision of Marxist epistemology, the moral gleam of selflessness that enhanced the ideology of the dissenting community, and the prism of aesthetic totality which granted legitimacy to the painstaking sacrifices that stood as the ethical laws of Communist activism of the 1930s.

CHAPTER FIVE

The Irrationality of Rationalist Discourse: A Phenomenology of Communist Propaganda

"We ought to be dreaming!" I wrote these words and became alarmed. It seemed to be that I was sitting at a "unity congress" and that opposite me were the editors and contributors of *Rabocheye Dyelo*. Comrade Martynov rises and, turning to me, says threateningly: "Permit me to enquire, has an autonomous editorial board the right to dream without first obtaining permission of the Party Committee?" He is followed by Comrade Krichevsky who (philosophically deepening Comrade Martynov who had long ago deepened Comrade Plekhanov) continues in the same strain even more threateningly: "I go further. I ask, has a Marxist any right at all to dream, knowing that according to Marx man always sets himself achievable tasks, which grow together with the Party?"

The very thought of these menacing questions sends a cold shiver down my back and makes me wish for nothing but a place to conceal myself in. I shall try to conceal myself behind the back of Pisarev.   (Lenin 1936, 180–1)

PART I

"Where Angels Dared to Tread and Marxists Feared to Go"

As we have seen in the foregoing discussion of Arnot's *Vindication*, revolutionary propagandists of the Second and Third Internationals helped to spawn a widespread belief that revolutionary rhetoric was ethically superior and untainted by the spurious character and mystifying forms of bourgeois ideology. This lent the rather facile presumption that mythical propensities are almost exclusively the property of bourgeois ideologues and that these deploy certain manipulative mechanisms of persuasion which are wholly absent among revolutionary propagandists, educated as they are in a rationalist, dialectical method of thought.

This position was of course not utterly pervasive, but neither was it wholly uncharacteristic. Its *residual* effect can be witnessed generations later in the writings of the literary critic and semiologist Roland Barthes. In his early phase of left-wing radicalism, Barthes theorized the concept of myth and defined it as a correlative of bourgeois ideology, as an all-consuming force in capitalist consciousness. Right-wing myth, he claimed, steals the object of its discourse in surreptitous fashion, dissimulates its semantic robbery, and naturalizes ideological, or desired, meaning by conferring the appearance of objective fact to subjective, partial claims. By contrast, revolutionary speech of the oppressed can only be poor, monotonous, immediate, unable to "proliferate ... it lacks a major faculty, that of fabulizing" (Barthes 1973, 147–8).

These assumptions are clearly Manichean and unsustainable. The discourse of revolutionary ideologues has not dispensed with, nor has it lacked, mythical structures of communication. Indeed, whatever the ethical rectitude, scepticism, and scientificity that one may ascribe to revolutionary doctrines, space must be granted for mythical possibilities which are not strictly identical with the fictional artifices of duplicitous rhetoric; on the contrary, certain manifestations of myth are the products of a social communication that expresses strenuous yearnings for social justice. Such aesthetic communication is, no doubt, invested with subjectivities and thus does not abide by any scientific precision. In its passion-wrought fabric, myth soars into heights of hyperbole and prophecy that are readily deemed distortions of truth. But this departure from pedantic naturalism could equally be seen as an aspect of political discourse which secures the hinge between theory and practice, between desire and actuality. Seen in this light, myth is the subjective imposition of coherence on a fragmented objective reality, an affective willing of history in which the finality of one's actions appears visible in advance and the unpredictability of contingencies brought under control.

As a "scientific" tract, the *Vindication* contests the irrationalist qualities of the conservative legacies of William Morris, seeking in the same thrust to purge itself of these ideological "contaminants." But it is debatable whether the scientific rationalist ethos of the tract can succeed in totally distilling itself of these alleged impurities. For example, has the martyr model fostered any greater possibility of overcoming limited bourgeois consciousness? Admittedly, he is intended to suggest some magnificent command of ethics and knowledge, achievable only through self-sacrificial praxis. But just as that martyr must surrender his own life existence to an ulterior cause, so the followers of that hero must (if they are to subscribe to the exemplary structure of individual commitment to collective ends) surrender a part of their own individual cognitive rationality to the possibility of a future Communist commonweal. If the martyr is the heuristic motif for grasping the dialectical relation between individual and common social cause (i.e. the sacrifice of self in favour of a higher social good), then the epistemological lesson that ought to have been drawn from this heroic principle is that of a dialectical relation where individual rationality is forfeited, or renounced to faith, yielding to an allegedly higher reason. Scientific rationalism represses this non-rationality yet remains ever-haunted by it.

In their concerted efforts to indict the idealist currents of capitalist society, Marxists were strict in their theoretical adherence to scientific rationality while seriously suspecting the realm of subjectivity: the mythical, the utopian, the religious, the aesthetic. But in pressing their fidelity to "dialectics" so absolutely, they at times trod upon their own toes, fostering a most undialectical antinomy between reason and affect.[1] While it would have been salutary for them to confront this radical split fully, it is also worthwhile remembering that in many instances history militated against their doing so.[2] In short, there are substantial reasons why a certain dogmatism crept into Marxist thought to keep apart the best of rationality from the worst of irrationalism and thus to render reason and affect not congenial cousins but feuding adversaries. Briefly, because Marxists waged a struggle against the curse of idealism – an idealism linked to the political and economic forces of reaction – they always sought to face the multifarious contradictions of reality as they were, refusing to submit to any deluding screens of idealist consciousness that might hamper the quest for fundamental social change. And in this mission they underscored the necessity of scientific doubt and clarity of perception in opposition to the wiles of a conservative rhetoric, which through blandishment and obfuscation helped to cement the reification of social consciousness in market society. (Cf. Marx 1843–4.)

Marxist thought interpreted the world as a dynamic, changing matrix, in which historical conditions were ever elbowing the perceptions of truth from their pedestal of security. And in taking praxis as its scientific measure, such a philosophy opposed any ideological institution that perpetuated visions of stasis and permanence, indeed any symptom or cause of false consciousness. *Process, dialectics,* and *history* were its buttresses while *identity, being,* and *eternity* were associated with the sublimations of an inverted human awareness, with a mentality disorientated by the spell of religion, utopia, ideology, nationalism, myth, etc. These forms of idealism imprint themselves in culture by eclipsing history, naturalizing its contradictions and subsuming them under a harmonious canopy of oneness and permanence. And because such forms of consciousness confer prior significance on ideas and spirituality, they could only be suspected by a materialist doctrine that upheld the fundamentally changing character of historical conditions as preeminent. Idealism was thus seen as the delusion that inhibited any radical political critique of capitalist society.

In large measure, Marxism was an "irreligious criticism" of alienation, that stifling opium of the people; it drove its "negative hermeneutic" (Jameson) into the stable comforts of the *status quo*, spearing it with the indictments of rebellious discontent. Indeed, one might say that the main aim of the Marxist doctrine was to eradicate all forms of idealism so that human consciousness might attain the moment in which the individual subject was somehow both cognitively and experientially at one with reality, and where all barriers of phenomenological or ideological deception could disappear.

But in this enthusiastic and laudable pursuit of the ultimate, there is a dash of fantasy; for this immanent identity between thought and practice is surely an ontological impossibility if not an unthinkable end of history. The very essence of our temporal, subject-object condition forbids an immediate and utter self-consciousness. Moreover, if, according to Marxian dialectics, grasping reality can only occur through mediation, then every mediation is itself an instance of partial, distorted vision, a *hic diabolic* which prevents us from squaring the circle; every moment of indirectness is a turn around a bend that precludes simultaneous, omniscient consciousness. Understanding the dialectics of social being and nature can thus only proceed with the aid of artifices of thought and action, ideal structures of totality which simulate a desired coincidence of theory and practice. This implies that one may not wish to endorse idealism, yet one must allow for the ideal moment that is indispensable to human self-consciousness.

Despite their intolerance of utopianism and mythical fabulation – elements apt to spawn a pernicious idealism – Communist ideologues could not avoid deploying symbolic structures of culture which Marxist theory might otherwise have repudiated as perilous fiction. In rhetorical or in merely discursive renderings, even the most impeccable Marxist philosophy resorted to the use of mythical representation. This did not mean that it would vitiate into yet another supine idealism but it did indicate an irrepressible desire in social being for *immediate* totality. Their mythical representation was of course no true realization of the urge for immanent subject-object unison, yet it was a reconciliation if not an artificial suture of that split fate in human existence; it was an aesthetic labour that constructed a simulacrum of an accomplished totality, an artefact in which the pulls of freedom and necessity appeared utterly resolved in a harmonious interplay of forces.

No doubt, as an identical subject-object which occludes historical contradictions and which posits a space of perfect self-consciousness, myth with its chimeric qualities seems to jar with the anti-idealist persuasion of revolutionary rhetoric. In reality, however, there is only an apparent discrepancy between dialectics and myth, between the materialist science of the one and the idealist artifices of the other. In fact, certain mythical structures of consciousness and of communication are inexorable realities, ever-present even within the rationalist spheres of political praxis. In this regard one must underscore the salutary, ideal moment in thought and activity and distinguish it from idealism *per se* – the condition in which the "ideal" wreaks havoc in its overwhelming predominance and uncontrollable force.

That Marxists evaded the problem of mythical culture, deriding it as "rotten magic," a phrase attributed to Lukács's attack on irrationalism (Rabinbach 1977, 15), could be understood as a precautionary measure against the hovering presence of fascism. Yet it may also be seen in terms of a long-held taboo[3] which had never been nor could ever (save with difficulty) be absorbed into the Communist rationalism which Engels had forged in his critique of utopianism. The problem of dogmatic rationalism can be witnessed most particularly among Communist literary critics and creative writers in Britain – individuals who did not theorize their attitude towards the irrational with the intensity of German philosophers such as Ernst Bloch (Christopher Caudwell's *Illusion and Reality* and his discussion of D.H. Lawrence and Freud in *Studies in a Dying Culture* are perhaps exceptions to this claim),[4] but were clearly uneasy with their status as Marxist poets. For in that posture, they were forced to confront that "unmanageable" couplet of science and utopia in which the sphere of rationality was held in great esteem while the terrain of irrational drives linked to traditional aesthetic practice was spurned as reactionary and subjectivist. Arnold Kettle's reflections on poetry and politics in the 1930s bring out the tensions and dilemmas of these Communist writers:

[O]ne of the recurring obsessions of many of the left poets was their unresolved doubts as to whether they ought really to be poets or politicians. Their books and letters are full of self-doubt. Spender writes a letter to Day Lewis (November 1938): "You seem to assume that, given the present situation, the only thing a poet can do is to merge himself in the working-class movement, completely." Edward Upward's autobiographical novels hinge almost entirely on the *choice* he felt he must make between being a poet and being politically responsible.

... Here were poets who wanted to be radical, felt deeply that capitalist society was rotten, but could only reach a certain point in their sense of political commitment, partly at least because they couldn't quite resolve the problem of writing poetry which they could feel was *really* [added emphasis] poetry, yet progressive. Because taking part in the "struggle" seemed to involve abjuring the only sort of poetry they could conceive of, they often felt themselves trapped by a false choice.

... there was a tendency (not discouraged by Soviet example) to oversimplify the relation between literature and politics and to want poetry to be "political" in a rather narrow "tactical" or propagandist way, which was not much help to artists who needed to develop their *art* as well as (indeed as part and parcel of) their political understanding.   (Kettle 1979, 91)

The sectarianism of the Communist party in the Third Period did not help poets resolve their conflictual attitude towards aesthetic practice. On the contrary, it would seem that the virtues of Communist activism and of Marxist scientificity became the essential criteria for defining progressive literature. Poetry had to be infused with a sense of mission. It had to remove itself from the realm of "luxury writing" (MacNeice) and, as Hugh MacDiarmid said in the *Second Hymn to Lenin* (1935), "maun cut / The cackle and pursue real ends."

The concept of literature held by the Communists was that it was decidedly not "above the struggle" as it was for F.R. Leavis's *Scrutiny* movement (cf. Wright 1979, 37–65). Rather its purpose was to avoid the contemplative, passive features associated with belletristic writing and become orientated towards the political issues of the day. *Left Review,* for instance, had no clear line, but seemed to adhere to three basic assumptions: (1) that all art is class art; (2) that social value is the proper criterion of art; and (3) that art is active and has a potential for serving revolution (Margolies 1979, 69). Yet a further criterion that marked the concept of Marxist literature was its scientificity. C. Day Lewis described the poet as the "scientist of words." Poetry "discloses for us emotionally, as science does intellectually, the hidden links in nature" (Margolies

1979, 70). Comparably, Douglas Garman called Christopher Caudwell's *Illusion and Reality* "not just another essay in aesthetic appreciation [but] … an attempt to give a scientific account of the origin of poetry" (Margolies 1979, 70). In brief, the awkwardness felt by Communists towards the aesthetic form is betrayed in their constant effort to "legitimize" the Marxist work of art, to render it scientific, politically sensitive, and committed, and finally to preserve its "salubrious" character from the "taints" of bourgeois art.

However, certain left literary critics were opposed to this Manichean division between Marxist and bourgeois aesthetics. Commenting in 1935 on the intelligentsia of Great Britain, Alick West took David Mirsky to task for the latter's one-sided appraisal of bourgeois intellectuals as literati, fallen into the abyss of irrationalism and potentially of fascist ideology. West argued that despite those reprehensible literary propensities which one may discern in Eliot and Pound's élitist coteries, it was important "to show the past in the richest light, for we need the past to fight the present and the past" (West 1935, 327). He accused Mirsky of indiscriminately dismissing everything traditional as bourgeois and fascistic, as well as of spawning a sectarianism "which would be well enough if we were going to have a Communist Day of Judgment tomorrow, with Marx in the place of Christ *à la* Middleton Murry" (West 1935, 327).

In privileging proletarian iconography and scientific Communist rhetoric over modernist subjectivism as well as over lyrical forms of ruralist sentimentalism (Samuel et al. 1985), Communists veered away from the élite intelligentsia (often rejecting their own bourgeois culture) and endeavoured to politicize art by rendering it the handmaiden of propaganda. This was an extension of their indictment of fascist and reactionary liberal ideologies. But in taking refuge from the emotionalism and decadence of bourgeois aesthetics, they failed to perceive the mythical and covertly sentimental components of their own tendentious writings. Despite their praxis-orientated ethos, they too were implicated in the use of "non-scientific" modes of ideological production. Arnot's *Vindication* is a case in point. It constitutes a paraliterary form that exhibits non-rational and aesthetic elements otherwise spurned by Communists in their battle against rivalling political ideologies.

The Dissenting Ideologue and the Problematic Hero

In promoting revolutionary internationalism and sectarian opposition to social democracy, Arnot was adamantly committed to fighting the nationalist institutions of the hegemonic ruling class. Simultaneously, the community which he addressed was implanted in the mainstream ideological infrastructures of bourgeois society. An acute disparity between his message and the sensibilities of his audience deprived him of a socially desirable form in which to express himself. In advocating destruction of the *status quo*, his rhetoric was strictly antagonistic and disruptive, relentlessly undermining the community's predispositions and cherished visions of society. On the other hand, the most effective and engaging mode of rhetorical persuasion for a given audience would have entailed a stimulation of nationalist feeling, a mirroring of the public's highest self-esteem. But such a tactic would have been ethically impossible for the Communist rhetorician who adamantly refused to engage in the propagandist expedients of his political adversaries. To adopt the niceties of nationalist rhetoric would have been propitious, had it been acceptable to the Communist Class-Against-Class policy. But it was not. The Comintern prescription that predicated absolute class struggle and suppressed nationalist sentiment also placed the dissenting rhetorician in a decidedly fraught state of tension and ambivalence.

Short of partaking in that repertoire of mainstream (and therefore often imperialist) Englishness, Arnot was compelled to create an *ersatz* community within his discourse, a community wrought of the dramatic workings of rhetoric. This in itself indexes the extent to which the political propagandist is more than a rationalist communicator; he is an artist and a master of dramatic narrative who reproduces the immediacy of the present with urgency and compelling force. In this respect, one might posit the rhetorical discourse as formally determined by aesthetic principles and thus comparable to a work of art. Indeed, I propose here that the polemic is a hybrid of a modern, marginal lyric mode and an ancient epic form.[5] In its tonal character, the *Vindication* is covertly plaintive. It possesses a polemical anger in which an "illicit" (because sentimental) lyricism is submerged. In its structure, however, the polemic seeks to explode the purely aesthetic parameters of an elegy or eulogy. For the revolutionary politics of the Communist pamphlet compel it to mediate with society and thus to relinquish the individualism of its subjectivist pain. But while the politically engaged quality of the pamphlet appears to quash its lyrical, subjectivist tendencies with an ideology of activism, such an insistent political philosophy paradoxically finds its origins in the very depths of sentimental grief that it seeks to hush. In short, the voice of polemical protest belongs to a figure who is alienated and acutely distressed by the *status quo*. In this sense, the dissenting rhetorician may be construed as the "problematic hero" (cf.

Lukács 1978), a solitary character, situated in opposition to his society and seeking integration therein, yet a figure who remains incompatible with his contemporary world, since he is subjectively anchored in some ancestral epoch of epic magnitude. The analogy posited here between the dissenting rhetorician and the problematic hero is not gratuitous. On the contrary, it facilitates a clearer portrait of the social character of the Communist ideologue: his underlying bourgeois individualism, his ethical discomfort with his modern age, his nostalgic melancholy for some precapitalist, if not for an alternative, society against which the turpitude of the present is continually judged. Being common to both the rhetorician and the problematic hero, these traits are significant in what they reveal about the respective figures as well as in what they divulge of the rhetorician's artistic and romantic sensibilities, otherwise unrecognizable given his removedness from the cloistered worlds of aesthetic pursuits.

The correlation between the revolutionary and the problematic hero challenges Dutt's presumption that a desired proletarian identity can be assumed unproblematically through immediate renunciation of bourgeois tendencies. It also suggests that the apparently anti-romantic rhetorician of Communist dissent remains fettered to the bourgeois forms of consciousness that he so repudiates in his political enemies.

In 1934, the Communist Arnot stands (like his literary equivalent, the problematic hero) as the only spokesperson of Morris's Marxism; his political act reflects his identity as a revolutionary bent on transforming society in the image of such ideological ancestors as Lenin, Marx, and Engels. Arnot assumes the posture of the mature Morris, who brings his murmurs of discontent to an activist pitch. Like Morris of *The Earthly Paradise* he is the "dreamer of dreams born out of ... due time" (Morris in Arnot 1934a, 12), to whom it does not suffice to demand why or whether he should "strive to set the crooked straight," but who proceeds to act upon the premise that it is imperative to do so at all costs.

As a polemicist, Arnot is thus a solitary figure (as is the problematic hero), always situated in opposition to mainstream society. Like the fictional protagonist, the polemicist has no official mandate from society, nor any prominent status save the one that he must invent or create rhetorically as the *ersatz* of an otherwise unacknowledged credibility (Angenot 1980). Thus, as with Lukács's problematic hero, the polemicist gives meaning to the outside world and to human experience through subjective wilfulness. As Jameson has it, "it is not the world from which such unity springs as in the epic, but rather the mind of the novelist

[or comparably of Arnot, the pamphleteer] which imposes it by fiat"
(Jameson 1971, 173).

For in his efforts to render the Morris legacy compatible with the
Marxist doctrine, Arnot seeks not only to enlighten his audience about
the identity of the hero but also to defend a laudable ethos transcending
the parochialisms and fetishisms of contemporary culture. And since it
is not from such a society that a meaningful paradigm emerges (or so
he thinks), then it is rather from a space apart, from the aesthetically
constructed universe of the pamphlet. There the problematic relation
between the ideologue and his community will be resolved. For where
there is no intrinsic common sense between rhetorician and national
community, it is incumbent on the ideologue to engender it. Such
authentic common sense is the socio-political equivalent of the natural
epic form, a literary genre based on a harmonious relation between the
individual, his inner consciousness, and the outer world. In this state
where, according to Lukács, "the soul does not yet know any abyss
within itself which may tempt it to fall or encourage it to discover
pathless heights, [where] the divinity that rules the world ... is not yet
understood by man, but is familiar and close to him as a father is to
his small child, then every action is only a well-fitting garment for the
world. Being and destiny, adventure and accomplishment, life and
essence are then identical concepts" (Lukács 1978, 30).

But homologies between the individual self and his outer setting mark
a perfection totally estranged from the modern consciousness, though
desirable in some subliminal nostalgic sense. The epic form, we may
say, is recuperated as a mock epic by the conservative bourgeois mind
that refuses to acknowledge the historical discrepancies between prelapsarian worlds and an age of "sinfulness," demoted from epic heights.
And in that refusal, the conservative outlook merely clings to vestigial
forms of unity and imposes them coercively upon the present. The
dissenting bourgeois mind (such as that of the problematic hero and
the dissenting ideologue) recognizes the historical disparities which
thwart the unproblematic unity between individual and society, between
subjective consciousness and objective reality. Yet underlying this alienating discomfort is the haunting desire to retrieve a sense of oneness.
Here the epic form is hankered after even while it can never be integrated
organically. Thus, in the case of the dissenting rhetorician, the epic
structure of heroic centrality is known to be impossible and consequently fosters protest and invective, the covert lament for an
unachieved (epic) hegemonic success.

The synthesis of the epic and lyrical forms, which we announced earlier as the constituent features of the polemic, represents the coalescence of two opposing conditions: central epic stature and peripheral lyrical dissent. Combined, these contending poles produce a negative heroic victory, an ironic exaltation of the degraded figure of protest. It is a triumph achieved through the formal qualities of the rhetorical discourse. For in the aesthetic world of the ideologue's polemic, the accidental and marginal character of the rhetorical voice is granted a necessary position of sovereignty and epic centrality. From the point of view of empirical society, the dissenting ideologue is but the quixotic speaker of an incomprehensible non-conformist manifesto.

Arnot's ambition to change society ideologically compares with the urge of the problematic hero who seeks to transform modern values and resurrect their lost authenticity. Such political fantasies are the drives of ideologues set against the predominant hegemony of their age. And in this course of action, both types are seen as mad in their chimeric fantasies. It is this defiant difference which separates them from their society and incurs the rigid gulf that voids them of a shared common sense with their public. It is this "otherness" which also thwarts their possibility of realizing (empirically) the epic greatness to which they consciously or unconsciously aspire.

But if it is the aim of such societal mavericks to overcome the hiatus between their ethical persuasion and the rest of society, then, short of a real actualizing of fantasy, they deploy aesthetic forms as the ritual gesture of their wish fulfilment. Both problematic hero and dissenting propagandist mould reality to suit their ideological desires through the creation of a mock world.[6] It is in this respect that we may now posit the rhetorician as a discursive craftsman or artist who faces the challenge of conquering his audience and bringing them under his ideological sway.

The Rhetorician as Political Artist

As a version of Lukács's problematic hero, the rhetorician has the task of overcoming his unofficial if not peripheral status, and awarding it some prominence. For what this dissenting stance represents is a position of strategic weakness which the rhetorician must dispel in the course of his discursive craft.[7] The dissenting rhetorician must earn his power and respect by struggling to clarify the paradoxes of his message. By contrast, a ruling-class ideologue such as Baldwin is, as it were, a mock-epic hero, endowed with hegemonic legitimacy. Thanks to his received authoritative status, he masters his public by appearing as the "chief of the common people," and by displaying a luxury of eloquence and panache. (Cf. Barthes in Sontag 1982, 138.)

Admittedly, while both types of rhetoricians are challenged by the problem of engaging with, and extracting the approval of, their respective publics, the dissenting ideologue is compelled to labour more strenuously for his rewards. The process of interacting with audiences is common to both rhetoricians, yet it is differentiated by degrees of difficulty. Such a process consists in a dialectical manœuvre of linguistic expression in which both the audience's sensibilities and the commonly held assumptions of truth and value are addressed. This implies that the rhetorical discourse must encompass both the individual needs of the audience and a generalizing statement that considers them in their totality. Yet the dissenting rhetorician's attempt to impose a judgment upon a wide variety of individuals, both specifically and generally, is an awesome endeavour, since he shares no veritable common sense with his public and is unable to accede to each and every addressee both simply and directly. Still, he acts as though he were an epic individual, heroically conquering his audience in single-handed fashion and compensating for his hardships by elevating his discourse to an idealist or aesthetic plane. In Kantian fashion, he reduces the complexity of objective conditions (namely the indeterminacy and motley character of the public) into an aesthetic entity. Here, he is able to grant himself, even if only with illusory results, a subjective control over reality.

By phenomenologically transforming his empirical audience from a heterogeneous anonymous mass into an ideal, normative addressee, the rhetorician's act could be described equally as a process of synthesizing the audience's universality (their magnitude in number) and their particularity (their various concrete subjectivities) into an aesthetic form. This arises when he converts cognitive logic into aesthetic judgment,[8] a shift that reconfigures "time," the causal condition by which objective judgments are formed and gathered into an intuited moment of coexistence. Here, what is successively apprehended (i.e. the individual members of the audience) for the purpose of crystallizing a logical judgment can be comprehended in one instant, in one thrust of intuition. Linear time is annihilated as an intensive moment is forged for aesthetic reflection. But in this instantaneous comprehension of multiplicity, determinacy is sacrificed (e.g. the differing individuals of the audience and their respective qualities are annulled). Contingencies are deleted as the perception of the aesthetic object is extracted from the successive flow of objectivity (historical conditions, social variations, etc.). The universality of the whole group is subsumed under a particular addressee. Thus the rhetorician shifts from appealing to an unmanageable multitude of persons to presenting a discourse that addresses the whole audience as a symbolic individual.

There are advantages in this aesthetic process and they are at least twofold. The rhetorician is able to focus and effectively target his rhetoric to a single point. This focus also affords his rhetoric a palpable immediacy which facilitates his audience's reception. This is the second asset. For if the rhetorician can succeed in granting his addressees the impression that each of them is a special participant within the whole community, then he has also fulfilled an important task: namely, to raise their interests and excite their subjectivities. Conversely, were he to regard them in a cognitive sense as but subordinate members of a whole, their sense of particularity and distinctive identity would not be gratified.

Admittedly, in rendering the empirical audience a normative ideal, the rhetorician's discourse does not address the individual interests of his public. Rather it provides a general sense in which each addressee sees his particularity as graced with heightened significance. And this "sense" can only be "purposeless," since it is imperative that the rhetorician deliver his claims in as impartial a manner as possible, thus catering to each and all in one utterance. Consequently, he commands his audience by accommodating himself not to their material everyday needs, but rather to a more universally or socially held assumption of well-being. It is for this reason that the ideal audience can be seen as expedient for the rhetorician, since once such an aesthetic subject is established then empirical details are swept aside and the essential structures of subjectivity are forwarded in their utmost clarity and simplicity, rendering the rhetorical project feasible according to its own internal laws.

Compounded with this aesthetic construction of the audience, the rhetorician ensures himself a heightened identity such that he may take command of the discursive event and secure the possibility – at least in his mind – of dominating his attentive public. For the degree of confidence and conviction with which he delivers his discourse will determine the extent of his narratorial authority and the possibility of disarming his addressees. In the course of persuasion, the important factor is not so much whether a correct political truth is being forwarded, but whether the discourse induces an audience to submit to an arbitrary rhetorical stance that can offer a readily accessible and coherent political vision.

The imposition of an authoritative-authorial voice is manifold. But in its incipient stage it is marked by the narratorial voice surrendering its own seemingly single identity to that of other voices from the past. It fashions a specific syncretic style of rhetoric which arises out of an intertext of other credible and revered figures from a cultural repertoire. Thus as Arnot defends his particular standpoint, he is compelled to invoke Lenin, principal hero of Communist tradition. For while Lenin is Russian, he is nonetheless appropriated as part of an epic from abroad and adapted to the national saga of British Communist experience. Recalling the 1930s, A.L. Morton writes: "One of the features of the earlier period was that we were still very much under the shadow of the October Revolution and inclined to look for ultimate truth across the water to the Soviet Union. Anything a Russian said was rather taken as gospel, which was not altogether sensible" (Morton 1985b, 22).

The passage from *State and Revolution* which Arnot uses as his springboard for the *Vindication* acts in the manner of Bakhtin's *author-itative discourse*, as the authoritative word from a "distanced zone organically connected with a past that is felt to be hierarchically higher" (Bakhtin 1981, 342). It is, so to speak, the word of the fathers, notably the Leninist heroes of the Russian Revolution. The excerpt from Lenin's pamphlet is thus endowed with "a lofty," "hieratic aura" (Bakhtin 1981, 342) which lends the *Vindication* an epic quality. And since the "world of the epic is the national heroic past ... the world of 'beginnings' and 'peak times' in that national history, a world of fathers and of founders of families, a world of 'firsts' and 'bests'" (Bakhtin 1981, 13), Arnot's discourse is, by extension, granted its own commanding power.

The importance of seizing the epic structure as a means of edifying a narratorial position resides in the fact that the epic is generally a complete form, and thus a constitutive principle whose *a priori* status is valorized as absolute. In this way, Arnot's discourse, which echoes Lenin's exalted pronouncement on canonizations, affords itself a sovereignty over other competing discourses on Morris's legacy. Indeed, the passage from *State and Revolution* comes to encapsulate the *primum mobile* of Arnot's own invective. For the *Vindication* passes through the legitimated territories of a Leninist tradition and circles back into the present, constituting a synthesis of Arnot's rhetoric with that of an ensemble of Marxist ideologues such as Lenin, Engels, and Morris himself. The teleology of Arnot's argument is not, therefore, unidirectional; it is rather a spiralling trajectory that entails temporal reversals predicated by his self-legitimation through the voices of senior ideologues. His rhetorical identity is far from being pure and unitary. Instead we find a symphonic coalescence of past and present, of universal and particular relations, as well as of epic authority and peripheral status.

But while Arnot's standpoint appears to be an arbitrary seizure of rhetorical authority, he is in fact subjected to certain laws inherent in the very act of his discursive delivery. Not even the endorsement of an epic revolutionary tradition will exempt him from mediating with the resistances which his audience poses in respect to his persuasive endeavour. The power which Arnot's authorial voice exercises, as he summons the authority of a legitimated culture to his defence, is a relational act of authorization which can only be earned through continual pacing and sensitivity to his public's desires and implicit demands. Arnot's apparently arbitrary power is thus delimited by unforeseen or even insuperable contingencies; and while it may be asserted that Lenin proffers Arnot a strengthened rhetorical posture, it is also plausible that Lenin's epic greatness is only recognized by a Marxist-Leninist audience. What of the foreignness of this hero? Does it not inhibit Arnot's contact with the English sensibilities of his following? Indeed, here is an instance of the resistances which the dissenting rhetorician encounters in his persuasive act and which he must deal with by partly acquiescing before those obstacles. The more he attends to the needs of his audience, the more power he can wield as a narratorial authority: e.g., he must give them forepleasures, incentives, and bonuses for granting him his shrift; he must create an aesthetic experience that will enthral them into his web of ideas. The more adeptly he constructs a world in which they experience a replenishment of their affective interests (aesthetic and cognitive), the more he can facilitate his persuasive project. It is to these aesthetic moments which he engenders that we must now turn. For embedded in his rhetorical strategy to entice his following resides the key to the queries: In what way is the polemical form mediated by non-rational experiences of perception? And in what manner can one claim that pleasure may be derived from the stringent character of a disruptive Communist diatribe whose rhetorical forms are derivative of a sublime outlook on reality?

PART 2   AFFECTIVE COMPONENTS OF
DISSENTING RHETORIC

Pathos as Unifying Sentiment

An important feature which has characterized the rhetorician's discursive techniques is his recurrent perceptual shift from cognitive to aesthetic judgments. Whether this concerns the manner in which he chooses to construe his audience as an aesthetic entity or whether it concerns his own status as a dramatic persona, embracing a tradition of Marxism-Leninism, the rhetorician's operation always entails a process of condensing empirical reality into symbolic units. Such an intensification of rhetorical material (including the participants in the event: i.e. the speaker and his audience) foregrounds the dramatic and performative dimensions of the rhetorical discourse whose economy of time and space is precisely what renders it immediately seductive. The continuity between the rhetorical mode and aesthetic principles is not incidental. Indeed, the aesthetic component which rhetoric borrows for its own purposes is vital to audience reception, as it provides paradigmatic unities that muster the fissiparous character of everyday life into visible and graspable wholes. This is a desirable feature for any discourse that seeks to mediate with its audience in rapid and all-consuming fashion. The aesthetic component contributes to the swift and absolute reception of the rhetorical message, since the laws of an aesthetic disposition (a disposition which participants in the rhetorical event are invited to share) predicate a quick and intuitive admission of information. Scientific scepticism is excluded from such judgments, since the divisiveness and disturbing details which it introduces would thwart the indispensable clarity, at times Manichean simplicity, by which the rhetorical form proceeds.

To produce the clarity of a rhetorical message (a condition claimed earlier on to be the necessary proviso for winning authority), the rhetorician must ensure that the contradictions of his marginal position, of his distinctively alien Communist message, and of his audience's multifarious subjectivities are all dispelled. His endeavour to assign roles to the constituent members of his discourse and sweep away the nebulous ground between participants cannot be realized unless he can insert a guaranteed pleasure principle, a note of promise, at the outset of his discourse. Such rhetorical gratification may only succeed if it is Arnot who defines his audience's desire by aesthetic or fictional fiat. For it is he who stipulates the rules that govern his mock world, a world generated by the unfolding narrative of his polemic. Only on this condition can he transform the empirical complexity of his object (his audience with all its variables) into an ideal addressee, and simultaneously clear his own anonymity and marginality of status by raising himself to the prominent height of magisterial author. It is this movement from the flux of everyday life to the timelessness of ideal structures that marks the transition from cognitive scepticism to aesthetic trust.

The rhetorical event is indeed a performance, and it seems appropriate to invoke Aristotle's dramatic couplet of pity and fear[9] so as to demonstrate the importance of the principles of pleasure and pain in fostering audience identification, the affective ground upon which Arnot's rhetorical "legislation" occurs. Let us proceed first with the concept of pity.

The *Vindication* opens with a mood of pathos as it embarks on an odyssey to speak the hitherto unspoken judgment on Morris's unacknowledged greatness as a Marxist revolutionary.[10] In addition, the pamphlet is crowned by an epiphany which prophesies retributive justice through the dirge for Alfred Linnell (composed by Morris in 1887 after Linnell's murder at Trafalgar Square). Morris's lament is imbued with dark diction, inspiring cataclysmic retaliation against the criminal murder of Linnell by the state. The dirge is also a poetic accoutrement to Arnot's defence of Morris and it serves to reinforce the rousing effect that a downtrodden subject bears upon his community.

Insufficiently praised and scarcely valued for his socialist activism, Morris, according to Arnot, would have had more influence on contemporary society were it not for the "veil" with which the capitalists surrounded him. More than any other leader, Morris was "subjected to that 'canonisation' of which Lenin spoke in *State and Revolution*" (Arnot 1934a, 4). Here Arnot takes the opportunity to construct a martyr out of the distorted posthumous image of the hero, implicitly rendering him the personification of a blighted truth. Described in the passive voice as "subjected to that canonisation" and "hoisted up to his niche as a 'harmless saint,'" Morris becomes the emblem of martyrized Marxism. His canonization by bourgeois admirers is ironically not a homage in Arnot's eyes, but rather the ideological crucifixion of a legacy which now begs redemption by an oppositional party.

If such canonization becomes the source of pathos through an intertextual invocation of Lenin on the fate of revolutionaries, then it is logical that this early plaintive note serves to instil the sentimental bond which Arnot requires for his rhetorical project. It is a ploy which both disarms and engages an audience, compelling them to focus attention on a specific subject – a victim of oppression assaulted by "relentless persecution" and "savage hostility" (Arnot 1934a, 3–4). This stress on the victimization of revolutionary legacies enhances the subjective appeal of Arnot's *Vindication*. For in his posthumous martyrdom, Morris's Marxist heritage is pitted against the "conspiring" bourgeois mythmongers. The latter appear as despicable enemies who by sheer contrast make the victim seem a repository of innocence and endearing powerlessness.

The text quoted from *State and Revolution* is undoubtedly grist for Arnot's mill. As Lenin's voice mingles with Arnot's in an elegy for the plight of revolutionaries, a "pathetic" tremor is injected through the recurring motif of "passivity" and "vulnerability." As the victim of slander, the Marxist memory of Morris is constructed as an anthropomorphized subject, continually at the mercy of mythmongers. This generates the aesthetic correlative of disarming innocence and vulnerability, conditions that necessarily beg the sympathy of an audience, and the guiding authority of some redemptive agent – ultimately, here, the narrator himself. For in producing a pathetic mood in his discourse, Arnot has implicitly also created the possibility of dispelling this aesthetic emotion. He has thus gained the role of narratorial saviour. By creating a "lack" at the outset, he is also responsible for the logic that will anticipate and fulfil this "fabricated" desire. The representation of martyrized Marxist teachings is consequently not an innocent beginning but the pretext for an ideological riposte, executed with forceful gusto. It is also the catalyst that sets the narrative in motion toward a predetermined goal.

Having secured his authority by summoning heroic models from the past, Arnot creates a universally shareable feeling of "lack" which further accentuates his authoritative posture as rhetorician. He is now doubly in command, steering his audience's subjectivity and enticing them to know more. The aesthetic powerlessness ascribed to the martyrized Marxist legacy of Morris impels an audience to adhere closely to the discursive narrative. For the audience will resolve its own inquisitiveness and sense of commiseration with the martyr if it abides by the rhetorician's unfolding tale. Here is a form of rhetorical barter in which Arnot guarantees his audience the redemption of the Marxist Morris while the audience recompenses Arnot with confirmation of his authorial power as narrator and saviour. Indeed, in announcing his promise, Arnot prepares to rise from the ashes of destruction – the Conservative distortion of the Marxist Morris – and provide a renewed legacy. This display of the rhetorician's capabilities is a linguistic feat emblematic of a veritable transformation of reality in what is essentially but an isolated thing, a mere pamphlet. Yet, in the same breath, the political tract is also an intensive totality[11] which refracts a whole world of political configurations.

In so far as the pamphlet achieves this poetic and phenomenological totality, it reproduces the mimetic unity of art through symmetry and cohesive argumentation. This patterned order is also embodied in the prefigurative vision of Morris restored to his Communist turf. With this symbol of retrieved harmony as a note of promise and pathos as its disarming mood, the *Vindication* is able to lead its receiving subjects to a point of suspended disbelief which concedes to the logic of the mock world. Of course, the advancement of such a perspective is only plausible if certain rules are obeyed, if certain artifices and responses to the laws of verisimilitude are applied. Arnot is careful in his portrait of Morris, showing as much the deficient and problematic facets of the hero as his laudable attributes. In the concluding passages of the pamphlet, he admits:

All this does not mean that William Morris had anything like the understanding of Marxism that was afterwards to be shown by the Bolsheviks. On the contrary, he allowed himself to be influenced by the Anarchists, who showed an anti-Parliamentary tendency, and several other similar tendencies – all of them (as Lenin was to note afterwards) a punishment of the movement for the sins of opportunism rampant in Hyndman and the Fabians … But these things no more entitle Morris to be canonised as a Reformist by two generations of the Labour Party and I.L.P. than Gorki's weaknesses would entitle him to be regarded as a White Guardist and a Menshevik.   (Arnot 1934a, 30–1)

With such qualifications, Arnot's message acquires a certain realism, a flexibility of argument which renders it decidedly more plausible. Indispensable to Arnot's project are leaps of faith which he must elicit from his audience and which permit him to posit his version of the Morris legacy as the guiding principle of a world view portrayed through the aperture of the pamphlet. Simultaneously, the audience must grant him the *a priori* assumption that his political voice has a scientific truth to convey and that his selective point of view is tenable.

To surrender to the rhetorical vantage point that Arnot is poised on exhibiting, the audience must comply with the system of rules which the pamphlet stipulates implicitly at the start of its narrative journey. Compliance with rules, or subordination to the laws of the argument, is a preliminary demand which Arnot imposes by fostering a sentimental aura of pathos that draws the receiving subject into identification with the glorified martyr, the revolutionary hero and his vilified legacy. But the leap of faith will not be readily induced with this alone. Coupled with the expedient use of pathos is the enforcement of a principle of terror which enables the rhetorician to further secure his rhetorical power. Pathos and terror, being mirror images of each other, respectively reflect the subjective and objective facets of the protagonist in crisis. While pathos draws audience attention to the subjectivity of the protagonist in distress, terror directs the public to the formidable and hostile nature of objective circumstances. Pity and fear, the two components of Aristotelian poetics which define the release of aesthetic pleasure through catharsis, thus prevail in the non-literary discourse as catalysts of cognitive persuasion, as elements which compel the audience to genuflect before the rhetorician's moral law.

Terror and the Dissonance of Rhetorical Invective

Attack as a principle of polemic was clearly manifest in Lenin's dealings with the bourgeois press ... He was never afraid of throwing down the gauntlet or making a public invitation to a polemical duel ... The tone of Lenin's polemic against the bourgeois and opportunist press was similarly one of attack. He appealed to his journalistic comrades to "hound them with all our might" and to fight the mean way that some papers have "of defending opportunism of the worst brand by means of sophisms." (Baluyev 1983, 89–91)

Following Lenin's tradition of rhetorical militancy and polemical vigour, Arnot's pamphlet complements its mood of pathos with argumentative retaliation against bourgeois reformist ideology. Yet, as in any assault, the blow to be dealt draws its impact from a measure of accrued venom, from psychic energy that precipitates action. In the pamphlet's overture, Arnot raises his polemical sentiment to a degree of palpable urgency, endorsing the rhetorical project and establishing the importance of his rallying call. The virulence and lyrical intensity of the discourse in these opening pages summon an audience to attend to the voice of a heightened political drama.

In its rhetorical insistence, the *Vindication* assumes a quality of tragedy where reality is polarized into extremes and a vision of truth is elucidated through the unadulterated clarity of dramatic forces. In tragedy, the power of enthralment is produced through aesthetic artifices which create a unique instant, a distinct temporal dimension that arises out of an extraordinary moment of crisis. "In the state of exception, the strength of real life breaks the hardened crust of mechanical repetition. Crisis as the *moment* of truth: the abolition of the ordinary rhythm of everyday life implies that metaphysical contraction of time – 'time deprived of temporality' – envisaged by Lukács in *Soul and Form*" (Moretti 1986, 42).

Like tragedy, the polemical form fashions an idiom that draws attention to itself. It marks boundaries beyond everyday language even while its style may be wholly demotic. In the case of the *Vindication*, acrimony and rhetorical fury enhance a demotic diction and act as the poetic substance of the polemic. These agitational features constitute the political lyricism of the pamphlet as it keeps itself at a remove from conventional aesthetic forms such as sentimental beauty and the flourishes of nostalgia and unctuous piety.

Just as the intensive language of poetry is rhythmically broken off from monotone everyday speech (cf. Caudwell 1973), so the polemical signature of the *Vindication* is characterized by its linguistic anger. Such a feature sets it off from the casual flow and routine language of calm bourgeois "neutrality." The dissenting style of the tract becomes a rhythmic and tonal departure from "normalcy," and, by extension, from the dominant hegemonic rhetoric of Conservative and Social-Democratic Morrisania. Thus, for a meteoric instant, the audience of the *Vindication* is made to sense the vibrations of the rhetorician's voice. In default of a substantial hearing, the latter must seize the moment he has within his discourse and maximize upon it to its fullest extent. Like the tragic form, the polemic speaks through a narrow aperture and under compelling conditions predicated by crisis and urgency. Like the tragic form, the polemic also exalts its own discursive truth, just as tragedy stimulates an audience to experience life with renewed and intensive value. Both genres thus draw a special attention to themselves with an epistemological superiority that thrives on critical and exceptional peaks of history and implicitly demeans the nebulousness of everyday life.

As we saw in chapter 3, Communist intellectuals believed in the scientific character of their work. Yet the *Vindication*'s inflammatory verbiage betrays a substantial lyricism. Despite his overt defiance of sentimentalism, Arnot unwittingly creates an inverted sentimentalism of political passion. The polemic is a political lamentation with epic desires; its sublimated bitterness turns grief into protest, and pain into a pleasurable anguish which is endemic to the poetry of martyr-worship. Consider once more the first lines of *State and Revolution* which Arnot quotes in the opening lines of his *Vindication*:

During the lifetime of great revolutionaries the oppressing classes have invariably meted out to them relentless persecution and received their teaching with the most savage hostility, most furious hatred and a ruthless campaign of slanders. After their death, however, attempts are usually made to turn them into saints, canonizing them, as it were, and investing their name with a certain halo by way of "consolation" to the oppressed classes, and with the object of duping them, while at the same time emasculating and vulgarising the real essence of their revolutionary theories and blunting their revolutionary edge.   (Arnot 1934a, 3–4)

If Lenin's diction and tonal exuberance verges on the hyperbolic, its rhapsodic flight must be viewed in terms of a lyrical ire which fosters the musical-cum-semantic swells of his rhetoric. Scientific as his discourse may be in political intent, its expression is at times poetic. The excerpted passage could be readily divided into two verses, the first of which treats revolutionaries in their lifetime, the second of which pertains to their posthumous reception. This division may of course be taken as simple grammatical or syntactical pattern, but beyond it lies a qualitatively distinct set of rhythms which fall into two parts respectively. In the first of these verses ("During the lifetime of great revolutionaries the oppressing classes have invariably meted out to them relentless persecution and received their teaching with the most savage hostility, most furious hatred and a ruthless campaign of slanders"), the defiling act by oppressing classes reproduces the effect of "relentless persecution" with a clearly defined crescendo, a tension rising to the climactic statement of "a campaign of slanders." The superlative attribute "most," which emphasizes the dire nature of each slanderous act, involving every possible facet of aggression (hostility, fury, ruthless conspiracy …), punctuates this spiralling trajectory as it moves towards its climax. In the second sequence (beginning with "After their death"), the rhythm changes and the prose assumes the movement of a maelstrom, replicating the long and tortuous descent, the posthumous degradation of "great revolutionaries" whose "revolutionary essence" is ultimately emasculated, vulgarized, and dulled.

Compounded with its prosody, Lenin's statement encapsulates a miniature narrative on the destiny of revolutionaries and their condemned status in bourgeois society. Thanks to the melodic features of this intense Leninist diction and the element of tragedy at its heart, Arnot equips himself with the material to fuel his own rhetorical lyricism. And whereas in earlier appraisals of this tenor we suggested that the pamphlet provided the rhetorician with a repository for expelling emotion (collective and individual), here we may say that the outpouring intends to move an audience through the dissonance of a lamentation. The polemical effusion is a melodic quality which activates the text and preserves the living note within the stultifying dead letter. (Cf. Bakhtin in Todorov 1984.) In this way, the urgency of the political message is maintained and made doubly decisive – indeed, as imperative as the aesthetic dichotomies which typify a genre that continually embraces the tense tango between life and death.

It is with this lyrical ambience that the state of aesthetic terror[12] may be conjured as Arnot raises his audience onto a plane that is several notches removed from everyday reality. Terror, of course, is not so much a natural force of evil, conventionalized in primitive literature with man battling against the hostilities of nature, as something that is ideological and inspired by the thunderous anger of the rhetorical voice and by the image that the latter creates of the mythmongers vulturing upon the Morris legacy. Terror also results from a punitive streak in the opening lines of the pamphlet. Here Arnot's source of discontent is swiftly transformed into an object of anticipated punishment as he proclaims, "this graven image of Morris has to be shattered before any estimate of him is possible. The myths built up about him have to be destroyed, especially the bourgeois myth on the one hand and the Labour Party–I.L.P. myth on the other" (Arnot 1934a, 4). As he exposes the "culprits" responsible for these fabrications, Arnot sees Stanley Baldwin as "impudent" and the Labour party affiliates as wilful in their misreading of Morris. "The early mythmongers of the ILP, all of them bitterly anti-Marxist, found it intolerable that an artist whom some of them regarded as the new Michelangelo or a new Leonardo da Vinci should be counted as a follower of Marx ... Starting from the axiom 'Morris not Marxist,' they then proceed ... to rule out all in his writings that is evidence to the contrary" (Arnot 1934a, 6).

In his indignation towards the anti-Marxist Morrisites, in his hatred of the hegemonic foe, Arnot polarizes the dramatic personae of his discourse, relegating the mythmongers to a demonic sphere and, by implicit contrast, privileging the Marxist community as the innocent victim of assault. Here the audience is led to accord sympathy to the revolutionary martyr figure (the anthropomorphized Morris legacy) and by extension to the authorial standpoint. In representing the political adversaries as hostile demagogues, Arnot invites his audience to relive the experience of loss and adversity in order to take refuge under the guardian wing of his own discursive judgment.

For rhetorical purposes, it is indispensable that the opening lines of the *Vindication* emphasize the assault on Morris's memory. This not only reinforces the elements of pathos and fear which capture the non-cognitive sensibilities of the audience; it also justifies Arnot's relentless drive to regain hegemonic control of Morris's legacy. The pamphlet must depart from the "wreckage" of a Marxist Morrisania (a moment of loss), so as to warrant a compensatory retrieval of lost totality – the "authentic" (Marxist) Morris. Such a process requires that Arnot eradicate all contradictions that might hamper his drive to assert that aesthetic control. His discourse must become totalizing and imperious, selecting material to satisfy his standpoint and affirm his sovereignty over the argument. This rhetorical absolutism, which shunts aside the potential contradictions of differing Morris legacies, can only be admitted once the identity of the political protagonist – the Marxist doctrine personified through Morris's legacy – is posited as a victim of slander, and thus as the deserving subject of wholesale applause. Simultaneously, the polemic wins its power and authority through the dissonance of the "formidable" rhetorical voice as it angrily casts its contempt upon the ideological enemy.

Morality as a Rhetorical Expedient

The urgency of the times and the marginal position from which he postures as a tribune of Marxism render Arnot's rhetorical enterprise more challenging than that of the self-assured and consensually approved Baldwin. But even in his marginality and dissent, Arnot must simulate the same authority which Baldwin wielded as he effortlessly dismissed Marxists as "crabbing" discontents. While Arnot may desire the power of his Conservative counterpart, he cannot exude the same rhetorical confidence and serenity. Still, he can introduce the force of moralizing speech as his weapon, particularly as such an idiom is effective in achieving rapid persuasion.

The moralizing aspects of the *Vindication* are not like Baldwin's calmly stated pieties. Rather they are aggressive assaults on the bourgeois institution. The Communist tract is punctuated with sniping resentment. Its polemical, plaintive strains are the undertones of a moralizing discourse. Emanating from an inferior position, the pamphlet voices its authority in a state of necessity and virtual panic; it thus resorts to the Manichean division of good and evil as its essential guiding structure. As he calls for a shattering of the Menshevik-Conservative Morris myth, Arnot pits the Marxist Morris, as a version of true judgment and ethical rectitude (awaiting its retributive justice), against the moral wrongs of its ideological counterparts. In this diametric opposition what was initially a mere symptom of anger and discursive disdain now becomes an instrument for facilitating the rhetorical flow.

Throughout the *Vindication* Arnot uses a judgment of taste as his determining standard of truth. He acts as the privileged spokesperson of a Communist creed, shedding light on the bourgeois Morrisania, not only to expose the misconstructions as insufficient or inaccurate knowledge but also to inject a moral castigation into his polemical challenge. To him, then, the bourgeois myths are not merely fallacious, but insidious and morally reprehensible as well. For more than malignings of Morris's legacy, these myths are seen as symptoms of glaring hypocrisy and duplicity. Where the bourgeoisie once defiled Morris ("relentless persecution is meted out"), they now posthumously praise him as a hero.

The *Vindication* addresses the cognitive but also moral problem of rhetorical deception. Intellectual dishonesty is ostensibly the nub of the polemic. But the affective tremors of the pamphlet suggest that Arnot's vehemence is due to more than a sense of pedantry over the "real" Morris. He is concerned with the "correct" knowledge of the Morris legend, not for purely intellectual ends but for practical, political ones. Beyond immediate representations of the hero, there are veritable hegemonic factors at stake: e.g. political betrayals of Communists by the "evil genius," Hyndman; the hegemonic appropriations of Morris's legacy by conservative institutions and their fawning reformist followers. These concrete political issues are embodied in the commemorative treatment of Morris, and in the manner in which his Communist identity is marred or effaced. Since the pamphlet does not regard the bourgeois myths as simply the products of poorly rendered knowledge, but as ethically distasteful acts of violence to truth (a truth determined by Marxist-Leninist values), Arnot's tone is necessarily charged with hostility and disdain, admittedly derivative of Morris's own words:

But now the Tory leader of the House of Commons – representatives of the capitalist class, "these foul swine" as they are called in *The Dream of John Ball* – has the impudence to scatter dirt over the memory of the man who said of Parliament that it was:

"on the one side a kind of watch committee, sitting to see that the interests of the upper classes took no hurt; and on the other hand a sort of blind to delude people into supposing that they had some share in the management of their own affairs." (Arnot, 1934a, 4)

And again, in a similar vein, he continues to rail:

They simply brush aside the Morris that was, and construct a Morris that never existed, a sort of sickly dilettante Socialist, as personally incredible as he would be politically monstrous. (Arnot 1934a, 5–6)

Glasier, who was busy re-making Morris in his own image – (see the ridiculous chapter on "Morris and Religion," where Glasier, himself deep in the swamp of religiosity, flounders pitifully around Morris's explicit statement: "I am what is called bluntly an atheist.") (Arnot 1934a, 7)

Systematically, the first chapter of the *Vindication* announces its Marxist-Leninist position by deflecting and morally spurning all other ideological appropriations of Morris. It is in this opposition between good and evil that discursive subjectivities take on a significant role in determining the success and contrived cohesiveness of the argument. For in casting scornful and contemptuous light on the bourgeois-reformist Morris worshippers, Arnot arrests his audience and draws them to his ideological camp.[13] By presenting his opponents as ethically disreputable, he applies a judgment of "distaste," repudiating the bourgeois mythmakers and relegating them to the nether sphere of immorality. His authorial "superego" leaves his audience in a blunt dilemma: either to remain disbelieving and alienated – indeed, exiled to the immoral flock – or to submit to the pamphlet's judgment and curl up in the blind comforts of a contrived social embrace where being morally good averts isolation and ensures that what is good is more pleasurable than what may or may not be rationally right.

In bringing morality to his service, Arnot's polemical form appears as an oracle of cognitive truth while in fact only constituting a relative epistemic view. But with an imperious moral stance, the pamphlet transforms opinion into doctrine and proclaims itself as truth by creating a boundary between a legitimated community and some non-conforming other. Inducing recognition rather than cognitive inquiry, Arnot affirmatively dons the ethical precepts of "virtue" lodged in the martyr hero and ostracizes all ideological elements averse to that revolutionary figure. His truth becomes the law of the whole – "his" whole – rather than the validity of the part, i.e. the marginal member of his mock world. Thus the tables are turned in the fantastic scenario of the polemic: where in reality Arnot is the pariah decrying the exclusive ceremony of the centenary, here he restores his desired centrality and shunts his enemies to the sidelines as a much-"deserved" punishment.

Urgency and the Polemical Form

In the modern world, only the historico-political actions which are immediate and imminent, characterised by the necessity for lightning speed, can be incarnated mythically by a concrete individual. Such speed can only be made necessary by a great and imminent danger, a great danger which precisely fans passion and fanaticism suddenly to a white heat, and annihilates the critical sense and the corrosive irony which are able to destroy the "charismatic" character of the *condottiere*.   (Gramsci 1971, 129)

The *Vindication* does not address its audience with the relaxed pace of an academic exegesis that patiently accommodates itself to the delays of numerous mediations. As a discourse that is subject to the constraints of an imperative propagandist duty, the tract cannot afford the academic leisure of arguing its point of view in procedural didactic fashion.[14] Nor would it seem apposite to do so, given the anti-esoteric slant of pre-scriptions to Communist intellectuals from the upper ranks of the Party. Instead the pamphlet must resort to the expediencies of moral coercion where a given audience is made susceptible not to total knowledge, but rather to the enticements of social harmony. The voice of morality masquerades as the messenger of mediated logic even while it attends to the pleasures of social belonging and collective oneness, providing but intensive totalities of information rather than comprehensive knowledge. It claims to speak on behalf of some absolute truth yet it never fully demonstrates the validity of its perspective. Rather, it establishes its centrality and veracity in *a priori* manner. Thus, if the polemic wills its message by dint of moral and aesthetic coercion, proclaiming its vantage point as a given truth, it achieves its persuasive force through assent; it expects and requires accord with its own judgment, since it wields the power of deciding not so much what is true as what is good or bad. On this ethical divide, its "moral" law annexes the audience by attending to the pleasure principle of sociability.

In determining the moral value and ethical stance of a Marxist-Leninist defence of Morris, Arnot is able to embrace or alienate his audience. For if the latter identifies with any figure other than the heralded protagonists of Arnot's mock world (i.e. Morris, Marx, Lenin,

Engels, Stepniak ...), it is apt to receive the same buffets from Arnot's authorial voice as the antagonists upon whom he casts his aspersions. It is here that rhetorical terror moves and manipulates an audience to align itself with the narrator's authority. For the pleasure of being in the mainstream of the community governed by the narrator depends upon two factors: the pressures which his morality imposes upon the individual, and the primacy ascribed to a senior culture of Marxist ancestors, whose doctrine serves as an ideological yardstick by which its followers may conform and integrate themselves into the discursive community. Social inclusion is thus a crucial element of the aesthetic pleasure which the rhetorician deploys. In the case of pathos, the audience anticipates its retributive justice in the form of moral gratification. As to the element of terror, an audience seeks authorial approval when it complies with a community through the irrational pleasures of blind faith.

Arnot's representative Communist propaganda both crystallized out of urgent conditions and transformed that urgency into a stylistic feature. The act of destabilizing popular consent with passionate rhetoric entailed a transformative purpose: to instil a Marxist-Leninist ideology into popular consciousness. But given the constraints imposed by the Comintern, and given fascist and reformist pressures militating against the Communist movement, this proselytizing impulse could only amount to an emergency measure. The rhetoric espoused was geared to the intensity of that historical period and to the dire nature of the prewar political conditions. Propaganda had an obligation towards immediate action. Delay, as R.P. Dutt insisted, was fatal.

Still, the commitment to scientific and objective information was firm. How then could Arnot's and other Communist tracts reconcile the urgency of their writing with ideal scientific treatises produced under conditions of leisure? Their dilemma was actually resolved, if only superficially, through the polemical form itself, an expedient which provided an audience with the illusion that the discourse had travelled the long route of scientific reasoning, while in fact persisting in using strategic short-cuts. In delivering a semblance of exhaustive analysis, of having sounded the depths of "knowledge" and "truth," the polemical genre reconciles its inherent needs to achieve its persuasive project both swiftly and totally; it satisfies its own needs to win immediate recognition and it also attends (albeit artificially) to the extrinsic, socially conditioned expectations that comprehensive knowledge be expressed.

As Arnot summons Lenin to his rhetorical aid, he employs a principle of pregiven assumptions.[15] The statement on revolutionaries and their fate in bourgeois society is taken as a universal paradigm which exempts Arnot from having to demonstrate his argument on a *tabula rasa*. The Leninist discursive tradition provides both Arnot and his audience with a convenient cushion of mental leisure upon which to lay their quizzical consciousness. And as such, their reliance upon a senior voice, implicitly a source of reverence, circumvents a more lengthy discussion which would otherwise be expected of Arnot's rhetorical performance.

But here in the locus of such unlaboured thought, Arnot's notion of truth is heralded as a purely rational validation. In fact, this apparently absolute truth also emanates from irrational sources, from the ontological response to pleasure and pain which in itself is linked to the inclusion and exclusion of individuals from society. For if Arnot's rhetorical success is ascertained by the pleasure he derives from his swift and effective persuasion, his audience is also afforded its pleasure in the effortlessness of their understanding. The accessibility of his assumptions gratifies Arnot in his persuasive project and reciprocally satisfies the audience as they enjoy the familiar references in his political message. Recognizing themselves in the rhetorician's mock world, they reinforce their own beliefs and sense of identity, overcoming their relative status as isolated individuals through the embracing force of the polemic's imaginary community. From this perspective, the mock world resurges with increasing poignancy as the rhetorical arena in which the ideologue manipulates human subjectivities and fundamental desires for recognition and social belonging. Indeed, the pleasure principle which he affords them, after trumpeting a formidable authorial voice of wrath, is all the more compelling, and readily induces them to submit to the laws of his discursive community.

What the rhetorical voice achieves, then, is the respect of its audience and a hierarchy of positions which ascribes power of knowledge to the author and an inferior but also resisting role to the audience. The latter is dominated and persuaded the more it is forced back into a regressive and quasi-infantile state of trust and need for societal inclusion. Arnot's rhetorical project proves ever more successful if he produces a cognitive dependency in his audience, if he is able to dispel the audience's sceptical and independent thought – that corrosive irony, as Gramsci has it – that might otherwise tarnish the polished surface of his polemical cameo.

Retributive Justice

Retributive justice is the anticipated pleasure that characterizes the *Vindication*'s persuasive power; it generates the gratification that justifies enduring painful struggle through (optimistic) belief in political salvation. In a contribution to the catalogue of "No Pasaran," the exhibition of the Spanish Civil War photo-reportage at Sheffield's Mappin Art Gallery (1986), David Mellor noted that the civil war's photo-reportage reached mass readerships across the world because of the authenticity and urgency of the photographer's existential involvement with the tragic scenes of massacre, "constituting photography's definitive break with the cool perceptions of modernism" (cf. Heron 1986, 23). Commenting on his analysis, Liz Heron remarked that the photographic image and its quality of freezing the intimacy of death and grief in the prolonged stare of the vicarious witness come close to a grim fascination that aestheticizes suffering and crystallizes it in the iconic character of its photo-journalism. "The clenched fists, the faces anxiously scanning the sky or contorted with grief, the body in combat, at the interface of death or victory, all occupy a continual present tense snatched from time: the meaning of lives is condensed in the drama of a decisive moment or a single gesture held out as an icon of heroism, suffering or revolutionary spirit" (Heron 1986, 23).

Such images become the emotive substance for reverence before the admirable patience of sufferers. The awesomeness of this heroism carries the memory of a conviction and hope for a better world, a hope that suggests how powerful the incentive of retributive justice can be in sustaining the faith of the people, in rationalizing their horrific plights as a prelude to redemption and in encouraging them to stand firm in the face of atrocity. Similarly, the *Vindication* manipulates this engaging affective principle of moral gratification, retrieved in some far-reaching and transcendent resolution of crisis, by punctuating its discourse with a variety of promises, thus recuperating the Marxist Morris, and ensuring that "neither the capitalist politicians, nor the official biographers will be able to rob the working class of his memory and his teachings" (Arnot 1934a, 5).

Through his invocation of Marx and Engels, Arnot's rhetorical appeal to his audience is similarly secured in his quotation from *The Communist Manifesto*, of which the crowning words are: "Proletarians have nothing to lose but their chains – they have a world to win" (Arnot 1934a, 15). The familiar reference to retributive justice is rehearsed in its most blatant and minimalist form. Sacrifice is so overwhelmingly presumed as a given mode of action that it is in fact annulled, and the duress of the struggle is abolished in the transcending moment of victory – "a world to be won."[16] As to the conquest of the Morris myth, the *Vindication* leaves its audience precisely on that final note of quasi-realized hope, stating its goal as a moral imperative: "It is high time that the Morris myth was destroyed; for the real Morris belongs to us, belongs to the revolutionary working class of Great Britain" (Arnot 1934a, 31).

Nor does the pamphlet end on the note of its own text; it derives further vibrations from the poetic finale of Morris's dirge honouring the martyr Alfred Linnell.

> Here lies the sign that we shall break our prison;
> Amidst the storm he won a prisoner's rest;
> But in the cloudy dawn the sun arisen
> Brings us our day of work to win the best.
> *Not one, not one, nor thousands must they slay,*
> *But one and all if they would dusk the day.*   (Arnot 1934a, 32)

The song exposes the final limit of workers' tolerance before authoritarian state oppression; but it responds with a sustained composure, prophesying unflinching resistance even in the face of some apocalyptic destruction.[17] Indeed, the ethos of this political stance is that of wholesale reversal which is predicated on total annihilation. Only this type of unmitigated victimization before the enemy will generate and thus warrant the brilliant return of the sun that may win the workers their "best."

As a statement that berates the offenders of a Marxist Morris legacy, the *Vindication* is a voice of protest but equally a declaration of imminent retributive justice that posits a higher satisfaction at the outset of its discourse. In surpassing the act of pure deconstruction, it projects a moral reward by conferring upon its own ideology a superior status and celebrating Marxism-Leninism in inverted style. But in its emergence from the world of protest, the tract carries an added rhetorical power; its intensity and compensatory action proffer positive value to the self-sacrificial character of the beleaguered and marginal movement of the political struggle. Comparably, if self-exile and self-restraint typified the nature of the Communist party under the strictures of the Comintern (1928–35), such sacrifices necessarily demanded recompense (cf. MacIntyre 1980; Howkins 1980; Samuel 1987). Thus, necessity was transformed into a virtue as the isolated condition of the Communist movement fostered a mentality of moral superiority. Conversely, participation in "bourgeois" culture implied ideological contamination. A preservation of Communist rectitude entailed a self-exclusion which endowed dignity upon those who subscribed to such an ethos of political separation. In this way, self-exile was cleared of any potential disgrace and transformed into the pride of an exalted martyrdom, not uncharacteristic of much Communist culture which collectively pitied itself for its history of suffering and revered itself for its untrammelled tolerance of setback and general discontinuity.

The revolutionary fighter and his martyrlike aspect constitute a determining principle of Communist mentality; he serves not only to depict the reality of social strife inherent in Communist historiography, but also to provide the relief of a transcending and retributive moral creed. Characterized by the martyr's profundity, historical clairvoyance, and laudable dismissal of phenomenal crises, the Communist political philosophy hinges on its compensatory moral overtones. Thus Arnot's tract exudes imminent gratification for his audience, granting them not only a promised truth – an objective and renewed Marxist Morris heritage – but also an elevated one at that. The singularity of Arnot's defence of Morris in 1934 beckons added applause, since his achievement is doubly strained by his individual and collective marginality in representing a dissenting Communist hegemony. This compensatory laurel, which an audience may objectively and vicariously confer upon Arnot's rhetorical enterprise, is seized by the polemicist himself as he transforms his peripheral appeal into an imperious, immanent, and triumphant voice of "truth," courtesy of the pamphlet's aesthetic retribution – the wishful promise, given both to himself and to his audience, to restore the Marxist Morris and dispel the ideological wrongs incurred by conservative Morrisania.

In so far as retributive justice grips the audience's narrative interest, it operates as a decisive lever in enforcing Arnot's principal message. Through the faith that it inspires in an audience, namely to concede to a morality of imminent reward, retributive justice acts as a law of equilibrium where debits are in the long term annulled. And in fostering a dependency on that future point of justice, rationale is invariably granted to the unknown, imposing, therefore, a non-rational acceptance of the absurdities and stresses relentlessly posed by the contingent present.

PART 3   THE SUBLIME HERO AND THE RHETORIC OF MARXIST THEORY

As rhetorical structures which enable the dissenting propagandist to win audience approval, pity, fear, morality, urgency, and retributive justice constitute both the intimidating and pleasure-forming devices which contribute to an affective discourse. But as elements that enable the rhetorician to foster an aesthetic mentality in his audience, these five categories are ultimately only the preparatory building blocks of the major non-rational component, the heroic principle. In his singular entity, the hero embodies these precusory forms, generating the ultimate instance of an aesthetic judgment through which the rhetorician transforms empirical reality from cognitive perception into an intensive totality. As he posits a normative addressee, the rhetorician comparably edifies himself as a representative of Marxist ideologues. In this, he prepares the audience's receptive attitudes for an aesthetic mode of perception, strongly determined by non-rational structures of consciousness. It is this frame of mind which permits the legitimate emergence of a heroic principle.

The figure of the hero serves to condense knowledge and facilitate cognitive reception. For the syntagmatic, or sequential, aspect of rationalist cognition is totalized into a paradigmatic unity, a rapid stroke of intuition that provides a preview of the associative chain of the doctrine as a whole. The hero is thus an aesthetic object that enables the receiving audience to organize its cognitive grasp of knowledge with a prefigurative sense of the entire philosophy. In addition, it is the familiar aspect of the hero, his human form, which offsets the estranging abstract and sequential logic imposed on an audience in the case of pure theory. The use of the heroic principle transcends Arnot's polemic. Indeed, one recognizes it in Gramsci's interpretation of Machiavelli's *The Prince*.

The basic thing about *The Prince* is that it is not a systematic treatment, but a "live" work in which political ideology and political science are fused in the dramatic form of a "myth." Before Machiavelli, political science had taken the form either of the Utopia or of the scholarly treatise. Machiavelli, combining the two, gave imaginative and artistic form to his conception by embodying the doctrinal, rational element in the person of the *condottiere*, who represents plastically and "anthropomorphically" the symbol of the "collective will." In order to represent the process whereby a given collective will, directed towards a given political objective, is formed, Machiavelli did not have recourse to long-winded arguments, or pedantic classification of principles and criteria for a method of action. Instead he represented this process in terms of the qualities, characteristics, duties and requirements of a concrete individual. Such a procedure stimulates the artistic imagination of those who have to be convinced, and gives political passion a more concrete form.   (Gramsci 1971, 125)

Lenin's *State and Revolution* functions comparably. Indeed, it is worth examining it closely, since it exhibits the peculiarities which the *Vindication* tends to assume in its rhetorical appropriation of revolutionary heroes.

The popular register of Lenin's pamphlet affords few opportunities for abstract verbiage. And yet the text remains philosophical in substance. Instead of highly wrought concepts unfolding in strictly logical fashion, we find aesthetic representations of dialectical materialism through the leitmotif of revolutionaries. In short, the pamphlet genre animates the often abstruse medium of theory through personifying techniques. Thus the opening paragraph of *State and Revolution* constructs a parallelism between the Marxist doctrine and great revolutionaries. This analogy broadens Lenin's claim that Marxism has been subjected to bourgeois distortion, misrepresentation, and general misapprehension; but it equally enlivens it through an elision that occurs in the description of the fate of revolutionary teachings:

What is now happening to Marx's doctrine has, in the course of history, often happened to the doctrine of other revolutionary thinkers and leaders of oppressed classes struggling for emancipation. During the lifetime of great revolutionaries, the oppressing classes have visited relentless persecution on them and received their teaching with the most furious hatred, the most ruthless campaign of lies and slanders … After their death, attempts are made to turn them into harmless icons, canonise them … At the present time, the bourgeoisie and the opportunists within the labour movement are cooperating in this work of adulterating Marxism. They omit, obliterate and distort the revolutionary side of its teaching, its revolutionary soul.   (Lenin 1932, 7)[18]

The subject in question is passive and non-human – Marxist and comparable revolutionary doctrines. Yet it is associated with the animating force of revolutionary thinkers, their defilement and institutional censorship. In the course of Lenin's rhetorical flourishes, this inanimate subject (revolutionary teachings) tentatively merges with the plight and essence of revolutionaries. In other words, Marxist political theory is ultimately construed as the butt of unmitigated persecution, of a "furious campaign of lies and slanders." Indeed, in this syntactical combination there is a convergence between the humanizing epithets and the abstract revolutionary doctrine. The teachings take on a life of their own, and not merely as "objects" but as virtual "subjects" endowed with a "revolutionary soul." In an aesthetic metamorphosis, the doctrine momentarily assumes a human face; Marxism is fictionally personified as a revolutionary hero, bringing the theoretical substance of Lenin's treatise to a more sensual rhetorical pitch; the use of the hero as a trope of political discourse becomes the aesthetic codifier of an otherwise arid conceptual exegesis.

This is indeed the model for Arnot's use of Morris as an aesthetic component which condenses knowledge (both of time and space) into a conceivable totality. In endowing the *Vindication* with its anthropomorphic appeal, Arnot must show Morris as the protagonist of a real and effective historical drama, exemplifying the concrete formation of a collective will (cf. Gramsci). Yet, like the Modern Prince himself, Morris cannot be a real person, only a complex structure. In this respect, the Communist Morris emerges as a Lukácsian typical hero who stands for something larger and more meaningful than his individual and isolated destiny. He is a concrete individual yet at the same time he embodies certain tendencies of a general collectivity (Jameson 1971, 192–6). But he is not any typical hero, for while he is endowed with a verisimilitude which is palpable and accessible to our perception, he is a fulcrum of identification which stands on the threshold of an abstract political philosophy that he harnesses semiotically in his sparse anthropomorphic form. Stripped of sensuous detail, the portrait of Morris remains estranged from immediate cognitive perception and in some sense from his claimants. There are few physical details offered to conjure up his identity: his traits are stark and etherealized into a realm of ineffability, a place beyond the "sensible"[19] world. As a martyr-hero, the Communist Morris is, consequently, ungraspable, save through intuitive or imaginative leaps.

As a structure of consciousness, such a hero compares with Benjamin's concept of the allegorical work of art, where allegory is "the privileged mode of our own life in time, a clumsy deciphering of meaning from moment to moment, the painful attempt to restore a continuity to heterogeneous, disconnected instants" (Jameson 1971, 72). Since the revolutionary cannot be grasped immediately, he is predicated on such a procedural phenomenology where it is imperative to use allegorical interpretation, to depart from the immediacy of sense perception and accept some radical break with conventional logic. For the revolutionary Morris is sublime in that his Marxist identity is not in tune with preestablished Morrisanias, with pregiven common sense. Arnot's dissenting rhetoric appears then as a "non-sense," a cognitive divorce which the allegorical mode of the sublime martyr-hero conveys in his very inexpressibility.

By contrast, Baldwin's representation of Morris produces a "beautiful" hero who incarnates a work of art in the symbolic mode, a mode which Walter Benjamin perceives as "the instantaneous, the lyrical, the single moment in time" (Jameson 1971, 72). As such, the symbolic form encapsulates meaning in a perfectly rounded fashion, leaving no space for misapprehension or further explication. The statesman's populist rhetoric adheres to platitudes and well-rehearsed assumptions; his hero necessarily appears as an immediately graspable object of perception. Arnot's revolutionary Morris, however, being allegorical, is abstruse and ambiguous. On the one hand, in a moment of naturalist verisimilitude, he colours and concretizes an abstract political philosophy with his anthropomorphic shape. On the other hand, he only grants a sparse sensuousness, quite removed from photographic naturalism. Were he gilded with the detail and flourish characteristic of conservative portraits, Arnot's Communist hero would lose his sublime character and sink into the immediacy of superficial phenomena. His sublimity is intended to preserve an aesthetic "asceticism" which ensures his aloofness and a hitherto unattained height; for only a martyr who has crossed over the threshold of death can pose as a prophet, illuminating the unknown utopia ahead. It is the magnitude of infinity at the frontier of which the sublime hero stands that grants him a yet unfelt and unexpressed greatness, one that triumphs, if only morally, over the parochialism of common sense and the realm of the sensible.

Severed into visually accessible and abstract facets, the sublime hero mimetically incarnates a structure of identification (his human form) and a relation of difference (his martyr aspect). In his vitality and activist life, he is immediately imagined. Yet as he sacrifices himself for some ulterior cause, his immediacy is dissolved into the nebulousness of death. Beyond this mortal threshold lies an infinity which must be totalized, awarded shape and palpability. But since the infinite is not part of the "sensible" world, it follows that the rationale which gives coherence to such unknown reaches is predicated on a metaphysical or "supersensible" contour. What cannot be seen must consequently be believed. In the concept of the martyr resides a principle of hope in which knowledge of the unknown is imposed through faith. For the material reality of death (i.e. the martyr's self-sacrifice) is annulled by a morality that justifies real loss as the necessary moment within a larger social process. The sublime hero is consequently the embodiment of a rationalist irrationality, a moral and thus seemingly rational cloak concealing an inner void or absence of reason.

As the semiotic expression of the unthinkable, the sublime figure consequently becomes the symbol of some superior ("immortal") rationality. He incarnates a dialectical epistemology which unifies identity and non-identity into a higher totality that transcends its warring inner forces. This sublation is the synthesis of individual identity and unknown otherness, aesthetically encapsulated by the martyr in his encounter with death, a conflictual juncture which is overcome by the moral virtue ascribed posthumously to the hero for his self-sacrifice. But if he is the aesthetic embodiment of a dialectical epistemology, he is not identical with that doctrine; his aesthetic form does not conform to that logic in any one-to-one relation. Logic and aesthetics are hardly coincident. But as a symbolic gesture, he nonetheless circumscribes that dialectical whole like a halo that encircles a negative space. Here his followers may visualize an encircling border around a totality which cannot be grasped save through tortuous mediations. Thus his subjects gain the illusory sense of mental control over a seemingly unknowable and unmanageable external world.

But in constituting that utopian urge, that shimmering ray of hope which enables followers to rationalize the absurdity of their discontinuous and nebulous present, he compels them to surrender their cognitive perception of historical immediacy and rise above the duress of crisis. In martyrlike fashion they are invited to overcome their individualism and conceive of their fate more broadly in terms of society and history. Such an ascetic submission by the individual to the community becomes the paradigm of a renunciation of personal scepticism in favour of a non-rationality. The paradigmatic structure of this process is the sublime hero himself whose anthropomorphic silhouette gives aesthetic form to an otherwise inaccessible and ungraspable infinity.

As the product of a dissenting ideologue, the martyr hero is a rhetorical device that issues out of the "problematic" character of a propaganda which is in search of an immediate, seamless unity of individual and community. In this search, the realization that such a totality is naïve and impossible within a dismembered and alienated society resurges fiercely. Despite this, the dissenter's rhetoric yearns for a prelapsarian simplicity, an identity that is sought, if only in fleeting instances, through the heroic form. Thus the martyr-hero, unlike the hero of earlier epics, is the result of a modern longing to recuperate that convergence between individual and society allegedly inherent in antiquity. Recognizing, however, the irretrievability of that societal unity, the martyr *projects* an alternative totality – not one of subject-object identity, but rather one of dialectical unity. (Cf. Lukács 1978b.)

Still, if this subject-object interaction produces a dialectical unity in aesthetic fashion, expressing the doctrine of a dialectical consciousness, the aesthetic moment cannot be readily translated into empirical conditions. For while the sublime hero is the allegorical structure for comprehending a set of subject-object dialectics, he is necessarily an intensive and extreme representation of reality. The object through which his identity is formalized is death. Yet such a polarity cannot be seen as the viable object through which human beings must objectify themselves. For that would merely prescribe a praxis of absolute self-destruction for each individual, an abnegation of humanity in the name of some higher but ultimately non-humanist cause.

The object of the hero's followers should not be death but rather society and history. The distinction between the sublime figure as exemplary model and the praxis of his subscribers has not always been clarified. In implicitly prescribing a dialectical unity between subject and object, the hero has posed significant difficulties for historical movements seeking to deploy him as an object of emulation. For example, neither Dutt nor Arnot is able to put forward a blueprint for transforming bourgeois intellectuals into Communist prototypes, into veritable proletarian heroes. Thus, they legislate exemplary individuals but always in a vacuum of polemical discourse that deletes the everyday aspects of revolutionary pursuits. A hero such as Morris would appear less than ideal were his personal confessions and weaknesses evidenced more readily. But Arnot never addresses Morris's dilemma in renouncing aesthetic preoccupations for the Cause. Morris's departure from artistic activity and his embrace of political activism is taken as a facile Hegelian negation of a negation, and the personal subjectivities and contradictions which haunt his politico-aesthetic ethos thereafter are short-changed. The hero unproblematically becomes a revolutionary socialist fighter, as if by some necessary teleology. Meanwhile, the weight of Morris's personal qualms regarding his martyr role as the backbone figure of the political and artistic movements which he founded is left untold. His correspondence with Georgianna Burne-Jones discloses some of these anxieties (cf. Boos 1982, 11), including his financial ease, the reservoir from which issued his extra power and material possibilities for the "revolutionary" task, but also the very source of his despair. In May 1889, in response to Joseph Lane, who had recently left the Socialist

League and criticized Morris harshly, Morris wrote: "you must make allowance for a man born and bred in the heart of capitalism, and remember that however he may rebel against the sham society of today we are all damaged by it" (Boos 1982, 13). Still, Morris's personal reflections on his quandaries are given a low profile in the *Vindication*, not to be sure for scholarly insufficiency but because the erection of a proletarian martyr-hero can only have rhetorical effect if he is presented as the symbol of a tragic austerity removed from the flux of routine life.

The sublime revolutionary hero can be misconstrued if he is not grasped as the *legislating* judgment that *directs* and shapes an empirical reality under his aegis. His formal qualities (i.e. his aesthetic embodiment of a dialectical unity) are removed from the realism of historical conditions so that a pure statement of "truth" may be expressed through his structure. But he is strictly unattainable and non-viable from an empirical point of view. He is not reproducible except as part of an aesthetic or tragic mentality that is irreconcilable with modern society. Instead, his purpose is to grant a moment of self-contemplation for activists caught in the relentless and all-consuming process of historical struggle. And in granting them a moment of leisure, a necessary break from the unceasing involvement in the travails of social action, where human subjects become engulfed in the myriad of life contingencies, the martyr figure poses as an icon of meditation. He is in himself, total and self-sufficient like a work of art under contemplative gaze. And in this respect, he offers his admirers a cultural objectification of themselves, an instant reflection of their *raison d'être* which otherwise could not be fathomed in the midst of fragmented mundane life.

But in so far as he is but a heuristic structure of consciousness, a form which illuminates the truth amid the complexity of dense and multiple appearances, he is an actor in a drama where the essential dialogue is one that is volleyed between himself as a tragic figure and death as his ultimate opponent. The dramatic setting in which the dialectics of the hero are played out produces an intensity in time, in urgency, and in absolute ethical meaning. The sublime martyr is the essence of a proletarian hero brought to his zenith. He embodies all those elements of the rhetorician's discourse which have been addressed thus far. Were one to amalgamate the aesthetic components that constitute the sublime hero's silhouette, one might envisage the pattern of distinctive parts thus: *pathos* and *terror* would determine the affective dimensions of an ancient tragedy from which the polemical genre springs and in which the sublime hero is implanted, *morality* and *urgency* would converge into an ethical idealism which underpins the ideological credo of the polemic. The imperative note of *urgency* inherent in the dramatic structures of the polemic would also provide the unspoken but irrationally felt authenticity of crisis as an ultimate day of judgment. *Retributive justice* would crest the polemic as the protest statement which serves to retrieve moral balance for the harsh losses inflicted on the protagonist of the discourse (the polemicist and his martyr subjects.) Thus the tragic hero would become the converging point of rhetorician and audience. With the heightened tragic self-awareness that is collectively reached (by audience and rhetorician) as an identification with the phenomenological trajectory of the hero, a metaphysical principle of retributive justice would reveal its imminent arrival and help sustain the faith of the audience in the reconciled though fateful circumstances of tragedy.

The sublime hero may consequently be construed as both the product and subsumption of all the constitutive forces of a tragic drama; he gathers the various components of social being (affective, epistemological, ethical, and metaphysical) into an absolutist prism of authenticated life where the shape and direction of existence is demarcated with utter clarity and best defined by a Manichean struggle of life and death. He is the prime catalyst of the tragic form, appropriated by his followers as an aesthetic means of governing objectivity. For by rearticulating life experience, he reenacts the adverse fate of humanity, fashioning it to suit human desire and the imperative need for self-affirmation.

This said, tragedy will not suffice in merely offering images of glorious transcendence of duress. It will also need to recreate the whole sequence of life in miniature, with its sacrifices and defeats, before it can muster forth the energy to invoke the poetic justice of heroism and tragic exaltedness. And for this reason, the mythical structure of the sublime hero contains within it not only the identical-subject object, the final flourish of martyrdom, but also the dialectical spiral of struggle as an imperative Calvary. As an ardent urge to prefigure the future and control the uncontrollable, the sublime hero may admittedly be idealist in bent; but his function as a utopian impulse is to energize social activity and to flesh out the dreams of humanity in concrete life. He responds to a subjective need that is profoundly ontological, and though irrational, hardly to be deemed incompatible with revolutionary discourse and its project of moving sentiments from torpor to praxis. Indeed, it is often the prefigurative and oracular character of this mythical being that facilitates the transmission of a Marxist theory of dialectics. For the delivery of a logic of dialectical materialism can only be enhanced by an expressive mode that is paradigmatic and thus capable of defining the whole sequence of the political philosophy through a microcosmic totality. The doctrine's believability and meaning are only fully seized when it can be held comfortably in a nutshell of thought.

Any rhetorical formulation of dialectics will imply a subjective reordering of temporality and epistemological perspectives. For in this process of representation, time is arrested phenomenologically and the dialectical process of life is extracted from its ceaseless adventures, thus allowing for a totalizing rendition of the theory. Then, with the hindsight of the owl of Minerva that takes flight at dusk, the theory, by means of a backward glance upon a historically prior moment, achieves its air of unity and completion, only to be thrust forward into a distant utopia as a beacon of guidance for social change.

For didactic, heuristic, or rhetorical purposes, the prefigurative and paradigmatic character of the sublime hero helps to trace a contour around the infinite complexity of reality. In this, it responds to the conditions of cognitive reception: the need to consolidate, to formalize and comprehend, to register subjectively the relentless and elusive movement of objectivity. Consciousness cannot assimilate or fully make sense of a flux of perceptions without organizing such data into unified structures of thought.

The utopian glimpse of political rhetoric is also an apparent cheat which coaxes the mind to leap over the otherwise necessary but tedious stations of an unfolding self-consciousness. Yet as such, this artifice is also the safety mechanism that helps social being resist the tedium of time's extensive convolutions and dialectical trajectory. Thus the phenomenological pretence that the whole can be visualized at any one point (be it retrospectively or prospectively) is none other than a hypostasis which is added to reality as an artificial means of perceiving the infinite with omniscience. But this contrivance is not necessarily pernicious. It is rather the screen which conceals the humiliating fact that we cannot apprehend permanent change with passive tranquillity and joyous immediacy. This mythical denial of the material contingencies and vulnerabilities of social being, this idealist foisting of desire upon an implacable and indifferent objectivity, is a human attribute of self-affirmation, a transcendence of external constraint. It defies an otherwise Nietzschean nihilism which thrives on a vortex of nothingness and hungers to destroy any trace of identity, indeed the very *telos* of social activity. In its sphere of aesthetic and moral constructs, myth (phenomenologically) subordinates necessity to human freedom and proffers the actors of history their possibility of visualizing both the route ahead and their defiant participation in the arena of action.

The presence of mythical forms (e.g. the sublime hero) in revolutionary rhetoric is not inconsistent with its theory, for every dialectical movement carries within it an instance of myth, and conversely, every myth is but an amplified instance of dialectics in aesthetic-dramatic shape. The spiral of dialectics, for instance, always arrives at a temporary stasis of serene perfection, a utopian ideal made possible by a stroke of irrationality – despite the rationalist character of dialectical materialism which seeks to annul all self-delusion and false consciousness. The unfolding of *History and Class Consciousness* is a case in point. Lukács's theory of revolution which pivots on the *Bildung*[20] of the proletariat follows a Hegelian trajectory, an ascending movement of the proletariat's subjective and objective aspects. Being both subject and object, this protagonist has the potential to hold a scientific standpoint of totality after having dialectically grappled with the forces of history, objectivity, and self-consciousness therein. Here, the attendant political, economic, and ideological struggles of the protagonist converge upon a perfect unity of theory and practice, a condition of identity that obliterates discrepancy and crystallizes conflict into a harmonious whole of subject and object, a consummate proletariat. But this entity which Lukács presents is ultimately an aesthetic construct, a flash of a utopian ideal that can only be grasped through a suspension of disbelief.

From a purist perspective, the collapse of the dialectical movement into a congealed instant of utopian perfection – an identical subject-object – appears to contradict the very purpose of dialectical materialism, namely to eliminate non-rationality from social consciousness. Did Lukács overlook this hitch in his own dialectical logic? And is this moment of non-rationality pervasive enough in dialectical thought to threaten the foundations of the philosophy as a whole? Hardly. We should only concern ourselves with the black hole of non-rationality that surfaces in dialectical thought if we remain undialectical about dialectics. Seen from another perspective, the static, utopian summit of the dialectical journey of the proletariat can be understood as a necessary illusion which acts rhetorically as the picture of a revolutionary destination, a home where one might come back to roost. For if, as Novalis has claimed, philosophy is a form of homesickness, so is the odyssey of the revolutionary proletariat, struggling and waiting to retrieve its hearth. But this home is paradoxically out of imaginative reach. The future (Communist) community is after all a black hole of unknowability, and all along, the identical subject-object of the proletariat has been (among other things) a means of blocking that darkness with a temporary totality, that of the social form of revolutionary consciousness. It is therefore the anthropomorphic silhouette more than any tapestry of utopian space that constitutes the material of radical propaganda. The classic motif is the martyr, the medium that best encapsulates the essence of dialectics in human shape. For the martyr is that figure who carries the interpenetrating tangents of subject and object in one thrust of being, facilitating an understanding of self-sacrifice as the humanist symbol of dialectical interaction itself. Recall Lukács's discussion of the exemplary revolutionary, Rosa Luxemburg (cf. Lukács 1971, 44), the anthropomorphic incarnation of a dialectical totality acquired through praxis. Recall the heroine's self-consciousness and rational lucidity. These prized features find their origins in Marx's definition of nineteenth-century proletarian revolutions, a portrait of unflinching Socratic self-examination, and intransigent, all-consuming pursuit of political truth. Proletarian revolutions, he writes,

criticise themselves constantly, interrupt themselves continually in their own course, come back to the apparently accomplished in order to begin it afresh, deride with unmerciful thoroughness the inadequacies, weaknesses and paltriness of their first attempts, seem to throw down their adversary only in order that he may draw new strength from the earth and rise again, more gigantic, before them, recoil ever and anon from the indefinite prodigiousness of their own aims, until a situation has been created which makes all turning back impossible and the conditions themselves cry out:
      Hic Rhodus, hic salta!
      Here is the rose, here dance!   (Marx 1977, 14)

As yet another example of dialectical theory expressed in rhetorical form, Marx's depiction of nineteenth-century revolutions heralds the Hegelian spiral that moves towards a self-consciousness purged of all epistemological myopia and incongruous reincarnations of tradition. Such a consciousness is the product of a relentless self-criticism and confrontation with the adversary that finally jettisons all reliance upon the matrices of past and future and achieves a self-possession that eclipses temporality. Following the imperative "Here is the rose, here dance!" the revolutionary subject enters into the eternal present of a performance, an existential equipoise of subject and object, an arabesque free of false props. Once more the coda of perfection emerges at the end of a tortuous cadenza of dialectical forces – a battle against the oppressive idealisms of alienated society. Of course, this culminating peak is but an artefact of desire. But as such, it is an aesthetic *tour de force* that resurges invariably at the apposite juncture of every dialectical sequence.

Considered closely, Marx's lyrical rendering of the dialectical spiral and its final resolution in the qualitative leap of the dance is but the ornamental side of Rosa Luxemburg's sublime endeavours and her eventual consummation of ethics in martyrdom. The image of the heroine's death and that of an exquisite balance signalled by the dance are two facets of the same instant of abstraction rendered aesthetically. In both cases, an artificial stasis is contrived to catch the best of proletarian praxis in a prism of totality. Nor is the rhetorical effect used for mere adulation of models of proletarian excellence. The utopian construct of the dance and Rosa Luxemburg *qua* martyr serve as measures of the absolute; they are ideal structures of thought and imagination by which lesser proletarian agents may judge themselves and steer their course through the duress of political action.

It is in the shift that political doctrine displays, as it moves from its pedestal of logic and enters the chariot of rhetoric, that the non-rationality of mythical expression comes to the fore. As Gramsci pointed out in respect to Machiavelli's *Prince*, political science assumes its most effective form when it dialectically weds science and ideology in the guise of a mythical being – an anthropomorphic entity that symbolizes both the rationality of a doctrine, and the initiative of individual agency and its mystique of heroic capability (Gramsci 1971, 125). For, if rhetoric is to bear an effect, it must not merely reproduce in ornate fashion the logic of its intended truth; rather it must destabilize the nonchalance of its public's mental attitude. And it can only do this once it has aesthetically reshaped the logic of political science into a dramatic scenario which eclipses calm rationalism in favour of the vitality produced by aesthetic devices.

It is not therefore surprising that among Marxist theorists, Rosa Luxemburg, Lukács, Marx, and the English Communists, the transmission of dialectical consciousness should assume an aesthetic shape – the proletariat as collective subject, a martyr who figuratively embodies in perfect unity the identity of subject and object. Clearly, the non-rational pause, the mythical structure which punctuates the logical concatenation of dialectics, is inescapable and not necessarily the mark of an insidious idealism. However, like any fairy tale, dream, or utopian mirage, the mythical entity is decidedly fleeting. Stretched beyond its historically specific moment, which may be no more than a flash, an instant of optimism, the sublime hero will lose his salubrious mythical force. He will merely lapse into a dogma and fail to offer an otherwise effective guideline for transformative praxis. Indeed, if the mythical entity slips into the rut of everyday life, then such a revolutionary ideal will not only become sclerotic and irrationally idolized, but his aesthetic qualities will jar with the detail and deficiencies of routine existence. His absolute perfection and martyr essence will be emulated doggedly, only to incur tragic defeat for his followers.

Indeed, it was precisely in public life (in Communist activist duty) that the attempt was made to reproduce the dramatic aura of the martyr, thus rendering political endeavours a means of authenticating individual experience and demeaning everyday needs and subjectivities. (Cf. Howkins's discussion of Edward Upward's trilogy *The Spiral*, Howkins 1980, 244.) Here the antinomies of bourgeois alienation were reproduced. As with the cleavage between the state and bourgeois society in which the former holds a spiritualistic and authentic relation to the latter as heaven to earth (cf. Marx 1843), so with Communist activists, the Communist party and its setting of ideal proletarian heroism stood in opposition to private individual bourgeois life as a celestial realm does to terrestrial existence.

This antinomic structure in revolutionary practice demonstrates that, despite their contestation of irrationalism, the Communist activists did not "cleanse" themselves of that canker from a "dying culture." The evasion of a sentimentalism linked to religiosity manifested itself in radical intellectuals abandoning their ivory towers and plunging into the political fray. Yet this sentimentalism that was shunned as the symptom of societal malaise was not truly jettisoned. Instead it was submerged into the undertones of the political journalism which Communist praxis entailed. By adopting non-fictional forms of public address and socially committed poetry (e.g. the pamphlet, political reportage, politically couched literary forms), Communist ideologues seemed to have dispelled the irrationalism which they denounced in their ruling-class counterparts, and in modernist literati. Yet, while appearing to have abandoned their ground of unconscious desires (surrendering it, according to Bloch, to fascist annexation), they in fact only buried their irrational drives – drives which resurfaced elsewhere in new incarnations. The latter consisted in a variety of persuasive discourses and political writings which were only apparently emancipatory. Here was a world of Communist aesthetic expression that seemed to flourish with impunity, since bourgeois individualism in the form of esoteric, intellectual, or artistic pursuits had been cast aside in favour of a "salutary" political practice. Shifting from the overtly aesthetic world of literary creativity to collective interaction with society, writers such as Edward Upward, John Cornford (cf. Howkins 1980, 244), and Arnot himself (who majored in literary studies at Glasgow) formed a wave of intellectuals who deserted élite culture. Their conversion to activism was based on the presumption that bourgeois individualism could be remedied through total immersion in politics. They did not, however, foresee that their idealization of activist roles became another aestheticizing, indeed reifying condition of bourgeois individualism. Their desired interaction with society was hampered by the ethical absolutism of their sectarian worship of heroic revolutionary warfare and of exemplary activists in whose image they pursued the Cause. Preoccupied with their moral posture as Marxist missionaries, they overlooked the necessity of addressing the vulnerabilities of the ordinary citizen,[21] his inability to pose readily as an epic hero of class war. Thus the proletarian model of William Morris, however dressed in Communist garb, however decisive in inspiring followers, did not and would not necessarily help dissolve the malaise of capitalist reification. For while his mythical stature galvanized and empowered his disciples to adopt dissenting values and manage the conflictual reality of political crisis, the hero could not ward against the possibility of being reified into an irrational entity himself by his most fervent claimants.

CHAPTER SIX

"England, Our England": The Sublime Poetics of Communist Community

In the last months of his life, especially, [Ralph] Fox's thoughts dwelt very much on the "great refusal" of present-day writers to face reality as a whole, the cynicism and atrophy which leave the way open for the enemy. This "fear of life, the effort to keep out of the community of humanity," means self-exile from the greatest spirits of all ages, from the "spiritual community binding together the living and the dead" which is our cultural heritage. "We would not be rejected from this community: and therefore do we hope," says Wordsworth. "Hope," writes Fox, "will return on that condition alone, that we are not rejected from the community." (Torr 1937, 6)

not english?
a Reminder for May Day

WHO are the english,
according to the definition of the ruling-class?
All you that went forth, lured by great-sounding names
which glittered like bubbles of crystal in your eyes
till they burst and you burst with them, shot to shreds
from one end of the shuddering earth to the other end,
shot that the merchant's pockets might clink and bulge,
shot that hoardings of imperial size
might fill each blank space of the motor-roads
with pink whore-faces beckoning the bankrupt to buy –
you are the english,

your ruling-class has said it,
you are the english,
keep then the recompense of a sounding name, for you have
nothing else.

Or you, the ragged thief, fruit of the press-gang, gallowsbird
flogged to a scarlet-breasted musketeer,
you, too, splintered your bones to build an Empire;
and now that names are lost in the desolation of moons
snow-drifting on the war-gnawed litter of history,
the dump of bones, you starveling, accept your share
with those whom the great-sounding names or greed
drew with drum-flams to death in distant places,
while Flanders mud flakes off the latest dump,
you are the english,
your ruling-class has said it.

And shuffle along you toilers on whose cowed faces
the heels of your betters have left bleeding badges
as proof of your allegiance. Shuffle along,
all you thrifty cotters saved from brotherhood by Wesley,
all you farmhands sweated out of thought,
all you slum-denizens humbly paying pence
to keep a bishop in Christian poverty,
all you shophands beaten over the brain
till you can only answer, "O let's go to the pictures,"
all you that lick the hand providing dope,
you readers of the national newspapers,
absorbing fascism and astrology
with your list of winners and hire-payment systems,
you are the english,
your ruling-class has said it.
Keep then the recompense of a sounding name, for you have
nothing else.

I call instead on those who are not the english
according to the definition of the ruling-class.
We'll step back first six hundred years or seven
and call up the peasants hoarsely talking under the wind,
their cattle stolen by the king's purveyors,

their wives deceived by whining hedge-priests.
Peasants, leaving your wattled huts to haunt
the crooked dreams of Henry with your scythes,
unrolling a long scroll you couldn't read
though you knew the word it held, not England,
but Justice – come, you peasants with hoof-smashed faces,
speak from the rotting wounds of your mouths, we'll understand,
prompting you with our anger.

I talked with John Ball, I was out with Jack Cade,
I listened to Wicliffe, I was burnt as a Lollard.
Come with us, peasants waking from fumes of charcoal,
into the wintry dawn, while the cattle stamp,
leap from your straw bed, leave the blowsy ale-wife,
someone has called and you have taken your fork
against the thundering cataphract of power.
When Adam delved and Eve span,
who was then the gentleman?
You are not english, peasant,
your ruling-class has said it.
Come with us then, for our love and our indignation
conjure you out of the dung, and we'll avenge you.
Come with us, peasant, we've the wind in our teeth,
we're out in the night, hunting, but not to trample
the crops of the poor, we have another quarry.
Rise up, peasants listening to the many voices,
fall in behind us, you are not english, comrades.

I call on those who left the little farms
and left the common lands at Parliament's voice
to chase the grave and comely henpecked king.
I call on Cromwell's Ironsides and the men
who listened to the many voices blown, distracted,
birdcries out of the thicket of blood-darkness,
and answered awry, glamoured by dark phrases,
the slaughtered Lamb, the flayed carcass of their lives,
the unremitting call to follow truth,
to follow a bond denying their present slavery,
broken by harsh echoes from the unploughed thicket.

Come, you Anabaptists and you Levellers,
come, you Muggletonians, all you Bedlamites,
fall in behind us, you are not english, comrades.

Come, you Luddites, come you men of the Charter,
singing your songs of defiance on the blackened hills,
invoking the storm, the whirlwind, being surer now,
deciphering at last the certain earth behind
the many voices confusing the moonstruck mind.
Come from the mines and the looms, come from the ploughlands,
come and tramp the streets of Birmingham and London,
the dragoons are waiting to split your skulls, my comrades
for you are not english, you angry millions, you workers,
your voice snarls in the clang of the flaring foundry,
your voice rips louder than raven-caws at the morning,
you are speaking out and you were not meant to speak,
you are waking, comrades,
you are not english now,
your ruling-class has said it.
You spoke at Glasgow and the Clyde when terrorism
was chaining all men in the roaring jail of war;
you will speak louder yet.

Stand out one of the men who were not english,
come, William Morris,
you that preached armed revolt to the workers and said
of the men who died for us in the Commune of Paris:
We honour them as the foundation-stone
of the new world that is to be.
You that cried out after Bloody Sunday:
Not one, not one, nor thousands must they slay,
but one and all if they would dusk the day!

And stand out, you the unknown weaver,
who wrote in the Poor Man's Guardian of 1832,
before Marx had shown us how the thefts were made:
The profit is that which is retained and never paid back.
There is no common interest
between working-men and profit-makers.

You were not english, we are not english either –
though we have loved these trees plumed upon the sunset
and turned back to the area-rails our prison-bars;
though we have followed the plough like a hungry rook,
with love for the brown soil slicing fatly away,
to haunt in the end the dingy rain of the street
where a prosperous spilth of warming music
trickled through drawn blinds on our beggar-senses;
though we have crept into the daisy-light of the dew
to wake once more in the dripping tenements;
though we have plucked hazelnuts in the lane of autumn,
making faces at the squirrel, to kiss between laughters,
that was not our land, we were trespassers,
the field of toil was our allotted life,
beyond it we might not stir though blossom-scents
left tender trails leading to the heart of summer;
though we have loved this earth where our sweat and our tears
drained through the thankless centuries, though we lay
long nights of agony digging our fingers deep
in the wet earth, yet the bailiffs evicted us,
it was all taken away, England was taken,
what little of it was ours in desperate toil
was taken, and the desperate toil remained,
and lanes of dank gloom where the echo of midnight falls,
a late wayfarer stumbling, leaving nothing behind
except the gaslight coughing and the crying child,
milk turned sour in the thunder-hour awaiting,
queues at the Labour Exchange while the radio squeals
in the shop nearby, and nothing remains, nothing
except the mad-faces forming from the damp-stains on the
plaster,
the scabs of sickness and the jagged edge
of tins in the bucket, and the knock on the door,
and the child crying and the bug-heats, hunger,
and the child crying,
and the radio-message through crevices of the dark silence,
Workers of the World ...
Listen, hold up your head, it wasn't the rat
whisking under the coal-scuttle, it wasn't the lodger
stealing back scared from the woman under the bridge.

In this hour even the flower-lips speak. It is
the augural moment declared by frenetic guesses,
come clear at last. The moon-slit whispers, the rafter
creaks to a new pulse stirring, the bough of silence
cracks with a quick decision, men softly creeping
through forests of hardship to surprise the drunken castle.
Lift up your head,
listen, you Rhondda miners, you Durham miners,
the radio-voice is seeping through the barriers,
Workers of the World ...
They are awake at Bleanleachan, men are stirring,
reaching out their hands, the moon sets in the coal-tip,
the fans of the air-shaft whirr like a giant breathing.
Come, changelings of poverty, cheated of the earth,
Albion or Land of Brut or Avalon,
Coal-ghetto that was once the Isle of Apples,
call it what you will, there must be in it
Soviet Republic.
England, my England –
the words are clear
Workers of the World, unite!
The voice comes pealing through the trumpet of the night,
You have nothing to lose but your chains!

The sunlight breaks
like waves on a shingly beach, sweeping the mountains
with more than the sough of pines.
This morning is of men as well as light,
its unity is born from the sweat of mingled toil,
it springs from the earth of action, it is ours
and England. We who made it, we are making
another England, and the loyalty learned
in mine and factory begets our truth,
this compact linking us to past and future.
The workers take the world that they have made!
unseal the horns of plenty, join once more
the severed ends of work and play; and if the thieves
challenge our coming, we have learned the might
of sledges falling, the turbine's fury, the craft
of dynamos winding energy from the elements.

In vain they turn their guns and poison gas on those for whom
electricity rears its unseen fortress,
the sun drops shrapnel of light upon their ranks
but feeds our renewed bodies; the womb of earth
cries for our seed. No others have the thews
to make this earth, this England, breed to her desire.
The disinherited are restored, our mother,
England, our England,
England, our own.   (Lindsay 1936, 353–7)

The years of the Popular Front saw the beginnings of a new attitude towards mobilizing popular consciousness. This altered strategy entailed relinquishing the purely negative stance of stringent internationalism (with its implicit suppression of national self-identification) and supplanting it with an alternative nationalism, one that would retain the virtues of Englishness while eliminating its attendant imperialism. But could this concerted effort to connect with the sensibility of the people prevent the ethics of radical dissent from blending with its adversary's discourse? In the process of forging a Communist Englishness (underpinned by class and national consciousness), dissenting propagandists faced the challenge of rearticulating and wresting the language of identity from conservative rhetoric without carrying over its ideology. It was a challenge that they virtually met during the Popular Front period, especially at the height of anti-fascist struggles, and most notably in Britain's war effort against Nazi Germany after 1941. In 1936, however, Communist propaganda was only just emerging from the shackles of an ascetic internationalism and opening its horizons to new forms of collective expression. The poem "not english?" (1936) by the Communist poet, historian, and social critic Jack Lindsay, is an example of that period of transition. Arching over two distinct historical junctures (the Class-Against-Class years and the Popular Front), it lyrically projects a dissenting national culture, adamantly united against ruling-class jingoism, yet still groping for an alternative vision of Communist Englishness. It is this Communist search for a political home of local English colour that "not english?" encapsulates: and it is the category of the sublime – in its diverse permutations and unfolding stages – that illuminates the rhetorical odyssey of propagandists expressing the hitherto unutterable marriage of Communism and nationalism. For the category of the sublime does not only reflect the hidden irrationality embedded in the worship of the martyr hero (cf. chapter 5), it also reveals the latent nationalist consciousness of a self-determining collectivity which seeks a suitable discourse of legitimation for its political empowerment.

In its resolute castigation of bourgeois nationalism, "not english?" represents the spawning of a Communist selfhood. But the emergence of a self-determining class, seeking to supersede the existing hegemony, does not arise of itself. It is contingent on the instrumental intervention of a rhetorician who urges the underclass to reconstitute itself: to depart from its rulers, to abandon traditional epistemologies (common sense), to reorientate itself through tumult and transition, and finally to redefine its coherence and *raison d'être* with assurance and self-possession. Indeed, in a flourish of revolutionary fervour, the rhetorician invites the oppressed social group to rehearse its plight and play out its drama of liberation on an imaginary public stage. His rallying call to arms, his lyrical protest constitutes a political *Bildung*,[1] not dissimilar to Arnot's *Vindication,* yet distinct in that it is highly conscious of its audience. However, as a didactic statement, it is hampered by a dearth of suitable signifiers. In this, the propagandist fails to summon forth a most crucial component of rhetoric – sensuous, perceptible images of a utopia which would readily capture the audience's imagination. He resorts instead to a tortuous phenomenological discourse that must reconcile dissonance with ideal form, dispersal and negativity with an allegorical projection of Communist commonweal. Only after dramatizing conflict and duress can the rhetorician register the collective identity of his disciples with palpable immediacy and thereby offer them their desired sense of authentic Englishness.

Symbolizing the unutterable, the boundless, and the incommensurable, the category of the sublime aesthetically portrays the ideologue's quandary. Radically in conflict with the sensible world, the sublime fails to find any objective (i.e. conventional) standards with which to consummate its judgment. But consummate its totality it must, and with this imperative it recedes into its own subjective interiority where objectivity is transcended and coherent meaning is secured in the Olympian heights of the supersensible realm. As "a magnitude which is like itself alone, ... not to be sought in the things of nature, but only in our ideas" (Kant 1951, 88), the sublime cannot express its meaning directly through signifiers issuing from the existing social or natural environment. Its judgment can only be formed once it has fiercely contested the sensible realm and endured a phenomenological transfer to another state of mind. The experience of the dissenting rhetorician is analogous; for once his condemnations of ruling-class nationalism (imperialism) have been

voiced, his redemptive political manifesto can no longer issue out of the
repertoire of the existing hegemonic discourse. Still, he must wrest the
legitimacy of Englishness away from the corpus of political duplicities
linked to imperialism while maintaining his recalcitrance in a gesture of
adamant dissent. Though his discourse remains fettered to a field of
communication dominated by the ideological foe, his break with mainstream ideology entails a poetic dismantling of commonsense forms of
totality, images of plenitude, harmony, and lyrical beauty. A dissonant
expression of anger and vengeance is formalized instead, circumscribed
and granted legitimate value under the aegis of a wholly distinct sphere
– an imaginary world wrought out of poetic artifice.

In "not english?" this ideological caesura with mainstream discourse
is produced specifically through an historical and dramatic break in the
poem's narrative. Transporting his following from the 1930s to the
fourteenth century, the ideologue performs a rhetorical "seance," invoking peasants and labourers in turn to rise out of history into the
timelessness of a poetic drama. As he dons the cloak of guardian angel
and stirs the peasants to join a movement of dissent, the rhetorician
cries out:

> Come with us, peasants waking from fumes of charcoal
> into the wintry dawn, while the cattle stamp,
> leap from your straw bed, leave the blowsy ale-wife
> someone has called and you have taken your fork
> against the thundering cataphract of power.

Arriving in the night to shake the peasants from their torpor and
rouse them to dire revolt, the ideologue deploys the technique of
nocturnal awakening as an aesthetic device by which to effect the
impossible. Indeed, like a conjurer, he draws his audience from out of
the dung and brings them into a dream-space outside everyday consciousness; here an as yet unrealized political movement is mustered.
From the depth of the night, from the inarticulate mutterings of the
wind, and from the hoarse and scarcely audible self-affirmations of the
peasants whom he coaxes to come forth, the audience is rallied together
through the atmospheric setting of blustery darkness. A luminous epiphany is coupled with the lucidity of a radio voice that peals through the
"trumpet of the night." Thus, as the hoarseness of peasant ire turns into
the clarity of the modern media, as the obscurity of history's countless
popular struggles crystallizes into the utopian projection of a renewed

England, the rhetorician's appeal increases its crescendo and visual sharpness to lend definite form to the otherwise amorphous underclass.

In spiralling through its stages of articulacy, "not english?" aesthetically replicates a surging revolutionary consciousness where scratchy voices of discontent evolve into defiant propagandist pronouncements such as: "Workers of the World ... ", "you have nothing to lose but your chains." The unfolding pattern parallels the developing clarity that governs the stations of the sublime, a judgment which stumbles in the foggy atmosphere of cognitive confusion in search of a moment of dazzling supersensible vision. Indeed, the relation between the *dynamic* and *mathematical* sublime, between the sublime imagination and reason, sheds light on *the relation between the propagandist and the emerging self-consciousness of his popular following.* This correlative structure between sublimity and political persuasion is less evident in Arnot's tract. For there the attempt to interact and reach out towards the audience is expressed through a portrait of Morris's sublime heroism. But in Lindsay's "not english?" the category of the sublime does not only serve to illustrate incommensurability, allegorical opacity, and the dissonance of class struggle. Here it is the distinctive moments of the dynamic and the mathematical sublime that foreground the *respective identities* of propagandist and audience. In Arnot's *Vindication*, this crucial relationship remains, at best, obscure. Lindsay's poem, by contrast, is a self-conscious poetic statement on the process of communication and of winning consent.

Given its tension between reason and imagination, the sublime provides the aperture from which to peer into the performative relationship between rhetorician and public. Indeed, in his aesthetic creativity, the rhetorician, like reason, must forge an imaginary identity from chaos incurred by societal transition; it is he who must effortlessly and imperceptibly reverse a conventionally meaningless concept such as "not english" into an accessible and, indeed, potent signifier – Communist Englishness – that will instil in his following their much-sought sense of fullfilment.

Resembling the external force of sublime reason, the propagandist plays an active role in facilitating his audience's mental grasp of the unfathomable destiny of political revolution. In keeping with the mentality of the Popular Front intellectual, he assumes a didactic and salvational posture as educator of the masses (cf. Coombes 1980.) But his task can only be achieved if he throws his following into a state of despair and confusion, forcing them to relive their oppression as agrarian

and industrial toilers victimized by immorality and pecuniary greed. To
intensify their feelings of anxiety and distress, he sensuously depicts their
precarious lives and the relentless buffets which they receive from a
merciless (social and natural) setting. Through images of peasants talking under the wind with "hoof-smashed faces," with "rotting wounds"
and "blowsy ale-wives," he reproduces the agony of a labouring class,
subjected to the brutal misery of "wattled huts," humiliating evictions
from the land and degrading endless toil. Retelling the narrative of the
oppressed, the propagandist creates an ambience of disarray and defeat,
a seeming doom which is imperative for the rhetorical project that seeks
to induce and capture trust from a vulnerable audience stumbling
pitifully in the debris.

After being raked over the coals for its cognitive failure, the sublime
imagination submits to reason wholly. It renounces its pride so as to
receive the only succour it can get, namely reason's redemptive gesture.
But the lapse of the imagination into a state of cognitive and affective
depression is also imperative for reason's final project: to assert itself as
the voice of an infinite totality. Reason's rise to prominence hangs on
the imagination's descent into the Hades of self-abnegation. Similarly,
the dissenter's following must rehearse the agony of its class narrative
and experience the distresses of its class oppression so that its surrender
to the ideologue will justify his rhetorical appeal and self-edification. It
is not incidental, therefore, that the rhetorician sows affective and
cognitive confusion into the consciousness of his public. Calling the
workers to sever relations with mainstream nationalists, he compels
them to recognize that it is not in their class interest to align with the
ruling class and its sycophantic followers. The working class must
determine its identity on the basis of its own class position and not of
some false concept of nationhood.

However, like the sublime imagination, the dissenting audience is left
with a disconcerting and disorientating representation of reality, one of
contending forces rather than of unity and coherence. For in demystifying the glories of capitalist Englishness, and in puncturing the fallacy
of some continuity of Englishness within the nation-state, the rhetorician makes it impossible for his public to construe the ruling class as
compatriots. Simultaneously, though, their dissociation from the hegemony and their loss of an official national identity leaves the dissenting
crowd (temporarily at least) in a state of limbo.

In this intensification of cognitive and affective unease, the audience's
interest cannot be sustained for long. Placed in the excluded position

of marginality, bewildered and pained by its own "pathetic" legacy of defeats and oppressed circumstances, the audience is unable to make sense of its destiny, indeed, of its *raison d'être*. Like the sublime imagination which fails to accept the ceaseless and painfully disruptive apprehension of the infinite (short of an immediate totality or form of intuition), the despairing audience of Lindsay's narrative cannot abide by the aesthetics of sheer loss, sacrifice, and gruelling adversity. Such discontinuity is akin to the cognitive processes of Kantian "understanding," a faculty which merely dissects reality and does not reintegrate the pieces into a humanly accessible form. The imagination would be totally destroyed if its perceptual faculties were continually subordinated to the privileged abstractions of rational understanding. Indeed, its mental block is conceivably a resistance to potential self-destruction. Comparably, the audience of a dissenting rhetorician would wither into lifeless resignation were it to adhere exclusively to images of martyrdom and devastated life – to semiotic forms of human agony and meaninglessness. Cognitively disturbed by the imagery which the rhetorician invests in his protest against English imperialism, the audience, like the sublime imagination, urgently requires some cognitive assistance. But since it has no guiding force other than the narrator/ideologue, it can rely on him alone for aid.

The rhetorician has thus to raise his protagonists from the murkiness and chaos of loss, lead them to regain their dignity, and enable them to acquire the status of tragic heroes whose moral triumph is intended to win the day. For having placed his audience in a state of discomfort, he may now afford himself the power to swoop in as a *Deus Ex Machina* and guarantee a promising *dénouement* to the fate of the proletarian subject. Thus he awakens the labourers from their torpor (symbolically, their resignation to fate) and inspires them to listen and raise their heads with pride, declaring:

Lift up your head,
Listen, you Rhondda miners, you Durham miners ...
They are awake at Bleanleachan, men are stirring,
reaching out their hands, the moon sets in the coal-tip,
the fans of the air-shaft whirr like a giant breathing.

Assuming a prompter's role, the rhetorician taps the proletarian energy of his audience through a vigorous rehearsal of their tradition of struggle. Variously, he imposes the much-desired rationale for an otherwise bewildering and unsettling history of loss. He offers a reason for overcoming conflict, yet simultaneously he justifies the sacrifices which are entailed in the praxis of martyrdom that is so pervasive among the early dissenters of English history.

> Come, you Luddites, come you men of the Charter,
> singing your songs of defiance on the blackened hills, ...
> Come from the mines and the looms, come from the ploughlands,'
> come and tramp the streets of Birmingham and London,
> the dragoons are waiting to split your skulls, my comrades ...
> come, William Morris,
> you that preached armed revolt to the workers and said
> of the men who died for us in the Commune of Paris:
> *We honour them as the foundation stone*
> *of the new world that is to be.*
> You that cried out after Bloody Sunday:
> *Not one, not one, nor thousands must they slay,*
> *but one and all if they would dusk the day!*

Martyrdom grants the rhetorician one of his principal expedients for rationalizing unrest and for engendering a paradoxical negative pleasure, a crown of moral gratification to an audience identified with the victims of class conflict. Sacrifice of this kind is certainly characteristic of a more general Communist mentality which Raphael Samuel has explored in his saga on the lost world of Communism: "Promethean ethics in which to take up arms against a sea of troubles was the highest test of Communist character. Passivity was 'ignoble,' the expression of a slave mentality. Resistance was heroic. Class struggle was both a universal condition and an absolute moral good. It was the 'real education' of the masses. It steeled the will and strengthened character. It made subaltern classes masters of their own destiny, arbiters of their fate. Morally too the struggle was redemptive, encouraging the individual to sacrifice immediate comfort for the sake of higher things" (Samuel 1987, 62).

But while rhetorical exhortations derivative of Promethean ethics refer to the real pangs of workers' oppression, in the poem such hardship is prized from its material source and becomes a virtual conceit. Images of misfortune and misery are transmuted into raging voices of fury. Cumulative examples of martyrdom, victimization and general pathos further the innocence of the community of workers, endowing them with a moral height and with a deserved promise of future reward. Their diligent toil and fidelity to each other is not only an emblem of virtue, but a fortitude that inspires belief in retributive justice, in some ulterior resolution of crisis. Thus the rhetorician can claim that "we who made it, we are making / another England, and the loyalty learned / in mine and factory begets our truth ..." By analogy, as the sublime imagination is tormented by its cognitive impasse, reason intervenes to persuade it that there is logic to the "madness" of its baffling object. Hope resides in a future or higher principle of meaning which will, through time, dispel the imagination's cognitive disarray, provided it surrenders its judgment to its rational superego. As to the Communist audience, we find its rhetorician reassuring the members of his ideological ensemble with sketches of a future commonweal; suddenly, recognition of the rugged experiences of activism and class unrest is eclipsed in honour of the forthcoming utopia, the advent of a new England.

What compels an audience to submit is not merely the moral pleasure resulting from its virtuous efforts, crowned by the golden innocence of suffering, but also a negative pleasure derived from ignorance and from the surrender of individual subjectivity and difference to the higher powers of "knowledge," to a community of moral laws and customs embodied in the *Deus Ex Machina*, the rhetorician himself. For with the ignorance or cognitive confusion displayed by a defeated audience, respect is aroused for a leader who assumes a posture of prophetic wisdom and far-reaching knowledge. Thus, the audience of a Communist propagandist event experiences peculiar delight in the awesomeness of a superior being who takes responsibility for its future destiny and who, therefore, becomes an absolute guarantor of security. Of course, his authority is contingent on preserving a portion of their ignorance and trust. For only then can he ensure that they surrender to his poetic contrivances.

Note the propagandist's imposition of meaning onto a fitful history of workers issuing from distinct chronological epochs. As he appeals to a set of martyred English toilers, he disentangles the proletarian identity from its ties with ruling-class nationalism, and graces them with the ennobling title of comrades. Yet this crowning title hypostatizes a spectrum of dissenting movements without due respect for their historical differences. Luddites, miners, men of Glasgow, peasants, and unknown weavers are aesthetically linked together into a celebrated non-englishness, into an unsung English radicalism. Still, this artifice, which has legitimated the negative relation of non-englishness, has also spawned an amalgam of forces which acquires an overriding social value, not merely of reaffirmed comrades but of transcending workers of the world. Such a supersession appears deeply gratifying in its moral empowerment, for the international dimension of the workers of the world has cemented and validated a community ethos by exceeding the parochialism of national frontiers. This new collectivity not only measures up to that of imperialist England, but indeed far surpasses it, both in number and in moral truth. In this rhetorical achievement, the ideologue creates a unified totality out of an otherwise dispersed series of counter-hegemonic forces; in so doing, he endows them with a renewed identity, one that is resurrected from their ashes of despair and brought to the far-reaching power of an infinity objectified in limitless internationalism. In this compensatory act which stills contradiction and gratifies his audience's wish for stable identity, he justifies their submission of trust.

This transcending effect can be clearly comprehended through the sublime aesthetic. For when an ungraspable object is presented to the mind and conflict arises between cognitive and aesthetic perception, between the understanding and the imagination, Kantian reason imposes a unifying logic to resolve the tension between the warring faculties. This unity crystallizes as a result of a pause secretly granted to the mind, a moment in which recapitulation and integration of perceptions can occur through a break of real time. In essence, reason compels aesthetic comprehension to suspend temporal progression and harness a moment of absolute timelessness through a denial of historical movement. In freezing time, this aesthetic consciousness creates space within the linearity of an ongoing process. Reason circumscribes a totality around the infinite and ever-moving universe of the supersensible realm in order to derive a logic from an otherwise elusive and unknowable reality. The imposition of unity and coherence on the unfathomable cosmos is thus merely an artifice of faith. For while reason parades as a form of veritable knowledge, it is in fact but a moral disguise of non-rationality.

The rhetorician's performance similarly involves suspending time. This offers the audience a necessary unity by which to grasp and believe in the validity of a difficult discourse: e.g., the justification of sacrifice in the cause of revolution, the depiction of an opaque Communist future, etc. Like reason, the rhetorician's rationalizing performance is determined by artifices that efface material discrepancies. His rhetorical address entails leaping over material causality and incurring a new temporal order as poetic refuge. "We'll step back first six hundred years or seven" and enter a timeless world where the ideologue can delineate a place apart from real history and thus, for a tentative, rhetorical instant, grant the impression of some unifying community of comrades. This aesthetic unity which he engenders saves the audience from bewilderment and moral gloom as they face their socio-political exclusion from mainstream society. Thus, the condensation of time into a "poetic" or imaginary space produces a vision of solidarity among distinct oppressed groups, just as "reason" creates a moral transcendence that sweeps the imagination up from its state of cognitive defeat.

Now while the audience's mental needs have been assuaged in the creation of an ideological community, the ideologue has yet to address his public's affective unease, to raise them from the mire of impotence and resignation to the heights of power and new-found autonomy. In a gesture of identification, he fuels his audience's rage and stirs their consciousness of history's martyr-ghosts. Having already rehearsed the pathos of their oppression, he is now compelled to harness their sentiments of self-pity and channel them to some concrete action, namely revenge. Protest and anger are consequently deployed as a mode of giving aesthetic form to anarchic emotion, and of simulating the fiery energy of rebellious conquest. Not only does the choleric tone of the ideologue's verse incite action, rallying the popular masses to the cause, but it infuses each member with an aesthetic power. Similarly every strenuous affection in Kant's sublime is an excitement of consciousness and an incitement to overcome obstacles. Wrath is specifically a trait of the dynamic sublime and it corresponds to a desire for transcendence or psychic redress, just as the aesthetic forms of anxiety of Communist propaganda more generally are the catalysts of inspiration, transformative action, and social praxis. The role of lyricized anger here recalls Arnot's Leninist polemic against the centenary's sentimentalism. The choleric tone in both writings functions as an impulse intended to galvanize social movements; yet it is also the dissonance of a counter-hegemonic voice that seeks to out-cry that pious and saccharine jingle of imperialist nationalist sentimentalism. Thus the songs of defiance which invoke the storm, the whirlwind, and the increasingly loud clamour of factory protest contain a pride expressed euphonically in the surging volume of rhetoric, a crescendo symbolic of desired hegemonic strength. The aesthetic contemplation of sublime storminess and fierce elemental rage suggestively depicts sentiments of worker resistance. Such adversity is ultimately transformed into a peculiar moral pleasure. For once the rude experience of revolutionary sacrifice is overcome by the calming attitude of a "rational" mind, the horror of tragedy is annulled and transformed into a stimulus which provokes an emotive exaltation from witnessing horror and pain. This Aristotelian catharsis purges all disquiet felt as a result of identifying with a tragic event. And it is precisely this type of tragic homeopathy which the propagandist has administered to relieve and resurrect its audience from crisis. For having dragged them through the depths of aesthetic misery, he is able to grant them the pride and moral satisfaction of enduring their struggles with enormous fortitude, a moral fibre rationalized as the necessary labour prefiguring utopian recompense.

Compounded with this catharsis is the explosion of the utopian light breaking "like waves on a shingly beach, sweeping the mountains / with more than the sough of pines." A cascade of joyful sentiments pours forth the vision of a long-awaited harmony: "the horns of plenty" are unsealed and "the severed ends of work and play" are joined once more. At this turning point, the audience is simply induced to believe in a utopia. One religious thrust of the imagination is all that is required as the last line of the penultimate verse ("You have nothing to lose but your chains!") abruptly enters the new luminous setting. There is no transition here other than a logic that claims that "the loyalty learned / in mine and factory begets our truth," a truth in which Mother England will restore her disinherited sons for having strenuously toiled the earth. An organic necessity is, therefore, mustered as the pseudo-rational proof and determinism of the workers' final reward.

But the unreality of this breaking-forth of sunlight from the darkness of historical struggles (a motif of luminosity depicting revolutionary consciousness) is not challenged by an audience identified with the proletarian protagonists. For the strain to find some resolution and respite in an oasis of hope has been so acute and painfully long (centuries long, as it were) that the arrival of the ideologue's retributive justice is but an amplification of catharsis and a welcome crowning to much labour and unreplenished yearnings. The sunlight, however, is not the light of everyday consciousness or of historical realism from which the poem took its initial register, and from which it subsequently plunged into the depths of nocturnal political desire. This new morning light is the consciousness of a community that is yet unconcretized in material terms; it is the light which pits good against evil as a moral system that radiantly drops "shrapnel of light upon their ranks" (the enemy), but "feeds our renewed bodies." Such a moral community is scarcely material, and yet its system of morality, which includes "us" and excludes "them," is powerful enough to sustain the faith of its members in a cause which is still remote and ungraspable. By legitimating the negativity of that Englishness (namely Communism) and by showing its logic, the ideologue has sought to convince a proletarian audience that English Communism is theirs to own.

As with sublime reason, the light portrayed in the poem is also that inner sight achieved from a wholesale leap into the darkness of faith, a faith in the promises of the rhetorician who has denounced capitalism's wrongs and (like reason to the imagination) imposed a metaphysics of inner vision. In this vision the political present is eclipsed and the virtues of past and future are prominently displayed as icons of an imaginative concentration, an irrationality that vindicates history's sacrificial lambs and heralds the cornucopia of future society. This sublime nationalist discourse seeks to persuade its audience of their authentic identity but cannot grant any immediate recognition of such a promise in palpable terms. Only submission to the belief that Communist nationhood can be consummated for the commonweal will sate the audience's desire for a much-sought *Sittlichkheit*. And this submission to faith will occur following a series of tortuous mediations of discourse traced along the odyssey of a tragic drama in which the labourers' harsh intimacy with the land and their thankless participation in collective struggles are imbued with pathos and suffering – enough misery to warrant their proud reclaiming of nationhood. In keeping with the Jobian ethos that the meek (or underclass) shall inherit the earth, the sublime provides the rationale for a compensatory justice. Such a moral law draws the victims of oppression from their "pathetic" depths to tragic self-awareness, indeed, to a revolutionary self-consciousness. And yet, despite this, their "deserved" right to a self-proclaimed Communist Englishness remains fettered to an imaginary place.

As the early Popular Front years manifest the first signs of an uninhibited reclaiming of national identity, "not english?" introduces the possibility of accommodating a nationalist consciousness to a revolutionary propaganda. And yet, even in 1936, Lindsay's poem shows that such an open declaration of Communist Englishness – of national identity – remains uncertain, lacking in legitimating signifiers and discursive forms, and restricted to hope more than actuality, to the imaginative force of poetry and less to the political arena. "not english?" also reflects the Communist's search for recognition from the working class. Rearticulated in Romantic and traditionally English cultural forms, nationalist consciousness seems to reflect the Communists' desire to reconcile their removed stature with their audiences, to integrate Communist politics with an English community and thereby merge the isolated intellectual activist with the masses. In effect, the yearning for an unalienated society where disparate, atomized forces (plebeian and intellectual comrades alike) may coalesce is exemplified by Lindsay's narrating figure, who rallies the elements of social discontent to a revolutionary collectivity. But as such the activist's desire remains encased within the prism of the poem, and fails, at this juncture at least, to be readily or fully concretized in real praxis.

Such desired bonding between intellectual and community is reflected in Lindsay's articles in *Left Review* which discuss the lost link between the poet's lyricism and society. In his *Plea for Mass Declamation*, Lindsay speaks of the driving force of capitalism which broke the sense of a homogeneous audience and dissolved the vitality of the speaking voice. For the "essential" thing – a linking of poetic form to the speaking voice in a socially valuable relation – was destroyed. The transformation of poetry into a commodity, he claimed, led to the separation of artist and audience, to an alienation between producer and consumer which was symptomatic of the Communist's isolation from the working class. In an endeavour to overcome this chasm, Lindsay proposes a definite course of action.

Here, then, I make my plea for Declamation, Mass Recitation, as the initial and primary form of our new poetry. For there we get the most direct contact with the new audience. Not that every poem can or ought to be written for mass-recitation; we must set as our goal the creation of a poetry that resumes and transmutes all the socially valid forms of the past with a new content, and seeks to go beyond them all with an enriched drama and lyric. But I claim for mass-declamation the position of norm in this new departure ...

For the peculiar nature of the social struggle of our day, as we near the terrible death-agonies and convulsions of Imperialism, demands of the poet that the core of his expression, his sense of the human whole, should be overwhelmingly political. He seeks contact with his audience in conditions of increasing danger; and his methods must be based on this fact. Mass declamation becomes the form of contact from which endless new developments can stem.   (Lindsay 1937, 516–17)

In a way, this type of political poetry may be construed as a propaganda with an immediate organic kinship between speaker and audience, a kinship made possible through the expression of political urgency. And while the polemical form thus far considered was replete with urgent vitality, it was an aesthetically created urgency induced through discursive flourishes. However, Lindsay's proposal for a more unified relation between poet/polemicist and audience is only viable under real conditions of crisis, such as those of the Spanish Civil War and the Second World War, with their devastating effect on even the more complacent sectors of British society.

The solidarity displayed by many Communist intellectuals towards the plight of people in Spain helped to secure a significant part of the anti-fascist campaign. It was this fraternal spirit associated with the symbols and experiences of those involved in the International Brigade that marked Lindsay's mass recitation, *On Guard for Spain* (published in *Left Review,* 1937 and, subsequently, as a penny pamphlet). The immediate context of the Spanish Civil War was essential for the successful outcome of such a mass declamation. Commenting on the *On Guard* performances, Jerry Dawson of Merseyside Unity Theatre recalls:

When we did *On Guard* the impact was almost always enormous. I remember when we played it to a meeting at Garston baths, I saw people in tears even at the mention of the name of certain Spanish towns, even just the list of names could achieve that, because they knew what had happened there. These audiences didn't see declamations as something arty, as poetry being recited to them, but as an emotional expression of things they'd come across politically in their newspapers.   (Watson in Mackie 1984, 69)

Through the success of *On Guard*, which was seminal in provoking other similar productions, the mass declamation became legitimated as a form furthered by the *Left Book Club* Poets Group, whose publication, *Poetry and the People*, was devoted to restoring the traditional link between poetry and the masses and to creating "poetry which by its clarity and compactness of expression stabs like a searchlight into the confusion and contradictions of our experience" (Watson in Mackie 1984, 70). Yet the proliferation of this form did not sustain the impact that *On Guard* had on audiences. For the identity which Lindsay's declamation established between conditions of production and conditions of consumption was no longer present in the postwar period. Thus Bill Schwarz has rightly noted, "If the Popular Front can ever be said to have emerged in Britain, it was during the War, which itself built on the mounting resolve of a broad, popular movement against fascism in which 'people' and 'nation' fused in a peculiarly intense, mobilizing combination. If the Seventh Congress of the Comintern outlined the strategic direction of a popular Communist politics it was the experience of the War itself which actually gave it substance" (Schwarz 1982, 57).

But the fusion between "people" and "nation" and most particularly between intellectuals and workers lost its vital bond by 1947–8 when a speedy decline ensued, destroying that significant but meteoric national-popular[2] movement. The latter was "sunk by the severities of the Cold War, smashed under the impact of Natoization, Marshallization and Britain's turn westwards for the special relationship with the USA" (Schwarz 1982, 58). It may also be adduced that the distinctive coalition of societal forces mobilized against fascism did not simply sever as a result of the Cold War. Indeed, under conditions of "normalcy," anti-state organizations such as the Communist party were already splintered along class lines. The shift in policy from the Third Period of the Comintern to the Popular Front and its effect on Communist propaganda reveals this clearly. In the early 1930s, the political mission of the Communist intellectual was to merge with the working class and denude himself of all cultural and professional privilege. By 1935 the aim and tone of Communist propaganda enabled the intellectual to assume the active role of distributor of knowledge and to preach through a liberal culture which the Class-Against-Class period had repressed. But if this intellectual emancipation from middle-class guilt privileged the ideologue's performance, potentially relegating workers to the status of mere recipients (Coombes 1980, 75) and aggravating class divides, the Spanish Civil War and Second World War contributed to the cosmetic dissolution of class distinctions. These two conflagrations were ironically conducive to the creation of genuine unity among disparate groups. However, such a situation only prevailed as long as worker-intellectual differences were masked by the compelling conditions of the anti-fascist struggle.

In a sense then, the war was a moment that removed bourgeois British society from its normalcy and thus from its inherent hierarchies, introducing the illusion of a level, "classless" community. But the urgency of the crisis was like an aesthetic dissociation from everyday life, where the rhythm and tempo of British class society were suddenly shelved, as a new, heightened and unified world of individuals interacted in a common purpose. In the light of its provisional and special quality, the war constituted an elevated and exceptional moment where possibilities previously desired could be fleetingly fulfilled. Yet simultaneously, if the creation of a genuine national-popular was contingent on the immediacy of the war and on the dynamic culture which had grown out of the war efforts, then it is logical that, in the postwar period, such a spectacular unity between middle- and working-class sectors should dissolve into its normal unbridgeable class divides.

CHAPTER SEVEN

"The Biting Edge of British Humour": The Sublime Patriotism of Cold War Communists

The enemies of Socialism and of the working class try to isolate us from the people by alleging that our ideas are foreign, not British, that Communism is a Russian invention. But look over the articles of William Morris in *Commonweal* and *Justice*, read his lectures to working men and others and you will [find] an inexhaustible source of evidence that Communism is as native to British soil as to Russian ... In order to advance the cause of Socialism, in order to bring Britain's cultural heritage fully into the battle of liberty and independence, we must find ways and means of bringing Morris – the authentic Morris – back to the British people. (Rothstein 1952, 42)

INTRODUCTORY REMARKS

The Communists of the 1950s inherited a mentality of excludedness from the 1930s. Yet this was not simply an ideological carry-over but equally a political actuality. The Cold War period isolated Communists, relegating them to the status of foreigners associated with Soviet Communism. Thus, despite the interim sequence of the war when Communists were more readily integrated into mainstream society (given their prominent anti-fascist activities and mobilization of popular support), these propagandists were once more isolated, as were their affiliates of the red decade. Unlike the latter, however, the Communists of the 1950s underscored the importance of articulating an English Communism while retaining a fervent internationalism. With the experience of the Popular Front, the practice of patriotic anti-fascist activity, nationalist sentiment lost some of its former offensiveness and an open self-celebratory English Marxism was adopted with *The British Road to Socialism*.[1] Ostensibly, this added dimension could have facilitated the possibility of winning consent through the expediency of the nationalist aesthetic forms of rhetoric which had been previously suppressed in the name of a proletarian internationalism. In promoting Communism through an idiom that was close to the people's indigenous sensibilities, propagandists could potentially dispel their reputation as sheer dissenters. Indeed, the national heritage could prove not only tactically but also humanly necessary: for to nourish the self-consciousness of popular sectors with familiar cultural icons would revitalize their sense of belonging and build those crucial bridges of common sense linking ideologues to their publics.

That is not, however, what happened. For the expanding national consciousness among Communists (witness the development of this phenomenon from the 1930s, through the Popular Front to the 1950s), which was linked to their strategy to win popular support, was also part of an impossible project to proclaim a radical Englishness with spontaneity and historical immediacy, with a power untrammelled by their subordinate status and by the strenuous ethical protest that they continued to voice against the ruling American and British hegemonies. Indeed, despite their wish to clothe Communist rhetoric in the raiment of popular beauty, their rebellious knight of sublimity reappeared, defending the integrity of Marxist ethics but scuttling the political endeavour to build consent through a veritable national-popular.[2]

The purpose of this closing chapter is to show that the unfettered deployment of nationalism and the liberating self-expression of 1950s Communist Englishness was only seemingly unproblematic. Through the aperture of E.P. Thompson's political address, "William Morris and the Moral Issues To-day" (Thompson 1951a, 25–30), I will argue that in spite of their exuberant national self-affirmation, the dissenting ideologues of the epoch could not adopt the aesthetic of beauty over the sectarian and ineffectual aesthetic of sublimity. The irreconcilable relation between Communism and populist nationalism stubbornly remained and so did the oppositional aesthetic correlative of revolutionary rhetoric. E.P. Thompson's speech provides a case in point as he seeks to instil a "beautiful," self-celebratory nationalist sentiment among Communists, but cannot bring this endeavour to its consummate pitch. For underpinning his discourse are the very politico-aesthetic contradictions of nation and class that dogged the ideologues of the 1930s. (Cf. chapter 3.)

In his speech on William Morris and moralism, Thompson affirmed Morris's politics, contributed to the anglicization of Communism, and proposed to revitalize Communist praxis. His political strategy recalls Arnot's appropriations of Morris during the 1930s.[3] This time, however, a nationalist idiom was vaunted vigorously[4] as the necessary means of inspiring the public with visions of an attractive commonweal. But the result was scarcely "beautiful." Despite much nationalist fervour, Thompson articulates a sublime patriotism that combines moralism and chauvinism in a bitter critique of contemporary society, overshadowing a truly celebratory and palpable depiction of Communist Englishness.

The aesthetic of dissonance and dissent, of opacity and non-contemporaneity, resurfaces here, forestalling the nationalist project of Communist ideologues and returning them to their familiar problematic stature (cf. chapter 5). With political ideals borrowed from the past, from an imaginary community of heroes removed from the altered sensibilities of Britain's postwar working class, Thompson's discourse of Englishness seeks public legitimacy. Yet its accompanying sublimity rehearses Arnot's polemical fire and is thus disjointed from the prevailing common sense of the 1950s, from its seductive amenities and sirens of luxury that drown out the moral righteousness and stringent poetics of bold revolution.

As an advocate of a political praxis that contests the tawdriness of capitalism, its rapacious consumerism and erosion of humanist ethics, Thompson betrays a preference for the "authentic" values of past traditions. His preference is suffused with a self-consciousness that is reminiscent of the conceit of hegemonic nationalism itself.[5] Thus, while radically opposed to bourgeois conservatism and to its attendant apologists (e.g. T.S. Eliot, Orwell, Koestler, and their American counterparts; cf. Thompson 1951a, 27), Thompson is of a Jacobinist disposition, both patriotic and élitist in his Romantic anti-capitalism. His discourse bears a sublime signature, a self-sundering aesthetic which increasingly reveals ambiguous ideological resonances. For though clearly an apposite symbol of Communist dissent, the sublime's Olympian tendencies draw it close to the threshold of a conservative aristocracy, thus putting into doubt the judgment's radical potential, and metaphysically suggesting a comparable ideological lapse in the revolutionary rhetoric of Cold War Communist patriots.

This closing chapter revisits the categories of sublimity and their role within the drama of dissenting ideologues. Pathos, terror, stern morality, retributive justice, and sublime idealism return as familiar actors in new apparel, the apparel of the Cold War. These same categories reveal the discursive measures taken by Communist ideologues to justify their

movement's legitimacy and daring nationalist energy. Yet in that justification, these aesthetic determinants also unravel that new-found spirit
and establish how sublimity and nationalist chauvinism eventually converge in a dissenting but abstract rhetorical unity – a unity which fails
to produce a much-sought national-popular derivative of the demands
and interests, the tastes and visions of the wider English public.

PATHOS, TERROR AND THE LEGITIMACY OF COMMUNIST PATRIOTISM

In an article treating the importance of Socialist Realism for the enforcement of Communist ideology (originally a lecture given at the summer
school on British cultural tradition), Alick West referred to a remark
made by Thompson in which the latter denounced the "inhibitions
which make us tongue-tied when we should be speaking with moral
passion" (West n.d., 79). Thompson also referred to a suspicion on the
part of Communists towards moral passion, and towards patriotism
generally. His claims were echoed by Alick West, who sought to reclaim
nationalism in defiance of the sectarianism which had hitherto weakened
and excluded Communists from the nation to which they belonged.
Indeed, for these ideologues, the possibility of expressing their national
identity uninhibitedly provoked a catharsis: "From [the] defeat of our
sectarianism has come a sense of release and festivity, so that the noise
of our voices raised in discussion and ceaseless argument has been, in
the phrase that Walter Pater used of children let out of school, like
'audible sunlight'" (West n.d., 79).

How was this exuberant patriotism possible? How were dissenters
able to openly voice their national-cultural belonging in the brilliant
resonance of "audible sunlight," when previously this expression represented a compromise to the bourgeois forces of reaction? It is in the
context of altered imperialist configurations of the 1950s that an explanation might be adduced. Firstly Communist national identity was in
solidarity with other oppressed peoples and generally linked to an anti-
imperialist cause of world peace. Secondly, Britain's imperialist status
underwent a dramatic change. Having lost large sectors of the colonies,
it stood in a subordinate position beside the august supremacy of the
USA. This enabled Communists to shift their most blatant protest from
domestic to foreign targets. In this shuffle, national borders acquired
distinctly different charges and the principal foe was defined as the
American imperialist threat. In the 1930s, imperialism instantly conjured

up Baldwinian conservatism and MacDonald-type reformism. In the 1950s, Englishness partially receded from its posture as the oppressor before the looming spectre of America's consumerist and aggressive culture of domination. In constructing Britain as the subject of an American plague, Communists (most prominently Thompson) created a martyr out of their aggrieved British heritage, heralding a Romantic anti-capitalist Britishness as superior and authentic. Thus, large portions of an otherwise conservative culture were appropriated and rearticulated unproblematically. The English heritage was not altogether jettisoned but rather recuperated, cast within a disarmingly "pathetic" role as a menaced species and thus made eligible for revolutionary recognition, indeed, for salvation. So long as English bourgeois culture (even the most oppressive within its own national setting) postured as a victim of capitalist vulgarization, it could accord with the justice-bent ethos of the Communist movement seeking to empathize with and rescue the colonized from genocide and the shackles of imperialism.

These altered political configurations can be witnessed in the renewed appropriation of Morris in the 1950s, a revival which marks a shift in Communist animosity towards the ruling class, an ideological sentiment directed increasingly towards America, and by extension a transfer of the class character of Communists of 1934 to their nationalist self-affirmation of 1951. Thompson's article "The Murder of William Morris" (Thompson 1951, 27) provides evidence of this ideological pattern. In rehearsing the arguments of Arnot's *Vindication*, Thompson's article details and dismantles the Conservative and Social-Democratic Morris myths in similar fashion to Arnot's tract. The distinguishing feature of Thompson's article (apart from its more extensive catalogue of myth-makers) is the change in identity of the principal Morris mythologizer. In 1934, the Social Democrats constituted the major adversary to Communism; the most insidious mythologizers were deemed to be Glasier and MacDonald-type reformists. In 1951, however, the principle foe is the imperialist USA; hence the American Morris biographer Lloyd Eric Grey is regarded by Thompson as the most condemnable of mythmakers. Thus, as anti-social-democratic feeling dictates the Communist disposition and rendering of Morris's politico-cultural status in 1934, so in 1951, the American threat determines the Thompsonian emphasis on the "pernicious" academic murder of William Morris through Grey's specious scholarly work.

At the stage of writing "The Murder of William Morris," Thompson had already begun clearing "the ground for a more extensive attempt at a positive assessment of Morris's theory and practice as a Socialist" (Thompson 1951, 27), implicitly sketching out the outline of the treatise that would become *William Morris: Romantic to Revolutionary* (1955). In this context, Grey's publication, *William Morris: A Prophet of England's New Order*, could only have provoked Thompson's revulsion before the ideological (and specifically American) burial of Morris's Communist political and theoretical work. The scholarly "murder" of Morris must have spurred Thompson to expose the nineteenth-century hero in ever more defiant and vigorous fashion, echoing the *Vindication's* vociferous protest. Arnot had done the pioneering spade work, and twenty years later, more than one voice (e.g. Rothstein, A.L. Morton, George Thomson) could resound with Arnot's original propagandist plea to resurrect Morris from the corrosive sentimentalism of Conservative and Social-Democratic myths.

These historical and ideological conditions underpin the use of pathos and terror in the cultural propaganda of the Communist party during the early 1950s. In April of 1951, the National Cultural Committee of the Party organized a conference in Holborn Hall, London, on the American threat to Britain's cultural heritage. Its purpose was to fight Americanization, to further popular understanding of Marxist-Leninism, and to render the working class the proud possessor of an English revolutionary tradition.[6] In this context, the legacy of William Morris was repeatedly affirmed to anglicize and endorse the political legitimacy of the much-alienated character of Cold War Communism. It was Thompson's address, "William Morris and the Moral Issues Today," that focused most centrally on the nineteenth-century figure, simultaneously presenting a critique of Americanization and debunking its stultifying and distorting effects on the authentic value of English Communism. Replete with sublime acrimony, his speech railed at the violence and cultural paucity of American culture as well as its genocidal character. Beside the terror of this looming enemy, English Communism stood enveloped in an aura of pathos.

As discussed in earlier chapters, one of the most powerful ways in which a polemicist is able to exalt his own ideological stance is by creating a "pathetic" ambience that captures audience sensibilities in a non-rational fashion, disarming them with a vicarious sense of helplessness that quickly begs some balm of compassion. A state of pathos affectively perturbs an audience and solicits its consolation and approval. To win such consolation is to secure a measure of trust and identification – a crucial leverage for political persuasion. It is therefore not surprising that Thompson employed this device with great flourish in his conference speech of 1951 when he addressed the USA's threat to British culture. Launching his discourse with an allegorical anecdote, he recounted the story of a dissatisfied American academic who dreams of renouncing the university profession in favour of testing his entrepreneurial skills at a meat business. Thompson's portrait foregrounds a crass capitalist mentality, one that is dismissive of the humanist values ascribed to erudition and scholarly knowledge and is entrenched in the race to invest in the postwar boom: "He squared his jaw above his virile cowboy-style shirt with the decision of a J.P. Morgan, banged his fist on the table, and glowered through his horn-rim spectacles. 'Boy I could have set up a *chain of slaughterhouses* throughout the Holy Land! My God, I could have *cleaned up!*'" (Thompson 1951a, 25). Afflicted with "Babbit-itis," the American glorifies the slaughterhouse business and fully endorses the essence of capitalism: "blood money," the exchange-value of war, cowboy imperialism, and a host of belligerent features encapsulated in the aesthetics of American popular culture. Thompson expounds on it thus:[7]

The "American dream" really is as childish and as debased as this and its poison can be found in every field of American life. Those who have never been to the United States and who fool themselves (like some readers of the *New Statesman*) that Hollywood, the Hearst Press and the comics, represent only a lunatic fringe of the American bourgeoisie, sometimes suggest that *Babbit* is an out-of-date joke on the 'twenties: unfortunately it only foreshadows the horror of to-day. In the last two or three years the dream of my Professor has acquired for me a terrible significance – and has revealed itself in a more terrible actuality for the peasants of Korea and the people of a threatened world.   (Thompson 1951a, 25)

Gripped by the alluring forces of this philistinism, the academic-cum-businessman is construed as an "abatteur" whose indiscriminate hand symbolizes the fatal bludgeon of America menacing a quaint, articulate, and sophisticated British culture, a culture deemed gracious and moral, yet vulnerable beneath the formidable shadow of an imperialist aggressor. Seeking to preserve that special finesse which age proffers British tradition (and which he finds wholly absent in the vacuity of American capitalist society), Thompson enacts a discursive duel that pits imperialist butchers against innocent victims, forging a "them" and "us" divide where "they" are decidedly philistine and "we" as British are exalted, rare, quasi-extinct as the bustards of another age.[8] The dichotomy is fundamentally a match between oppressors and oppressed, where Americans hold a monopoly over imperial power while English Communists possess control over a political pathos reinforced by Thompson's references to the Third World casualties of American genocide, a pathos in which the portrait of American violence sanctifies both the victims and their British sympathizers.[9]

Our morality is based on one principle only – man, his real suffering and his real happiness. No matter how often they say "freedom" we say that the burning of Korean villages with jellied petrol bombs is a vile and inhuman practice. No matter if the B.B.C. drones on about "western democracy" night after night it still will not alter our sympathy for the trade unionists imprisoned and shot in Spain or Greece, or our knowledge that the instigators and propagandists of a new world war are setting themselves against all the canons of elementary human fellow feeling by which the common people of every land have learnt to live.   (Thompson 1951a, 28)

By associating Communist morality with the righteous struggles of Third World peoples and their martyrdom in the face of war and want, Thompson endows his movement's nationalism with the salutary virtues of humanitarian ethics, wholly different from the empty moral (read nationalist) rhetoric of the American adversary and its English allies. The contrast between the terror of the American war-machine and the pathos of the fallen and besieged lends Thompson's Communism an innocence and popular rectitude which exculpates it from any charges of hypocrisy and hollow idealism characteristic of bourgeois nationalist discourse – a discourse typical of a whole tradition of Conservative and Labour politicians "who ... buttered their careers with 'idealistic' phrases – the MacDonalds, Snowdens, Morrisons, and the rest who ... kept the people occupied with star gazing into the 'moral' firmament while they themselves ... climbed into comfortable positions" (Thompson 1951a, 28).[10]

But the pathos which Thompson deploys in defence of his advocacy of moral fervour (read nationalist fervour) is in part a means of recuperating with impunity the (scorned) ideological expedient of nationalism. If there are any lingering sentiments of distrust and inhibition regarding the appropriation of Englishness, the use of pathos is both purifying and chastening; it assuages the sceptical and recalcitrant Communist who clings to the sectarian anti-nationalism of the 1930s. If Englishness can be subsumed under the abstract concept of culture, anthropomorphized as an innocent victim and terrorized by foreign powers, even the crimes of its own domestic imperialism are tentatively effaced in that idealized posture of cultural fragility and edified beauty. Simultaneously, as a reinforcement of English worth, this pathos is also the affective component which warms Thompson's passionate retaliation. It is an aesthetic device which delineates the odiousness of the political enemy, contrastingly reinforces the innocence of the English Communist community, and galvanizes the tribune to triumph over the adversary, if only through verbal trenchancy. But as a device, pathos is exclusively directed at the converted to condone a self-affirming Communist nationalism; it serves to dispel a collective guilt and discomfort which might hauntingly surface should moral fervour be construed as narcissism or a compromise to the conservative hegemony. The "pathetic" rendering of the Communist identity and the terrifying howl of the enemy are affective elements which must, according to Thompson, be restricted to the converted audience. When the propagandist appeals presented at the cultural conference are aired more publicly before the people (the non-converted community), they must transform pathos into a spirit of defiance and inspiring optimism. For the plaintive sensibility associated with Communist propaganda is now deemed ineffective; the perennial negativity of radical protest fails to elicit ideological support. Pathos must in some sense be transmuted into a positive and victorious quality, and in that alchemy will pass through the ironic channels of satire and caustic humour, the distinguishing trait of British retaliatory strength which Thompson advocates as an imperative response to Americanization:

[L]et us not be too heavy-handed about it. It is necessary for us to understand the full seriousness of the threat to our culture, and to have the facts and figures before us. But we will not defeat this threat with facts and figures alone, and we have on our side in this fight one great resource, and that is the healthy sense of ridicule within our people. This has been shown with great effect already by the response which Unity Theatre has won with their show, *Here Goes*. It was shown again this morning by Peter Major, when he used the weapon of satire in the attack upon the American comics. What we should remember is that, when we use this weapon, our battle is already half won. For a very long time the American, whether tourist, or business-man, or pettifogging academic, has been – sometimes unfairly – an object for ridicule amongst our people. I do not suggest that we can laugh the American threat away: but we should keep the biting edge of British humour sharp, and turned in that direction. (Thompson 1951a, 25–6)

Such an endorsement of ridicule is symptomatic of a siege mentality, the combative disposition of the peripheral subject who must resort to the realm of discourse to preserve his sense of righteousness and simultaneously strike the enemy with rhetorical buffets. Discursive jousting indexes the ideologue's threatened condition, as well as his ensuing ardour to win public legitimacy for an otherwise unheard political protest against the powers of the ruling class. In urging his following to launch an inveighing riposte against the loathed American enemy, Thompson vindicates the rectitude and viability of Communist praxis; but he also betrays a chronic marginality which even his polemical rage cannot dispel.

SATIRE AND THE LIMITS OF ACRID LAUGHTER

The weapon of satire, as Thompson has it, embodies the awkward reconciliation of protest and celebration. A sharp critique of existing bourgeois society combined with the comic relief of satire produces the fantasized triumphalism typical of the besieged. For humour or the parodic form is the latter's measure of dignity when it seeks to celebrate its identity without protest. Yet when a defiant battle against the oppressor is waged, satire combines protest with comedy into its own dissenting mode of victory. Mockery becomes the aesthetic means of flouting the enemy; in an imaginary overcoming of distress, the peripheral subject is thus able to fancy himself capable of epic strength and achievement. But even in this confident and empowered posture, he retains his commitment to a counter-hegemonic stance, and thus cannot fully realize any veritable political centrality.

As a tribune of a subordinate political movement, Thompson embodies such a *problematic* (Lukács) subjectivity and takes a dire stand against the British state, and against the American "rape" of British culture. But as he advocates the use of a "healthy ridicule" as a retaliatory weapon, he also recognizes the limits of the satirical mode which forestall a veritable epic self-affirmation. For in aiming to out-manoeuvre the foe, he seeks to herald a spirit of Communist optimism which transcends the heckling character of satire as well as the residual defensiveness and persistently plaintive tendencies of orthodox Communist rhetoric. Thus he writes: "When we take the message of this Conference back to the people let us keep the positive note in the foreground. For goodness sake, don't let us fall victims to gloom and defeatism ourselves and appal our audiences with only a catalogue of American penetrations. And don't let any of our opponents be given a chance to sneer that the

Communists and their friends have found one more thing to be *against*"
(Thompson 1951a, 29).

Thompson's strong reaction against the negativity of Communist
ideologues is conversely a comment on their inability to speak liberally
about Englishness without the forbidding taboo of national identification. His rhetoric is an implicit critique of the sectarianism of the 1930s
and its propagandist silence over the national question, its refusal to
project visions of a future society save through obscure allegories and
political abstractions. Indeed, it is that aesthetic of sublime recalcitrance,
that negative tenor associated with the Communist movement's virtual
embeddedness in the practice of protest, that he yearns to erase, so that
a more affirmative and enticing Communist profile may be vaunted
before the ranks and the larger popular community.

Thus while satire may be deployed as the signature of the dissenting
subject, confidently and ebulliently assaulting the political opponent
with tones of comic wit, its healthy ridicule is also a weapon of attack
that remains shipwrecked on the side of negativity and risks lapsing into
a pit of emptiness in the aftermath of its acerbic assault: "Let us always
remember that it will be useless to try to resist the American threat if
we can only replace it with a vacuum: and that, while we may win some
local gains of a negative kind, the only lasting victories will be where –
whether in scholarship, or dance tunes, or philosophy – the American
threat is driven out by a development of the living British tradition"
(Thompson 1951a, 29).

But in joyously recuperating the cultural treasures of a revolutionary
heritage, Thompson does not necessarily strike the much-sought positive
note of Communist propaganda. For the residual irony and sublime
acrimony of satirical Communist discourse can scarcely be distilled into
an unhindered and purely self-celebratory nationalism without a radical
transformation of the socio-political conditions of society at large. Only
a reversal of material forces which would shift peripheral movements to
centre stage and marginalize the existing ruling class could ensure the
transformation of the invective of Communist Englishness and produce
a festival of self-affirmation.

THE IMPOSSIBLE QUEST FOR THE BEAUTIFUL

In abandoning the apologetic and defensive attitude of the Communist
movement, Thompson claims that it is imperative to speak out uninhibitedly about British historical traditions – in short, to dramatize and

project the meaning of English Communism as articulately and unashamedly as possible. In Lindsay's poetic terms, it is to raise the mutterings of revolutionary Englishness to their consummate moment of expressive clarity, and to address the British working class positively. To rail derisively and satirically at the enemy will not suffice. Communism must be capable of unfurling its wings without the ideological fear of capitulating to the adversary or of losing the exemplary robustness ascribed to traditional revolutionary rhetoric.

Thompson's sublime patriotism was coherent so long as it abided by its inherent tendency towards satire and feisty polemic. Its rebellious form and pugilistic spirit rehearsed Arnot's sublime vituperation and protest of the 1930s. But the positive note which Thompson seeks to promote among his comrades can scarcely coexist with the dissonance of sublime Communist propaganda. The aesthetics of passionate dissent are in radical conflict with the beautiful, with the niceties of a nationalist discourse that sensuously evokes the desired splendour of a Communist commonweal. Still, it is the aesthetic modality of harmony and pleasing form which Thompson yearns to recuperate as he quotes Harry Pollitt's recollection of Morris's writings, recollections recorded in Pollitt's autobiography, *Serving My Time*: "There is not half enough of this type of propaganda to-day. We have all become so hard and practical that we are ashamed of painting the vision splendid – of showing glimpses of the promised land. It is missing from our speeches, our Press and our pamphlets, and if one dares to talk about the 'gleam,' one is in danger of being accused of sentimentalism. Yet I am convinced it was this kind of verbal inspiration that gave birth to the indestructible urge which helped pioneers of the movement to keep fight, fight, fighting for freedom, when it was by no means as easy as it is to-day" (Thompson 1951a, 29).

But no sooner has it invoked Pollitt than Thompson's appeal to Communists to revive the gleam of Morrisian and other socialist propaganda is hoist with its own petard; the delineation of a Communist Englishness (glimpses of the promised land) proves to be but a resurrection of the past, of "our own history and cultural achievements, ... forgotten revolutionary *traditions*" [added emphasis], whose implicit prophecy of a future commonweal only reinforces the Communists' refusal to draw positive substance and regenerative moral fervour from the present. For the present is the site of hedonism, consumerism, private interests, and the insidious glamour of American capital which captivates the popular imagination but which is aesthetically distasteful to Communists of the epoch. Their loathing is manifest in remarks such as Sam Aaronovitch made during his address to the Party conference of 1951: "I would say this in closing: Lenin said, 'We have national pride, therefore we hate our slavish past.' To this let us add 'and we hate our slavish present.' The picture we have revealed in this report of the U.S. 'way of life' and its invasion of Britain, can only arouse disgust and shame in the hearts of the British people" (Aaronovitch 1951, 22).

But the refusal to attend to the present, however vile and shameful, renders the gleam of such dissenting propaganda all the fainter; for the possibility of affirming a Communist nationalist consciousness is undermined by an ideological distancing, an ethical and aesthetic self-removal from popular taste. With its sublime autonomy and defence of values that scorn the mediocrity of Americanization, mass commodification of culture, and the erosion of ethical purity, Communist propaganda perennially forges its own, idiosyncratic culture by adulating a politically vibrant and robust prewar working-class identity, mythologized as the epitome of English dissent. Admittedly, the idealized radical heritage furnishes the necessary ideological architecture upon which to build hegemonic confidence. Yet the self-possession is cloistered in an archaic Communist castle, endowed with its selected literary tradition and estranged from the real social clamourings for pleasure and private comforts that consumerist society persistently and rampantly caters for. Paradoxically, as Bill Schwarz has pointed out (cf. Schwarz 1982), conservatives from the Scrutiny Movement and Communist intellectuals, such as E.P. Thompson and his affiliated colleagues of the Historians' Group of the Communist Party, display a convergent distaste for the "bland allure of post War affluence" (Hebdige 1982, 199). The conservatives were most concerned with the spectre of anarchy and its imminent destruction of past cultural stability, a preserve of an élite levelled by capitalist commodification. The Communists were perturbed by the lost vigour and depoliticization of the working class, its surrender to the delights of television, high wages, and materialistic aspirations. In this context, the aesthetic of beauty emerges as an ideal which corresponds to the commercial sensibilities of an Americanized popular culture, one which Hoggart described with disdain as a "shiny barbarism," "the ceaseless exploitation of a hollow brightness," "a Candy Floss World" (Hoggart in Hebdige 1982, 199). Such a counterfeit beauty of tinsel and profit cannot be espoused by the Communist rebels of the 1950s, however much they feel liberated in their new-found sense of nationalist self-affirmation. Their counter-hegemonic stance can only preclude the possibility of sustaining a wholly "positive note" and mellifluous rhetoric. Indeed, Thompson's repeated references to Morris's writings fail to be anything other than discursive appeals aflame with sublimity. Morris, the Romantic figure from the past, bequeaths a faint hue or gleam of ruralist beauty but ends up being overshadowed by a persistently provocative rhetoric which Thompson perpetuates by drawing upon Morris's most militant statements: "It is to stir you up not to be contented with a little that I am here tonight." And in another address which Thompson quotes, Morris proclaims:

I hold that we need not be afraid of scaring our audiences with too brilliant pictures of the future of Society, nor think ourselves unpractical and utopian for telling them the bare truth, that in destroying monopoly we shall destroy our present civilization ... If you tell your audiences that you are going to change so little that they will scarcely feel the change, whether you scare anyone or not, you will certainly not interest those who have nothing to hope for in the present Society, and whom the hope of a change has attracted towards Socialism ... And certainly the Socialists who are always preaching to people that Socialism is an economic change pure and simple, are very apt to repel those who want to learn for the sake of those who do not.   (Morris in Thompson 1951a, 30)

If Thompson's discursive cullings issue primarily of out a Morrisian protest which uninhibitedly flourishes its sword to bring not peace but the disconcerting news of formidable revolution, then the lyrical note of beauty which Thompson wishes to instil in the "People" with its positive notes and harmonious cadences will be necessarily drowned in the grating atonality of political dissent.

SUPERIOR PATRIOTISM AND ITS SUBLIME MORALITY

In foregrounding Morris's feisty countenance, Thompson eclipses the bucolic romanticism linked to the hero's "beautiful" aesthetic *œuvre* and returns to the élitist sublime, to a mode which ascribes rectitude and supreme value to another sphere of time and space detached from the parochialism and the constraining parameters of the *status quo*. Despite strenuous efforts to invoke the repressed patriotism of the 1930s, Thompson's discourse remains fundamentally moral and abstract in its Englishness. Suffice it to note how he edifies the historical past as an

absolute standard of judgment embodied in continual references to
Morris's political thought.

I would like to refer once again to the man who, above all others, ... was
accustomed to go straight to the point in any matter he took up, and when he
had occasion to write of America at the time of hysteria accompanying the
judicial murder of the Chicago Anarchists, he dealt with the American bourgeoisie's pretence of democracy thus:

"a country with universal suffrage, no king, no House of Lords, no privilege
as you fondly think; only a little standing army, chiefly used for the murder of
red-skins; a democracy after your model; and with all that a society corrupt to
the core, and at this moment engaged in suppressing freedom with just the
same reckless brutality and blind ignorance as the Czar of all the Russias
uses."   (Thompson 1951a, 26)

   In resurrecting the wisdom of a spiritual father, Thompson legitimizes
his own denunciation of America's pseudo-democracy. The revered
luminary lends a tacit inspiration which encourages a similar course of
polemicizing against the ruling powers, a defence of "authentic" democracy against the sham liberties of bourgeois society. As a David pitted
against the enormous odds of an imperialist Goliath, Thompson and
his movement require this type of historical precedent to endorse their
position. Thus, sublimity resurges in the form of a superior moral
capability and a self-affirmation which serve as the compensatory
empowerment of the besieged political community. But only at the level
of an exalted ethical stance can an ideologue such as Thompson suggest
any superiority over the capitalist fortress. Communist self-vindication
enhances its ideological posture by marshalling its authenticity beside
the falsity of the adversary. But the assertion of moral righteousness is
coupled with an effort to win political legitimacy under conditions
which continually militate against Communist survival. Idealism ensues
as Thompson's Manichean discourse casts the English Communist identity in the role of crusader for truth, beauty, and goodness while American culture is deemed a moribund condition and set in dire contrast
with the "desires of another people who see a richer life, [and] ... who
have warmer ambitions for Britain than those of tedious insolvency and
rearmament" (Thompson 1951a, 30). This categorical division between
"us" and "them" glorifies the ethics of English communism by depicting

them as vital and regenerative expressions of life, rather than as capitalist and decrepit symbols of death. The binary opposition has a compelling categorical clarity that morally coerces its audience to choose the humanist option and eclipse any alternative.

Yet while Thompson's category of life is overwhelmingly seductive, it is associated with a healthy English fibre of resilient humour which does not pit life against warfare, but aesthetic, verbal ripostes against veritable aggression. British warfare is discursive, and thus allegedly salubrious and ingenious for its masterful satire, its "healthy sense of ridicule," and its moral endurance. Implicit here is the idea that British culture carries a moral and intellectual acuity which brutish American philistinism simply lacks, and that by dint of such superiority, British Communists may fight against American imperialism with ever more impunity, since reason is on their (English) side. Such a moral and thus humanist value which Thompson ascribes to the English Communists (and perhaps even to Englishness in general) suggests that the English civilization is endowed with sparkling wit and spiritual verve, rendering even those English imperialists slightly less loathsome than their American counterparts.

In his counterpoint of Englishness versus otherness Thompson ultimately stylizes the home team as a humanist crowd with comic wryness that is laudable for its moral triumph over circumstance. But under the instrumental power of his satirical polemic, the humanism he advocates is not always coherent. For the allegorical assault on the philistine American academic condemns its victim mercilessly. It thus endorses the use of a punitive discourse in the aesthetic sphere of the polemic, in a mock world where Communist ideologues are deemed unsparing conquerers of American aggression.

Where the Manicheism of Thompson's rhetoric crystallizes a pattern of diametrically opposing identities, it also eludes the discrepant particularities that make up who "we" and "they" really are. This vacant and idealist projection of "us" and "them" lapses into the pit of abstractions which Thompson so fiercely denounces in later years in his appeal to the concrete and sensuous renderings of objectivity (cf. Thompson 1978). The opaque construction of "us" and "them" also conditions his converted and non-converted audiences to construe reality in reified terms, deleting class factors and homogenizing parties into abstract entities defined in purely national terms. As the Manicheism of polemical forms disguises discontinuities with a homogeneous mask, so

Thompson often imposes a uniformity of Englishness upon the notion of "the people" (cf. Thompson 1951), relegating Americans and their culture to absolute decadence.

Such abstracting tendencies within the polemic militate against a revolutionary consciousness. But they also replicate the very structures of bourgeois political economy that underpin the American imperialism which Thompson eloquently derides, namely the subordination of use-value to exchange-value. For the suppression of particular and sensuous differences which define the variegated character of a national community – streaked as it is with gendered, racial, and class distinctions – and their subsumption under the general title of Englishness reproduce that exploitative subjection of human labour to sheer numerical and profit-determined values of exchange. Indeed, on an ideological level, Thompson's dichotomous rendering of Englishness and Americanness entails the creation of a political exchange-value which validates and empowers "us" – the English people – through discursive pathos and satirical artifices of polemical vituperation, gathering each and all into one abstract nationhood that is instrumentally deployed in the struggle for political hegemony. Simultaneously, this exchange-value is a hollow form of Englishness forged by Communist predilections for a syncretic, romanticized, prewar English identity. It is a title emptied of the material culture of the 1950s, purified of the apathy and eroded class consciousness of that postwar era, and structured according to principles of Communist dissent that are estranged from the lived experiences of the working class of that period. In the widening gulf between popular culture and the idealizing propensities of anti-capitalist ideology, Communist ideologues dissolve any genuine interaction between themselves and their audiences, engendering a compensatory reward of exclusivity that not only weakens the force of their propaganda but produces a social hierarchy of leaders and led that is wholly anathema to the egalitarianism of Communist ethics.

THE SUBLIME IDEALISM OF RETRIBUTIVE JUSTICE AND THE ARISTOCRACY OF RHETORIC

As a delegate of a marginalized community, Thompson shows that despite difference and subordination, an ideological departure from the mainstream does not imply defeating self-exile but rather a self-removal which anticipates the returns of some ulterior higher justice. The particular conditions of marginality which constrain an ascendant group also kindle its sense of mission and self-liberation, goading it to act with energy and resolute defiance. The self-distinction and apparently dele-terious isolation in which a dissenting movement is lodged imply neither permanence nor resignation. Rather, they are the preparatory stage for overcoming crisis and conflict. Such transcendence is not strictly mate-rial, yet it is necessarily moral in its sense of imminent triumph and retribution. Since the battle waged by this feisty collectivity occurs in the moral space of an ideological mock world, the victory which is achieved is but aesthetic. It cannot be otherwise, since the values of this dissenting group are polarized and radically dissociated from the "shod-diness" of existing capitalist society. In their ethical ideals, Communist tribunes exile themselves to a world of non-contemporaneity beyond real human interaction, defeating their initial motive to communicate and rally popular social forces to the cause of peace and social equality. Thus the mission of 1950s Communists is scuttled by its aesthetically purist decrees and acerbic rhetoric that avoids grappling with the limi-tations of common sense (fetishistic thought). As Gramsci remarked, criticism of the capitalist world cannot arise *ex nihilo* but only from a dialectic between the immediacies of the existing world and some future utopia. "For it is not a question of introducing from scratch a scientific form of thought in individual life, but of renovating and making 'critical' an already existing activity" (Gramsci 1971, 330–1). Thompson, like the movement as a whole, breaks with the popular culture of postwar cap-italism and perpetuates a categorical antagonism between the revolu-tionary prophecy of an abstract future, delivered by the oracles of retributive justice, and the contemporary evils of imperialism, with its "spreading taint of death" (Thompson 1951a, 30). In doing so, he is apt to commit the error that Gramsci warns against: the introduction of a "scientific (or utopian) form of thought into everyone's individual life" without extracting its critical import from the terrain of common sense. In short, while reformism and conciliatory dialogue are not strategies for Communism (i.e., the overthrow of imperialism), *neither* is the reifi-cation of social forces into fixed polarities of time (corrupted present versus glorified future) and social relations (corrupted populace versus an abstract popular entity). These generalities and dichotomies only con-tribute to the mystified consciousness of those sectors that would oth-erwise be rallied democratically to the cause of social revolution.

In his mission to "change the people," Thompson endeavours to extricate the working class from the tangles of capitalist society by catapulting them into their optimum status as "the people," the authentic

democratic identity, emblazoned with an aura of ethical rectitude, regenerative power, and retributive promise. But in the Manicheism of his
nationalist discourse, both abstract adversary and idealized people are
polarized beyond any encounter or mediation. So too the veritable
people of the 1950s, who "had little desire to know their past – only to
escape from it, into 'affluence' and 'apathy'" (Schwarz 1982, 65), can
scarcely accede to the exemplary category of the people which Thompson associates with healthy visceral moralism. (Cf. Thompson 1951a, 28.)
As Bill Schwarz points out, Thompson's ethical idealism and his
demand for authentic proletarian values are incongruous with the working class of the 1950s; his absolutist values can be seen as potentially
reactionary in their utter disregard of the real working class of that
period. Thus Schwarz writes: "E.P. Thompson's talk on 'William Morris
and the Moral Issues of today'... by its tone illuminates some unex-
pected convergences with the bleak *Scrutiny* outlook: 'In place of the
great proletarian values revealed in class-solidarity and militancy, we now
have, even among sections of our own working-class movement, the
values of private living growing-up – the private fears and neuroses, the
self-interest and timid individualism, fostered by pulp magazines and
Hollywood films'" (Schwarz 1982, 64–5).

   Caught between the warring arguments and blandishments of capitalist and Communist rhetoric, it is unlikely that Thompson's audience
would have sustained a strong interest in the persistently judgmental
tenor of his discourse, which condemned the shoddiness and degenerate
propensities of the present in favour of some *mightier, truer past*. Like
sublime reason, Thompson features here as the ideologue-philosopher
who comes with a verbal sword to thrash common sense, to rid it of its
obscurantism and redeem the vulnerable populace with inspiring blandishments. But his redemptive efforts are aristocratic (cf. Gramsci 1971,
204–5) and foreclose the possibility of engendering a real democratic
movement; his following is always compelled to surrender irrationally
to his judgment, proffering faith like the imaginative faculty of the
sublime and thus abnegating itself before the rhetorician's oracle of
"truth." Here, the faith that is surrendered is doubly accentuated by the
very rhetorical position of the dissenting ideologue, who, short of epic
(hegemonic) strength, seeks centrality in a world apart where he can act
with imperiousness and panache. Yet this world apart is invisible,
because moral; it is part of a metaphysical space which can only be seized
through non-rationality. Such a rhetoric compels an audience not merely
to forfeit what is familiar and immediately graspable (their everyday

outlooks), but also to reach out towards a cognitively estranging world beyond, a world which has no palpability save moral superiority. A rhetorical contract of this kind is somewhat of a bribe that hinges on aesthetic purism, on a tragic (categorical) mentality that blatantly pits life against death, compelling "all those who, in whatever way, desire a richer life, all those who have warmer ambitions for Britain than those of tedious insolvency and rearmament, all those, indeed, who desire any life at all" to be won to "our side" (Thompson 1951a, 30). For as Thompson states in detail,

Never has there been a time in the history of the world when the real moral issues before man have been clearer. Perhaps the issues are so clear and so big that we sometimes fail to grasp them. We are offered Life or Death. On the one hand, the spreading stain of corruption and defeat in culture and human endeavour, on the other the liberation of the creative energies of whole peoples. On the one hand the burnt earth and steaming seas of a devastated planet, and on the other the flowering of wastes deserted by man for many hundreds of years. This is the only choice before man. The defenders of American capitalism have nothing whatsoever to offer the people, but more work, and more poverty, and at the end of it, Death in a desperate and indiscriminate war. Beneath all the nice quibbles about means and ends, all the clever things which Orwell or Koestler or Eliot or their American counterparts have to say, will be found the same facts: napalm, the Hell Bomb, and the butchers of Syngman Rhee. (Thompson 1951a, 27)

With this, he produces an intimidating choice between a subscription to capitalist decadence, oppression, and violence and the pursuit of a Communist life. But in his insistence that the people purify themselves of their vulnerabilities to capitalist life-styles so as to become authentically human, he coerces his audience to abandon their worldly possessions and materialistic propensities and follow the opaque but vital Communist commonweal. This surrender entails both an audience's renunciation of its existing ethos and a suspension of scepticism – indeed, a double capitulation to the moral laws of the dissenting propagandist. It is an ideological submission that also foreshadows a mystified consciousness in which a public adheres to the promises of its ideologue with a religious acceptance that obliterates temporal contingencies and reifies the vision of an ideal community as the oasis of plenitude and social well-being. Indeed, the propagandist devalues the contemporary bourgeois world, while simultaneously elevating the

Communist world to a height that can only be acceded to through an epistemic break. The latter consists of an erasure of the horizontal flow of temporality and an edification of the imagined sphere in which a sense of community is "neither primarily geographical nor social, but involves the 'vertical' linking together of all believers through as it were a common pinnacle of sacred beliefs" (Kitching 1985, 108).[11] Thus, in promoting his own views (sacred beliefs of a kind), Thompson quotes Morris: "We will produce no more for profit but for use, for happiness, for LIFE" (Thompson 1951a, 27). The category of life is clearly Thompson's most persuasive blandishment, but it remains as abstract and abstruse to the receiver as the empty phrases of conservative nationalist rhetoric ("moral values," "freedom and democracy," "the western way of life," etc.).

Just as in a religious genuflexion, where an audience submits to a priestly class mediating between lower sectors and the "pinnacle of divine Providence" (Anderson 1983), so a political following irrationally proffers wholesale trust and approval to the dissenting rhetorician who straddles the here of his audience's immediate experience and the tomorrow of their ideological hopes and aspirations. Such a submission recalls the vertical (religious) consciousness inherent in ruling-class nationalism, where time is eclipsed and superseded by reified and reifying space. This incipient religiosity is in no way restricted to a conservative ideologue, but manifests itself equally in the iconoclasm of a dissenting rhetorician. For it is not the content or ethics of a discourse that dictate its disengagement from the fetishisms of bourgeois consciousness; rather it is the rhetorical relationship between ideologue and audience that is decisive. Where the delivery of knowledge is apportioned in aesthetic unities and disarming structures of literary expression that distract an audience from assessing the contradictory and recalcitrant force of material reality, a subjective idealism surfaces, creating an imaginary tableau that overshadows actuality and holds the consciousness of the public in the grip of an entrancing belief.

Admittedly, the reception of ideology necessarily entails various suspensions of disbelief; these are the concessions made to a propagandist in exchange for some invigorating ideological message. However, at the point in which political discourse routinizes its suspension of critical thought, at the point in which the aesthetics of propaganda exceed their role as catalysts of persuasion and unifying common sense, they contribute to the sundering of the rhetorical community and foster a priestly class of ideologues. Here the relationship between leaders and led reaches

an untenable bifurcation: the receiving audience loses its active participatory force while the ideologue rules imperiously as if the discourse
were his sceptre. Dissenting propaganda resembles the relation between
the capitalist and the worker, where the latter loses his control over the
means of production, and the economic system takes on the guise of
an irrational, seemingly autonomous structure. In such discourse, the
audience loses its hold over the means of ideological production, turning
passive and contemplative before the crystallized "truth" of a rhetorical
form whose imperious authority is but the subjective will of an ironic
hero in epic disguise.

CONCLUDING REMARKS

Under conditions of crisis, ideological disarray, and marginality, the
dissenting propagandists of the 1950s could not be immune to the Class-
Against-Class dogmatism which they renounced officially. However
much they professed to enjoy the delights of an emancipatory nationalism, of a Communist Englishness, they did not ultimately relinquish
the ethical ardour of their erstwhile praxis. A merely mechanical appropriation of nationalist sentiment could not alter their ideological identity
and their standing among the popular sectors. What determined their
possible success or failure in creating a truly democratic movement was
rather the particular nature of their dissent. Aloof from the immediacy
of the historical period, they were unable to implement a nationalist
discourse, either a populism or a national-popular; the sublime could
only resurface anew with familiar ethical prohibitions and constraints.

Given the isolating realities of the Cold War, the Communists displayed a potent voluntarism, often accompanied by a rigid and dualist
ethical rectitude, an abstract idealism (cf. Lukács 1978) which granted
them a sense of political capability derivative of the virtue and zeal
invested in their imagined community. But if the abstract nature of their
political imaginings held at bay the discrepancies of their objectively
marginal status, it also rendered impossible the salutary patriotism (the
democratic movement) which they sought to realize. For the more
Jacobinist and élitist they were in respect to Americanized British culture, and the more they spurned the enthralling force of commodity
fetishism to which the popular taste fell prey, the less integrated and
viable was their nationalist project. Indeed, the abstract and judgmental
character of their sublime patriotism recreated in inverse fashion the
reifying and irrational structures of consciousness encapsulated by the

beautiful aesthetic of bourgeois ideology (ruling-class nationalism). In claiming this, I do not mean to conflate the political rhetoric of Communists with the practices of Conservative and Liberal ideologues; for while the latter endorsed the capitalist political economy, the former were conscious of its utter undesirabilty. Nonetheless, being part of that world order, the Communists were also subjected to the pressures of alienation, of ideological ostracization as well as to the debilitating split between public and private life spawned by capitalist society. Nonetheless, the simultaneous identity and difference of the aesthetic moments of beauty and the sublime symbolically demonstrate both the radical ventures and limited possibilities of Communist rhetoric, be it Class-Against-Class or patriotic. For the sublime judgment cannot offer anything more than an epistemological model for an alternative society. And even then it remains inadequate, since its idealism is inexorably impregnated with the effects of reification. This also implies that Communist propaganda and its sublime renderings cannot redress society by way of radical rupture from existing capitalism. Nor can such a rhetoric harshly denounce all bourgeois common sense as contaminating and as dispensable false consciousness. For such a twentieth-century Jacobinist discourse is fundamentally embedded in the terrain of bourgeois consciousness, however much it seeks to unfurl wings and take to utopian flight. And in that attachment, it must necessarily grapple dialectically and interactively with the constraining tendencies of its own capitalist context. As Lukács pointed out, the false consciousness in bourgeois society cannot be addressed "in an inflexible confrontation of true and false. On the contrary, it requires us to investigate this 'false consciousness' concretely as an aspect of the historical totality and as a stage in the historical process" (Lukács 1971, 50).

By creating an antinomy of authentic versus false consciousness, Thompson's speech at the Communist cultural conference of 1951 reproduced the dualisms of bourgeois thought; in marking an insuperable barrier between conscious intellectuals and "spontaneous" masses, it foisted a moral *ought* upon his audiences while eclipsing the mediations necessary to transform society historically from within its own frontiers. Admittedly, writing during the Cold War era may have warranted the use of idealist discourse if only as a measure of self-defence and self-legitimation.[12] An abstract concept of the people or an abstract populism (cf. Schwarz 1982, 80) furnished an ideal structure of popular approval for Communists even where there may have been precious little real support. (Cf. Samuel 1987, 60.) But the final repercussion of this propagandist artifice was that the dissenting rhetorical form succumbed to the tendencies of ruling-class nationalist ideology. It lapsed into a fetishistic consciousness which focused narrowly on the aesthetic *phenomena* of nations, eclipsing their material labour and social relations and rendering them homogenized communities pitted against a unitary foe. Thus Thompson's attack on the American threat to Britain assumes the form of a war waged (with an arsenal of "authentic dance tunes" and indigenous philosophy) on a depraved culture of violence, rather than a battle fought against the real machine of imperialism and finance capital. Ironically, such a political consciousness marks the dissenter's return to an idealism which his sublime gesture sought to dispel in its original impulse of political and ethical revolt. This idealism harbours all the elements of a nationalist sensibility which takes its cue from the commodity relations of the modern market. It is to this that we now turn in a culminating analysis of aesthetics, nationalism, and political propaganda.

Conclusion

In their enthusiastic embrace of Englishness, Communist propagandists of the 1950s appeared to shed the ideological prohibitions of the Third Period of the Comintern. The suppressed ideology of nationalism could finally be espoused with alacrity and purpose. Overtly, one might say that the erstwhile sectarianism of the 1930s had been renounced in favour of a more relaxed and flexible Communist doctrine which reconciled nationalism with internationalism, and transformative praxis with affirmative politics. But this remains an impressionistic observation and one which abides by the surface appearances of official history. Closer scrutiny shows that the newly adopted nationalism of the period was steeped in an ethical idealism reminiscent of the 1930s. Witness the discursive motifs of sublime aloofness, of self-righteous martyrdom, as well as the opaque projections of future commonweals, *inter alia*. Reappearing in new configurations of nationalist discourse, the sectarianism of the 1930s was jettisoned in word but not in deed. Conversely, the Class-Against-Class dogmatism of the 1928–35 period may be construed as a form of proto-nationalism or political chauvinism (in the apparel of internationalist sensibility) preserved in its bud by the censorship of Comintern policies.

Given such ideological continuity between epochs, the more liberal attitude towards nationalism could not supersede the propagandist quandaries of Communist ideologues of the 1930s; the Cold War period relegated Communists once more to a peripheral political movement, oppressed by a powerful Anglo-American hegemony and subjected to all the discomfiture and impotence of marginality. Thus, in affirming their Englishness, it was not the redolent category of beauty which Communist ideologues plucked for their rhetorical bouquets but the sublime thorn of romantic dissent. Within cloistered halls of oratory they applauded and promoted the wisdom of William Morris's radical Englishness, but their political discourse remained caught in the cage of their utopian and retrospective visions, replicating a sublime disposition that was never fully at one with itself and thus always secretly, if not subconsciously, emulating the symmetries and equipoise of the hegemonic beautiful, the emblem of an entrenched ruling class.

Bifurcated by its moral élitism and its critical assaults on dominant ideology, the sublime articulates the Communists' wayfaring intellectual character, drawn to the people in idea, yet in practice often removed from that plebeian force. As an aesthetic insignia that reflects their persistently dissenting verve, it nonetheless discloses their aching homesickness, their covertly *nationalist* desire to be reintegrated within the hearth of a larger community. But this return to a hitherto "blasphemous" ideology neither brings them closer to the conservative political hegemony nor makes them any more comfortable in their recalcitrant posture. Nor does it revolutionize their ethos. On the contrary, what is revealed is a propagandist form that recedes into its own moral sphere of self-vindication. Such dissenting propaganda escapes the reality of its subordinate status through its projection of an imagined community that transforms objective contingencies into subjective law, fictionally resolving the social group's sense of impotence and defeat. The ideal community proffers the illusion of an epic triumph and is thus the aesthetic terrain upon which political consciousness is cultivated, nurtured, and brought to ideological consummation; it serves to compensate for the absence of any real hegemonic power, and as such it is fuelled and intensified by a highly potent morality, an idealism that enables the ascendant political group to fantastically realize its desires for societal renewal. There lies the *formal* and non-rational character of propaganda which produces a simulacrum of collective identity, an intensive and utopian representation of social cohesion. Through an overpowering pleasure that seizes the individual in his state of civic or ideological affirmation, this imagined community phenomenologically brackets out the gap dividing political desire (freedom) from actuality (necessity); by distilling the plangency of the aggrieved, it gathers their sentiments onto a plateau of self-possession, a defiant protest where consensus prevails against a demonized foe. Unity is secured in that adversarial attitude, and in the belief that retributive justice will crown the ascendant movement with moral victory.

With this conviction, Communist propaganda not only produces the social cohesion necessary for its ideological success (namely its capacity to console and sustain powerless peripheral groups), it also lends a seemingly cognitive consistency and definition to the content of political rhetoric. Communist propaganda of the 1930s and 1950s sought to delineate an unfathomable utopian commonweal. But in that endeavour it circumscribed a spatial contour around the unknowability of the *Noch nicht* (Bloch), the opacity of a future social order. Such dissenting rhetoric did not actually grasp the future save through a moral system which irrationally and categorically predic(a)ted the redemptive character of a Commmunist society. With fervour and adamancy, an Arnot, a Lindsay, or a Thompson could dictate that reason lay in the madness of historical struggles and adversities besetting the popular class, and that some retributive justice would yet emerge as an ulterior salvation. Through this commitment, the rhetorician would be inspired, despite fierce odds against him, to wage a battle against the ruling-class hegemony and reassure himself and his following of their movement's political strength and legitimacy.

There is a decidedly modern sensibility in this Promethean act of defiance. For the recurring characteristic of such rebellious discourse is its vigorous sense of agency and self-possession. As it encounters threat and adversity, it shows a creative capacity to construe itself in an epic crusade, teleologically marching towards victory. Simultaneously, this forceful self-vindication is coupled with introspection. Like the modern subject that is continually reevaluating his identity (having relinquished the markers set by tradition, and the securities of the outer world, be they religious, epistemological or other), Communist propaganda is primarily coloured by its collective isolationism. Its yearning for the warm hearth of hegemonic communities is sublimated in the form of an imaginary world order, designed to act as a slavishly approving witness to its every claim. Here lies its intrinsic capacity to engage in aesthetic labour and to transmute the political alienation of its following into a seemingly glorious self-sufficiency, an independence particularly characteristic of modern subjectivity. Such an autonomy results from a wizardlike alchemy that summons an imaginary fellowship to proffer its community a sense of oneness with an ideal place.

As with modern subjectivity that yearns for a liberating individualism but is riven by the pain of homesickness, so dissenting propaganda ambitiously and confidently departs from familiar harbour but suffers from its lost moorings. Its longing for a distinctive autonomy is embittered by its inability to consummate its subjective goals (i.e., its aspirations to actualize an alternative political order) amid the insurmountable

obstacles of the outer world. Dissenting propaganda reflects the alienation of a bourgeois society in which public and private spheres, state
and civil society are abstracted away from each other; universality and
particularity never mediate or reach any close encounter. And since the
unity of these alienated poles is neither naturally given nor produced in
sui generis fashion as a self-generating objective structure, propaganda
must achieve it through some practical, self-legitimizing and self-
enhancing intervention, indeed, through the *fabrication* of an idealist
unity which abstractly (but never truly) brings private and public life
into a societal harmony underpinned by a sense of sublime duty and
ethical obligation. Thus, where the sublimity of dissenting propaganda
only witnesses fragmentation on the turf of existing society, it projects
a supersensible community predicated by its self-affirming rationality.

Meanwhile Conservative propaganda grants the illusion of being
snugly ensconced in its home, integrated with prevailing common sense
in a *natural* and seemingly premodern organic unity. Yet despite this
rhetorical countenance, it is no less wrought of artifice and no less
modern in its individualism. Its centrality and legitimacy are also self-
imputed, yet the distinctively mellifluous ease with which it proclaims its
identity simulates an innocence germane to a naïve epic past, an era that
is free of the cumbersome quandaries of *problematic* (Lukács) subjectivity. Deploying the category of beauty for its persuasive ends, Conservative propaganda dispenses with self-justification – precisely because a
judgment of taste cannot be subject to dispute – and produces a
discourse which parades as transparent and universally accessible to its
following. Inventing an Arcadia and heralding it as its childhood of
delightful spontaneity, Conservative ideology continually bathes its audience in illusions of authenticity, in configurations of organic community
which like the aesthetic judgment hanker after some past bliss while
only achieving the sentimental constructions of a modern abstract
beauty.

In essence, it is Kant's aesthetic judgment which articulates the
paradigmatic aspect of modern subjectivity, and analogously of (both
Conservative and Communist) propaganda. Annexing power, self-
sufficiency, and crowning dignity for its own ends, the aesthetic
judgment traces the schema of a subjective consciousness that refuses
individual enslavement to some higher governing body. Operating in
part inductively, this judgment must search for a universal structure and
subsume it under its particularity. In this logical manœuvre the aesthetic
judgment summarily portrays the desired autonomy of the modern

ideologue who mentally appropriates the vast political universe and sweeps it under his wing, swelling his paltriness into epic glory. In this the aesthetic judgment illustrates the shift of the peripheral activist to his desired hegemonic point of centrality, a position which proffers him not only a simulated public legitimacy but also an equipoise that is secured when the subject has finally plotted his imaginary ground and established his sense of place. By contrast, the Conservative ideologue, who appears already well established on home turf, appropriates the aesthetic judgment to reassert his hegemonic confidence. Constructing his discourse out of irrationality, he dismisses conflictual objectivity, spins his ideology in accordance with personal fancy and in conformity with the laws of social taste. (Recall Baldwin's anecdotal mythologizing of Morris.) But this Conservative propagandist will nonetheless assume the air of defending tradition and replicating a given repertoire of "facts" as a seemingly spontaneous rehearsal of age-old custom and common sense. Thus, where both dissenting and Conservative ideologues are modern individualists, only the former will forthrightly mark his sense of autonomy and radical rupture with the *status quo*. The Conservative, despite his initiative and bold agency, gingerly subdues his ambitions and dissimulates a wholly possessivist spirit under the fraternal bonds of community.

Paradoxically, in his radical vanguardism and heroic agency, the Communist ideologue displays the mentality of the modern sovereign individual more overtly though not more essentially than does the Conservative ideologue. In his rhetorical endeavours, the dissenting ideologue, together with the collective identity to which he ascribes an ethical autonomy, resembles the prototype of emerging capitalism who, short of veritable democracy, substitutes an intensive individualism for societal community. But such autonomy never really achieves the self-sufficiency that it appears to project. The Communist rhetorician may recognize his dependence on the proletarian mass to whom he preaches, yet, like the modern subject who denies his collective genesis, the ideologue eclipses the matrix of social relations which constitute his rhetorical intervention; in this he subsumes the real power of collectivity under his own singularity and fancies himself single-handedly empowered, not unlike the self-asserting aesthetic judgment which gracefully secures its worth through a subjective universality.

This form of rhetorical idealism is a validating process which finds its most expansive configuration in the phenomenon of nationalism, a phenomenon whose compensatory secular religion lends a unified and coherent identity (albeit ideological) to the otherwise fissiparous and disorientated character of modern society. In this regard, Raymond Williams points out that

it is capitalism, especially in its most developed stages, which is the main source of all the contemporary confusions about peoples and nations and their necessary loyalties and bonds. ... it is, in the modern epoch, capitalism which has disrupted and overridden natural communities, and imposed artificial orders. It is then a savage irony that capitalist states have again and again succeeded in mobilising patriotic feelings in their own forms and interests. The artificialities of modern nationalism and patriotism, in states of this kind, have then to be referred not to some intellectually dissolving universality, but to the precise and powerful functions which, necessarily in the form of artifice, they are now required to perform.   (Williams 1983, 184)

Accurate as Williams may be in reflecting on the irony of capitalism's successful manipulation of nationalist sentiment, the consideration is perhaps less astounding if one grants that collectivities of whatever kind function ontologically as both material and epistemological validations of individual subjectivity. And if it is the advent of capitalism that renders the nation-state the most distinguishing but also the most totalising of societal units (Smith 1983), indeed the "objective" or socially accepted yardstick for individual self-legitimation, then it can also be understood that the artificial boundary of the nation-state sweeps up the feeling of real community experience into its higher form and acts as a continual usurper of the rhetoric of social bonding. Under capitalism, nationalism is the defining magnitude of societal identity; as such it is but a glorified aesthetic judgment, a value by which individuals display their social being through idealist constructs of irrationality. For just as the aesthetic judgment is a category of taste which unites a community through the abstract agreements of consensus, so nationalism is an ideology that interprets society as a modern state bonded by an *invented Gemeinschaft*, by a communitarian spirit that is abstractly inserted into political discourse. Both the aesthetic judgment and the phenomenon of nationalism are categories which harness society's longing to reconstitute a prescient community. And despite the chimeric nature of such an urge, these categories artificially allow the "golden" unity of some past Arcadia to appear in modern apparel. But such a fancy emerges through a violation of historical continuity where an abstract concept of societal totality is foisted on the present from a previous epoch, irrespective of the empirical resistances of the immediate world. The superimposition of an ideal sphere upon actual reality does not produce any mutual interplay of individual and community; it only creates an *abstract measure* of such a possibility, a guiding principle or form to emulate. Thus nationalism may be understood as an ideology which provides the "point fixe" and "spiritual point d'honneur" by which alienated individuals and collectivities find their orientation – yet always through the coercive imposition of social convention and alien form on individual difference and subjectivity. The sentimental nationalism of Baldwin's rhetoric *and* the tragic feelings of Communist sublime sacrifice are the idealized subjectivities, the *glorified* sigh of the oppressed, never their veritable emotions and experiences. Nationalist consciousness forcibly weds the universal – the grand title of citizen, or heroic revolutionary – to the particular individual through an unhappy marriage of convenience.

Railing against this discrepant feature of modernity, the Communist sublime is an aesthetic mentality that *nonetheless issues from* the political and economic infrastructures of the existing capitalist order, and it cannot elude the matrix of its own conditions however much it contests the excesses and artifices of conservatism. The Communist sublime possesses a vigorous selfhood and self-differentiating impulse, symptomatic of the bourgeois epoch itself; as such the category is invariably implicated in fostering and perpetuating the phenomenon of nationalism. Nor is this utterly surprising. Emerging at the juncture of historical transitions to capitalism, the discourse of nationalism finds itself anchored in the bedrock of commodity relations, in the homogenizing structures of exchange value; but its efflorescence also occurs as a product of a surging self-consciousness in modern subjectivity, a subjectivity that reflects the ethical voluntarism, the political autonomy, and the rights of citizenship promoted by eighteenth-century bourgeois revolutionaries. As ancestors of the Communists of the 1930s and 1950s, these Jacobins mark their identity at the crossroads of phenomenal societal change, reaffirming their selfhood all the more powerfully through the consummate language of nationalist ideology. Granting the individual his sense of wholeness, freedom, and self-reliance, their rhetoric is inextricably connected with a self-determining consciousness and with an established practice of political dissent pitted against the reactionary tradition of an old regime. It is thus only logical that the Communists of the 1930s and 1950s should have covertly or overtly adopted a nationalist rhetoric even as they promoted a Class-Against-

Class position or a recalcitrant anti-imperialist Cold War stance. For whether ruling-class or oppositional, the discourse of nationalism is fundamentally linked to the gratification of a public's desire for freedom, for autonomous subjectivity – be it civic dignity or revolutionary heroism. It is a rhetoric which, in spite of its sleights of hand, endows its following with a participatory status, a performative role that draws an audience into communion with its discursively imagined nation or commonweal. Here is the public's occasion to simulate an aesthetic identity, a dignified and immortalized selfhood secured through the narcissistic display of self before otherness.

It is not surprising, then, that the legacy of William Morris appealed both to Conservative and Communist claimants. Its national/ist signature lent a stabilizing value by which unstable political movements could secure their foothold, bolster their legitimacy, and effectively stem any undercurrents of political distress. In this, the battles over Morris's cultural importance have differed widely, but their immovable feature, and thus their common bond, remains the man's Englishness. Whether mutedly or dissonantly expressed, Morris's national identity served each claimant and enabled him to empower his own vindicating stance. And it was the aesthetic judgment of beauty – correlative of nationalist consciousness – which appeared as most expedient for the rhetoric of Morris admirers vying for hegemonic power. But in so far as nationalism was associated with the irrationalist consciousness spawned by commodity fetishism, with the duplicities of liberal democracy and the treacheries of Social Democrats of 1914–18, its advantages remained ethically unacceptable to Communist ideologues of the 1930s. Ruling-class nationalism was most conducive for those competing forces that possessed the privilege of endorsing their position in the name of commonsense values already tacitly entrenched in social consciousness (cf. Baldwin's establishment rhetoric); where values had yet to be defined, tortuously or covertly through ideological mediations, as in the case of dissenters, the force of nationalist discourse was diminished.[1] Thus Arnot's defence of Morris's *indigenous* revolutionary heroism was substantiated through an ascetic aesthetic of stringent activism and internationalist praxis. And Thompson's advocacy of Communist Englishness was rendered through the evocation of Morris's nineteenth-century political energy and moralism. But these covert configurations of nationalism were disjointed from the present, always hankering after a restoration of justice at some future hour. Until that time, however, the ideological function of Communist propagandists never quite secures the perfect balance of democratic nationalism that it seeks (i.e. that delicate unity of Marxist principles and popular consent). Instead, the rhetorical forms of nationalism that Communist discourse adopts (whether directly or indirectly) necessarily fall prey to the proliferating reifications of the commodity form if only because nationalist consciousness issues out of the capitalist market itself.[2] Indeed, whether ruling-class or counter-hegemonic in political stance, the ideologue creates a general accord based on aesthetic principles which *interpellate* (Althusser) an audience to envisage its (existing, imminent, or desired) freedom and to grasp some real or metaphysical concept of place as a site of belonging. In doing this, he invariably fosters a nationalist subjectivity that is bound to the idealism of capitalist relations. This contiguity between nationalism, propaganda, and the market is best exemplified in the concept of propaganda as a medium of communion with the converted. Here an ideologue flatteringly narrates a redemptive epic saga, inserts his audience into a heroic tale, and exalts their subjectivity, gracing them with the status of a chosen élite. Yet the tale is none other than a *glorified* rendition of their way of life, be it the asceticism of Communist Party life or the conservatism of Baldwinian ruralism. In the construction of a communitarian space, the ideologue invokes the ensemble of beliefs and moral values that are already endorsed by his audience, and crystallizes these into a prism which refracts back to that social group a luminous symbol of their agreement. As such, this agreement is an intangible and inaudible abstraction which always eludes the concrete particularities of their real social condition. Somewhat like a vortex whose centre is but a whirring void of energy, consensus (or the commonsensical rendering of the ideal community/nation) is a contrivance, an untouchable *thing in itself*. It is not a real set of accords, but rather an inspirational idea of absolute societal harmony which, while empty of concrete substance, nonetheless offers itself as a *Sollen*, a model of community relations and the emblem of how societies wish to regard their collective identity under times of duress. Thus the political utopias of Baldwin, Arnot, Lindsay, and Thompson are constructed out of judgments of taste (beautiful or sublime) whose disinterested status renders them *sensuous abstractions* of social accord, not materially palpable but morally and affectively compelling.

Precisely because of its elusive character, the idea of the nation or the sublime world of Communism appears as a simple but mysterious thing. Its mystery closes it off from immediate understanding and lends it the appearance of a finished product. Indeed, the fetishism of this ideal

space (the crowning moment of nationalist consensus) compares readily
to that of the commodity, to that apparently thing-like entity whose
exchange-value obliterates real labour and produces a pleasurably expedient but false immediacy. Whether ruling-class or Communist, the
ideal community (a nation or political party) appears as a unitary and
inexplicable value of seeming spontaneous generation. Its tranquil surface conceals a turbulence of social, economic, and political contingencies where an audience is coaxed to surrender personal interests in the
name of some higher commonweal. The latter stands as a communitarian integration of individuals; but it is only thus as an object whose
members are subsumed under its aegis. When one can no longer tell
the dancers from the dance – when, for instance, activists are utterly
identified with the Cause – then their higher ethical community of
Communism appears as an objectification and even as a cannibalization
of its very producers, only then does it emerge as a context free of social
substance, as a viable and instrumental exchange-value. In this abstract
form, the imagined community proffers its self-sacrificing followers the
opportunity to resubjectify themselves, to appropriate the value of
nationhood, or Communist solidarity, for their own self-enhancement.

Thus as a tacit accord embodying the most cherished virtues of a
society, the imagined community stands as a structure of legitimation,
used for self-sustainment and self-empowerment. Having been objectified through that unfortunate sacrifice of individuality, it is then
reclaimed and deployed for underscoring the value of each of the
subjects who originally forfeited their immediate interests for its larger
cause. By way of a violent phenomenological twist, each subject seizes
the ideal community as a piece of property, as a type of insurance policy
against subjective dissolution, appends the ideal qualities and sum total
of its beauty (landscape, national character, noble spirit …) to his
individual persona and graces him with a set of wondrous virtues which
serve to transform his mortal condition from paltriness to permanence,
from insignificant particularity to enduring universality. The concept of
belonging to the nation/community is but a euphemism for a certain type
of empowering ownership. Participation in the social ensemble or self-
sacrifice for the cause is contingent on an ideological reward, namely
the reaping of value and legitimacy from that ideal property – the
imagined community.

Thus even the ethical rectitude promoted by Communist party doctrines may be construed as a form of ideological property and indeed
the very moral reward that a propagandist will proffer his following to

win political recognition and support. Given in return for the commitment and abiding faith of the recruit, such a reward is ultimately a type of individualistic freedom germane to bourgeois idealism. It is a promise that can only be granted through the aesthetic sphere of a political message, and not beyond those parameters. For by creating a dramatic stage out of a discourse, an ideologue is able to render his audience not merely recipients of the idea of some utopian commonweal but, more important, authors and actors of the very harmony that they seek. He engenders the perfect conditions in which to enable them to foster, master, and accomplish their own destiny with a seeming free will that aesthetically vanquishes the concrete contingencies of mundane life (e.g. in the case of Communists, Party wranglings, political strife, defeats imposed by industrial action, etc.). Yet this ideological craft is nonetheless paradoxical. For as it lends its audience a feeling of autonomy and singular capability, it also subjugates this public to an alienation that ultimately subverts the liberty that was promised at the outset. For the often rhapsodic blandishments of a nationalist, self-affirming discourse lead the individual to construe himself as heroic; yet such an extraordinary flourish of identity is an illusion of independence controlled by the authorial ideologue. The unique moment of sovereignty that the individual enjoys in the course of the propagandist event ultimately imprisons his inquisitive consciousness. Left self-deludingly free of the constraints incurred by his society, the individual is equally bereft of the knowledge of social relations and contradictions that underpin this euphoric and dramatized moment of liberty. Such a freedom is truly of a Kantian nature; it is one that jettisons all discrepancy in favour of an idealist and undialectical totality. Instead of promoting a Hegelian autonomy which would compel recognition of necessity, the ideologue inserts his public into an aesthetic sphere where temporality is ground to a halt, where timelessness freezes the movement of social reality, erases the tensions of everyday life, and edifies a dizzying beauty of purposive totality. This inebriating pleasure is an immediate, reflexive but also vacant liberty that is ultimately dissolved into a pitiful subjugation. For the more the public feels the utopian *élan* of this hollow aesthetic liberty (witness the glory and sense of untrammelled identity created by nationalist or revolutionary euphoria), the more it suspends disbelief, surrenders to the ideologue, and submits a truer freedom to the controlling strings of its authorial master – the rhetorician. What we discover in the rhetoric of Baldwin's pacifying discourse are the charms of ruralism and quaint nostalgia which imperceptibly disengage the audience from their sense of individual rationality. The pleasurable imagery and tone with which Baldwin caresses his following incurs an oblivion which guards his rosy idealism from the disconcertingly discrepant terrain of reality. Thus, suspended in the imaginary community of his speech, an audience is ever at the mercy of the ideologue's persuasive manœuvres, and specifically, in the case of Baldwin, such manœuvres are viscerally powerful.

In a comparable manner, the sublime force of Communist rhetoric (Arnotian or Thompsonian) arrests its audience through the determining structures of classical tragedy. By extracting their sensibilities and realist consciousness from the sphere of everyday life, such propaganda compels a following to genuflect before the formidable capability of radical martyrs, to capitulate irrationally to the ideologue's discursive world, and to identify with the empowering and emancipating feelings of self-sacrificial sublimity. But by inflating the public's pride in that magnificent and impossible defiance of material reality, the Communist ideologue enables his audience to enjoy its sense of prominence and grandeur, its freedom and invincibility exclusively within the terms of the idealist message. Only within these confines can the wonder of the sovereign, rational being be conjured. Each member of the audience may only win the reward of a much-promised liberty if he conforms to the spatial and temporal caveats of the political narrative and to the presupposition that all scepticism must yield to a wholesale trust in the ideologue's convictions.

Forced to adhere to an external law and to a standard of beliefs that are consensually predetermined as the barometers of *truth and validity*, the public slips into a rut of alienation. Its own sense of originality is dispelled. Its distinctness and plurality are dissipated in the vapour of conformity to the principles of the Communist Cause. While it may achieve its desired freedom and self-sufficiency, such a public only manages to secure an abstract sense of sovereignty. Concrete, sensuous, everyday-life identity is surrendered to the standard status of citizen or revolutionary activist – to an elevated, but hollow, moment of social dignity with which the modern subject clothes himself in times of critical occasion. Liberty, the pinnacle of ethical personhood, is thus granted when the individual is removed from his own *terra firma* – his ground of certainty, personal experience, and immediate needs – and lodged on the soil of another's territory, the soil of Communist praxis. Estranged from his own cognitive terrain, the individual is catapulted onto the ideologue's turf and made to feel liberated of all material constraints, even though fettered to the ground of that discourse. The glories of a vindicated identity, of an epic stardom, may be vicariously experienced in the worship of great political heroes or in sublime scenarios of martyrdom. Yet such exhilaration occurs only momentarily and within the prism of aesthetic, intensive events that are overshadowed by the larger cage of a defeating alienation – a quasi-religious subordination to the universalizing laws of some higher rhetorical figure.

In animating a public's selfhood, political discourse will perhaps never elude a utopian dimension, an idealism whose aesthetic impulse fosters a necessary inspirational flame: the irrational optimism of the will. Yet this aesthetic dimension can also be stretched out of proportion and inhibit the revolutionary character of dissenting propaganda. In a sense, the polemical form which constitutes the essence of counter-hegemonic discourse is wrought out of aesthetic determinants that impose a hierarchy on relations between ideologues and their following. Infused with dramatic intensity, and rigidly opposed to the messy materialism of everyday life, the poetic artifices of rhetoric militate against the necessary mediations which accompany revolutionary praxis. These discursive components contribute to a mystification of audiences such that a following may be enticed – indeed, mesmerized – by the spell of an enchanting ideologue and his construction of an ideal community. In the case of Communists, the imagined society could never be articulated with sensuous immediacy, but was subsumed under the form of a sublime hero (cf. Arnot's rendering of Morris) or an abstract populism (cf. Thompson's reference to Englishness through the voice of the *people*). Consequently, in assuming the silhouette of popular heroism, the imagined community of Communism served as the territorial marker of political identity, the frontier between *us* and *them* which enhanced the collective ego, and relegated otherness to some equally abstract force of hostility.

Incarnated as the proletariat or the English people, this collective ego eluded concrete specificity and was always something of a thing-in-itself. The real public, the veritable masses whom Communists sought to gather under their wing, were imagined, and (whether consciously or not) used as things for "us" to delineate the optimum character of Communist identity. But in themselves they were unknowable. And so, in their abstracted identity, the real popular community remained beyond the boundaries of any revolutionary mediation intended to crystallize a national-popular, "an organic unity between theory and practice, between intellectual strata and popular masses, between rulers and ruled" (Forgacs 1984, 93). Such a dialectic conceived by Gramsci would be the result of intellectual forces combining with popular sectors whose collective identity was engendered from their *own initiative and creative energy*, and less from the voluntarist stroke of an élite of political rhetoricians. For as he argued, one must struggle against "false heroisms and pseudo-aristocracies, and stimulate the formation of homogeneous, compact social blocs, which will give birth to their own intellectuals and their own commandos, their own vanguard" (Gramsci 1971, 204–5).

Still in default of veritable political strength, and if only to survive historically, it was precisely an imagined community, an aesthetically projected vanguard, that proffered Communist rhetoricians such as Arnot, Lindsay, and Thompson their *confidence* and *sense* of an eventual triumph over the capitalist system. Their rhetoric applied well to moments of crisis when the duress of class struggle justified the use of inflammatory imagery sparked in the name of a higher ethical rectitude; but beyond a certain historical peak of militant energy, long-term hope could not be secured (even among the converted) without an anchorage in the imagery of everyday Englishness, of particular experiences that marked people's private interests and needs. Abstract or moral prescriptions addressed to their own constituencies were appropriate in times of great historical drama, but in periods of greater economic ease, such as after the Second World War, sublime discursive raptures could only fall upon deaf ears. The unimaginable sphere of Communism could only wither in the minds of sceptics, disillusioned radicals, and a working class coopted by the commercial enticements of American wealth. After the heat of social tumult, what was to prevent such an aesthetic call to arms from dissolving into a solipsistic incantation of outmoded revolutionary cries, meaningless to a complacent and depoliticized lower social class? What was lacking in the structures of dissenting rhetoric was an *immediately* accessible vision of alternative possibilities, a vision which spoke directly to the contemporary tastes of the day – yet one that was neither sentimental in its embellishment of the *status quo* (i.e. Baldwin's England) nor irrational in its leap into the mythical regions of historiography and futurism (i.e. Communist Englishness). Yet such an immediacy had been coopted by the ruling-class culture, whose overwhelming imperialism virtually absorbed all other political dispositions, leaving them always subordinate to that of the *status quo*.

The question persists. What would it have taken to enable dissenting propagandists to enforce their radical doctrine pervasively in the idiom that would have been both critical yet sufficiently grounded in common sense to supersede the chasm of irrationality that separated them from their public? To have acceded immediately to the sensibilities of mainstream bourgeois society would have implied collapsing into the inimical practices and ideology of the hegemony. To have asserted difference and ethical rectitude would only have widened the gap between the morality of the educators and the alleged profanity of the masses. So, perhaps all that remains is the humbling recognition that any attempt to bring about sweeping revolutionary change to British society depended on altered historical conditions, on the elimination of an imperialist legacy that ever stymied the project of radical movements. Short of this, British Communist propaganda could only be a voluntarist activity, not a veritable transformative praxis.[3] As an aesthetic, dramatic situation it could only serve as a catalyst in times of upheaval and imminent chaos, when what persuaded was not so much a visible utopian community (although that communitarian future was certainly seductive) as the pressure that crisis imposed on individuals as an all-compelling objective force. Revolutionary propaganda could only invite an audience to relive the narrative of its class situation in its duress and triumphalist euphoria. Still, while this aesthetic experience did not alter reality, but only bolstered the morale of the troops, such optimism remained an indispensable moment of emancipation, and as Ernst Bloch had it, "the strongest and best thing [the Communists had. For] ... Reason cannot blossom without hope, and hope cannot speak without reason: both must operate in a Marxist unity; no other science has a future, no other future has science" (Bloch 1971, 33).

Appendix:
A Word on Morris the Propagandist

In an appendix to *The Unpublished Lectures of William Morris*, E.D. Lemire lists 578 meetings at which Morris spoke between 1883 and 1896. (Cf. Lemire 1969.) Of these numerous addresses, multiple open-air speeches were unpublished. As Arnot noted in his *Vindication*, the Conservative and Social-Democratic canonization of Morris's *œuvre* tended to eclipse his activist writings in favour of his more literary and formalized texts. Those vital and lively propagandist discourses, often delivered at mass rallies, remain hidden in the pages of *Commonweal* of the 1880s and 1890s. Meanwhile, A.L. Morton's compilation of Morris's political lectures represents an assortment of formal and leisurely paced addresses which lack the energy and robustness of his open-air propaganda. His lectures and open-air speeches seem to bifurcate into two distinct types of discourses: those directed at middle-class publics on the one hand, and those geared to working-class audiences on the other. As Morris grew cognizant of the class character of his propagandist endeavours, he also became more sensitive to the appropriate discursive register which he needed to adopt in order to elicit popular consent.

In his pre-socialist phase, he postured in Victorian fashion, seeking a delivery that was formal and definitive. (Cf. *Hopes and Fears for Art* [1882].) In a letter to Georgianna Burne-Jones of 10 August 1880, he wrote that he would complete a further two lectures and then transform the whole series into a book. But this formalization of political experience was soon to yield to the vitality of sheer propagandizing. "Morris lost all traces of the 'Grand Manner' and all consciousness of any audience but the one in front of him. To become an agitator, a Marxist revolutionary, he gradually changed all aspects of his public effort ... He learned that when the object is to move people, to convince them, one must give up the luxury of final statements" (Lemire 1969, 16).

Aware of his own position of wealth and material ease, he made a concerted effort to raise the consciousness of the popular masses through a genre that subordinated literary perfection to simplicity and concreteness. He was often apologetic for his repetitive discourse, but his search for a direct quality of rhetoric resulted in more powerful and animated propaganda, one where the local character of his audience was immediately and concretely addressed. By contrast, those socialist lectures which were finally compiled for posterity were directed at a middle-class audience, and thus more "academic" in style and argumentation. Strangely, however, Morris's first encounter with political public life inspired him to write one of his most celebrated and remarkable pieces of propaganda, a discourse pregnant with the features of dissenting rhetoric. Addressed to the "Working-men of England," his manifesto entitled *Unjust War* (cf. Henderson 1950, 388–9) was written during his involvement in the "Eastern Question" between 1876 and 1878. In joining the Eastern Question Association, Morris campaigned against Disraeli's alliance with the Turks, following the disclosure that Turkish mercenaries had committed atrocities upon the Christian population of Bulgaria. Disraeli threatened to drag Britain into a war with Russia so as to preserve the rule of Turkey in the Balkans. Although Morris did not necessarily grasp all the complexities of this Oriental imperialism, he was conscious of the repugnant character of a war which would serve the exclusive interests of England's imperial position in India and the holders of Turkish Bonds. (Cf. Morton 1979; Thompson 1976.)

Despite Morris's scant experience in political proselytizing, the manifesto *Unjust War* is a consummate piece of dissenting propaganda. It harbours all those hallmarks of the rallying cry; it is an appeal which forms the basic genre of Communist propaganda of the twentieth century. Launching with a note of dire urgency, it prods its public into action, guaranteeing an imminent cataclysm should the popular masses remained mired in torpor. Like the rhetoric of Arnot's *Vindication*, Morris's manifesto gathers its momentum with insistent and pulsating rhythm, relentlessly announcing imminent disaster: "war prices, war losses of wealth, and of work, and friends and kindred. We shall pay heavily and you the working-classes will pay the heaviest." Interpellating the underclass and warning them of their potential suffering, he endows them with a foreboding pathos (you shall pay the heaviest), a condition which he encourages them to transform into heroism or conversely into exalted martyrdom. For they are implicitly the chosen protagonists, delegated to engage in mass action. And to convince them of this imperative duty, he spells out the implications of the cost of standing quiescent before the otherwise inevitable juggernaut of imperialistic war. "And what shall we buy at this heavy price? Will it be glory and wealth and peace for those that come after us? Alas! no, for these are the gains of a just war, but if we wage the unjust war that fools and cowards are bidding us wage today, our loss of wealth will buy us fresh loss of wealth, our loss of work will buy us loss of hope, our loss of friends and kindred will buy us enemies from father to son."

Morris's warnings are aimed at demystifying the false and hollow patriotism of a war which ultimately crushes the insurrection of oppressed peoples – victims of profit and despotism who resemble his very own public. Creating a common bond – the imagined community – of oppressed subjects, Morris sets up the characteristic "us" ("you")/ "them" dichotomy where the imperialist authors of foreign policy are joined to the "thieves and murderers of Turkey" standing menacingly over the downtrodden of eastern Europe, but implicitly, by extension, over "you," the "Working-men of England."

Still in his Liberal phase, Morris's manifesto deploys the expedient discourse of patriotic address ("Working-men of England") while distinguishing itself from an English imperialism, and, in its denunciation of political rulers and profiteers, prefiguring Lindsay's Popular Front poem, "not english?": "And who are they who flaunt in our faces the barrier inscribed on one side English Interests and on the other Russian Misdeeds? Who are they that are leading us into war? Let us look at these saviours of England's honour, these champions of Poland, these scourgers of Russia's iniquities! Do you know them?"

As imperialism is demystified, an "authentic" Englishness is implicitly edified in the potential role of the "Working-men of England": they who hold the ethical banner of a just war against the immorality of profit-mongerers. As with his claimants, Morris's political tract is imbued with a moralizing rhetoric that not only pours scorn on the Conservative leaders of oriental imperialism but also dictates the public's political choice by admonishing any submission to the forces of oppression. Just as with his political disciples, Morris deploys morality in order to spurn the enemy and cast him in an evil light, wholly set against the universally held virtues of human freedom and "the hope of the world," and thus forbids his public to identify with that party of heartlessness and unethical destruction: "Shame and double shame, if we march under such leadership as this is an unjust war against a people who are not our enemies, against Europe, against freedom, against nature, against the hope of the world."

In a vein not dissimilar to Rosa Luxemburg's and Lenin's denunciations of the treacherous pacificist rhetoric of social democratic leaders of the First World War, Morris discloses the hypocrisy of an imperialist leadership that unscrupulously pursued its stake in the Middle East: "these men, if they had the power (may England perish rather!) would thwart your just aspirations, would silence you, would deliver you bound hand and foot for ever to irresponsible capital – and these men, I say it deliberately, are the heart and soul of the party that is driving us to an Unjust war:– Can the Russian people be your enemies or mine like these men are, who are the enemies of all justice?"

In the genre of the twentieth-century dissenting tract, Morris's manifesto weds the Aristotelian categories of tragedy to a projected triumph, a final resolution in which the "strenuous opposition" of the "Working-men of England" is said to prevent the English government from wrapping "England and Europe in an Unjust War." Thus pathos and terror, urgency and morality, as well as the propagandist promises of a retributive justice (cf. chapter 5), combine to form the tense unity of a political drama. With its vibrating language, moral texture, and nationalist sentiments, such discursive form seductively captures its target audience – the "Working-men of England" – goading them to proclaim their protest with ever more vigour.

Notes

1 Cf. Max Weber's notion of "disenchantment" (Weber 1918, 129–56).

2 It was during the First World War that leaders of the Second International compromised their commitment to internationalism and to the cause of the proletariat. In 1914 allegedly pacifist leaders betrayed their working-class following, when they abided by the bellicose pursuits of their national bourgeoisies and, despite hollow humanitarian rhetoric, justified the imperialist project of the Great War. The more genuine socialists harshly criticized this conduct. Lenin in particular declared the necessity of creating a new International (the Comintern or Third International, founded in 1919). The Second International persisted through various incarnations (cf. Joll 1968; Cole 1963), while the Third International forged its association of workers in sharp defiance of its predecessor, privileging the statutes of internationalism over ruling-class nationalism. This new association aimed to avoid a repetition of the events of 1914, asserting that it would not splinter or abandon its spirit of devotion to the internationalist cause as the Second International had so "shamefully" done (Claudín 1975, 16). For more detail see chapter 3.

3 For the purposes of this book, I refer to ruling-class nationalism as "Englishness." The concept of Englishness was a fundamentally imperialist construction of national belonging, with exclusive and excluding features often derivative of highly privileged and idealized regions of England such as Stanley Baldwin's beloved Worcestershire – his home county and, in his mind, the jewel of the nation.

There is a field near me at home more than a mile long, curving through woods down to the river, which I never enter without feeling that I have stepped back into the days of Chaucer. It would never surprise me to meet his pilgrims ambling on their palfries over the greensward.

Today, to us exiles, thoughts of Worcestershire in spring pluck at our very heart-strings. We who are confined to London see the verdure of the Evesham Gardens, the blossom of the Pershore plum. We see the cherry orchards from Bewdley to Tenbury. We see pear and apple blossom everywhere, and we can smell the hopyards in the autumn ... a circle of beauty which I defy any part of England to match.   (Baldwin 1927, 279–80)

However charming and seductive the delights of English ruralism, Baldwin's uninhibited chauvinism goes against the grain of the internationalist spirit of Communists of the 1930s.

4 For a detailed discussion of Morris's numerous other activities, see Thompson 1976.

5 For reviews of the exhibition at the Institute for Contemporary Art, see, *inter alia*, Shorter 1984; Fuller 1984; Gravett 1984.

6 In the 1930s, although Leninism (cf. Rothstein 1927, 214–21) and the Paris Commune (cf. Morton 1937, 113–14) were considerable models for revolutionary action, Communists also sought to integrate these teachings into British culture. Cf. section "Translating Bolshevism into English" in Fox 1932, 204–7. The campaign to anglicize Communism continued with ever greater fervour in the 1950s. See chapter 7.

7 "Scientific rationalism" refers to the doctrine that underlies the "theoretical revolution that Marxism had to carry out in relation to the revolutionary praxis of the proletariat; that is, the transition from Utopia or ideology to scientific socialism" (Sánchez Vázquez 1977, 127).

8 Wrangles over Morris's romanticism and scientific rationalism are paralleled by a history of ideological battles within Marxism itself. See the debates over scientific versus humanist Marxism in Anderson 1980; Richard Johnson et. al. n.d.; Mike Johnson 1982; Schwarz 1982; Childe 1948.

9 Here I draw upon Lukács's *Ontology of Social Being: 3. Labour,* in which he claims that labour is the model for all social being. He bases this assumption on Marx's belief that "[l]abour ... as the creator of use-values, as useful labour is a condition of human existence which is independent of all forms of society; it is an eternal natural necessity which mediates the metabolism between man and nature, and therefore human life itself" (Lukács 1980a, iv).

Lukács subsequently concludes on Marx's ground that social being is distinguished by its capacity for epistemic projection of goals. Here, an essential aspect of labour (and thus of social being) is assumed to be the presence of teleological positings (i.e. positing of goals). As a model for social practice, labour and its teleological category can be seen as "an indelible component of any kind of thinking, from everyday conversation through to economy and philosophy" (Lukács 1980a, 3–4). In this vein, propaganda, which seeks to achieve effects on public consciousness, incorporates features of the basic category of labour, namely that of positing goals.

10 For a contrastive discussion of ideology as a form of distorted consciousness (Marx), and as a positive, identificatory process (Gramsci), see Larrain 1983.

11 In his *History and Class Consciousness* Lukács develops a theory of reification which specifies the implications of the commodity form and extends these to an analysis of the effects of the capitalist mode of production on all spheres of society: law, politics, religion, and everyday life. Reification is derivative of the specific separation of the worker from his means of production. This results in a seemingly free worker whose labour power assumes the character of a commodity, rationalized, quantified, and measured for its exchange-value. As to the human sensuous experience of labour, and the immediate relation of the labourer to his product (i.e. use-value), it is utterly demeaned. In capitalist society, claims Lukács, use-values are subordinated to exchange-values. Such a factor is responsible for engendering reification, a condition determined by economic relations of production that atomize human identities by alienating them from the reality of their own social processes. "The mechanised system of production, like the market itself, comes to confront the worker as pre-existing and self-sufficient," functioning in accordance with nature-like laws (Bernstein 1984, 8). This naturalizing effect results in a pervasive idealism in which individuals perceive reality in abstraction from concrete historical and material contingencies.

12 For an analysis of the Janus-faced aspects of bourgeois ideology, its capacity to dangle tantalizing emancipatory promises while maintaining a restrictive and powerful hold over public consciousness, see Eagleton 1990, 102–19.

13 An example of this can be found in the Third Period of the Comintern where political information was administered to popular sectors in accordance with executive rules legislated by the Communist Party. The mode of propagandist delivery was determined not by the most expedient rhetorical tactics, but rather by the content of public discourse, an often repetitive declamation on the ideological tenets of ethical integrity,

political heroism, and the immediate economic interests of the working class. But this rhetoric was also delivered in formulaic fashion. In 1932, Idris Cox criticized the content of revolutionary propaganda, claiming that "there is a tendency for all Party speakers to talk in the same abstract vein" and to disregard the local character and problems of each community being addressed (Cox 1932, 551–3). Thus by taking as given the manner in which knowledge would be received, Communists produced Marxist tracts in conformity with their ideological principles; yet they left unprobed the question of the public's reception of agitational propaganda.

14 In their respective articles on Communist propaganda of the 1930s, Jack Cohen and Idris Cox are critical and conscious of its weaknesses, raising some important problems such as its abstract character and disconnection from the specific experiences of the working class. See Cox 1932; Cohen 1932. However, their discussion of the deficiencies of Communist propaganda still betrays their predilection for a correct scientific discourse, one aimed at securing convincing arguments but not always geared to the question of the public's specific sensibility and desire for recognition.

15 I address the tension between the aesthetical and ethical nature of Communist propaganda throughout the book, but particularly in chapters 3, 4, and 5. For a discussion of the ethico-aesthetic relation in Kant's dynamic sublime, see Makkreel 1990, 85.

16 Until Kant arrived on the scene, German aesthetics was a discipline which concerned itself almost exclusively with the system of rules and criteria of taste that enabled one to create and emulate works of art. Aesthetics corresponded to the descriptive system which evaluated objects of beauty wherein the concept of beauty *per se* was unquestioningly admitted. Kant introduced a "Copernican Revolution" which entailed a radical questioning of the basic structures of consciousness "on which every aesthetic perception and every designation of an item of nature or art as beautiful or ugly rests" (Cassirer 1981, 308). The significance of this shift in thought lies in its interrogation of the socially "given" objects of aesthetic apprehension (objects of beauty, for example) and in the ensuing pursuit of the question, not of what we know but of how we know it. This transition in thought marks a movement from dogmatism to critical inquiry. In so far as Kant's *Critique of Judgment* provides the basis for a systematic analysis of aesthetic creation and perception, it is also useful for conceptualizing ideological (propagandist) production itself. The reader will no doubt understand that, having appropriated Kant's third *Critique* for the purposes of illuminating the workings of political rhetoric, I am in no way espousing a Kantian philosophy even while many of Kant's political and

epistemological theories are consonant with or parallel to critiques of contemporary society.

17 Whereas in the Third Period of the Comintern (1928–35) the Communists perceived social democracy or "social fascism" to be their principal enemy, in 1935 at the start of the Popular Front, they relinquished their sectarianism. Without seeking to dissolve their distinctive revolutionary identity, they sought to forge alliances with Social Democrats and other elements of the Labour movement, for as the Second World War drew near, they deemed their real adversary to be fascism. For more details see Dimitrov's speech at the Seventh Congress of the Communist International (Dimitrov 1935a and Fyrth 1985).

18 If this book were a work of art, it would seek to produce typical figures (cf. Lukács 1963) out of the respective protagonists: Arnot, Lindsay, and Thompson. But since the genre of the scholarly monograph forbids fictional representation, it cannot consummate this typical form, "which would be neither the average nor the mathematical mean" (Királyfalvi 1975, 80). For the typical constitutes one of those aesthetic determinants that "best mediate the individual (e.g. the historical 'here and now') and the universal (e.g. the essential, although not in the metaphysical sense). In creating the typical, the artist embodies in the destinies of certain concrete men the most important characteristics of some historical situation that best represent the specific age, nation, and class to which they belong. The result of this mediation of the individual and the universal preserves and deepens both, so that the type is more and better (aesthetically) than either or both separately" (Királyfalvi 1975, 80). In default of producing this aesthetic form, this book gestures towards it even in its non-fictional mode, seeking to lay down the guidelines for an articulation of some essential facets of Comintern, Popular Front, and Cold War propaganda.

CHAPTER ONE

1 In using the term "ideologue" throughout the book, I do not impute to it any specifically negative connotations. I intend it to mean "propagandist" in a generally neutral sense.

2 "Mock world" is a term borrowed from Caudwell's *Illusion and Reality* to signify man's plastic relation to the outer world. This is most readily explained in respect to art, where art becomes an "affective experimenting with selected pieces of external reality" (Caudwell 1973, 296). Caudwell sees this process as equivalent to scientific experimentation that is set up

in a laboratory. Such a context for manipulating reality through artifice (aesthetic or scientific) constitutes the domain of the mock world. For in the laboratory of art (or science), some aspect of external reality is imitated; in short, a small, artificial world is wrought. But what characterizes this mock world is the active manœuvres of the artist, who contrives his reflection of reality to suit his desires. Thus in each production of a mock world, a "'fake' piece of the world [is] detached so as to be handled conveniently, and illusory in this much, that it is not actually what we meet in real life, but a selection from external reality arranged for our own purposes. It is an 'as if'. In the same way the external reality symbolised in scientific reasoning, is never all external reality, or a simple chunk of it, but a selection from it" (Caudwell 1973, 296).

3 "Propaganda" is taken here to be affected by alienation in so far as it constitutes a mode of communication that is always partial and bereft of hegemonic consensus. Simultaneously, propaganda seeks total approbation but, short of veritable conditions by which to receive this unanimous nod of consent, it asserts its claims dogmatically. In this respect it does not dialogue or mediate with its audience. Rather it imposes its claims with voluntarist force and, in subjectively idealist fashion, separates out the relationship between ideologue and audience into a radical antinomy.

4 The reference to "naïve" and "sentimental" is drawn from Lukács's discussion of Schiller's delineation of ancient and modern poetry (naïve and sentimental respectively): "In his great treatise, *On Naïve and Sentimental Poetry*, Schiller distinguishes two types of poets: those who are in union and accord with nature, and those who only seek this unity. The philosophical and historical foundation of this typology is the distinction ... between antiquity and the modern age ... Schiller's conception of the fundamental difference between the two periods is that the culture of the capitalist division of labour engenders this dissociation of reason and sensibility and thus estranges man from nature. So long as this estrangement does not manifest itself historically, as in the case of the Greeks, the poet can remain naïve. But when it is present, when the poet seeks to surmount it through art, when his creativity does not derive from a unity with nature, but from a yearning – unrealizable for him – after this unity, then he is modern, sentimental" (Lukács 1968, 118–19).

5 Although the analytic of the beautiful contains other moments (i.e. "relation to purpose" and "modality"), I restrict my discussion here to the two sections of the first book, namely, "quality" and "quantity."

6 In his definition of Kant's notion of concept formation, Cassirer provides a useful historical perspective (from Aristotle through Spinoza) on the evolving philosophies of the concept and its attendant ontological aspects. (Cf. Cassirer 1981, 276–87).

7 Cassirer observes that "the Kantian insistence on disregarding all interest leaves full and unhampered room for the activity of the imagination; only the activity of the will and the activity of sensory desire are routed from the threshold of the aesthetic on methodological grounds. Adherence to immediate attraction and imediate need is precisely rejected thereby, because it hems in and stifles that immediate life of the representation, that free figuration of the formative imagination which constitutes for Kant the special characteristic of the artistic" (Cassirer 1981, 312–13).

8 Subjective universality constitutes the process through which the aesthetic judgment validates itself in default of conceptual proof. Requiring assent rather than objective endorsement of fact, the aesthetic judgment imputes a universal voice to its claims, an idea of utter consensus which grants it a universality, yet an aesthetical or subjective universality based on a unity of social tastes rather than on the coherence of material objectivity. As Kant has it, "the judgment of taste does not postulate the agreement of everyone (for that can only be done by a logically universal judgment because it can adduce reasons); it only imputes this agreement to every-one, as a case of the rule in respect of which it expects, not confirmation by concepts, but assent from others. The universal voice is therefore only an idea (we do not yet inquire upon what it rests)" (Kant 1951, 50–1). For more discussion of this point, see Cassirer 1981, 318–24.

9 For a similar interpretation of the relation between aesthetic pleasure and social inclusion within the community, see Popov 1990, 293.

10 I use "purposiveness" in the manner that eighteenth-century philosophers construed it and as interpreted by Cassirer to mean: "the general expres-sion for every harmonious unification of the parts of a manifold, regard-less of the grounds on which this agreement may rest and the sources from which it may stem ... A totality is called 'purposive' when in it there exists a structure such that every part not only stands adjacent to the next but its special import is dependent on the other. Only in a relationship of this kind is the totality converted from a mere aggregate into a closed sys-tem, in which each member possesses its characteristic function; but all these functions accord with one another so that altogether they have a unified, concerted action and a single overall significance" (Cassirer 1981, 287).

11 It should be noted that the aesthetic judgment is in fact a reflective judgment, a mental activity which entails a classificatory procedure where: (1) reflection moves from the particular to the universal; (2) the universal or general law is not given prior to the reflective judgment, but only after and as a result of that judgement. In this, the reflective judgment is counterposed to the constitutive judgment in which the particular follows the conceptual logic of a preestablished universal law; and most important (3) even though the universal law is not given as a concept or law at the start of the reflective operation, there is nonetheless an indeterminate principle of coherence, a purposiveness which regulates the logic of the reflective judgement. (Cf. Ferry 1990.) This purposiveness is a cognition in general, which Terry Eagleton compares to a "Heideggerian 'pre-understanding' that the world is the kind of place we can in principle comprehend, that it is adapted to our minds even before any determinate act of knowing has yet taken place" (Eagleton 1990, 85). Thus, a purposive synthesis of an object can be conjured up in the imagination from a matrix of preexisting meanings that are intrinsically suggestive of totality.

12 Here and in what follows throughout the book, I am ascribing certain features to the judgment of the beautiful (i.e. deception, fetishism, obscurantism, etc.) which are not a reflection of the judgment *per se*, but rather a comment on the manner in which its intrinsic properties lend themselves to rhetorical exploitation in political (and specifically conservative) ideology.

13 Whereas "objective purposiveness" implies a totality of relations, defined in accordance with a definite purpose (i.e. the perfection of an object), "purposeless purposiveness" is a formal purposiveness which is independent of interests (Kant 1951, 63). Rudolf Makkreel adds an interesting interpretation to this definition: "an important, though generally unrecognized, feature of this purposiveness without a purpose is its life-enhancing character. Aesthetic pleasure heightens the sense of my existence, furthers my feelings of being alive, and is therefore significant. While the disinterestedness of aesthetic pleasure involves an indifference to the existence of the object judged, it does not require me, the judging subject, to be indifferent to my own existence" (Makkreel 1990, 92).

14 Aesthetic judgments cannot be consummated short of a harmonious convergence between subjective perception (the imaginative grasp of an object) and normative structures of objectivity which enable such a perception to be understood collectively (commonsensically). Unity and form are what endow aesthetic judgments with their social/objective, and thus communicable, character.

15 "Reason" is not only removed from experience but is solely concerned with directing the understanding towards "a certain unity of which it has itself no concept, and in such manner as to unite all the acts of the understanding, in respect of every object, into an *absolute whole*" (Kant in Cassirer 1981, 204).

16 In a similar vein, Thomas Weiskel points out that the imagination's cognitive defeat is a necessary failure in the teleological unfolding of reason's self-edification. "The cause of the sublime is *the aggrandizement of reason at the expense of reality and the imaginative apprehension of reality*" (Weiskel 1976, 41). The cognitive-cum-perceptual dissonance experienced by the imagination is resolved in order to consummate the judgment. But as Weiskel suggests, if the final prestige is proffered to reason, then the imagination (despite its moral empowerment) can be construed as a casualty in the edification of reason's patriarchal power. Analogously, one might infer a comparable relationship between the submitting audience and the self-enhancing ideologue; for where the audience is ethically vindicated as a virtuous subject awaiting its moral grace, the ideologue wins substantial and concrete power from the consensus which he harvests in his rhetorical persuasion. Simultaneously though, as Rudolf Makkreel points out,

> [h]owever much the imagination is used to serve reason in the sublime, aesthetically it remains a function of reflective judgement. As such, it must draw back from the kinds of limitless goals that reason can project by itself. In the sublime, therefore, the imagination presents our supersensible destination, not only as morally transcending nature, but also as the human form of nature in us. The judgment of the sublime has "its roots in human nature," and the imagination may project only within the limits of human possibility.
>
> Ultimately, the "determining ground" of all aesthetic judgment is located in what Kant calls the "supersensible substrate of humanity." This substrate of humanity also underlies the *sensus communis* (common sense) which is the transcendental principle of the judgment of beauty. (Makkreel 1990, 86)

So comparably, the audience in a propagandist event will draw its sense of purpose and justification from an abstract morality imposed by the ideologue, yet a morality which is, in the last instance, derived from a fundamental ethical common sense. Reason is, like the ideologue, the deliverer and tribune of an ethos, whose transcendent height is but the cloak of a "supersensible substrate of humanity," a commonsensical ideology held in popular thought, namely values which exalt human subjectivity and moral dignity over the threateningly anti-human force of infinity. Thus the imagination's capitulation to reason is partly a self-preservational impulse; for its belief in some higher totality constitutes an attempt to rationalize its own perceptual sacrifice, indeed to construe its loss of sensible vision as a heroic, moral capability.

17 A concrete example of the dynamic sublime is the celebrated "heath" scene in Shakespeare's *King Lear*. Here the rude elements of nature awaken the king to his moral sensibilities, to his potential for dominating the horror of the elemental forces (their fierce quality and awesome magnitude) through a powerful strength of mental calm. Similarly, as Makkreel has it, "The sheer power of nature exhibited in a hurricane or a waterfall tends to make man regard himself as insignificant. Yet it can also cause him to reflect on his own power and locate 'in himself a sublimity of disposition' which is superior to mere physical power and conformable to rational law" (Makkreel 1990, 84).

18 The audience to which a propagandist preaches is most often an audience that is inherently sympathetic to the appeals of the propagandist. For propaganda functions not as pure cognitive persuasion, but as a means of "boosting the morale of the troops," of invigorating the self-consciousness of an already converted community.

CHAPTER TWO

1 In her talk on the BBC (February 1934), Morris's daughter, May, introduced her father to the public exclusively in terms of his aesthetic *œuvre*. She referred regretfully to Morris's political activities, claiming that these public duties tore him away from the quiet pleasures of his artistic work. "I have been asked to speak to you about my father, William Morris, poet, decorative artist and pioneer of the arts and crafts movement, champion and protector of ancient buildings, master preacher and prophet ... If you go round the Exhibition opened today at the Victoria and Albert Museum to celebrate his Centenary, I think you will be struck by the infinite variety of the work done by him and his friends and the high excellence of it ... the work done was serious and became tradition, laying the foundation for the Arts and Crafts movement in England" (Morris 1934).

The Morris centenary also celebrated the man's art and design work in areas beyond central London. In February, at the Bodleian in Oxford, English drawings were displayed among some first editions from the Kelmscott Press. In March, Walthamstow held a Children's Pageant, which G.E. Roebuck saw as contributing significantly to society's appreciation of art: "As great an undertaking, but one by force of circumstance foreshortened in duration, was the splendid exhibition representing the arts and craft world done in our many schools. The Baths Hall was filled to over crowding with a mass of work, in itself but a fragment of what could have been presented, and ... most artistically arranged to mark the progress of idea and application throughout the school life of children ... [T]here was an artist in every man, ... each had a subconscious tendency to create the beautiful ... All these institutions, schools and popular means to artistic expression we possess to day...proceed directly from the devotion of Morris to his ideals ... and nothing could have more fittingly marked his Centenary than this mass display of creativity of children who owe their joy and opportunity to the life and labours of their great fellow citizen" (Roebuck 1934a).

2 For references to Morris's political history, see chapters 3, 4, and 5.

3 For more detail on Morris's thoughts on revolutionary social change, see his lecture "How We Live and How We Might Live," *Commonweal* 1887 in Morton 1979, 134–58. See also chapter 3.

4 Cf. Introduction, note 18.

5 According to Tom Nairn, the Royal Society of St George was founded in 1894 "in the floodtide of imperialist delirium. Its aim was aptly conveyed by the first number of its journal, *The English Race*: 'There is some fear that the English stock is getting deficient in that healthy and legitimate egotism which is necessary to self-preservation ... The Englishman must assert his indefeasible birth right'" (Nairn 1981, 258).

6 For a detailed definition of the qualitative and quantitative aspects of the judgment of taste see Kant 1951, 38–43 and 45–7 respectively.

7 See Kant's discussion of the "lively play" of the imagination. (Kant 1951, 77–81)

8 In commenting on several passages of ruralist nationalism, including the famous excerpt from "On England," Patrick Wright states: "This interpretative stress on the senses, on the experience of meanings which are vitally incommunicable and undefinable, may only seem clear as an example of what Hermann Glaser once described – albeit in a very different national context – as the 'deadening of thought through mythicising vagueness.'" Wright indicates that the celebrated passage from "On England" vaunts an "'indivisible heritage' as a kind of sacrament encountered in fleeting if well remembered experiences which go without saying to exactly the extent that they are taken for granted by initiates, by true members of the ancestral

nation" (Wright 1985, 83). Implicit here is the notion that any "authentic," sensuous perception of Englishness must invariably be commonsensical, that is, grounded in the filial inclusion that the individual experiences within his community as a true member of the ancestral nation.

9 "The death of Mr. William Morris, ... removes from the world a man whom we do not hesitate to call a great artist. A poet, and one of our half dozen best poets, even when Tennyson and Browning were alive; an artist whose influence is visible almost everywhere; a craftsman who devoted himself, in a commercial age, to the union of arts and crafts, it may be said of him, with little or no exaggeration, that he adorned all that he touched. And if another famous epitaph may be allowed to suggest itself, we should say that, while his best work – a poem of his own, or a volume from Kelmscott Press – is often present on our bookshelves, most of us find something in the nature of a monument to Mr. Morris in the better taste of our domestic surroundings. It is seldom, indeed, that an Englishman is an artist of this type ... No one who has witnessed the Arts and Crafts Exhibitions, which he helped to promote ... will deny that he possessed and effectively used a remarkable diversity of gifts. To these he added a strenuous and outspoken English nature, such as rarely combines with typical artistic temperaments." (*The Times* 1896)

CHAPTER THREE

1 Arnot was a prolific journalist, particularly for the *Labour Monthly*. See bibliography for further details.

2 Arnot's anti-Social-Democratic persuasion, accented as it was by historical experience and memories of the diplomatic negotiations of the First World War, constituted an important part of his attack on the centenary event; it was compounded with his hostile attitude towards Stanley Baldwin (cf. Arnot 1936a), the Conservative leader who defeated the workers in 1926, a strike in which Arnot was a prominent activist. (Cf. Hayes 1987; Farman 1972.) The pamphlet on Morris represents, therefore, one of Arnot's many efforts to take issue with the ruling class as a whole. Through his executive role in the Party, and in conformity with the policies of the Comintern, he sought to alert the working-class movement to the duplicitous character of Conservative and reformist rhetoric. See the unfolding discussion in this chapter.

3 On this subject of journalism and the bourgeois press, see also Dutt 1932, 325–31; Madge 1937, 279–86.

4 In a similar vein, Caudwell applies Engels's discussion of socialist utopianism to a critique of the petit-bourgeois epistemology of H.G. Wells. Any cooperative endeavours undertaken by utopian socialists, Caudwell claims, "each with their precise but widely differing ideas ... can but result in a general cloudy vagueness inhibiting action" (Caudwell 1938, 74).

5 In respect to this whole discussion of the "gentle socialist," consider Bertrand Russell's reflections on Trotsky's analysis of the politics of the British Labour movement: "To hope to achieve Socialism without republicanism is the sort of thing that could only occur among English people ... Another important point is illustrated by the analogy of Cromwell, upon which Trotsky dwells at some length. Cromwell, unlike most of the Parliament men, expressed a preference for soldiers convinced of the justice of the cause rather than 'gentlemen' and only by this means succeeded in achieving victory in spite of the opposition of his superior officers. In our day in England, there seems to be hardly anyone whose belief is ... sufficient to make him indifferent to 'gentlemanliness'; certain Labour leaders are constantly led into weaknesses by the desire to have their opponents consider them 'gentlemen.' They do not realise that the ideal of a 'gentlemen' is one of the weapons of the propertied classes; it precludes dirty tricks against the rich and powerful; but not against the poor and the oppressed. This weakness is peculiarly British. Our British passion for inconsistency and lack of philosophy is leading the Labour movement astray ... The Russian Communists have achieved what could never have been achieved by men who were content with a hotch potch of amiable sentiments. It is useless to pretend for instance that Socialism is merely Christianity carried out consistently ... And we British, like the young man who had great possessions, are prevented from thinking clearly by the vague realisation that if we did, we would have to abandon our imperialism; it is only by a skillful muddle headedness that the Labour Party can inveigh against imperialists while taking care to retain the Empire and carry on the tradition of oppression as the late government did in practice" (Russell 1926).

6 Brecht's notion of estrangement derives from his theatrical method, which was characterized by a "gestic style." This style consisted in dramatic devices that explicated to the audience the development of the action. In this respect, Brecht sought to avoid the production of illusionist theatre that encouraged uncritical identification with the emotions of dramatic personae. Instead, as Brecht put it, "What is involved here is, briefly, a technique of taking the human social incidents to be portrayed and

labelling them as something striking, something that calls for explanation, not just to be taken for granted, not just natural. The object of this 'effect' is to allow the spectator to criticise constructively from a social point of view" (Brecht in P. Johnson 1984, 77).

In this light, it may be argued that Arnot's anti-sentimental tract shares features of this estranging "effect," since it adamantly aims to instil a critical social consciousness in the public mind.

7 Socialist realism was an aesthetic doctrine announced in 1934. It entailed infusing a Marxist-Leninist line into art and propaganda. With Marxism as its philosophical basis and the education of the masses as its principal end, the main feature of this aesthetic ethos was the accurate reflection of society in works of art with special emphasis on optimistic, vigorous heroes and their healthy pursuit of a revolutionary process (Királyfalvi 1975).

Lukács has noted that while socialism should be the main perspective of socialist realism, the apprehension of this final goal as anything other than a "general concept" or abstract value can lead a literary work to produce a sentimental portrait of its subject-matter. "In socialist realism, as in all other literature the perspective must be of modest proportions, growing out of the characters and actions of the individual work (as in Sholokhov's *The Quiet Don*), not out of the optimism or wishful thinking of the artist because 'reality, independently of thinking, independently of the writer, goes on its own way.' Since in his opinion, very few works of art have been able to achieve the integration of the socialist perspective with the other requisites of reflection, Lukács sees socialist realism as 'a possibility rather than as an actuality'" (Királyfalvi 1975, 69).

8 According to the Soviet film-maker Sergei Eisenstein, "montage" is an idea that arises from the collision of independent shots whose counter-action constitutes a "dramatic principle," linked primarily to "form" and not to plot. Eisenstein's theory is based on a dialectical approach which asserts that cinematographically an idea emerges out of movement from the process of superimposing, on the retained impression of the object's first position, a newly visible, further position of the object. From the superimposition of two elements of the same dimension arises a new, higher dimension (Eisenstein in Leyda 1949).

9 "Intertextual" refers here to Bakhtin's definition of the utterance where the relational and living aspects of discourse are contrasted with the logical and purely formal relations of linguistics. Arnot's intertextual chorus, consequently, consists in the various voices from history which he invokes in his polemic to legitimate or identify his persuasion. The reference to

past texts is historically determined and far more than incidental verbal resonance.

10 Arnot's pamphlet is bent on achieving a "realist" perspective in Lukács's sense. Here a dialectical relation is proportionately wrought out of the universal and particular aspects of the depicted subject (William Morris, the Marxist hero). Without entering into a full-scale definition of Lukács's concept of realism, suffice it to note that this notion constitutes an attack on a variety of "anti-realist" aesthetic philosophies (e.g. modernism, surrealism, naturalism, expressionism, existentialist literature) which tend to distort a proportionate representation of reality either by lapsing into the morass of life's particular phenomena and portraying these in their surface sensuousness as in naturalism, or by wholly dismissing external reality and fostering escapist fantasy as in surrealism.

According to Lukács, the problem with the artists of "modernism" is that "they are unable to see correctly the relationship between essence and phenomenon, seeing them only as opposites, exclusives, or rigid contradictions. The recognition by the artist that their relationship is dialectical and that both are part of objective reality, rather than being mere products of the human consciousness, is a primary requisite of realistic art" (Királyfalvi 1975, 63).

11 It must be stressed that Communist sensibility was not bereft of a utopian urge. As argued below, Communists espoused a distinct aesthetic form of utopia germane to the category of the sublime. See chapter 5.

CHAPTER FOUR

1 In one respect, the *Vindication* is intimately bound up with the problem of knowledge. It professes to deliver an alternative but authentic version of Morris's identity. It presumes to offer an infallible redressal of hitherto propounded narratives and recollections of Morris. But fundamentally, Arnot's version is not distinct from other contending positions, at least in so far as the Communist tract is one more self-proclaimed truth. In this respect, Morris perplexes his claimants and biographers. However, the quest for the real Morris is not the concern of the book; the aim is rather to address the relation of Morris's claimants to Morris and his legacy. This investigative reversal *à la* Kant's Copernican revolution consequently shifts the analysis from a description of an impenetrable empirical fact (e.g. the "authentic" Morris) to an assessment of the subjective relation which propagandists hold towards their object of praise.

2 For a discussion of Party organization and the indoctrination of new recruits, see "Osip" 1926, 187–90.

3 For a depiction of critical self-consciousness in the ideal revolutionary mentality, see Rosa Luxemburg's *The Junius Pamphlet*. Describing the proletariat, she writes: "Gigantic as his problems are his mistakes. No firmly fixed plan, no orthodox ritual that holds good for all times, shows him the path that he must travel. Historical experience is his only teacher, his *Via Dolorosa* to freedom is covered not only with unspeakable suffering, but with countless mistakes … Self-criticism, cruel, unsparing criticism that goes to the very root of the evil is life and breath for the proletarian movement" (Luxemburg 1915, 7).

4 In describing the ethical and political responsibilities of the revolutionary, Lenin states that "the undisputed and fundamental duty of all Socialists [is to] reveal to the masses the existence of a revolutionary situation, to make clear its scope and depth; to awaken the revolutionary consciousness and the revolutionary determination of the proletariat, to help it pass to revolutionary actions, and to create organizations, suitable for the revolutionary situation" (Lenin 1940, 13).

Also, in a characteristic definition of the exemplary revolutionary type, Rosa Luxemburg writes of the German Social Democracy that "it was not only the strongest body, it was the thinking brain of the International as well. Therefore the process of self-analysis and appraisement must begin in its own movement, with its own case. It is in honour bound to lead the way to the rescue of international Socialism, to proceed with the unsparing criticism of its own shortcomings" (Luxemburg 1915, 9).

5 For a comparable example of an ideologue's political dynamism and intensity, see the use of repetition and pulsating rhythm in the opening paragraphs of *The Junius Pamphlet* (Luxemburg 1915, 5).

6 Morris's tempestuous fits have been frequently depicted even by his most affectionate admirers. E.P. Thompson in particular has offered accounts such as this: "Morris presented a face to the world made up of bluff, self-assertive decision, vigorous application to detail, matter-of-fact workmanship. He was damned if he would let anyone take *him* for an ineffectual aesthete. 'I sits with my feet in a brook,' he used to recite, 'And if any one asks me for why / I hits him a crock with my crook / For it's sentiment kills me, says I'" (Thompson 1976, 88).

7 It is worthwhile noting that, according to A.L. Morton, Arnot was "certainly one of the most erudite of the early British Communists and in addition he was for some considerable time the representative of the CPGB on the Comintern in Moscow, and that in the late 1920s and early 1930s

when Leninism was most uncompromising. He was also an assistant editor of the *Labour Monthly*, Palme Dutt's most active colleague" (Morton 1987). In the light of these comments, it is not inconceivable that Arnot espoused Dutt's counsel to intellectuals with a fervour equal to that of Dutt himself. Moreover, being one of the more erudite of Communist intellectuals, Arnot would have no doubt confronted the problem of exclusive professionalism as a recurring point of conscience.

8 Heller's discussion of the bourgeois citizen reveals an ethical attitude similar to that of the Communist revolutionary martyr. Both citizen and martyr subscribe to a sense of Kantian duty, an ethical devotion which one may well-nigh say is under the aegis of the categorical imperative.

9 This justification of crises typifies Luxemburg's rhetoric. Witness her claim that, despite enormous difficulties, shameful moments of defeat, and recurring mistakes, the German Social Democracy's efforts were not in vain (Luxemburg 1915, 17). Similarly in her speech "Order Reigns in Berlin," she writes of the failure of the leadership of German Social Democracy: "the leadership can and must be created anew by the masses and out of the masses. The masses are the crucial factor; they are the rock on which the ultimate victory of the revolution will be built. The masses were up to the task. They fashioned this 'defeat' into a part of those historical defeats which constitute the pride and power of international socialism. And that is why this 'defeat' is the seed of future triumph" (Luxemburg in Howard 1971, 415).

In a comparable vein, Dimitrov, speaking on fascism and the working class's duty to supersede crises and transform them into victory, claims that "It is only the revolutionary activity of the working class which can help to take advantage of the conflicts which inevitably arise within the bourgeois camp in order to undermine the fascist dictatorship and to overthrow it" (Dimitrov 1947, 24).

CHAPTER FIVE

1 For examples of the undialectical duality of science and utopia in Marxist thought see the Marxists of the Second International.

2 The fight against idealism can be witnessed in a variety of contexts as a campaign against fascism or imperialism. For specific British examples see the writings of British radicals of the 1930s: Edgell Rickword, Christopher Caudwell, Robin Page Arnot, *inter alia*.

3 In respect to this taboo, see also E.P. Thompson's remarks of 1976: "What Goode seems to be doing is like so many before him, and like myself in

1955, running away from the acceptance of Utopianism as a valid imaginative form, because of a fright given to us by Engels in 1880. (1880 is the date of the first French edition of *Socialism: Utopian and Scientific*.)" (Thompson 1976, 797).

4 In Germany, the problem of Marxism and its relation to irrationality was vigorously debated between Ernst Bloch and Georg Lukács. (Cf. Bloch et al. 1977.) Bloch's *Heritage of Our Time* (1934) constituted a polemic against the irrationalism of Marxist rationalism. In it he claimed that Marxists had surrendered the aesthetic and affective terrain of tradition to fascist colonization; they had abandoned the matrix of irrational human drives (which Bloch saw as genuine strivings for community and emancipation), the realm "where angels dared to tread but Marxists feared to go" (Rabinbach 1977, 15). In probing what Lukács referred to as the dark hiatus of irrationalism (Rabinbach 1977), Bloch wondered whether Marxist theory could offer an alternative ideological landscape to that of fascism and whether Dionysian dreams could be transformed into revolutionary ones.

5 My definition of the interpenetrating genres of the polemic is based on Lukács's typology of literary forms, most specifically that of the novel (cf. Lukács 1978.) No doubt, while the equivalence advanced here between the polemic and the novel is not absolute, on a general level, it does offer the possibility of construing the polemical form as a genre of a dissenting voice, of a marginal and thus lyrical author who desires epic (or hegemonic) power not unlike the yearnings of the novel's "problematic hero." (Cf. Lukács 1978.)

6 Cf. chapter 1, note 2.

7 I owe the notion of "discursive craft" to Paul Ricœur's *Hermeneutics and the Human Sciences*. (Cf. Ricœur 1981.)

8 For a useful distinction between aesthetic and cognitive perception, see Cassirer 1981: "[Cognitive perception is an] exposition of an unbroken coherence of conditions, which can be conceived as the analogue of a connection between premises and conclusions. One experience is joined to another in a kind of dependency relation, in which both relate to each other as ground and consequent. The aesthetic grasp of a whole and its individual partial moments, on the other hand, excludes this kind of view. Here the appearance is not dissolved into its conditions, but it is affirmed as it is immediately given to us; here we do not become swamped in conceptual grounds or consequences, but we stay with the thing itself, surrendering ourselves to the impression that the pure contemplation of it arouses. Instead of analysis into parts, and their superordination and

subordination, here it is proper to grasp them all together and unify them in an overall perspective for our imagination; in place of the effects, through which they link into the causal chain of appearances and are prolonged therein, we focus on the value of their sheer presence as it is disclosed to intuition itself" (Cassirer 1981, 309).

9 Hans Jauss usefully highlights the position of the ancient Greeks on the sensuousness of language and its effect on audiences. With specific reference to Gorgias and Aristotle, Jauss argues that rhetoric draws upon the aesthetic component of catharsis in tragedy (with its attendant elements of *phobos* [shudder] and *eleos* [wailing]) in order to transform the passionate interests of an audience into new convictions. The significant element here consists in the communicative function of catharsis, a function which for Gorgias is directly relevant to the devices of rhetoric. For Aristotle, however, catharsis remains purely aimed at the aesthetic liberation of the mind of a viewer with no ulterior ends. But it is with Gorgias that the pleasure of affective experience assumes a more subtle complexion. The enjoyment of speech pattern and poetic resonances and the disarming effect of pathos brought to its tragic pitch of cathartic relief correspond to the trajectory of persuasion. Thus as Jauss argues, "Gorgias illustrates the curious persuasive power a speech can attain through pathos and ethos and by creating cathartic pleasure show the ambivalence of the aesthetic lure: rhetoric can 'present the unbelievable and unknown' and change a person's beliefs. In trials, it can sway many 'even if it is not truthful,' can affect the soul as poison can the body, be well intentioned and charm the listener but also lead him into evil" (Jauss 1982a, 24–5).

10 Arnot's stress on pathos is not untypical of much revolutionary rhetoric. A classic example may be found in Rosa Luxemburg's *The Junius Pamphlet*, where she describes the shameful crisis and defeat into which the German Social Democracy was plunged during the First World War: "The deepest fall, the mightiest cataclysm. Nowhere was the organization of the proletariat made so completely subservient to imperialism. Nowhere was the state of siege so uncomplainingly borne; nowhere was the press so thoroughly gagged, public opinion so completely choked off; nowhere was the political and industrial class struggle of the working class so entirely abandoned as in Germany" (Luxemburg 1915, 9).

11 Lukács uses the term "intensive totality" to denote the manner in which a work of art should reflect reality.

> The work of art must … reflect correctly and in proper proportion all important factors objectively determining the area of life it represents. It must so reflect these that this area of life becomes

comprehensible from within and from without, re-experienciable, that it appears as a totality of life. This does not mean that every work of art must strive to reflect the objective, extensive totality of life. On the contrary, the extensive totality of reality necessarily is beyond the possible scope of any artistic creation; the totality of reality can only be reproduced intellectually in ever-increasing approximation through the infinite process of science. The totality of the work of art is rather intensive: the circumscribed and self-contained ordering of those factors which objectively are of decisive significance for the portion of life depicted, which determine its existence and motion, its specific quality and its place in the total life process. In this sense the briefest song is as much an intensive totality as the mightiest epic. The objective character of the area of life represented determines the quantity, quality, proportion, etc., of the factors that emerge in inter-action with the specific laws of the literary form appropriate for the representation of this portion of life.

... the goal of the work of art is depicting that subtlety, richness and inexhaustibility of life ... and bringing it dynamically and vividly to life. (Lukács 1978a, 38)

12 By aesthetic terror I am referring to the kind which is experienced in Kant's sublime, a distanciated, affective experience which is not felt as a confrontation with physical danger but is distilled from the imagining of peril into a sense of awe and respect.

13 Another example of the way in which the polemicist organizes his audi-ence into followers and traitors can be seen in Lenin's writings on Kautsky's treacherous Social Chauvinism. Delivering his critique with anger and contempt, Lenin's invective asserts its truth by hounding those like Kautsky who have defiled and marred the Marxist doctrine and stifled real revolutionary praxis. Witness the trenchant repudiation of Kautsky in "The War and the Second International," which must have compelled an audience to take refuge under the authorial wing of Lenin's discourse lest it endure a similar rejection to that of Kautsky himself.

Kautsky has degraded Marxism to unheard-of prostitution and has become a real parson. The parson tries to *persuade* the capitalists to adopt peaceful democracy – and calls this dialectics ... The parson consoles the oppressed masses by painting the blessings of this ultra-imperialism, although he has not even the courage to say that it can be 'achieved'! Feuerbach was right when, in reply to those who defended religion on the ground that it consoles the people, he pointed out the reactionary meaning of consolation: whoever consoles the slave instead of rousing him to revolt against slavery aids the slave-owner.

All oppressing classes need two social functions to safeguard their rule: the function of the hangman and the function of the priest. The hangman is required to quell the protests and the indignation of the oppressed; the priest is required to paint for them the prospects of mitigation of their sufferings and sacrifices ... while preserving class rule, and thereby to reconcile them to class rule, wean them from revolutionary reaction, undermine their revolutionary spirit and destroy their revolutionary determination. Kautsky has turned Marxism into a most hideous and stupid counter-revolutionary theory, into the filthiest clericalism.   (Lenin 1940, 26–7)

14 See also Luxemburg's "To the Proletarians of All Countries," where her sense of urgency is an implicit critique of over-theorization and verbosity. "Therefore we call out to you: Fight! Act! The time of empty manifestos, of platonic resolutions and resounding phrases is over: the hour of action has come for the International. We urge you: Elect workers' and soldiers' councils to take over political power and work with us toward peace" (Luxemburg in Howard 1971, 355–6).

15 Lenin uses the same technique of summoning examples from history as a means of condensing and legitimizing his arguments about the "renegade" Kautsky. Invoking the figure of Hyndman as a precedent that implicitly characterizes the betrayals of Kautsky himself, Lenin writes: "It seems only yesterday that Hyndman, who turned to the defence of imperialism prior to the war, was regarded by all 'respectable' socialists as an unbalanced crank, and nobody spoke of him otherwise than in a tone of disdain. Now the most eminent Social-Democratic leaders of all the countries have sunk to Hyndman's position ... If you are convinced that Hyndman's chauvinism is false and fatal, does it not follow that you must direct your criticism and attacks against the *more influential* and more dangerous defender of such views, viz., Kautsky?" (Lenin 1940, 7).

16 Retributive justice is a recurring theme of revolutionary rhetoric. In "Order Reigns in Berlin," Rosa Luxemburg closes with these words of warning to her enemy, the forces of law and order that quelled revolution and resistance: "'Order reigns in Berlin!' You stupid lackeys! Your 'order' is built on sand. The revolution will 'raise itself up again clashing,' and to your horror it will proclaim to the sound of trumpets: *I was, I am, I shall be*" (Luxemburg in Howard 1971, 415).

Also in "To the Proletarians of All Countries," Luxemburg proclaims:

What the ruling classes are preparing under the name of peace and law is only another work of brute force from which the hydra of suppression, hate, and new bloody wars will rear its thousand heads.

Only socialism can achieve lasting peace, can heal the wounds of mankind, can make blooming gardens of the waste fields of Europe, trampled by the apocalyptic horsemen of the war. Only socialism can renew tenfold the destroyed productivity, can awaken all the physical and moral energy of mankind, can replace hatred and discord by brotherly solidarity, by harmony and respect for every human being.   (Luxemburg in Howard 1971, 354–5)

17 Note the use of a characteristic apocalyptic discourse in Luxemburg's *The Junius Pamphlet*, quoted from the German party papers of 26 July 1914. "If destruction takes its course, if the determined will for peace of the German, of the international proletariat, that will find expression in the next few days in mighty demonstrations, should not be able to prevent the world war, then it must be at least the last war, the *Goetterdaemmerung* of capitalism" (Luxemburg 1915, 15).

18 This translation of Lenin's *State and Revolution* differs slightly from the one cited in Arnot's *Vindication*. Since Arnot only furnishes an excerpt and no source, I am compelled to cite the translation offered by International Publishers (New York), in order to include more of Lenin's text.

I should add that the divergence in translations does not alter my analysis of the poetic character of Lenin's polemic.

19 By "sensible" I intend "perceptible through the senses."

20 I use *Bildung* in the general sense that James Schmidt defines it: "the process by which an individual is 'formed' or 'cultivated' within a social collectivity." This interpretation coincides with the meaning of *Bildung* broadly understood in late eighteenth-century German philosophical discourse. For a more detailed discussion of the term's nuances, see Schmidt 1975, 2–40.

21 Alun Howkins discusses how members of the Communist party felt unable to measure up to the standards of true activism and political commitment. After nearly twenty years of membership, he reports, Bob Dark wrote: "'During all my years as a member of the party I frequently had an uneasy feeling that my personal life was not all that was expected of a Communist. And if I was not happy about it neither was the Party. On and off my home and family came under severe criticism from other party members.' Criticism could go further. Ernie Trory, a prominent Brighton Party member, was occasionally in trouble because in the opinion of the

branch he was spending too much time in pubs and playing cards"
(Howkins 1980, 244).

CHAPTER SIX

1 Cf. chapter 5, note 20.
2 I use "national-popular" in Gramsci's sense to mean a form of hegemony
that forges links with other classes, and which transcends a narrowly political concept of domination. By infusing other classes with a sense of
shared interest, this type of control generates a national-popular "collective
will" among various social strata. The creation of a national-popular in
Italy, as Gramsci saw it, meant overcoming the divides that separated a
whole set of dominant-subordinate relationships, including intellectual
élites versus popular masses, high versus popular culture, philosophy
versus common sense, etc. A national-popular would override these alienating disparities and "construct an educative alliance between them … an
'organic unity between theory and practice, between intellectual strata and
popular masses, between rulers and ruled' which constitutes democratic
centralism" (Forgacs 1984, 93). In Britain, as in Italy, the acute separation
between intellectuals and people rendered the challenge of a national-
popular all the more significant. Here was a project whose aim was to dismantle the *status quo* (i.e. the existing conservative hegemony) and
supplant it with a new social order. The national-popular represented the
collective will by which the building of class alliances towards an alternative hegemony could be achieved.

CHAPTER SEVEN

1 *The British Road to Socialism* was a program that the Communist party
adopted during the Cold War period. As Schwarz indicates, the "programme … dropped the Party's commitment to soviet power (i.e. soviets
or workers' councils as an alternative to parliament), bound the Party to a
strategy by which Britain would reach socialism 'by her own road,' and
outlined the parliamentary route to socialism based on a 'broad popular
alliance' in place of the soviet scenario of dual power. It declared that 'the
people of Britain can transform capitalist democracy into a real People's
Democracy, into the democratic will of the vast majority of her people'"
(Schwarz 1982, 54–5).
    This nationalization of socialism in Britain took on a particularly cul-
turalist profile, readily evidenced by Alick West in his essay entitled *The*

British Road to Socialism. Here, West stresses the importance of the program for the revitalization of British national culture, a forum by which intellectuals and popular sectors could form a collective unity. To him, "The British Road to Socialism" was a "piece of creative Marxism ... [being] national in form and socialist in content" (West n.d., 80): "What is at stake in the fight for *The British Road to Socialism* must be the content of our work. And we must measure the truthfulness of that content by our national tradition. We have realized this week more deeply than ever before with what intensity of vision the great writers of the past penetrated to the essence of the society of their day, how they exposed its abuses with all the truthfulness then within the scope of man's knowledge, and attained in their work the highest peak of humanism then possible ... Like the great writers of the past, and as Lenin demanded of the tribunes of the people, we must speak through our art *to all*" (West n.d., 85–6).

2 Cf. chapter 6, note 2.

3 In 1952 Morris also stood out as the inspiring luminary of a conference organized by the National Cultural Committee on the revolutionary facets of the British cultural heritage.

> Among those who are nearest and dearest to us are those who associated themselves with the struggle of the modern industrial working class, with the beginnings of Socialism in this country. The greatest of these was William Morris and I am not sure whether we yet realize all the grandeur of this man.
>
> He is one of those rare figures in cultural history who served the people to the very last ounce of their physical strength and in all their thought and creative work took the people as their inspiration and their judges.   (Rothstein 1952, 39)

4 For an even more blatant expression of nationalist fervour during the conference, see Sam Aaronovitch's opening address entitled "The American Threat to British Culture" (Aaronovitch 1951, 3–22).

5 Similarly, in defining the British cultural heritage, Aaronovitch vaunts a galaxy of writers with a patriotic zeal reminiscent of the conservative William Morris centenary of 1934. Citing the names of great authors, artists, scientists, and economists, Aaronovitch concludes: "Just the bare roll call is enough to rouse one's pride" (Aaronovitch 1951, 16).

6 Although Lindsay, *Arena*'s editor, specified in his prefatory comments that the threat to British culture comes from the "reactionary elements now dominant in U.S.A." and that there was "no question of an attack on American culture as such" (Lindsay 1951, 2), most of the contributions to the conference did not make this distinction so clearly; in fact,

their decidedly anti-American rhetoric overshadowed any nuance or qualification.

7 In slightly cruder but comparable terms, Aaronovitch depicts the American way of life as "a glorification of the almighty dollar and of so-called private enterprise ... an incitement to racialism and hatred of national minorities ... [a daily worship] of violence, brutality and gangsterism" (Aaronovitch 1951, 4).

8 The reference here is to Thompson's "Open Letter to Kolakowski," a polemical address in which he uses disarming tones of pathos and postures as a lonely bustard, on the ground, "awaiting the extinction of my species on the diminishing soil of an eroding idiom, craning my neck into the air, flapping my paltry wings. All around me, my younger feathered cousins are managing mutations; they are turning into little eagles, and whirrr! with a rush of wind, they are off to Paris, Rome, to California" (Thompson 1978, 319).

9 The logic which underlies Thompson's identification of Third World suffering with the threatened condition of Englishness is echoed by Aaronovitch when he states that "American racialism is a war weapon being employed ... in Korea. It helps to corrupt young Americans for a war against the peoples of Asia. From 'nigger' to 'gook,' from lynching in the American south to the bestial murder and rape of the Korean people, is only a step. It should sober us to think how short the step is from 'gook' to 'limey'" (Aaronovitch 1951, 5).

As the last of the Mohicans, the Thompsonian bustard abides uncompromisingly by his British soil, the locus of a culture now fading, now threatened by the superficial but engaging attractions of American values. In his letter to Kolakowski, Thompson contrasts this feeling of the increasing rarity of Englishness with the imperious enticements of Western modernity; it is an opposition which Thompson forges between himself and his opponent, not unlike the discursive dichotomies of his speech on William Morris in 1951.

10 Similarly, Aaronovitch opposes a genuine nationalist self-determination to the profit-oriented patriotism of Labour leaders and Tories who "openly betray Britain's national interest." He refers to these men as "salesmen" who "must have lost all national pride. Men who would barter away for a few dollars our economic and political independence" and who would not "hesitate to squander our cultural independence" (Aaronovitch 1951, 14). These men, he suggests, are also those who have drawn upon the established rhetorical traditions of British imperialism where "A Northcliffe, cradled in hatred for the Irish national movement, created the yellow,

jingo press, [where a] Kipling sentimentalizes colonial wars, [where a] Joseph Chamberlain lyricizes over 'the Anglo-Saxon race, so proud, so tenacious, self-confident and determined ... which will infallibly be the predominant force of future history and universal civilization'" (Aaronovitch 1951, 14).

11 I am borrowing here from Kitching's discussion of Benedict Anderson's concept of imagined communities.

12 It should be noted that my critical assessment of Thompson's lecture at the *Arena* conference is not intended as an unmitigated assault on Thompson's whole *œuvre*; it is only a comment on his writing at the particular historical conjuncture of 1951. His many later works certainly do not suffer from the Manichean divisions and chauvinism that are present in the 1951 essay. On the contrary, Thompson's *œuvre* as a whole is clearly one of the finest examples of British historical scholarship. In short, while I am critical of Thompson's Cold War lecture, the discussion in this chapter in no way diminishes my admiration for the richness of his political thought and the vibrance of his engaging prose.

CONCLUSION

1 Propaganda can only be successfully wielded in capitalist society if it employs a system of aesthetic devices which elicit non-rational reception. The hegemonic ruling class wields the largest control over these "structures of feeling," most particularly those of an immediately apprehendable nationalism: a mirroring of society in its most exalted colours. The ruling class, which, as Marx claimed, owns the means of production, consequently also owns the means of mental production. This is not only a comment on the ruling class's power over the production and dissemination of knowledge; it is also a statement that the ruling class is capable of heralding its own ideas as the ideal expression of society's generally disparate streams of culture. The ruling class is endowed with the privilege of delimiting right from wrong and good from bad because it possesses not merely monetary strength but also authority over society's ideological presuppositions. For the ideas of the ruling class are unfolded within the parameters of a dominant common sense. And from this preliminary condition (i.e., that the *a priori* structures of consciousness are the irrational matrices of approval and consent), ruling-class propaganda proceeds to generate ideas in perpetual accord with the predisposition of society's mainstream thought. For it is through the universal acceptability won by such ruling-class ideas that an ideal expression of the dominant material

relations can crystallize. This ideal expression corresponds to what Gramsci calls an optimum principle of fixed proportions. Drawing from Pantaleoni's "Principles of Pure Economics," Gramsci establishes that the science of organizations can be extrapolated from the theorem of fixed proportions in order to demonstrate how political movements define their effective ruling ability. In political administration, this fixed quantity is evidenced through capable leaders and their constitution of a particular social group, an ensemble that is judged according to its quantitative relations – in short, according to its adequate membership. Of course, as Gramsci notes, "it must always be borne in mind that a recourse to the theory of fixed proportions has only a schematic and metaphoric value. In other words, it cannot be applied mechanically since in human collectivities the qualitative element (or that of the technical and intellectual capacity of the individual components) is predominant, and cannot be measured mathematically" (Gramsci 1971, 190).

Thus when a ruling class deploys the optimum principle of fixed proportions to endorse and metaphorically demonstrate its viable ideology, it does so not by expressing the contradictions of society but by occluding them, consequently producing the representation which most conforms to the culturally and historically specific configurations of a given nation-state. In other terms, fixed proportions are the scientific laws of the aesthetic category of the beautiful whose symmetry and internal consistency constitute the measurement of judgment which a given community has assumed to be absolute. Such laws of physics (proportion, equilibrium, and balanced interactive components such as chemically compatible substances congealing and reacting in fruitful fashion) are the basic foundations of an aesthetic category which determines a ruling-class rhetoric, endowed precisely with traits of verbal equipoise and societal centrality. These signal the harmonious appearance of neatly carved hierarchies whose class relations are treated as part of a symmetrical structure rather than as antagonistic forces of conflict.

By contrast with the proportionate aesthetic features of a ruling-class identity, the dissenting class or social group is decidedly disproportionate, for it does not subscribe to the laws of society's fixed proportions, to that common sense of optimum values. But if the aesthetic character of this counter-hegemonic group is one of discontinuity and imbalance, it is also one of negative proportions. In short, an optimum principle is operative within the science of an anti-statist organization, but such an optimum is fixed within a sphere apart from hegemonic common sense. Thus, it is the judgment of the sublime which defines the fixed proportions of a counter-hegemonic group as the negation of a negation, as the balanced totality derived from negativity. Here "sense" must be derived from "non-sense," whereas with ruling-class rhetoric, "sense" is automatically invoked from common sense.

2 For an exploration of the relation between the market and nationalism, see Browne 1991, 91–120.

3 As Marx has it, transformative praxis entails changing reality materially, not ideally through the aesthetic realm of ideas. Unfortunately, while propaganda is able to incite action and move the public heart and mind, it does not abide by the important maxim that the educators should also be educated, that they should enter into dialogical relation with their followings and thus break the rigid divides that separate rhetorical discourse from the flux of political reality.

Bibliography

Aaronovitch, Sam. 1951. "The American Threat to British Culture." *Arena* 2, no. 8 (June/July): 3–22.

Anderson, Benedict. 1983. *Imagined Communities*. London: Verso.

Anderson, Perry. 1980. *Arguments within English Marxism*. London: Verso.

Angenot, Marc. 1980. *La Parole Pamphlétaire*. Paris: Payot.

Arac, Jonathan, ed. 1986. *Postmodernism and Politics*. Minneapolis: University of Minnesota Press.

Arendt, Hannah. 1982. *Lectures on Kant's Political Philosophy*. Sussex: Harvester Press.

Arnot, Robin Page. 1922. "Communism and the Labour Party." *Labour Monthly* 3, no. 1 (July): 9–18.

– 1922a. "The Future of the Labour Party in British Politics." *Labour Monthly* 3, no. 6 (Dec.): 329–41.

– 1923. "The Anti-Communist." *Communist Review* 4, no. 1 (May): 114–21.

– 1923a. "The Labour Movement and the Unemployed." *Labour Monthly* 4, no. 3 (March): 147–60.

– 1923b. "The Labour Party's Approach to Power." *Labour Monthly* 4, no. 6 (June): 329–39.

– 1924. "Labour Tastes Power." *Labour Monthly* 6, no. 3 (March): 171–6.

– 1926. *The General Strike*. London: Labour Research Department.

– 1927. "The Labour Party of the Future." *Labour Monthly* 2, no. 9 (Oct.): 106–9.

– 1931. "Ten Years." *Labour Monthly* 13, no. 7 (July): 417–27.

– 1934. "1914 and 1934." *Labour Monthly* 16, no. 8 (Aug.): 488–96.

– 1934a. *William Morris: A Vindication*. London: Martin Lawrence.

– 1936. "The English Tradition." *Labour Monthly* 18, no. 11 (Nov.): 693–700.

– 1936a. "Thieves' Cant." *Labour Monthly* 18, no. 1 (Jan.): 40–3.

– 1938. "Britain the Centre of Gravity." *Labour Monthly* 20, no. 8 (Aug.): 483–8.

– 1939. "Crusade for Defence of the British People." *Labour Monthly* 21, no. 1 (Jan.): 20–5.

– 1940. *Twenty Years: The Policy of the Communist Party of Great Britain from Its Foundation July 31st, 1920.* London: Lawrence and Wishart.

– 1941. *Forging the Weapon: The Struggle of "The Labour Monthly" 1921–1941.* London: Labour Monthly.

– 1943. *There Are No Aryans.* London: Labour Monthly.

– 1945. *May Day.* London: David S. Smith.

– 1947. "Retrospect on H.G. Wells." *Modern Quarterly* 2, no. 3: 194–207.

– 1951. *Unpublished Letters of William Morris.* Series no. 6. London: Labour Monthly.

– 1954. "Lives of Labour Leaders." *Marxist Quarterly* 1, no. 1 (Jan.): 57–61.

– 1955. "William Morris Communist." *Marxist Quarterly* 2, no. 4 (Oct.): 237–45.

– 1964. *William Morris: The Man and the Myth.* London: Lawrence and Wishart.

– 1985. Oral interview taped by Ann Schuman for the Author, Oct.

Ashleigh, Charles. 1926. "Lenin's Last Speech." *Communist Review* 6, no. 9 (Jan.): 393–6.

Attfield, John, and Stephen Williams, eds. 1984. *1939: The Communist Party and the War.* London: Lawrence and Wishart.

Bakhtin, M.M. 1981. *The Dialogic Imagination.* Edited by Michael Holquist and translated by Caryl Emerson and Michael Holquist. Austin: University of Texas Press.

– 1984. *Rabelais and His World.* Bloomington: Indiana University Press.

Bakhtin, M.M./P.N. Medvedev. 1985. *The Formal Method in Literary Scholarship.* Translated by Albert J. Wehrle. Cambridge, Mass.: Harvard University Press.

Balakrishnan, Gopal. 1995. "The National Imagination." *New Left Review* 211 (May/June): 56–69.

Baldwin, Stanley. 1924. "On England." *On England and Other Addresses.* New York: Books for Libraries Press, 1971, 1–9.

– 1924a. "Rhetoric." *On England and Other Addresses.* New York: Books for Libraries Press, 1971, 93–7.

– 1925. "Truth and Politics." *On England and Other Addresses.* New York: Books for Libraries Press, 1971, 75–92.

– 1927. "Worcestershire." *Our Inheritance.* Toronto: Ryerson Press, 1928, 277–83.

– 1927a. "Books." *Our Inheritance.* Toronto: Ryerson Press, 1928, 284–97.

– 1927b. "Among Scientists." *Our Inheritance.* Toronto: Ryerson Press, 1928, 268–74.

– 1933. "Our National Character." *This Torch of Freedom: Speeches and Addresses.* New York: Books for Libraries Press, 1971, 7–14.

– 1935. "This Torch of Freedom." *This Torch of Freedom: Speeches and Addresses.* New York: Books for Libraries Press, 1971, 3–6.

– 1937. *Service of Our Lives.* London: Hodder and Stoughton.

Baluyev, Boris. 1983. *Lenin and the Bourgeois Press.* Moscow: Progress Publishers.

Barilli, Renato. 1989. *Rhetoric.* Minneapolis: University of Minnesota Press.

Barthes, Roland. 1973. *Mythologies.* Selected and translated from the French by Annette Lavers. London: Paladin Books.

Beardsley, Monroe C. 1975. *Aesthetics from Classical Greece to the Present.* Alabama: University of Alabama Press.

Beiner, Ronald. 1983. *Political Judgement.* London: Methuen.

Bell, Mackenzie. 1896. "William Morris: A Eulogy." *Fortnightly Review* (Nov.): 693–702.

Bender, John, and David E. Wellbery, eds. 1990. *The Ends of Rhetoric.* Stanford, California: Stanford University Press.

Benhabib, Seyla. 1986. *Critique, Norm and Utopia.* New York: Columbia University Press.

Benjamin, Andrew, ed. 1991. *The Problems of Modernity: Adorno and Benjamin.* London: Routledge.

Benjamin, Walter. 1969. *Illuminations.* New York: Schocken Books.

Bernal, J.D. 1952. *Marx and Science.* London: Lawrence and Wishart.

Bernstein, J.M. 1984. *The Philosophy of the Novel: Lukács, Marxism and the Dialectics of Form.* Minneapolis: University of Minnesota Press.

Bernstein, Richard J., ed. 1985. *Habermas and Modernity.* Cambridge, Mass.: MIT Press.

Bhabha, Homi K. 1990. *Nation and Narration.* London: Routledge.

Blackburn, Robin. 1988. "Raymond Williams and the Politics of the New Left." *New Left Review* 168 (March/April): 12–22.

Blatchford, Robert. 1896. "William Morris." *Clarion,* 10 Oct., 324–5.

Bloch, Ernst. 1971. *On Karl Marx.* New York: Herder and Herder.

– 1977. *L'esprit de l'utopie.* Paris: Gallimard.

– 1987. *Héritage de ce temps.* Paris: Payot.

– 1988. *The Utopian Function of Art and Literature.* Translated by Jack Zipes and Frank Mecklenburg. Cambridge, Mass.: MIT Press.

Bloch, Ernst, et al. 1977. *Aesthetics and Politics.* Translated by editor, Ronald Taylor. London: NLB.

Boos, Florence. 1982. "William Morris's Socialist Diary." *London History Workshop* 13 (Spring): 1–17.

– 1983–4 "Victorian Response to *Earthly Paradise* Tales." *Journal of the William Morris Society* 5, no. 4: 16–29.

Boos, Florence S., and Carole Silver, eds. 1990. *Socialism and the Literary Artistry of William Morris*. Columbia: University of Missouri Press.

Boston, Richard. 1984. "Seeking a Hand-Made Utopia." *Guardian*, 17 March, 17.

Bottomore, T.B., and M. Rubel, eds. 1965. *Karl Marx: Selected Writings in Sociology and Social Philosophy*. Harmondsworth: Pelican Books.

Branson, Noreen, and Margot Heinemann. 1973. *Britain in the 1930s*. London: Panther.

Breuilly, John. 1982. *Nationalism and the State*. Manchester: Manchester University Press.

Briggs, Asa, ed. 1962. *William Morris: Selected Writings and Designs*. London: Penguin.

Briggs, Asa, and J. Saville. 1971. *Essays in Labour History. 1886–1923*. London: Macmillan.

Browne, Paul. 1991. "Individu, classe, sexe, communauté. Essai sur la dialectique de la modernité." *Carrefour. Revue de réflexion interdisciplinaire* 13, no. 2: 91–120.

Buci-Glucksmann, Christine. 1980. *Gramsci and the State*. Translated by David Fernbach. London: Lawrence and Wishart.

Bürger, Peter. 1984. *Theory of the Avant-Garde*. Minneapolis: University of Minnesota Press.

Carpenter, Edward. 1896. "William Morris." *Labour Leader*, 19 Dec., 1.

Carr, E.H. 1982. *Twilight of the Comintern: 1930–1935*. New York: Pantheon Books.

Cassirer, Ernst. 1955. *Philosophy of the Enlightenment*. New Haven: Yale University Press.

– 1963. *The Myth of the State*. New Haven: Yale University Press.

– 1981. *Kant's Life and Thought*. Translated by James Haden. New Haven: Yale University Press.

Caudwell, Christopher. 1938. *Studies in a Dying Culture*. London: Bodley Head.

– 1949. *Further Studies in a Dying Culture*. London: Bodley Head.

– 1973. *Illusion and Reality*. London: Lawrence and Wishart.

Centre for Contemporary Cultural Studies. 1978. *On Ideology*. London: Hutchinson.

Chambers, Ross. 1984. *Story and Situation. Narrative Seduction and the Power of Fiction*. Minnesota: University of Minnesota.

Childe, Gordon. 1948. "Marxism and History." *Modern Quarterly* 3, no. 2.

Clark, Jon, Margot Heinemann, David Margolies, and Carol Snee, eds. 1979. *Culture and Crisis in Britain in the 1930s.* London: Lawrence and Wishart.

Claudín, Fernando. 1975. *The Communist Movement: From Comintern to Cominform.* New York: Monthly Review Press.

Cohen, Jack. 1932. "Critical Thoughts on Our Agitation and Propaganda." *Communist Review* 4, no. 6 (June): 292–7.

Cole, G.D.H., ed. 1934. *William Morris: Stories in Prose; Stories in Verse; Shorter Poems; Lectures and Essays.* London: Nonesuch.

– 1963. *The Second International. A History of Socialist Thought: Vol. III, Part 1.* London: Macmillan and Co.

Collette, Carolyn P. 1983–4. "William Morris and Young England." *Journal of the William Morris Society* 5, no. 4: 5–15.

Collins, Richard. 1990. *Culture, Communication and National Identity. The Case of Canadian Television.* Toronto: University of Toronto.

Communist Leadership. 1948. *A Three-Lesson Syllabus.* London: Farleigh Press.

Communist Party. n.d. *Dialectical and Historical Materialism. An Introductory Course in Five Parts.* London: Farleigh Press.

Coombes, John. 1980. "British Intellectuals and the Popular Front." In Gloversmith, *Class Culture.*

Cooper, Emmanuel. 1984. "News from Somewhere." *Tribune,* 16 March.

Cornford, John. 1933–4. "Left?" *Cambridge Left* 1, no. 2 (Winter): 25–9.

– 1934. "The Struggle for Power in Western Europe." *Cambridge Left* 1, no. 3 (Spring):49–58.

Coupe, Lawrence. 1984. "From the Aphrodite to Arena." In Mackie, *Jack Lindsay.*

Coutts-Smith, Kenneth. 1976. "Theses on the Failure of Communication in the Plastic Arts." *Praxis* 3:77–97.

Cox, Idris. 1932. "The Need to Improve the Character and Content of Revolutionary Propaganda and Agitation." *Communist Review* 4, no. 11 (Nov.): 549–53.

Crane, Walter. 1896. "An Artist's Reminiscences." *Justice.*

Crow, Dennis. 1978. "Form and the Unification of Aesthetics and Ethics in Lukács's *Soul and Form.*" *New German Critique* 15 (Fall): 159–77.

Cunninghame-Graham, R.B. 1896. "With the North-West Wind." *Saturday Review,* 389–90.

Daily News. 1896. "Death of Mr. William Morris." 5 Oct.

Daily Telegraph. 1896. "William Morris." 5 Oct.

Daily Worker. 1934. "William Morris: His Centenary Celebrated Today; a Vigorous and Courageous Revolutionary." 24 March, 5.

Dale, Peter Allan. 1977. *The Victorian Critic and the Idea of History.* Cam., Mass.: Harvard University Press.

Davies, Andrew. 1984. "Jack Lindsay and the Radical Culture of the Forties." In Mackie, *Jack Lindsay.*

Davis, Helen, and H. Kemp. 1934. "The Rise and Fall of Bourgeois Poetry." Part I. *Cambridge Left* 1, no. 3 (Spring): 68–77.

Day Lewis, C. 1935. "Revolutionaries and Poetry." *Left Review* (July): 397–402.

de Man, Paul. 1984. "Phenomenality and Materiality in Kant." *Hermeneutics: Questions and Prospects,* edited by Gary Shapiro and Alan Sica. Amherst: University of Massachusetts Press, 121–44.

Dent, Bob. 1984. "Morris's Times." *Peace News,* 20 Jan., 10–11.

Dimitrov, Georgi. 1935. "A Speech before the Soviet Writers' Association." *Left Review* (June): 343–6.

– 1935a. "The Present Rulers of the Capitalist Countries Are But Temporary, the Real Master of the World Is the Proletariat." *Resolutions: Seventh Congress of the Communist International.* New York: Workers Library Publishers.

– 1947. *United Front against Fascism.* New York: New Century Publishers.

Dobb, Maurice. 1922. "Communism or Reformism." *Communist Review* 2, no. 4 (Feb.): 273–97.

Dumont, Fernand. 1993. *Genèse de la société québécoise.* Montréal: Boréal.

Durkheim, Emile. 1985. *Les formes élémentaires de la vie religieuse.* Paris: Presses Universitaires de France.

Dutt, C.P. 1926. "The Bourgeois School of Journalism." *Communist Review* 6, no. 9 (Jan.): 424–8.

Dutt, Rajani Palme. 1931. *Capitalism or Socialism in Britain.* London: Communist Party of Great Britain.

– 1932. "Bourgeois Journalism and Our Press." *Communist Review* 4, no. 7 (July): 325–31.

– 1932a. "Notes of the Month." *Labour Monthly* 14, no. 1 (Jan.): 5–15.

– 1932b. "Intellectuals and Communism." *Communist Review* 4, no. 9 (Sept.): 421–30.

– 1934. "Notes of the Month." *Labour Monthly* 16, no. 10 (Oct.): 583–98.

– 1934a. *Life and Teachings of V.I. Lenin.* New York: International Publishers.

– 1935. *Fascism and Social Revolution.* New York: International Publishers.

– 1946. "The Power of Marxism." *Modern Quarterly* 1, no. 3 (Summer): 3–19.

Dzienidok, Bohdan. 1972. "The Cathartic Compensatory Effect of Art and the Aesthetic Experience." *Actes du VIIe congrès d'esthétique,* 228–32.

Eagleton, Terry. 1990. *The Ideology of the Aesthetic.* Oxford: Blackwell.

– 1990a. "Nationalism: Irony and Commitment." T. Eagleton, F. Jameson, and E. Said, *Nationalism, Colonialism, and Literature,* introduction by Seamus Deane. Minneapolis: University of Minnesota Press, 23–39.

Editorial. 1890. "The Paris Commune." *Commonweal,* 29 March, 101.

Editorial Comment. 1937. "Ralph Fox: A Tribute." *Left Review* (Feb.): 2–7.

Editorial Retrospective. 1938. *Left Review* 3, no. 16 (May): 957–6.

Editorial Review. 1926. "In Memory of Lenin." *Communist Review* 6, no. 9: 389–90.

Eisenstein, Sergei. 1949. In Leyda, *Film Form.*

Ellen, Geoff. 1984. "Morris the Revolutionary." *Socialist Review,* March, 26–7.

Ellis, Benedict. 1947. "Poetry Read Aloud: The Creative Influence of the Audience." *Our Time* 6, no. 3: 57.

Emerson, Caryl. 1986. "Outer and Inner Speech." In Morson, *Bakhtin.*

Emerson, Caryl, and Michael Holquist. 1986. M.M. Bakhtin, *Speech Genres and Other Essays.* Austin: University of Texas Press.

Engels, Frederick. 1880. *Socialism: Utopian and Scientific.* Peking: Foreign Languages Press, 1975.

Erdman, David, ed. 1965. *The Poetry and Prose of William Blake.* New York: Anchor Books.

Farman, Christopher. 1972. *The General Strike: May 1926.* London: Rupert Hart-Davis.

Femia, Joseph V. 1987. *Gramsci's Political Thought.* Oxford: Clarendon Press.

Ferguson, Frances. 1992. *Solitude and the Sublime.* London: Routledge.

Ferry, Luc. 1990. *Homo Aestheticus.* Paris: Bernard Grasset.

Fischer, Ernst. 1963. *The Necessity of Art.* Harmondsworth: Penguin.

Fogarasi, A. 1932. "Reactionary Idealism and the Philosophy of Social Fascism." Translated by Jack Cohen. *Communist Review* 4, no. 2 (Feb.): 92–8.

Forgacs, David. 1984. "National Popular: Genealogy of a Concept." *Formations of Nation and People.* London: Routledge and Kegan Paul.

Forman, Buxton. 1896. "William Morris." *Illustrated News,* Oct., 456.

Foster, Hal, ed. 1983. *The Anti-Aesthetic: Essays on Postmodern Culture.* Washington: Bay Press.

Fox, Ralph. 1921. "The Realism of Revolt." *Communist Review* 2, no. 1 (Nov.): 9–13.

– 1932. "Comrade Stalin's Letter and the C.P.G.B." *Communist Review* 4, no. 4 (April): 199–207.

– 1935. "Henri Barbusse." *Left Review* 2, no. 1 (Oct.): 3–6.

Fuller, Peter. 1984. "William Morris: Revolutionary Socialist or Aesthetic Conservative?" *Antique Collector* 4: 80.

Fyrth, Jim. 1984. To the Author, 17 Nov.

– ed. 1985. *Britain, Fascism and the Popular Front.* London: Lawrence and Wishart.

Gadamer, Hans-Georg. 1976. *Philosophical Hermeneutics.* Translated and edited by David E. Linge. Berkeley: University of California Press.

– 1976a. *Hegel's Dialectic.* Translated by P. Christopher Smith. New Haven: Yale University Press.

– 1986. *The Relevance of the Beautiful.* Cambridge: Cambridge University Press.

Gallacher, Willie. 1948. *Hansard,* 22 Jan., 482–3.

Garman, Douglas. 1936. "Book Reviews on Revolutionary Art." *Left Review* (Jan): 180–3.

Gellner, Ernest. 1983. *Nations and Nationalism.* Oxford: Blackwell.

Gilmore, Michael, T. 1978. "Eulogy as Symbolic Biography: The Iconography of Revolutionary Leadership, 1776–1826." *Studies in Biography,* edited by Daniel Aaron. Cambridge, Mass.: Harvard University Press, 131–57.

Gloversmith, Frank, ed. 1980. *Class Culture and Social Change.* Brighton: Harvester Press.

Goodwin, Barbara, and Keith Taylor. 1982. *The Politics of Utopia.* London: Routledge.

Gramsci, Antonio. 1971. *Selections from Prison Notebooks.* London: Lawrence and Wishart.

Gravett, Paul. 1984. "William Morris Today." *Peace News,* 13 April, 19.

Gray, Robbie. 1984. "The Victorian Visionary." *Marxism Today,* March, 30–3.

Greenfeld, Liah. 1992. *Nationalism. Five Roads to Modernity.* Cambridge, Mass.: Harvard University Press.

Greig, Lindsey. 1984. "William Morris, Forgotten Revolutionary." *Socialist Worker,* 31 March, 11.

Grey, L.E. (pseudonym for Grennan, M.R.). 1949. *William Morris: Prophet of England's New Order.* London: Cassell.

Hannigan, D.F. 1897. "William Morris, Poet and Revolutionist." *Westminster Review* 147, no. 2 (Feb.): 117–19.

Harvest Home. 1896. "The Burying of William Morris under Kelmscott." 7 Oct.

Hayes, Eddie. 1987. To the Author, 3 June.

Hebdige, Dick. 1982. "Towards a Cartography of Taste 1935–1962." *Popular Culture: Past and Present,* edited by Bernard Waites, Tony Bennett, and Graham Martin. London: Open University Press, 194–218.

Hegel, G.W.F. 1830. *The Encyclopaedia of the Philosophical Sciences, Part 1. Logic.* Translated by William Wallace. Oxford: Clarendon Press.

Held, David, et al. 1983. *States and Societies.* Oxford: Open University and Martin Robertson.

Heller, Agnes. 1979. *A Theory of Feelings.* Assen, The Netherlands: Van Gorcum.

Henderson, Philip, ed. 1950. *William Morris. Letters to Family and Friends.* London: Longmans.

Heron, Liz. 1986. "In the Blinking of a Lens." *New Statesman,* 18 July, 23–4.

Hill, Christopher. 1985. To the Author, 6 Nov.

Hinton, James. 1981. "Roots of British Communism." *New Left Review* 128 (July/Aug.): 88–92

Hirschkop, Ken. 1986. "Bakhtin, Discourse and Democracy." *New Left Review* 160 (Nov./Dec.): 92–113.

Hobsbawm, E.J. 1990. *Nations and Nationalism since 1780*. Cambridge: Cambridge University Press.

Hohendahl, Peter Uwe. 1977. "Introduction to Reception Aesthetics." *New German Critique* 10 (Winter): 29–63.

Holub, Robert C. 1984. *Reception Theory. A Critical Introduction*. London: Methuen.

Horvath, G. Paloczi. 1946–7. "Irrationalism in Contemporary Bourgeois Folklore." *Modern Quarterly* 2, no. 1 (Winter): 16–29.

Hough, Graham. 1979. *The Last Romantics*. London: Duckworth.

Howard, Dick, ed. 1971. *Selected Political Writings of Rosa Luxemburg*. New York: Monthly Review Press.

Howell, David. 1986. *A Lost Left. Three Studies in Socialism and Nationalism*. Manchester: Manchester University Press.

Howkins, Alun. 1980. "Class against Class." In Gloversmith, *Class Culture*.

Hyndman, H.M. 1896. "William Morris." *Justice*, 10 Oct., 4.

Ingarden, Roman. 1973. *The Cognition of the Literary Work of Art*. Evanston: Northwestern University Press.

Institute for Contemporary Art. 1984. "William Morris Today." London: Institute for Contemporary Art.

Ivornel, Philippe. 1986. "Paris, Capital of the Popular Front." *New German Critique* 39 (Fall): 61–84.

Jackson, T.A. 1924. "The Message of March: The Commune and After." *Communist Review* 4, no. 11 (March): 468–74.

– 1926. "Historical Materialism." *Communist Review* 7, no. 1 (May): 39–47.

Jameson, Fredric. 1971. *Marxism and Form*. Princeton: Princeton University Press.

– 1972. *The Prison-House of Language*. Princeton: Princeton University Press.

– 1981. *The Political Unconscious*. London: Methuen.

– 1990. "Modernism and Imperialism." T. Eagleton, F. Jameson, and E. Said, *Nationalism, Colonialism, and Literature*, introduction by Seamus Deane. Minneapolis: University of Minnesota Press, 43–66.

Jauss, Hans Robert. 1982. *Toward an Aesthetic of Reception*. Minneapolis: University of Minnesota Press.

– 1982a. *Aesthetic Experience and Literary Hermeneutics*. Minneapolis: University of Minnesota Press.

Jay, Martin. 1984. *Marxism and Totality. The Adventures of a Concept from Lukács to Habermas*. Berkeley: University of California Press.

Jebb, P. 1926. "The Transition to Socialism." *Communist Review* 7, no. 5 (Sept.): 218–24.

Jenkins, Alfred. 1985. To the Author, 27 Aug.

– 1987. To the Author, 16 June.

Johnson, Mike. 1982. "The Problem of Science within English Marxism." Stencilled Occasional Paper. History Series no. 58. Birmingham: Centre for Contemporary Cultural Studies.

Johnson, Pauline. 1984. *Marxist Aesthetics.* London: Routledge and Kegan Paul.

Johnson, Richard, et al. 1982. *Making Histories.* London: Hutchinson.

Johnson, Richard, et al. n.d. "Economy Culture." Stencilled Occasional Paper. History Series no. 50. Birmingham: Centre for Contemporary Cultural Studies.

Joll, James. 1968. *The Second International 1889–1914.* London: Weidenfeld and Nicolson.

Jones, Mervyn. 1984. "Humane Socialist." *New Statesman,* 23 March, 12–14.

Kant, Immanuel. 1950. *Prolegomena to Any Future Metaphysics.* Translated by L.W. Beck. Indiana: Bobbs-Merrill.

– 1951. *Critique of Judgement.* New York: Hafner Press.

– 1986. *Critique of Pure Reason.* Translated by Norman Kemp Smith. London: Macmillan.

Kay, John. 1984. To the Author, 11 Nov.

Kaye, Harvey, and Keith McClelland, eds. 1990. *E.P. Thompson: Critical Perspectives.* Philadelphia: Temple University Press.

Kedourie, Elie. 1966. *Nationalism.* London: Hutchinson.

Kellner, Douglas, and H. O'Hara. 1976. "Utopia and Marxism in Ernst Bloch." *New German Critique* 9 (Fall): 11–34.

Kenez, Peter. 1985. *The Birth of the Propaganda State.* Cambridge: Cambridge University Press.

Kettle, Arnold. 1979. "W.H. Auden: Poetry and Politics in the Thirties." In Clark, *Culture and Crisis.*

Királyfalvi, Béla. 1975. *The Aesthetics of György Lukács.* Princeton: Princeton University Press.

Kitching, Gavin. 1985. "Nationalism and Instrumental Passion." *Capital and Class* 25 (Spring): 98–116.

Klingender, F.D. 1935. "Revolutionary Art Criticism." *Left Review* 2, no. 1 (Oct.): 38–40.

Klingender, F.D. 1943. *Marxism and Modern Art.* London: Lawrence and Wishart.

Klugman, James. 1969. *History of the Communist Party of Great Britain Vol. 2, 1925–26: The General Strike.* London: Lawrence and Wishart.

Knox, Israel. 1936. *The Aesthetic Theories of Kant, Schopenhauer and Hegel.* London: Thames and Hudson.

Kohn, Hans. 1965. *Nationalism: Its Meaning and History.* Princeton: D. Van Nostrand Co.

Kurrik, Maire Jaanus. 1974. *Literature and Negation.* New York: Columbia University Press.

Labour Research. 1984. "William Morris' 150th Anniversary." 73, no. 3 (March): 72–4.

Langan, Mary, and Bill Schwarz, eds. 1985. *Crises in the British State 1880–1930.* London. Hutchinson.

La Pensée. 1946. "Marxism and Ideology." *Modern Quarterly* 1, no. 2: 27–42.

Larrain, Jorge. 1983. *Marxism and Ideology.* London: Macmillan.

Leatham, James. 1934. *William Morris, Master of Many Crafts.* London: Deveron Press.

Lemire, Eugene, D. 1969. *The Unpublished Lectures of William Morris.* Detroit: Wayne State University Press.

Lenin, V.I. 1910. "L.N. Tolstoy." *Sotsial Demokrat* 18 (16 Nov.). In Lenin, *Collected Works* 16, 323–7.

– 1924. "Ramsay MacDonald and the Third International." *Labour Monthly* 6, no. 3 (March): 140–57.

– 1924a. "English Pacifism and English Aversion to Theory." *Labour Monthly* 6, no. 10 (Oct.): 612–18.

– 1932. *State and Revolution.* New York: International Publishers.

– 1936. "What Is to Be Done?" *Selected Works* 2. London: Lawrence and Wishart.

– 1940. *The War and the Second International.* London: Lawrence and Wishart.

– 1940a. *Opportunism and Social-Chauvinism.* London: Lawrence and Wishart.

– 1963. *Collected Works.* Moscow: Foreign Languages Publishing House.

Lentricchia, Frank. 1983. *Criticism and Social Change.* Chicago: University of Chicago Press.

Lewis, L. 1946. "The Great Moral Muddle." *Modern Quarterly* 1, no. 4 (Autumn): 55–71.

Lewis, Roger C. 1987. "Arcadia or Utopia." *Journal of the William Morris Society* 7, no. 2 (Spring): 15–25.

Leyda, Jay, ed. 1949. *Film Form.* New York: Harcourt Brace & World.

Lindsay, Jack. 1936. "not english? A Reminder for May Day." *Left Review* 2, no. 8 (May): 353–7.

– 1937. "A Plea for Mass Declamation." *Left Review* 3, no. 9 (Oct.): 511–17.

– circa 1946, n.d. *England, My England.* London: Fore Publications.

– ed. 1951. *Arena* 2, no. 8.

– circa 1951/2, n.d. "Some Aspects of Socialist Realism." *Essays on Socialist Realism and the British Cultural Tradition.* London: *Arena.*

– 1954. "The Commune of Paris and English Literaure." *Marxist Quarterly* 1, no. 3 (July): 169–80.

– 1961. *William Morris, Writer.* London: William Morris Society.

Litzenberg, Karl. 1936. "William Morris and the Reviews: A Study in the Fame of the Poet." *Review of English Studies* 12, no. 48 (Oct.): 413–28.

Lukács, Georg. 1921. "The Problem of Communist Organization." *Communist Review* 1, no. 6 (Oct.): 41–9.

– 1963. *Asthetik, I. Die Eigenart des Asthetischen-Werke,* Bde. 11 & 12. Neuwied: Luchterhand.

– 1963a. *The Meaning of Contemporary Realism.* London: Merlin Press.

– 1968. *Goethe and His Age.* London: Merlin Press.

– 1971. *History and Class Consciousness.* London: Merlin Press.

– 1974. *Soul and Form.* London: Merlin Press.

– 1977. *Lenin: A Study in the Unity of His Thought.* London: NLB.

– 1978. *The Theory of the Novel.* London: Merlin Press.

– 1978a. *Writer and Critic.* London: Merlin Press.

– 1978b. *The Ontology of Social Being: 1. Hegel's False and His Genuine Ontology.* London: Merlin Press.

– 1980. *The Destruction of Reason.* London: Merlin Press.

– 1980a. *The Ontology of Social Being, 3. Labour.* London: Merlin Press.

– 1981. *Philosophie de l'art (1912–1914): Premiers écrits sur l'esthétique.* Paris: Klincksieck.

Luxemburg, Rosa. 1915. *The Junius Pamphlet.* London: Merlin Press, n.d.

MacIntyre, Stuart. 1975. "British Marxism 1917–1933." Ph.D. thesis. Cambridge University.

– 1980. *A Proletarian Science, Marxism in Britain, 1917–1933.* London: Lawrence and Wishart.

Mackail, J.W. 1912. *The Life of William Morris.* London: Longmans, Green & Co.

Mackie, Robert, ed. 1984. *Jack Lindsay: The Thirties and Forties.* Institute of Commonwealth Studies, Australian Studies Centre, University of London.

Mackie, Robert, and Neil Morpeth. 1984. "From Nietszche to Marx: The Passage and Formation of Jack Lindsay." In Mackie, *Jack Lindsay.*

Mackintosh, J.P. 1977. *British Prime Ministers in the Twentieth Century* vol. 1. London: Weidenfeld and Nicolson.

Madge, Charles. 1937. "The Press and Social Consciousness." *Left Review* (July): 279–86.

Makkreel, Rudolf A. 1990. *Imagination and Interpretation in Kant.* Chicago: University of Chicago Press.

Manchester Guardian. 1896. "William Morris." 5 Oct.

Margolies, David. 1979. "*Left Review* and Left Literary Theory." In Clark, *Class and Crisis.*

Marx, Karl. 1843. "On the Jewish Question." In Karl Marx, *Early Writings.*

– 1843–4. "A Contribution to the Critique of Hegel's *Philosophy of Right.* Introduction." In Karl Marx, *Early Writings.*

– 1844. *Economic and Philosophical Manuscripts.* In Karl Marx, *Early Writings.*

– 1934. *The Eighteenth Brumaire of Louis Bonaparte.* Moscow: Progress Publishers.

– 1964. *Pre-Capitalist Economic Formations.* Edited by E.J. Hobsbawm. New York: International Publishers.

– 1977. *Capital* vol. 1. London: Lawrence and Wishart.

– 1977a. *Grundrisse.* Harmondsworth: Penguin Books and *New Left Review.*

– 1981. *Early Writings.* Translated by Rodney Livingstone and Gregor Benton, with an introduction by Lucio Colletti. Harmondsworth: Penguin Books and *New Left Review.*

Marx, Karl, and Friedrich Engels. 1958. *Selected Works* vol. 1. Moscow: Foreign Languages Publishing House.

– 1975. *Œuvres Choisies.* Moscow: Progress Publishers.

– 1978. *Feuerbach. Opposition of the Materialist and Idealist Outlooks.* Moscow: Progress Publishers.

Mayakovsky, Vladimir. 1928. "The Death of Lenin." *Communist Review* 6, no. 9 (Jan.): 412–18.

McCall, Colin. 1984. "The Rebel Designer." *Yours* 2, no. 6 (March): 2–3.

McLennan, Gregor. 1982. "E.P. Thompson and the Discipline of Historical Context." In Richard Johnson, *Making.*

McLennan, Gregor, David Held, and Stuart Hall. 1984. *State and Society in Contemporary Britain.* Cambridge: Polity Press.

Mellor, David. 1986. "Spanish Civil War and Photoreportage." Cited in Heron, "In the Blinking."

Minogue, Kenneth. 1987. *Nationalism.* London: Methuen.

Mirsky, David. 1935. "Intelligentsia." *Left Review* 1, no. 4 (Jan.): 117–22.

Moretti, Frank. 1986. "The Tragic World View." *New Left Review* 159 (Sept./Oct.): 39–48.

– 1987. "The Spell of Indecision." *New Left Review* 164 (July/Aug.): 27–33.

Morning Post. 1934. "Genius of William Morris: Mr. Baldwin's Vivid Tribute." 10 Feb.

Morris, A.J. 1974. *Edwardian Radicalism.* London.

Morris, May. 1934. *BBC Talk.* Saint Aldates, Oxford: Shakespeare Head Press.

Morris, William. 1889. "Under an Elm-Tree; or Thoughts in the Country-side." *Commonweal* (6 July). In *Political Writings of William Morris,* edited and with an introduction by A.L. Morton. London: Lawrence and Wishart, 1979, 214–18.

– 1887. "Unjust War. To the Working-men of England." In Henderson, *Letters.*

– 1890. *News from Nowhere or an Epoch of Rest.* Edited by James Redmond. London: Routledge and Kegan Paul.

Morson, Gary Saul. 1986. *Bakhtin. Essays and Dialogues on His Work.* Chicago: University of Chicago Press.

Morton, A.L. 1937. "What an Admirable People." *Left Review* (March): 113–14.

– 1945. "A Scale Model of the Future." *The Language of Men.* London: Lawrence and Wishart.

– 1952. *The English Utopia.* London: Lawrence and Wishart.

– 1953. "Utopias Yesterday and Today." *Science and Society* 17, no. 3 (Summer): 258–63.

– ed. 1977. *Three Works by William Morris.* London: Lawrence and Wishart.

– 1978. *The English Utopia.* London: Lawrence and Wishart.

– ed. 1979. *Political Writings of William Morris.* London: Lawrence and Wishart.

– 1984. To the Author, 9 Dec.

– 1985. To the Author, 6 Oct.

– 1985a. "Morris, Marx and Engels." *Zeitschrift für Amerikanistik.* 33lg, Heft 2: 145–52.

– 1985b. "The 1930s." *Bulletin of the Marx Memorial Library* 106 (Spring): 20–5.

– 1986. "Morris, Marx and Engels." *Journal of the William Morris Society* 7, no. 1 (Autumn): 45–54.

– 1987. To the Author, 5 May.

Morton, Vivien, and Stuart Macintyre. 1979. *T.A. Jackson: A Centenary Appreciation. Our History* 73.

Mosse, George L. 1975. *The Nationalization of the Masses.* Ithaca: Cornell University Press.

Münster, Arno. 1985. *Figures de l'utopie dans la pensée d'Ernst Bloch.* Paris: Aubier.

Nairn, Tom. 1973. *The Left against Europe?* Harmondsworth: Pelican Books.

– 1981. *The Break-Up of Britain.* London: Verso.

Naylor, Gillian. 1981. "No Drawing Room Sort of Man." *William Morris and Kelmscott.* London: Design Council.

Negt, Oskar. 1976. "The Non-Synchronous Heritage and the Problem of Propaganda." *New German Critique* 9 (Fall): 46–70.

Newbold, J.B. Walton. 1923. "The Baldwin Ministry." *Communist Review* 4, no. 3 (July): 109–14.

Newman, Teresa. 1984. "Wallpaper and Propaganda." *Journal of the William Morris Society* 6, no. 1 (Summer): 10–17.

Obituary. 1896. "The Late Mr. William Morris: Interment at Kelmscott." Walthamstow: *William Morris Gallery Collection.*

Ollman, Bertell. 1976. *Alienation.* Cambridge: Cambridge University Press.

"Osip, Flying." 1926. "Building the Party." *Communist Review* 7, no. 4 (Aug.): 187–90.

Owen, A.E.B. 1987. To the Author, 14 May.

– 1987a. To the Author, 9 June.

Pall Mall Gazette. 1896. "William Morris." 5 Oct.

Pascal, R. 1948. "Synopsis of Contributions of Prof. Georg Lukács and Ernst Fischer to the Wroclaw Conference 1948." *Modern Quarterly* 4, no. 2 (Spring): 253–8.

Pêcheux, M. 1975. *Les vérités de la Palice.* Paris: Maspero.

Pelczynski, Z.A., ed. 1984. *The State and Civil Society.* Cambridge: Cambridge University Press.

Pollitt, Harry. 1940. *Serving My Time.* London: Lawrence and Wishart.

Popov, Stefan. 1990. "Community and Utopia: A Transcendental Deduction." *Philosophy and Social Criticism* 16, no. 4: 291–301.

Postgate, R.W. 1922. "The Fall of the Commune of Paris." *Communist Review* 3, no. 2 (June): 77–89.

Priscott, Dave. 1985. "Comments." In Attfield and Williams, *The Communist Party.*

Progressive Review. 1896. "William Morris: Poet, Artist and Craftsman and Social Reconstructor." 1, 148–52.

Rabinbach, Anson. 1977. "Unclaimed Heritage: Ernst Bloch's *Heritage of Our Times* and the Theory of Fascism." *New German Critique* no. 11 (Spring): 5–21.

Reid, Betty. 1985. To the Author, 21 Aug.

Reisner, Larissa. 1921. "The Heroic Sailors of the Russian Revolution." *Communist Review* 1, no. 1 (May): 3–6.

Richir, Marc. 1991. *Du sublime en politique.* Paris: Payot.

– Rickword, Edgell. 1934. "Straws for the Weary." *Left Review* 1, no. 1 (Oct.): 19–25, reprinted in *Literature and Society.* Manchester, 1978.

– 1935. "Art and Propaganda." *Left Review* (Dec.): 43–5.

Ricœur, Paul. 1981. *Hermeneutics and the Human Sciences.* Translated by J.B. Thompson. Cambridge: Cambridge University Press.

Rochlitz, Rainer. 1983. *Le jeune Lukács.* Paris: Payot.

Roebuck, G. 1934. *Some Appreciations of William Morris.* London.

– 1934a. *The Waltham Forest Guardian.* 13 April.

Rothstein, Andrew. 1927 "On Lenin's Method." *Communist Review* 2, no. 10 (Nov.): 214–21.

– 1952. "William Morris Belongs to the People." Britain's Cultural Heritage. *Arena*, 39–42.

– 1956. "The Great Pioneer." *Labour Monthly* 38, no. 3, 133–9.

– 1985. To the Author, 26 Sept.

– 1987. To the Author, 23 June.

Russell, Bertrand. 1926. "Trotsky on Our Sins." *New Leader* (Feb.): 26.

Rust, William. 1949. *The Story of the Daily Worker.* London: People's Press Printing Society.

Sacks, Peter M. 1985. *The English Elegy.* Baltimore: Johns Hopkins University Press.

Said, Edward. 1983. *The World, the Text and the Critic.* Cambridge, Mass.: Harvard University Press.

– 1990. "Yeats and Decolonization." T. Eagleton, F. Jameson, and E. Said, *Nationalism, Colonialism, and Literature*, introduction by Seamus Deane. Minneapolis: University of Minnesota Press, 69–95.

St. James's Gazette. 1896. "William Morris: Personal Characteristics." 5 Oct., 10.

Samuel, Raphael. 1980. "British Marxist Historians 1880–1980." *New Left Review* 120 (March/April): 21–96.

– 1986. "The Lost World of British Communism, Part I." *New Left Review* 154 (Jan./Feb.): 119–28.

– 1986a. "Staying Power: the Lost World of British Communism, Part II." *New Left Review* 156 (March/April): 63–113.

– 1987. "Class Politics: The Lost World of British Communism. Part III." *New Left Review* 165, (Sept./Oct.): 52–91.

Samuel, Raphael et al., eds. 1985. *Theatres of the Left 1880–1935. History Workshop.* London: Routledge and Kegan Paul.

Sánchez Vázquez, Adolfo. 1973. *Art and Society: Essays in Marxist Aesthetics.* Translated by Maro Riofrancos. London: Merlin Press.

– 1977. *The Philosophy of Praxis.* Translated by Mike Gonzalez. London: Merlin Press.

Sara, Henry. 1926. "The March Past." *Communist Review* 6, no. 11 (March): 491–5.

Scheu, Andreas. 1896. "In Memory of William Morris." *Justice* 17 Oct., 6.

Schiller, Friedrich. 1980. *The Aesthetic Education of Man.* New York: Ungar.

Schmidt, James. 1975. "The Concrete Totality and Lukács' Concept of Proletarian *Bildung*." *Telos* 24: 2–40.

Schuman, Ann. 1985. To the Author, 17 Oct.

– 1987. To the Author, 12 June.

Schwarz, Bill. 1982. "The People in History: The Communist Party Historians' Group, 1946–56." in Johnson, *Making*.

– 1984. "The Language of Constitutionalism." *Formations of Nation and People*. London: Routledge and Kegan Paul, 1–18.

– 1985. To the Author, 13 Sept.

– 1987. To the Author, 1 May.

Scott, H.G. 1977. *Soviet Writers' Congress 1934*. London: Lawrence and Wishart.

Seton-Watson, H. 1964. *Nationalism and Communism*. London: Methuen.

– 1977. *Nations and States*. London: Methuen.

Shaw, G.B. 1896. "William Morris as a Socialist." *Clarion*, 10 Oct.

– 1896. "William Morris as Actor and Dramatist." *Saturday Review*, 10 Oct., 385–7.

– 1966. *Morris As I Knew Him*. London: William Morris Society.

Short, John Rennie. 1991. *Imagined Country*. London: Routledge.

Shorter, Eric. 1984. "A Mish-Mash on Morris." *Daily Telegraph*, 15 March.

Showstack Sassoon, Anne. 1982. *Approaches to Gramsci*. London: Writers and Readers.

Simon, Roger. 1985. To the Author, 29 Aug.

Skelley, Jeffrey. 1987. To the Author, 24 March.

Sketch. 1896. "The Late William Morris." (Oct. 7): 439.

Smith, Anthony D. 1983. *Theories of Nationalism*. 2nd edition. London: Duckworth.

Socialist Standard. 1984. "Morris and the Problem of Reform and Revolution." (Feb.): 23–7.

Sontag, Susan, ed. 1982. *A Barthes Reader*. London: Fontana/Collins.

Soper, Kate. 1987. "Marxism and Morality." *New Left Review* 163 (May/June): 101–13.

Speaker. 1896. "In Memoriam William Morris." 10 Oct., 391.

Spectator. 1896. "William Morris." 10 Oct., 478–9.

Spittles, Brian. 1988. "Twentieth Century Perceptions in *News from Nowhere*." *Journal of the William Morris Society* 7, no. 4 (Spring): 19–24.

Spriano, Paolo. 1985. *Stalin and the European Communists*. London: Verso.

Standard. 1896. "William Morris; Poet, Artist and Socialist." 5 Oct.

– 1896a. "The Death of Mr. William Morris." 7 Oct.

Starr, Mark. 1922. "Communism and Christianity." *Communist Review* 2, no. 3 (Jan): 228–31.

Stead, C. 1935. "Writers Take Sides." *Left Review* (Aug.): 453–62.

Strachey, J. 1935. "The Education of a Communist." *Left Review* 1, no. 3 (Dec.): 63–9.

Symonds, Anthea. 1984. "Science, Planning and Socialism." Ph.D. thesis, Centre for Contemporary Cultural Studies, University of Birmingham.

Sypher, Eileen. 1976. "Towards a Theory of the Lyric: Georg Lukács and Christopher Caudwell." *Praxis* 3: 177–8.

Taylor, Charles. 1991. *The Malaise of Modernity*. Concord, Ontario: Anansi Press.

The Times. 1896. "Death of William Morris." 5 Oct.

– 1934. "William Morris: The Legacy of Beauty; Mr. Baldwin's Tribute at Exhibition." 10 Feb.

– 1934a. "William Morris: The Centenary Exhibition." 9 Feb.

– 1934b. "English Drawings at the Bodleian: Relics of William Morris." 9 Feb.

– 1934c. "A William Morris Exhibition." 11 Jan.

– 1982. "Battling over the Memory of William Morris." 11 Dec.

This Morning's News. 1896. 3 Oct.

Thompson, E.P. 1951. "The Murder of William Morris." *Arena* 2, no. 7 (April/ May): 9–28.

– 1951a. "William Morris and the Moral Issues To-day." *The USA Threat to British Culture, Arena* 2, no. 8 (June/July): 25–30.

– 1976. *William Morris: Romantic to Revolutionary*. New York: Pantheon.

– 1978. *The Poverty of Theory and Other Essays*. London: Monthly Review Press.

– 1980. *Writing by Candlelight*. London: Merlin Press.

– 1994. *Making History: Writings on History and Culture*. New York: New Press.

Thompson, E.P., and Dan Smith, eds. 1981. *Protest and Survive*. London: Monthly Review Press.

Thompson, J.B. 1990. *Ideology and Modern Culture*. California: Stanford University Press.

Thomson, George. 1946. *Marxism and Poetry*. New York: International Publishers.

Todorov, Tzvetan. 1984. *Mikhail Bakhtin, the Dialogical Principle*. Translated by Wlad Godzich. Minneapolis: University of Minnesota Press.

– 1982. *Theories of the Symbol*. Translated by Catherine Porter. New York: Cornell University Press.

Torr, Dona. 1937. "Ralph Fox and Our Cultural Heritage." *Left Review* (Feb.): 6.

Tuck, J.P. 1934. "English Criticism and the Soviet Writers' Congress." *Cambridge Left* 1, no. 3 (Spring): 4–13.

Tuckett-Gradwell, Angela. 1985. To the Author, 13 Oct.

– 1987. To the Author, 16 June.

Verney, E. 1927. "Flashlight on Lenin the Man." *Communist Review* 7, no. 9 (Jan.): 415–23.

Vogler, Thomas. 1986. "Romanticism and Literary Pasts. The Future of the Past." *New German Critique* 38 (Spring-Summer): 131–60.

Vološinov, V.N. 1986. *Marxism and the Philosophy of Language*. Translated by Ladislav Matejka and I.R. Titunik. Cambridge, Mass.: Harvard.

Waites, Bernard, et al., eds. 1982. *Popular Culture: Past and Present*. Milton Keynes: Open University Press.

Walthamstow Forest Guardian. 1934. "William Morris Centenary, Some Reflections of an Onlooker." 13 April.

– 1934a. "Walthamstow and William Morris" 23 Feb., 9.

Watkinson, Ray. 1971. "William Morris in the Year of the Commune." *Labour Monthly* 53, no. 12 (Dec.): 547–53.

– 1986. To the Author, 29 Dec.

Watson, Don. 1984. "Jack Lindsay: Poetry and the Spanish Civil War." In Mackie, *Jack Lindsay*.

Weber, Max. 1918. "Science as Vocation." *From Max Weber: Essays in Sociology*. Translated, edited and with an introduction by H.H. Gerth and C. Wright Mills. London: Routledge and Kegan Paul, 1948, 129–56.

Weinroth, Michelle. 1984. "William Morris: Haunting the English Culture." *Hard Times. Zeitschrift der Deutsch-Englischen Gesellschaft* (Berlin), 25 (April): 10–12.

– 1991. "La communauté idéale et le discours révolutionnaire." *Carrefour. Revue de réflexion interdisciplinaire* 13, no. 2: 50–67.

– 1992. "Les apories de la propagande communiste britannique des années trente." *Discours social/Social Discourse* 4, nos. 1–2 (Winter/Spring): 147–70.

Weiskel, Thomas. 1976. *The Romantic Sublime*. Baltimore: Johns Hopkins University Press.

West, Alick. 1935. "David Mirsky's Onesided Picture." *Left Review* 1, no. 8 (May): 324–8.

– 1936. "Communism and Christianity." *Left Review* (Jan.): 174–6.

– 1948. "Marxism and Culture." *Modern Quarterly* 3, no. 2 (Spring): 118–28.

– n.d. "The British Road to Socialism." *Essays on Socialist Realism and the British Cultural Tradition. Arena*, 78–86.

– 1975. *Crisis and Criticism*. London: Lawrence and Wishart.

Westminster Gazette. 1896. "William Morris: A Few Reminiscences." 5 Oct., 1.

Williams, Bert. 1932. "Lenin, Luxemburg and the Fight for Revolutionary Marxism." *Communist Review* 4 (Jan.): 12–23.

Williams, Raymond. 1961. *The Long Revolution*. London: Chatto & Windus.

– 1963. *Culture and Society 1780–1950*. London: Chatto & Windus.

– 1975. *The Country and the City*. London: Paladin.

– 1976. "Notes on Marxism in Britain since 1945." *New Left Review* 100: 81–94.

– 1977. *Marxism and Literature*. Oxford: Oxford University Press.

– 1981. *Politics and Letters*. London: Verso.

– 1983. *Towards 2000*. London: Chatto & Windus.

– 1989. *Resources of Hope*. London: Verso.

Winter, Jay. 1974. *Socialism and the Challenge of War*. London: Routledge and Kegan Paul.

– 1987. To the Author, 30 June.

Wolff, Janet. 1981. *The Social Production of Art*. London: Macmillan.

Wood, Allen W. 1990. *Hegel's Ethical Thought*. Cambridge: Cambridge University Press.

Wood, Ellen Meiksins. 1982. "The Politics of Theory and the Concept of Class: E.P. Thompson and His Critics." *Studies in Political Economy* 9, 45–75.

Wood, Neal. 1959. *Communism and British Intellectuals*. London: Gollancz.

Wright, Iain. 1979. "F.R. Leavis, the *Scrutiny* Movement and the Crisis." In Clark, *Class and Crisis*.

Wright, Patrick. 1985. *On Living in an Old Country*. London: Verso.

Yeo, Stephen. 1978. "A New Life: The Religion of Socialism in Britain 1883–1896." *History Workshop Journal* 4 (Autumn): 5–55.

Young, Kenneth. 1976. *Stanley Baldwin*. London: Weidenfeld and Nicolson.

Žižek, Slavoj. 1989. *The Sublime Object of Ideology*. London: Verso.

Index